My Exaggerated Life

My Exaggerated Life

Pat Conroy

As Told to
Katherine Clark

THE UNIVERSITY OF SOUTH CAROLINA PRESS

Publication is made possible in part by the generous support of the
University Libraries, University of South Carolina.

© 2018 Katherine Clark

Published by the University of South Carolina Press
Columbia, South Carolina 29208

www.sc.edu/uscpress

Manufactured in the United States of America

27 26 25 24 23 22 21 20 19 18 10 9 8 7 6 5 4 3 2 1

Library of Congress Cataloging-in-Publication Data can be found at
http://catalog.loc.gov/.

ISBN: 978-1-61117-907-1 (cloth)
ISBN: 978-1-61117-908-8 (ebook)

This book is dedicated
to the memory of
PAT CONROY,
whose friendship changed my life.

Contents

Introduction

A story untold could be the one that kills you.

PAT CONROY, *Beach Music*

Pat Conroy is a famous, best-selling, beloved American author who has won a place in the hearts of millions of readers with his books *The Great Santini, The Lords of Discipline,* and *The Prince of Tides,* among many others. Pat Conroy was also an American original: a military brat, an adopted son of the Carolina lowcountry, a starting point guard for a Division I college basketball team, a self-made writer, a champion of the underdog, and a friend of little people. Many know and love this man's work, but most will not have had an opportunity to get to know the inimitable man himself. The purpose of this book is to capture Pat Conroy in full measure, so that readers who never met this singular American character will have their chance to encounter him in these pages and experience something of what it was like to hear his stories in person, as only he could tell them.

Conroy's readers will already know a great deal about the author's life from his autobiographical fiction and nonfiction. We will learn a good deal more from the inevitable scholarly biographies that will follow in due time. This book does not attempt to supplant or compete with an academic rendering of Conroy's life and in fact strives to avoid too much overlap with well-known Conroy lore and previously published material. When a major subject of Conroy's life—like his mother's death, for example—receives scant attention in these pages, that's either because Conroy has written extensively on this subject in other works, or because he was not interested in addressing it here. What this book seeks is not to offer a comprehensive accounting of the author's life, but to preserve the voice, the character, the personality, and the humanity of Pat Conroy in the amber of his own spoken words.

To that end, no one actually wrote this book. I interviewed Pat Conroy for about two hundred hours and edited the transcripts of our recordings into a narrative that hews as closely as possible to the tone and spirit of Conroy's words. My job was to select and structure the text on the page, but what's on the page is Conroy speaking. Here Conroy is the narrator of his life, not the scholar of it. It was not my job to be the scholar of his life here either; that enterprise is for a different book. My role was simply to be an editor who enabled Conroy to be Conroy. And when Conroy is being Conroy, I find him an extremely reliable and credible narrator, but the fact remains that the narrative here is his life as he remembers it and chooses to tell it. On the one hand, I am certain that Pat made a disciplined effort to be as accurate and honest with me as he could be. On the other hand, I am equally certain that some of the stories he told me reflect how a writer's imagination takes hold of real events and makes them better in the telling over years of retelling.

In editing our transcripts, my philosophy was to let Pat be Pat on the page as he was in our interviews, because this kind of book should provide a warts-and-all portrait of a character, along with the gaffes and all narrative of his life, as straight from the horse's mouth as feasible. My responsibility is to share what he told me, because this represents what readers would have heard for themselves if they had met Pat at Griffin Market or sat with him on his balcony as he told stories. And this is the purpose of the book. Instead of hewing literally to any factual record, an oral biography is designed to convey many other kinds of truths about character and voice. What's in these pages offers a glimpse into Pat Conroy's psyche and the emotional reality he lived with from day to day, year to year.

Here is Pat's philosophy on the subject of his own nonfiction, including the interviews we recorded for this book: "In memoir, you better make sure you're dealing with the truth as best you can tell it, as best you can carve it out, as best you can remember it. The problem is, once it's in a book, it's going to sound like the whole truth, and it's not going to be. It's the truth as best I can put it together. But it's not going to be the whole truth, because everybody's version of what happened is a little different; and it's not going to be the literal truth because I don't have a recording of my life." He also noted: "My answers can change on a daily basis. I can say something portentous as though I'm giving the final benediction on something, and then I will say something completely different the very next day."

Memoirist and novelist, Pat Conroy was also a raconteur who delighted audiences as well as friends and family with his storytelling. Not every writer is a great raconteur, just as not every raconteur has the ability to be a good writer. In fact the first oral biography on which I collaborated came into being because the black midwife Onnie Lee Logan did not know how to write. On the other hand, she was a great storyteller out of the oral tradition of the African American South, in which knowledge and information are stored and passed down through stories told and repeated over generations. The Capote-esque bon vivant Eugene Walter of the second oral biography I worked on was a good writer who produced a few novels and poems, but these did not come close to his brilliance as a raconteur whose stories captured the brilliance of a uniquely well-lived life.

Likewise, great writers are often not great talkers. William Faulkner, for example, was notorious for being taciturn in public and speaking only in monosyllables. He preferred to listen and observe, especially when others were doing the storytelling on the front porch of the general store or at the hunting lodge where he was a regular guest. He internalized the stories told by the raconteurs in his family and community and later spun them into literary gold, but he himself was much more writer than raconteur.

Pat Conroy was one of those rare beings whose gift with the spontaneous spoken word equaled his skill at crafting the written word. However it is not Conroy's celebrity as an author that makes him a great subject for an oral biography. In fact I prefer unknowns as subjects and was initially leery of any project involving a famous person. The first two subjects of the earlier oral biographies I worked on had both done great things with their lives against huge odds, but not to the point that the world knew who they were or what they'd done. This anonymity did not bother either of them or detract from their own sense of personal success. Both individuals had a strong sense of identity that empowered them to pursue lives of great meaning and fulfillment. One lesson of these lives is that the inner conviction of being "somebody" is more important than the celebrity bestowed by public opinion or acclaim. Then, through the act of narrating their life stories, both these "nobodies" showed the world what it means to be somebody.

Although Conroy believed he was destined to remain a nonentity, he became famous before he was thirty when his book about teaching black students on a Gullah sea island was adapted into a movie in which the handsome Hollywood star Jon Voight played the role of Pat Conroy, or Conrack. This was the beginning of a string of books and then movies based on the books, which all added to his renown. In the midst of increasing fame and success, Pat lived an outsized life, full of well-publicized conflict and drama. He loomed larger than life in the public imagination as a heroic figure who achieved mythic proportion even before he died.

But in contrast to those "nobodies" who knew they were really somebody, Pat Conroy was a somebody who could never get over the feeling that he was nobody but "that beaten kid and the boy who could not defend his mother." He was haunted by the fear that life would eventually punish him and make him suffer for the way the world had mistakenly crowned him a personage. Ironically in this case, it was Conroy's insistence that he was a nobody like all mere mortals that makes him a great subject for oral biography. Although he may have been a legend in his own time, he was not a legend in his own mind. Pat Conroy saw himself as a flawed human being who was blessed with great good luck in his professional career and cursed with self-inflicted wounds in his personal life. To the extent this book conveys Pat's own image of himself, it will demythologize that mythic figure of the public imagination. For him this project was not about myth making, but about truth telling. This is not to say that some of his stories don't contain mythologized elements that have accrued over years of retellings. It's to say that Pat's mission here was not to build his legacy, but to bare his soul. In our interviews he could not have been less concerned with burnishing his legend, polishing his image, or trumpeting his masculinity. The great charm and power of his character is this ability to reveal himself utterly in naked humanity. Just as he advised other authors to do in their writing, Pat went deeper and deeper into himself in our talks. At one point he told me he had not gone as deeply into himself since he'd last been in therapy with his psychologist, Marion O'Neill, whom he credits with saving his life. As our interviews came to an end, he observed, "I have blurted out my entire life to you nakedly and unashamedly when I should have been ashamed." Actually I think the sharing of his inner self and its stark truths is his finest act of heroism.

I got to know Pat Conroy partly because he had read and admired the oral biography I did with Eugene Walter, whom he knew. After several years of a long-distance friendship conducted on the telephone, Conroy remarked one day that if I'd been recording our conversations, I'd have a book by now. It wasn't too long after he made that remark that I began recording our conversations.

When someone once asked him why he collaborated with me on this book, Conroy replied, "My vanity got the better of my false modesty." Although I love that response, I believe he was being—as usual—comically self-deprecating. A more serious and true answer to that question can be found I think in *The Lords of Discipline*, when the protagonist Will McLean reacts to the cruelties and injustices he experiences by vowing to himself: "*I shall bear witness against them.*" Conroy himself suffered cruelties and injustices throughout his life, from the time he was a child beaten by a violent and abusive father. The man who emerged from the crucible of chronic trauma was a warrior of words, determined to bear witness to the wrongs inflicted on the innocent and vulnerable by the corrupt and powerful. Pat Conroy never stopped being such a warrior, never ceased in his mission to bear witness against all kinds of evil, both individual and institutional. His desire to do this book with me was an extension of this mission, especially as he realized there were many aspects of his life to which he had not yet borne witness. But it was never vanity or ego that drove him to share so much about his life with his readers. Rather it was a desire to put the pain he had endured to good use, and share it with others whose own pain might be diminished as they read about his.

Then there is also this: Pat just loved to talk. He had a "compulsive need for friends and good conversation," as he says about himself in *The Water Is Wide*. "I love people and collect friends like some people collect coins or exotic pipes." A friend of his once explained that Pat conducted a major part of his social life on the telephone, and after a day of writing, when he was exhausted from his labors and in need of human contact, he would start calling friends. For many years his number-one "telephone friend" was the cartoonist Doug Marlette, whose nephew Andy reports, "They were talk-on-the-phone-every-day-for-hours best friends. I do not know what they talked about other than everything. National headlines and college basketball." It was not long after Doug's death in a car crash in 2007 that I met Pat and was added to his roster of "phone friends." When I began receiving calls from him two or three times a week for an hour or two at a time, I realized that Pat Conroy lived his life through words, first in his writing and then in talking. He particularly loved conversing on the phone, I think, because it was a way of interacting entirely through words. It was another forum for telling stories, another exercise in language.

In his books the author wanted to give vent to anguish and suffering, but the man who called me on the phone wanted laughs. Laughter was a tonic he needed to share with someone, especially after a day of wrestling with his demons alone in the writing trenches. But the kind of tonic that worked for him did not come cheaply or easily. The laughter he needed had to be well earned, and it came from telling tales of the abyss—of pain, grief, sadness, despair, disappointment, failure, folly—and finding the words that made comedy instead of tragedy out of the human predicament. He referred to it as his "high gross comedy."

As Andy Marlette observed, he loved to talk about absolutely anything, especially if a good story could be made out of it. He also loved to joke and tease, to rail playfully against fate and the gods and whoever or whatever rubbed him the wrong way. But when someone or something rubbed him the right way, he was exuberant in his delight, lavish with praise. When it came to literature, life, and human nature, he could decry the worst and celebrate the best with equal fervor.

On a fellow writer he didn't like: "He's one of two men who gave me the address of his tailor in London." (That right there is one of the best put-downs I've ever heard, but there's more.) "He was one of two men who wanted me to get nightshirts, and I said, 'You mean those things you wear in *Night before Christmas and All Through the House*?' He says yeah. I said, 'I can't imagine my bride from poor Alabama, me lumbering toward her with a lustful look in my eye, wearing a nightshirt and one of those hats.'"

On his friend Jonathan Carroll's novel *The Land of Laughs:* "I started reading it, and on about the tenth page, one dog starts talking to another, and I thought, 'Oh, fuck.' Yet, I couldn't wait to hear what the dog said! And I realized I was hooked. It's a great book; I love that book."

Although he had significant and necessary enmities—with racists, bigots, censors, and bullies—Conroy was much more lover than hater. Jonathan Carroll used to tease him for his "life-embracing quality," his "gulp-down-the-world, glory-in-the-world-and-all-its-fruits attitude." Doug Marlette used to joke that Pat "let everybody into the ark eventually." Pat told me, "Doug teased me hilariously. He said, 'You've wrapped yourself around all human life, embraced it all—the good, the bad, the idiots, the disgusting—and in the end of this full Conroy embrace, you let them all into the ark." About himself Pat said: "I am a great appreciator. When I appreciate something, if it excites me, if it stimulates me, I can show that. I've taken great joy in the world, in a lot of what I found in it. Landscapes, geographies, cities, travel, great food, great wines, great books. I've loved it all." Perhaps the best thing about conversing with him was being infected by his enthusiasms.

Participating in a conversation with him was like playing a sport; it was a verbal tennis game. He was nimble and agile, always able to get to the conversational ball and keep the rally going, or hit a winner. He relished the challenge of whatever came back at him from the other side of the net. Doug Marlette used to say that Pat had "the quickest response time of anyone." Coming up with the perfect one-liner, clever rejoinder, or witty remark only after the moment had passed was never his problem. Wisecracks were his specialty, and they were always as perfectly timed as they were original.

About our project he said, "I'll try to think deep thoughts, and I will try to be witty, literate, hilarious, and of the ages. That is what I'll try to be." And that is what he was, whether trying to rise to some occasion in our interviews, or just calling me "to gossip and bullshit," as he put it.

Although I spent a very limited amount of time in person with Pat Conroy—who lived two states away—we developed a close friendship because it evolved through his favorite medium, the elixir of words. He once even told me I was better on the phone than I was in person. (He later claimed that was a joke, but I don't believe him.)

A few of our recorded conversations took place in person, but most took place over the telephone, just as our friendship itself had developed. From March 2014 through August 2014 we spoke every day, Monday through Friday, at 9 A.M. my time, 10 A.M. Conroy's time. These conversations lasted an hour to an hour and a half. Usually I was greeted as Madame Ice Pick, Lady Rottweiler, or Dr. Bust-My-Balls, and invited to "proceed with the evisceration, open me up and see what's there with your probing, tooth-pulling, ball-breaking questions of the morning." He used to complain that he had lost a best friend and gained a grand inquisitor who came with scalpel, blades, and Roto-Rooters to "excavate" his "worn-down body." At the end of the hour, Conroy was apt to say something like, "Let me ask you this: after this depth charge into my belly, what do I do with the flood of intestines spilling over the side of my bed? What do I do with my heart in my hand, pumping its last few beats before I recede into a terrible life? My eyes are bleeding out of my head; my eyeballs are down to my belly button. What do I do about all that? Take an aspirin and go back to bed?"

Madame Ice Pick I may be, but I would never lay claim to being an oral historian, as I've had no formal training or education as such. I am simply someone who knows how to operate a recorder (barely), and enjoys these opportunities to take the fundamental elements of narrative captured on recordings and shape them into a book. This is what Pat required of me: "I don't want a boring book to come out of this. And I don't want people to think, 'He even *sounds* fat.'"

Readers familiar with Conroy's written works will find his speaking voice radically different. In his novels and memoirs, Conroy's authorial style is poetic, lyrical, beautiful, and elegiac. His lush prose often contains an ode to a special person or place. His plots involve high drama and tragedy. In contrast his speaking voice is breathtakingly blunt, uncommonly candid, and filled with casual profanity. This was the Pat who talked with me on the phone, smoked cigars with his best friend Bernie Schein, ate lunch with the guys on Thursdays at Beaufort's Griffin Market, and watched the sunset with his wife on their balcony. In person (or on the phone), Pat's brutal honesty and raw candor about himself and his life's many struggles and conflicts could make your sides split with laughter. Throughout this narrative, the animating force of the spoken language is Pat's own brand of gallows humor. While his subject matter was usually dark, his tone was usually comic, and his self-deprecating theme was ever what a fool he was for having lived such "a wretched and maggoty life." One parallel I do find between his writing style and speaking voice is that he enjoyed being over-the-top in both, although in his books this heightened the drama of his dark material, whereas in person it made you laugh. Judging from just his books, the reader might never know how much Pat enjoyed making people laugh. But in person, this is what he liked to do, with himself as the butt of most of his jokes and the humor coming at his own expense.

Although there are many tragic figures in Conroy's canon, and his life constantly cast him in the role of the Prince of Pain or the Prince of Tears, the person I got to know, and the one who materializes in these pages, is a man with a merry heart. And it was this merry heart that enabled him to survive the many great fights of his life, including the fight for his own survival. When I commented on this in one of our interviews, Conroy told me, "Thank God I have a sense of humor. I think it has saved my life. If I had not had a sense of the absurd, I swear to God, I would have been dead long ago."

About his writing Conroy said, "Every book I've written has been called forth from a dark side of me." I think he's right, and because he confronted that dark side of himself and his life in his writing, he was able to carry a merry heart into the world, and that's what he brings into this book as well. In one of our interviews, we discussed the biblical proverb "A merry heart doeth good like a medicine, but a broken spirit drieth the bones." Although Pat scoffed at the idea that he possessed a merry heart, this is precisely what his multitude of friends has come to know and love about him. When someone asked his wife, Cassandra King, what it was like to live with such a tortured soul, she replied that Pat was one of the most good-natured people she'd ever known. His psychologist Marion O'Neill told me that Pat possessed "an underlying positive-ness about life," and she went on to say, "That's what has kept him alive. He has a tremendous sense of humor, which is part of his positive-ness, part of what's kept him going." Pat's broken life led to a succession of books, but it did not produce a broken spirit.

> PC: You call this merry? My God, you must have come out of the prison system of Alabama.
>
> KC: I don't think a merry heart is one that has never experienced darkness. I don't think you can be a merry heart unless you have experienced darkness. You've got to know the darkness, you have to have struggled with it, and you have to have transcended it before you can say you have a merry heart. A heart that's just happy and bubbly and has never encountered darkness: that is a shallow heart, not a merry heart.
>
> PC: I'm sitting here thinking of the next brutal piece about myself being thrown up—oh yes, that Southern American dimwit who thinks and brags that he has a merry heart, ha-ha-ha-ha.

Nevertheless that heart of his was merry, and it was huge. A case in point, from a story his daughter Megan tells: Once when he dialed the wrong number trying to reach a friend and found himself on the phone with a complete stranger, a little old lady, he spent an hour and a half in conversation with her. After learning she didn't have a car and needed to go to the store, he asked for her grocery list. This was Pat. He reached out to everyone he met, and if he found something he could do for another person, he did it. The main benefit fame offered him was to make it easier to fulfill his natural impulse to do anything for anybody.

But Pat was uncomfortable being thanked, recognized, or even noticed for his bigheartedness. After a ceremony in his honor, he complained to me, "If I have to hear one more time about my fucking generosity of spirit, I'm going to quit going to these things." Although he had a well-earned reputation for being pugnacious and combative, he actually had the soul of a teddy bear but liked to present himself as if he were always the grizzly he could indeed become when leaping to the defense of a friend or one of his many good causes. "Behind all that thunder, you're just pure honey," is as true a statement about Pat Conroy as it is of Jack McCall in *Beach Music*. The gruffness, sarcasm, and crankiness Pat employed as decoys for the gentleness and tenderness at his core were hilariously transparent to those who knew him. I called it his mock curmudgeon routine, which is on ample display in these pages. His widow, Cassandra King, has also pointed out that these pages do not do justice to her husband's boundless kindness and generosity, and that's because Pat Conroy was much more likely to think of himself as an asshole than as a kind and generous man. His humility and genuine—not false—modesty would never have allowed him to think of himself in such positive terms. Others' voices can and do say those things about him, but his own voice could not. My advice to the reader who did not get to see the twinkle in his eye, the tongue in his cheek, and the smile playing about his lips, or hear the underlying snicker in his voice, is not to be fooled by the crusty manner he enjoyed using in conversation, including our interviews. Pat's humor and goodwill are always bubbling right below the surface when not erupting in plain view.

It was the great good fortune of my life to become friends with Pat Conroy. It was a tremendous privilege to spend hours on the telephone with him, either recording, or just listening and laughing (and wishing I were recording). Now the reader will get to spend happy hours listening and laughing and, afterward, will no doubt feel the same gratitude I always did for the gift of Pat Conroy's conversation, which never shied away from tales of misery and woe, and also never failed to lift the spirit.

After I let him know I'd completed work on the book, Pat Conroy sent me this e-mail, reprinted here verbatim:

dear katherine,I,pat conroy,being of sound mind and fat body,do ssolemnly swear that I haveneither heard of nor ever spoken to the disreputable woman named katherine clark.these assertions will become clearer when I file my defamation suit against her.I will prove in an open court of law that none of the statements in her scurrilous texts were ever spoken,thought or expressed by me.you will soon be hearing from my bloodthirsty lawyers who will go after possession of your bayside mansion and your ten thousand dollar dog.congratulations,katherine.you worked your ass off and all I did was run my mouth.great love,pat conroy

Katherine Clark

Prologue

When you've got a father who beats you, as a kid you think it's your fault. You develop a self-destructive belief that you're no good. The conflict Pat's always had is whether he's worth anything or worth nothing.

MARION O'NEILL, Ph.D., ABPP, clinical psychologist

My father confused me about what it meant to become a man. From an early age, I knew I didn't want to be anything like the man he was.

PAT CONROY, *My Reading Life*

I had the greatest childhood on earth, because Santini beat the shit out of me, then the Citadel beat the shit out of me, so I was ready for life. The Great Santini taught me everything I needed to know about how the world would treat me. He taught me everything life could hurt me with, crush me with, throw at me; there were no surprises that life got to throw at me because I'd grown up with the Great Santini. And if that wasn't enough, I was sent to the Citadel, where I got my nose rubbed in shit for four straight years. The Citadel was the greatest college I could have gone to, because whatever Santini did not teach me, the Citadel, with its avid cruelty and amazing capacity for sadism, taught me the rest of it. It was a great way to go out into the world. Conroy is terrified of everything, suspicious of everything, doubts everything. Many people go out looking for the best, sort of expecting the best to happen. They don't know that life is going to beat the shit out of you. I was expecting it. I expected every bloom to fall. I braced myself for it.

The worst thing about Dad was you never knew when he was going to blow. He had a fuse that could be lit any minute, over nothing at all. You never knew what was going to get to him; you never knew. At a basketball game when I was a freshman in high school, they had waxed the floors of the gym, and my shoes were sliding to where I almost did the splits. I got called for traveling three times before I got used to this floor. After the game, when I got outside, Dad knocked me to the ground. He was left-handed, and when it came from the left, that was when he got you good. He never let you see it coming. You didn't know when that blow would be coming. But you knew it would come. It would come.

My very earliest memory is of sitting in a high chair while Dad was beating Mom, hitting her and slapping her to the floor. She was screaming. I felt this flush on my face—didn't know what it was—and what I was feeling was anger, but I had no words for it. Also a terrible sense of helplessness, which I've had for the rest of my life.

The first time he hit me was when I did something like cry—because I was still a kid in diapers—and BAM. What was unusual about Dad: he always went for the face. I don't remember him ever swatting me on the behind. Do you know how much it hurts to get hit in the face? Of course I cried a lot more, and that infuriated him much more, and then, "Peg, you better shut this kid up or I'll shut him up." Dad's very effective way of stopping a kid from crying was to beat him. When I was older, Dad would lift me up by the throat and beat my head against the wall, bam bam bam bam. And, "I told you not to do this," bam bam bam bam bam. I'd be up there, strangulated, red-faced, and then Dad would give me the command, "You better get that fucking look off your face."

Nobody ever spent the night with me; I could not risk it because we didn't know when Dad would go off and beat us up, or beat up Mom in front of our friends. And I couldn't spend the night with people because I was a bed wetter until about seventh grade. Later in life, I developed hearing issues. Now I don't have hearing issues; I'm deaf. The ear doctor said, "Have you ever had trauma to the head?" I said, "Dad used to knock me around a lot and beat my head against the wall." She said, "That's trauma to the head."

Life with Dad completely uncentered me. My sense of self was damaged beyond repair. I have a mass of anxieties and insecurities which lie upon a plate inside me like wiggling eels. I will never get over my ruined boyhood. The trauma is always with me. I carry it like a camel's hump.

There's nothing I can do about it. It's always on my back. I can write myself blind, but I will still be that beaten kid and the boy who could not defend his mother. I can feel it right now, the anxiety I felt when I'd see Dad coming home. And every moment of my life I feel the lack of confidence. My childhood fear of Dad has translated into the adult fear of failure, which is with me always, along with feelings of shame and humiliation. Avoiding failure and shame has been the ultimate, grandest motivator in my life.

I wonder why I'm not a lunatic in an insane asylum looking up at the moon and baying like a dog. But what this has led to is despondency, despair, drunkenness, and oh my God, many, many marriages. I've had breakdowns and crackups. I am a two-time loser at suicide. Both times I thought I had killed myself. I thought I had taken enough pills, but I always woke up days later. It was chemistry that defeated me. You cannot imagine what a low feeling that is. Everything is lost, and then you can't even commit suicide? Give me a break. I was thinking it's a fairly easy thing to do. A lot of people do it successfully, and to go around as an unsuccessful suicide adds a layer of cowardice to your psychosis. Whatever is driving you crazy, it simply adds to your burden of contempt for yourself.

~

I have compassion for where both my parents came from. They came from nothing. Dad was one of these dimwitted Chicago Irish Catholics. The Irish liked to beat the shit out of everybody they meet, including their own children. And "Conroy" means "hound of the battlefield" in Gaelic, so I guess that's what my father was trying to live up to. My mother came from the poorest possible white South you could come from. She almost starved during the Depression. World War II pulled them both out of where they came from, gave them opportunities that had never been there. Can you imagine having gratitude toward a world war? But Dad becoming an officer in the Marine Corps, and Mom marrying into the officer class would have been impossible without World War II.

Don Conroy was not a good father, but he was one hell of a fighter pilot. His job was killing people. He didn't have one human feeling about the enemy he killed. During the Vietnam War, he thought we should just nuke North Vietnam. "Why do we have nukes? Why lose one American boy when you have a nuke?" I said, "Dad, that's a little extreme," and he said, "Ends the war. No more Americans get killed. Nuke 'em." That was my Dad. When he talked about dropping napalm on a battalion of North Koreans, he'd laugh as he'd tell how they would try to brush the napalm off their burning clothes, because it's a jelly. My father would say, "It don't work that way, you don't brush it down." Dad found it hilarious that they simply spread the napalm more on their body.

When he caught another battalion moving across the Naktong River, he talked about going back and forth to make sure he killed all three hundred guys. My little cousin Johnny would always say, "How do you know they were dead, Uncle Don? Maybe some of them were hiding in the bushes." My father would say, "Nope, I checked, I got 'em all." And Johnny said, "Some of them could have been in the weeds." He said, "No, I went down low, I checked." And Johnny said, "What was it like down there?" The river was red with blood, and Dad was seeing arms and legs and heads and feet floating down this river. He had torn them apart. "You were up too high in your plane, Uncle Don, you couldn't see everything." And he'd say, "I'm sorry, I wasn't that high; I got down low. I checked it out; I got 'em all."

How did they expect this guy who was a blunt instrument by birth, with an IQ of about 90, to come back from that? "Hi, son, want a ride to Cub Scouts? Want me to pick you up from the Little League, son, and then maybe we'll go out and get a hot dog? That sounds like it will hit the spot, doesn't it, son?" My father was more likely to say things like, "I love to drink gin because I know it's going to make me mean. And sometimes I love being mean. There are times I want to be mean. Sometimes you just love the feel of being the meanest guy around."

My sweet brother Tim had a theory that Dad was born a really nice kid in Chicago, and then because of his Irish society and the poverty of his childhood during the Depression and getting beat up by his father, it changed something in Dad, and this really great, great kid turned into something different. You know, Dad was a great kid turned bad by environment and experience. Dad was always making his growing up sound like this brutal deprived childhood: he couldn't come in till after dark because they only allowed five kids into the apartment. They had nine, so the four oldest would stay out all night until they could sneak up and go to bed.

So Tim says, "Here's my theory about you, Dad. You were the sweetest guy on earth, but your father beat you up, and society got to you, you went through the Depression, your family was starving, you had to work when you were ten, and you got scared. So in Chicago if you get scared it makes you mean, and you start getting into fights, and you got into fights when you played basketball, but that was just because you were frightened, and it had nothing to do with anything else but survival. And that's my theory of you, Dad."

Dad said, "Negative. I was the meanest fucking kid they've ever seen in Chicago. I was the meanest little cocksucker you ever met, son."

It was after a game that he could be particularly savage. He could really be mean after you played a game. I hated Dad going to a game, picking me up from practice. I think picking me up from practice was the worst. I usually got belted on the way home. I got slapped after more basketball and football practices than you can imagine. He loved doing it in front of other people, because the humiliation was ten times worse. But the problem was, he could be mean anytime. It didn't seem to require very much, and it seemed like he was proud of being mean. He had a need to be mean and to act out of that meanness. He swatted me to the ground in the Gonzaga High School parking lot on letter night after the athletic banquet when he thought he saw me doing something wrong. Bam, I'm down. I get up, and bam, I'm down again. Some tough Italian, Irish, and Polish fathers, who knew me from playing ball and did not know who he was, were pulling him off me.

My Great Dog Chippie had the only natural reaction to Dad possible: she wanted to kill him. It was my sister Carol's theory that Chippie could sense evil. Anytime Dad drew near this dog you'd hear *Grrrrr-rrrrr.*

~

My mother was a gorgeous woman; she dressed impeccably; she was exciting; she read everything that came out; she had ambitions for her children. She wanted all of us to go to college; she wanted me to be a Southern writer. Mom really wanted that; that was repair work for her. She bought books all the time, and in the way I was raised by Mom, fiction was something totally real. When a book got to Mom she would talk about it and act it out. I remember in some book she was acting out the mental breakdown of a six-foot-six giant. I remember the rhythm of her voice, and I can still hear it. So at least in my misguided, misled childhood, a rhythm for language was built in there somewhere from Mom's voice reading to me. She would change intonations, and when there was a male speaking she would lower the register of her voice; the princess would get her most charming voice; the frog prince, he'd get a squawky voice. Whatever she was reading was something we would talk about, and Mom could always go, "Now, doesn't that man remind you of so-and-so in *To Kill a Mockingbird*?" And "Doesn't so-and-so remind you—?" So, for us it was a nice way to grow up, where literature seemed like part of our life.

Unfortunately, she was married to a one-celled animal. But she played the game. She obeyed the code of silence. She never uttered one word about how Knocksy Boy let loose on the house. As Mom said, "How would I make a living, how would I feed all of you?" I just didn't see what else she could do—a woman, not college educated, with no skills whatsoever. I think that kept her. Her not knowing what to do without him, because going back to Piedmont, Alabama, was not a big option with her. Later, when I saw Piedmont as an adult, I grew affectionate toward my mother for her choice of never taking me there.

I just adored her, and I do not think I would have survived without her. She fought for me; I've always remembered that. She'd pull him off me, knowing that she was going to get it herself. That became a definition of courage to me. I think I've stuck my nose into a lot of shit because Mom was like that.

Ours was a family in danger from the beginning, although I think my parents loved each other. But possibly the coming of kids interfered. Seven children; six miscarriages. I think Mom's love of me was too much for Dad. Me coming very early was too much for him. They got married in 1944, and I was born on October 26, 1945. Then there were too many of us. Mom was overwhelmed. We moved too much. We were always at new schools; we didn't know anybody. All the kids are screwed up because we came through Mom and Dad. That was a difficult country to travel in.

Dad eventually broke all our spirits. Carol is mentally ill, and Tom had a violent suicide. Carol was the smartest girl in the world until Dad broke her spirit. I saw her being driven crazy day by day. She is the first guard dog who barked. When Dad came home, Carol would give out the warning: "Godzilla is home!" We'd all go hide. I was like a sheepherder, moving. I could get the kids running. We had hiding places everywhere we went. Carol told me, "Our parents are crazy, and we've got to be careful." She based that on watching *Father Knows Best* and *Leave It to Beaver*. Instead of the father coming to the dinner table in a coat and tie and the parents treating the children so kindly, Dad comes home drunk from Happy Hour at the Officers' Club, Dad hits us, Mom gets mad at Dad, and we run to our rooms.

Kathy went to bed at six after dinner every night so she wouldn't experience anything that happened to her brothers and sisters. And she never laughed out loud, which she said was a way to not be noticed. She saw that I laughed and got hit. Carol laughed and got hit. So she developed, along with my brothers Jim and Mike, silent laughter, where they could break up but no noise would come out of their mouth. To this day we've never heard Kathy laugh.

And our poor, innocent Jim, who's now the dark one. Jim had something that almost no Conroy has had: he had a really good image of himself, the first full-fledged ego we produced. Bright and sunny, had a great personality, slaughtered in hell, with Dad slowly breaking his spirit, slowly Jim being beaten down from that ebullient, boyish, effulgent, filled-with-light kid that he was, and by the time Dad was finished with him, Jim walking around as though he lived inside a cage. It was horrible to watch. Dad turned Luke Skywalker into Darth Vader in about a two- or three-year period. Jim is now the snarling, irascible, nothing-good-can-happen man he is today. Then Tom, the kid who was schizophrenic, marinated in the Conroy family madness and got no help, did a back flip off a fourteen-story building.

But we were looked upon by the priests and nuns as the perfect Catholic family. Mom and Dad with a million kids lined up in our cheap clothes from the PX, the boys with our butch Marine Corps haircuts, the girls wearing their librarians' eyeglasses with fins on them. A T-shirt I wore five years before is on Tim; Tom's wearing shit that I threw away. The perfect Catholic family.

⁓

I went to eleven schools in twelve years and lived in twenty-three places before we moved to Beaufort, South Carolina, when I was fifteen. I was born in Atlanta, and six months later Dad is stationed at El Toro. That's where fighter planes are. And that's where I got my accent, because I learned to talk in California. I should be talking like my brothers and sisters, because all the places we lived were well below the Mason-Dixon Line, and the farthest north we got was the suburbs of Virginia. But after California, which I barely remember, I talk like Hopalong Cassidy instead of a Southerner. Otherwise, my mother made sure she was raising me as a Southerner. Mom was, in her phony but understandable way, drawn to the soft backlit South that she wanted so much to believe in, because she thought Dad's overcharged Yankeedom was a form of low-class behavior.

In 1946–47, my father made the Naval Olympic basketball team, which had all the best players in the Marine Corps and Navy. At that time they organized teams, met for a tournament, and whoever won went to the Olympics. So Dad followed his team, which assembled in Annapolis, Maryland, at the Naval Academy, and we went to live in— why we did this I don't know, but this is my parents—Manassas, Virginia. Carol was born there when I was one and a half. Then I think we may have gone back from Annapolis to California.

We came back for the Korean War in 1950 to live with my grandmother Stanny in Atlanta, and I went to Sacred Heart for kindergarten. Dad was deployed for almost two years in Korea. O, happy day; happy day. I loved it when Dad was called overseas in the military, whether it was Vietnam, Korea, or Mediterranean cruises. Carol and I used to pray for war every year. We didn't care where the war was fought; anywhere in the world was fine as long as Dad was taken out to fight and we would go back to Atlanta to live with Stanny or down to Orlando to live with Aunt Helen. These were always the most peaceful years in our lives, and later Mom would say these were the greatest years of our lives. I wish it had happened more. I loved those years. When he was gone I was the happiest boy on earth. What would have been heaven is if there had been WWIII and Dad would be gone for four years in a row.

But Dad came back in '52 and I went to first and second grade in New Bern, North Carolina, where the air base at Cherry Point is. Mike and Kathy were born in Cherry Point Hospital. In third grade we moved back to Atlanta for six months because Dad went off somewhere. I hoped it was some war that he would be fatally wounded in, but he was not. He came back, and we moved in the middle of the year, which was rare for us, to Camp Lejeune in Jacksonville, North Carolina. What a Godawful place. That's when I changed schools from St. George to Infant of Prague, and that was when a serious dip in my education took place, because in Atlanta we had not started multiplication tables, and in Jacksonville, North Carolina, they were already past division.

So that was third grade. Dad gets another job flying at Cherry Point, which is all of fourth grade. Jim was born in that year. Fifth grade, we went to Orlando to spend the year with Aunt Helen and Uncle Russ and the Harper boys when Dad was overseas on a Mediterranean cruise. In '56, '57, '58, Dad commuted to Washington and Quantico, and we lived in two different houses on Culpeper Street in Arlington, Virginia. My brother Tim was born at the Bethesda Naval Hospital in 1957.

At that time, unknown to us all, Dad was Navy intelligence besides being a fighter pilot. The Marines had to have two areas of specialty because it was a small service. So Dad spent a few years as a spy. He told me later he delivered documents to a used car dealership in Maryland and took me with him, because it looks good to have a kid, like you're not spying. You find the car, the trunk's open, you put these documents or a briefcase inside it. He said that happened during the Suez crisis. He was on duty the night the news came in that Francis Gary Powers was shot down over the U.S.S.R., and he had to go directly to the White House to report to Eisenhower.

That was sixth, seventh, and eighth grades, and oh my God, he got me good in those years. He got the whole family good that first year.

That's the year Mom stabbed him, when they got in a fight because he refused to come sing happy birthday after Mom lit the candles on Carol's cake. My most charitable read on it is that it was the stress of Intelligence work. My most uncharitable read that my brothers and sisters all share: Tell us the year he wasn't an asshole.

In '59 Dad goes back to get his college degree at Belmont Abbey College outside Charlotte. One of the worst years also—he was around the house all the time, and it was the smallest house we ever lived in. But I went to Sacred Heart for my first year of high school, and I loved it there. I just loved it. Then Mom came in with the great news that we were leaving, and I collapsed. I said, "Hey Mom, I really like it here. I could stay here." Several families offered to have me stay, live with them, and go to the high school. I thought, how great—it would get me out of this. I had never told anybody that I was being raised by the Joker, but these families came rushing forward: let Pat live with us. But then Mom said, "Your father says he loves you too much."

That next year he was the worst I remember him being. He was at the Pentagon, and that was my year of Gonzaga High School. God, that was a hard year. Of course, we argue about which was Dad's worst year and admit there's much competition. But Gonzaga High, that year of Washington, I really got knocked around. I think Dad had a high-powered job, and he was just a nightmare.

I loved Gonzaga, although the commute nearly killed me; Joseph Monte nearly killed me; the studying nearly killed me. Joseph Monte was the first great intellectual in my life. Everything Monte said was brilliant. He brought passion into everything he did, but it was in a low-key and very cerebral way. The first day he walked in class and said, "What a shame none of you has read over a thousand books. Then we might begin to have a conversation." And of course, the kids thought what an asshole. I'm thinking, God, I'd love to have a conversation with this guy. He encouraged the living hell out of me. I can't tell you how good that guy was for me. He had a way of marking A+ double credit for imagination. I was off and running with that. Here's how life sometimes works out: in 2005 when I received the F. Scott Fitzgerald Award for lifetime achievement, the presenter was Joseph Monte.

But that was a hard year. I carpooled with a Marine major who got me in the Naval Annex, and then I caught two buses to Gonzaga. This was in the worst traffic on earth, Washington, D.C., and it took me about two hours to get back and forth to school. I had to play three sports, and then three hours of homework a night really took some acrobatics from me. I was exhausted the whole year. That was the last year Mom had a baby so I was awakened in the middle of the night.

We get orders again, and I'm sent off into the arms of Gene Norris at Beaufort High School. I fell in love with Beaufort when I saw it, and because I don't come from anywhere and am part of nothing, I pretended I was part of it. Beaufort was the golden place under the sun that I came to when I was fifteen. This place that I'd never heard of in my life surrounded me with friends that I still have. Gene Norris was a prince among men. Gene was the kind of teacher who made you want to do great things for him because you adored him and you loved him. The first paper I wrote for Gene, he handed it back and said, "Boy, you're something, aren't you? You ain't nothing. You're something." He found something in me, and it was thrilling to have been identified, to have been spotted. You know, "I see you, boy." I was seen; I was seen. What he would always teach is: literature and art can change your life. They change everything about you and the way you see the world.

Gene started taking me out, and he'd say, "Boy, you want to go ramblin' this weekend?" Sure, Mr. Norris. Dad went crazy. "Peg, are you nuts? You got this faggot taking our son to antique shops?" "He's a very nice man, Don. He's taken an interest in Pat." And I flowered with Gene. I was looking for role models of men who were not vicious, for a gentle kind of man.

Two years there and then I take my next grand step into the total dissolution of my life when I march through the gates of the Citadel, which is the end of the story of my sad educational life.

⁓

Some military brats love it that they get to see new places and remake themselves every year. If they screwed up in one place they could do better at the next place and create themselves anew. I hated moving, easing our way from one shit for a town to another shit for a town. I was a shy kid and wouldn't make friends until sort of in the March–April period, and by then Dad would get orders, and we'd go again. The military brat always knows when orders have been cut in Washington. Mom and Dad are whispering in the kitchen: "When do we tell the kids we're leaving? They won't be at this school any longer, and we just got here nine months ago, Don." "Hey, tough shit. These are orders from the Pentagon. What do I do, tell them to go fuck themselves? No, we gotta hit the road." I never even saw anything grow; I saw nothing make it from one season to the next.

It really got to me for the first time when we spent our year in Orlando with the Harper family. Dad was completely absent, I got completely comfortable in the school I was going to, and we were living around lakes. Orlando was a beautiful town back then, lovely beyond measure, and that was a good life.

What the Conroy kids loved about Uncle Russ and Aunt Helen's house is that nothing ever changed, not a piece of furniture, the deer heads on the wall, *The World Book Encyclopedia.* I saw a rug going into the house in 1955 that was there when Aunt Helen died in 2000 sometime. I still dream about the pattern in that rug. They had a pepper shaker that was a rooster and a salt shaker that was a hen, and we all looked on these as talismans of sameness, of belongingness. It was a real house, instead of these places where you live on bases. For us it was just magical.

I dreamed of a life like that, and every time I ran across it, I ached for what I knew I would never have. We lived in ugly houses, Quonset huts, and trailers. What I wanted was a nice house, normalcy of some sort. I wanted the salt and pepper shaker; I did. I really wanted it. I longed for that and hungered for that. The moving around we did when I was a kid gave me an incredible, extraordinary need for a home.

We never lived in places that were ours, and neither of my parents ever had much taste. The first portraits on the wall my mother did after she discovered painting by numbers. Even as little as I was, I saw that they were perfectly hideous, but Mom considered them beautiful. One was of the Blessed Mary, and the other was Bozo the Clown. These portraits hung on our walls for years, as though we had acquired them from a castle in England. Taste is a thing that accrues over generations, and my mother had a long way to go.

When I was in fourth grade at Annunciation School in Havelock, North Carolina, outside Cherry Point, my mother was on some kind of committee for the Officers' Club, and they were having a party at the general's house. My mother had taken me over because the general's son, Rebel Moore, was my age and he needed a playmate during this party. Rebel had the nicest house on the base, and as we were getting ready to go outside, I noticed my mother in the dining room looking at the pictures on the wall and studying them. Mrs. Moore, the general's wife, had not come down yet; she was still getting ready upstairs. Mom was the first to arrive so she could bring me to play with Rebel. So I saw my mom going from picture to picture in the dining room, and I realized what she was doing was comparing it to what she had on her walls. Mrs. Moore was a Southern woman of impeccable taste—she had come from one of those families—and one of the things she had was portraits of her children, those little blond portraits that are in every Southern household. Mom was zeroing in on this, taking in the whole thing. She'd study it and try to memorize it. That's how she learned; that's how she did it.

So, the Lady of Guadalupe went off our wall; Bozo the Clown went off the wall; Jesus went off the wall; the paint-by-numbers went off the wall. All those disappeared. Now, the problem was, Mom did not have the money to do what the general's wife could do. But there were several times Dad left during the year to go to Europe, Asia, a Med cruise—whatever. Mom sent him photos of herself and the children and asked Dad to get some portraits made from them, because they're cheaper over in Europe. Dad writes, says, "I got portraits of you and the kids coming in."

Well, these portraits come in, and Mom opens up the box, so excited. Then she has a stunned look on her face, a look of complete appallment, a desperate embarrassment. Carol and I are sitting there, and Carol says, "Mom, what's wrong? Let's see." "No, I'm not going to show you." But Carol was always a troublemaker, especially when it came to poking holes in Mom's image of herself. So Carol unwraps the portrait of me, and I start screaming. It's not that I don't recognize myself. I do recognize myself, but I am a young Japanese boy. My eyes are dark brown, and I am as Japanese as Emperor Hirohito. Carol is a fat little Japanese girl with big cheeks, dark brown eyes, and black hair. Mom looks like a geisha girl. Well, she hid those portraits, and we never saw them again. When Mom's taste got better, the stuff got better, but taste was still a problem.

~

Except for two years at Beaufort High School, I went to Catholic schools all my life, and the Catholics got me. They fucked up everything connected with my dick and my brain. In sex education class, the nuns taught sex like it was something Tasmanian devils did to each other. Sister Skalaska made the vagina sound like a sewer pipe leading to hell. She told us about the hideous smells and said, "I know you young men would never even think of putting your fingers in this." She made it sound like the most repulsive thing you could do. She made the male organ sound like a rhinoceros schlong, like some loud beast you must learn to control, but of course it's uncontrollable when confronted with a sewer-like vagina. The nuns made the girls think there was going to be this beast waiting for them in bed. He was going to come on like a Tyrannosaurus rex. "You must give of yourself because of children, but if it's not giving you children, you can't do it."

On the playgrounds at school while all these boys and girls raced around having a ball, the nuns were watching with their peregrine eyes for any sign of sexual intent or a hard-on. When the bell rang, you had to freeze wherever you were, as though you had been turned into a pillar of salt, and you're suddenly Lot's wife. So you freeze in midstride or bent over double and remain locked in these positions until the nun clangs her bell, and then you walk to get in line. They had us completely trained.

But all of a sudden, I wake up one night to find I have a dick. I am completely stunned by the power of this thing, the power of this urge, which the Catholic Church simply tries to make you a soldier against when it comes up to you. No one had told me about nocturnal emissions. I thought I was bleeding to death. This was in ninth grade. God, it feels good to bleed to death. I touched some of the blood and saw it was white. It was a complete shock to me. All of a sudden something clicked: This is what they've been talking about. This is it. This is the great sin. This is what the nuns are worried about, the priests are worried about. And of course it's easy to be good when you don't have that to worry about. It's really easy to be a good Christian boy. But to suddenly have this Vesuvius located directly inside you which you had no idea was there, no idea would explode out of you, changes everything. I could have been a priest if not for that. Still, I was the most virginal, ridiculous teenage boy who ever lived, the most Catholic kid in America, an altar boy from fourth grade all the way through the Citadel.

They scare you to death when you're a little kid; that's what the Catholics do to us. I was a little second-grade kid, and these nuns had Joycean powers of description about what hell was like. And I thought, Hmmm. It ain't worth it. You mean I got to be good or I go there? I found it difficult when I was in second grade hearing that if I fucked up at all I would burn in hellfire for all eternity. I remember burning myself on a match, and I found it rather painful, and then I thought, you know, this will end. But all eternity? I thought a school day lasted a long time, and I'm thinking good God Almighty, all eternity? This is a God you do not want to piss off. It just terrified me. All I could see were these nightmare scenarios of me playing with my small Chihuahua-size dick and God spying me when he was taking a smoking break.

In the time I grew up, you could go to hell and burn in eternal fires for eating a piece of ham on Friday. If you did not eat bream, trout, mackerel, or herring, which my mother solved with fish sticks, you could go to hell, and I'm thinking, that is serious. The Catholics certainly gave us a sense of sin, of borders that we shouldn't cross, and if we did, we knew we were displeasing not just the priest, not just our parents; we're displeasing God. And if we did that, where were we going? To HELL. They're very clear.

I am a nonbeliever in converts to Catholicism, because if you weren't there in the trenches with an Irish nun giving you brain damage for not turning in your homework, I'm sorry, you're not Catholic. These converts will Aquinas you to death, St. Augustine you to death, Thomas More you to death. It drives me crazy. There is nothing I believe in less than a Catholic conversion. Robert Coles—give me a break. Walker Percy—kiss my ass. In America you cannot be a Roman Catholic unless you were beaten up by a mustachioed three-hundred-pound nun when you were an eight-year-old boy. If you don't have that experience, you don't know anything about the religion. For those who do have that experience, our souls are unrecapturable after a Catholic childhood. They got their hooks in me, and that's it. First they get the dick, then they get the brain, and you don't ever get them completely back. It is all a story in being fucked up, completely screwed up, nuns teaching me sex. I am lucky one of those priests did not fuck me. Because in my life that would have been it.

~

I never rebelled in any way that I can remember. And I wasn't a kid that did a lot wrong. I wasn't a mischievous kid; I wasn't a kid that got into trouble. This is what always got to me: I was a dream kid, a goody-goody kid. Anybody would have loved to have me as a kid. I would see kids I went to school with get drunk on the weekend and wreck their cars, and I would think, my God, my father would kill these guys. There'd be a murder on his hands. But I played the game as it was written out for me. I was simply a cadet taking orders. We were all a minor branch of Dad's command.

But I just could not measure up to my father. I could not do it, and I tried. I really tried. But I always let Dad down. One time Dad picked me up at a game in his uniform from some school in Dumbfuck, South Carolina. Our school had earned a record; I think I scored forty-three points. Dad screamed at me all the way back for not playing defense, just screamed. In the thirty miles he just screamed. "Scouts aren't gonna like you! You can't play defense!"

There was nothing I could do to impress my father, nothing I could do to make him think I was successful. I played three sports; I was in a million activities. They had me totally under their control: I couldn't drive; I couldn't date. But my overachieving-ness did not bring me any kudos. Finally, with Mom one time, I said, "What in the hell can I do? I'm president of my senior class; I've lettered in three sports. And there's no way to please him; there's nothing I can do."

Mom was my cheering squad, my marching band, my everything. But I would never tell Dad anything because this brought out his meanness toward me. He would say, "Who gives a shit? Who cares? I hate guys that brag about themselves. You win medals, you keep your trap shut. That's part of the game." So I learned to tell Dad nothing.

There was a fight my mother and father had over me, a war for a son's soul. I had to play basketball like a tough guy because I was little, but I always put out a hand and helped guys up off the court. My father hated it; my mother loved it. Sportsmanship was big with her. And I wanted to be a man like my mother admired, the kind of guy that women didn't have to be terrified of, somebody that didn't beat you up. Dad felt sportsmanship was the realm of the complete pussy. "Don't give 'em a hand up. Give 'em a hand, and when they try and use it, you slap 'em back down on the floor." It used to enrage him that I'd knock guys down and then stick out an arm and pull them up. He hated that. Nothing made my father more unhappy with me than my winning all sportsmanship awards ever offered in my direction my entire life. Dad would say, "Oh, yes, my son. The pussy award always goes to him." And he'd say, "If you were a Chicago boy, you'd throw it back in their face. I'd break the jaw of the guy that gave me the pussy award. I don't want to win the pussy award; I want to have guys down there bleeding on the floor beside me after I've put them on the deck." And then of course, when I won it at the Citadel, he went nuts. He just went crazy. "You won the pussy award at a military college?" He just could not ever let that go.

Dad would always say, "I'm not raising a household of lovers; I'm raising fighters. I don't want no hand-holders in my fucking house. You give me a hand-holder I'm going to kick your ass out of the house. No hand-holders." But Mom won. I became a good sport because my father was a bad sport. I hated the model of manhood Dad presented for his sons. Guys who beat up women don't impress me much. Guys who beat up kids don't impress me either.

⁓

I was always walking into the first day of a completely new school and environment without knowing a soul. I will always be walking into the first day of a completely new school without knowing a soul. That is how I walk the earth and always will. Sports was my way of walking into a new school and making sure they had to deal with me somehow. The coach had to talk to me; teammates had to talk to me. I got to Beaufort, and in the first game I scored twenty-eight points. The next day everybody knew my name. I was asked to spend the night with Bruce Harper, who was handsome, vice president of the student council, and seemed like a huge big shot to me. That all changed my life, and that was because of sports.

What had happened was I had grown into the body I was going to carry into manhood without realizing it. I was still a skinny kid, but I'd become a strong kid I didn't know about. When that first game was played at Beaufort High School, I could tell they'd never seen black kids play basketball, and that's who I'd played against. That's how I'd learned. In sixth, seventh, and eighth grade, I used to go to the ghetto near our house in D.C. and pray that they didn't have enough people. When I played I was called "that fucking white boy." "I'll take the fucking white kid," or "the white fuck." "Come here, white fuck." In Beaufort I could hear them saying, "He plays nigger basketball." It occurred to me I was the best player on the court. I could see it in my teammates' eyes; I could feel it in the crowd.

The next day, I walk into class, and Gene Norris goes, "Oh, Lord, I think a star is coming into class. I've never met a star before. To have a real star in my classroom, it just makes me humble." Then Gene puts me up for president of the senior class. I had no idea who anybody was, but they voted for me because I was an athlete.

Sports gave me a way to like myself, because I never saw myself as the worst athlete out there, and generally I was okay. I was never a great athlete, but a little better than most; never the fastest, but the third fastest. It gave me a feeling that I was doing really well at something. Still, Dad denigrated everything I did. "Who wouldn't do well against these rednecks? These kids barely know how to put on their tennis shoes. These ain't Chicago boys. Chicago boys would eat you alive."

My father was a great athlete and a great basketball player, but he didn't teach me or any of his sons. We learned by ourselves without Dad's help, in fact with Dad mocking us every step of the way. When I played basketball with Dad, he'd say, "Okay, come on, pussy." And then what did he do? He wouldn't guard me. He'd start slapping me in the face. He'd just slap me and slap me and slap me. I couldn't go right, I couldn't go left. I just had to stay there getting slapped until I gave him the basketball and walked off the court. And he'd say, "What a mama's boy. I tried to make a Chicago kid out of you, and you don't have it in you." He'd say, "Southern pussy."

It seemed to bother Dad more than anything else that I had some success in basketball, a sport that he had great success in. It became a threat to him, my coming into my own as a basketball player. It made him furious instead of giving him any sort of pride. He would not come to the games, or he'd come and scream at me all the way home. On the court I'd hear my father scream at me when I'd pull a guy up, "I'd have stomped his face!" Then he'd be yelling for the other team to embarrass me. "Knock Conroy down! Kick him! Deck Conroy! Put him on the court! Put him on the ground! Break his leg!" I don't think he wanted another hotshot in the family besides himself.

But he could not take it away from me, because with sports, you have numbers. You have statistics. I knew what Dad had averaged in high school. He knew it, and he knew that I knew it. I averaged eighteen points my first year, twenty-two the next year, and he had never done that in high school, although he was a much better athlete, much bigger and stronger. But I was quicker and faster and often the top scorer. So I had statistics I could throw at Dad. If I threw them too hard, he'd kill me, so I didn't. But he knew what they were. Dad would do his stuff—"You're the MVP? What a shitty team that was"—but it didn't dim that for me. With writing, there were no statistics. And my father: "I can't wait to tell the boys in the squadron that my son is writing poetry." If I had something published in the literary magazine, he'd go, "Mom, your favorite faggot just published another poem."

~

I do not know when it was that Dad applied to the Citadel for me. All I know is I had already graduated from high school, I was not accepted to a college, and Dad would not talk about that with me. I spent a horrible summer after I graduated without having even applied to a college, and when I asked Dad about it, he said, "Shut the fuck up. I'm working on it." I was fairly hysterical about my future because I didn't seem to have one. As far as I knew I was not going to college the next year because I had not applied anywhere. Later I learned that Dad was hoping for a basketball scholarship, and I didn't get one. I thought of joining the Marine Corps; that was my backup plan.

Then finally, in the middle of the summer, at the all-star game in Columbia at the University of South Carolina, I find out that the Citadel is taking me as a walk-on in basketball. This coach says to me: "I want to welcome you, Pat. You're in the Citadel family now." I didn't even know an application had been sent. I found out later that the Beaufort Citadel Club put up $500 for me, and General Edwin Pollock, who later said that getting me into the Citadel was the worst decision he ever made in his career, got them to deduct $1,000 from my tuition. So it had taken all this time to cobble together the money. Mom told me they didn't have to pay anything for the first year, which is an expensive year because of the uniforms. Then they gave me a basketball scholarship at the end of my freshman year.

Imagine my joy at finding myself at the Citadel after a childhood like mine. It was worse than Dad. But you know, that is what I went through, and it doesn't do me any good to regret it; it doesn't do me any good to think of what might have been. I used to dream that going to Harvard would have solved many of my problems. Of course it wouldn't have. I know that now. Nothing could have solved my problems. And the Citadel is what I got, that is what I endured, that is what I didn't like, and that is ultimately what I wrote about.

I went up there with eleven or twelve guys from Beaufort High School; we were in the freshman class together. So I thought I was going to have a whole bunch of friends that year at the Citadel. At the end of the year, I look around, and I was the only one left. I was the only one from that group who graduated.

I actually left before school even started. Mom put me on a train for two and a half days from Omaha, Nebraska, where Dad was stationed at Offut Air Force Base. It turned out I was early, and the only freshman on campus. I walk over to the barracks, and a group takes me and racks my ass. I'm completely brutalized that first day. Then they kick me out: Get outa here toe-head; get outa here waste wad. I'm exhausted, and I didn't know what to do or where to go. I walked to Highway 17 with my suitcase and hitchhiked to Beaufort, where I find Gene Norris eating a hamburger at the Shack with Bill Dufford, who was the principal of Beaufort High School. Gene is furious with me because he thinks it's the only way I'm going to go to college.

"Gene," I said, "I'm sorry. I just didn't like it. I didn't like it at all." And I get, "You little scallywag, you didn't give it a chance. You didn't even last one night. Your father's going to kill you if he doesn't get to me first. That's the only chance you have for a college education." He arranged for Ray Williams, who was a senior at the Citadel, to take me back up to Opening Day the next morning.

My view of the Citadel was shaped forever, whether this is fair or not, by the cruelty of the plebe year. I was not expecting the savagery of the plebe system I walked into, mainly because they all lied about it. They all said hazing is not allowed. It's against the law in South Carolina. But the Citadel did not mind breaking that law. So I get to this place where all the knobs are starving and upperclassmen are screaming at us night and day, making us do pushups till we vomit. Then they'd march you out to the marsh and let the no-see-ums and mosquitoes eat you up. It was ferocious, and it was beyond anything I had ever been prepared for, even by my father. It was institutionalized brutality, a complete anarchy of abuse.

The pure aggression of male society is a terrible thing. The rack line is a terrible thing; they'll get you and make you do pushups till you drop. They will make you do anything until you collapse physically before them, then they scream and humiliate you. Being in the barracks was like being on the island in *Lord of the Flies*. Young men will do anything bad as far as you'll let them. The only thing holding anybody back at the Citadel was they could not kill you. That was the point they could not go to. But that's the only thing I saw holding people back.

There are always one or two people Citadel guys never forgive, who went overboard, who were too sadistic, where it became too personal. There are guys I haven't forgiven today for what they did to me in the plebe system. All Citadel graduates have at least one guy they'll hate for the rest of their lives. We all got one. We'd like to kill him ourselves and not just hear that he dies. We'd like to murder him. The guys who were just doing their job, who were just playing the game—you don't hate them. But the guys who took it to this sadistic level that only the plebe system is capable of—God, you hate them.

So I had entered into a force field of terror. I was scared the whole time I was there. The freshman year at the Citadel absolutely traumatized me. It was like being hit by a tidal wave; I was in a state of shock the entire year. At the end of the year, my coach said I went quiet, that I quit talking. He said they were more worried about me than anybody they'd ever had in the basketball program. I clammed up; I wouldn't talk to my teammates; I just shut it off.

The mystique of the system is that they tear you down and then they build you back up into men. They break you down completely and then rebuild you into a Citadel man. They get you, you're a piece of shit, and by the time they finish you, you're a rare Carrara marble. Harsh discipline makes the man, and all that. Blatant cruelty is not only lionized; it's like the trail to sainthood. It is the noblest thing you can do. You're taking this poor knob and making a whole man out of him.

God forbid if you're ugly or fat or skinny or pimply. One poor kid was nicknamed Death Warmed Over. He was so ugly, they couldn't stand looking at his face in mess, so they made him put a bag over his head with holes cut in where his eyes and mouth and nose were, and he had to eat under the table for the entire year so he would not make the upperclassmen gag at the sight of him. That was good for him psychologically, don't you think? They were making a whole man out of him.

I didn't buy anything about the plebe system. It just seemed like cruelty for no reason. It was pure harassment, nothing else. I did not believe in that road to leadership. Why did the Citadel think the plebe system makes good men? Why would anybody think that anything good could come from such cruelty? I don't remember having any moments of courage. I was as weak and cowardly as my father always thought I was. I was proving what a loser he always knew I was. I didn't feel magnified or glorified or feel I was making a better man out of myself. I was just simply terrified and brutalized. I never felt the things other guys told me they felt, that they were on their way to becoming a whole man at the Citadel. That philosophy did not make it to me. My military philosophy is that my platoon that loves me will annihilate your platoon that hates you. An officer eats only after his men are fed; an officer sleeps only after his men are down for the night. I do not believe discipline and torture need to go together.

I think six hundred were in our freshman class; 240 graduated. They wiped us out in droves that first year. And these were good guys any school would be proud of; they just could not take the cruelty. Some of these were skinny kids or fat kids. I was a jock, and I couldn't take it. All during that year, fathers had to come get their poor kids and take them home. It was the worst thing you've ever seen: boys crying, fathers crying. And I knew the kid's story—he cracked under pressure and couldn't take it anymore. I remember on Hell Night seeing them lined up in the dorm with their suitcases. They could not wait to get out of there.

Here's how I account for the fact I stayed: He was about six-four, 235 pounds, with the temper of Zeus. I could not have that scene. If I quit the Citadel, I could imagine Dad beating me up all the way home as he spread out for me all the deficiencies I brought to manhood. I could just hear it: You weren't man enough. It would have been a nightmare trip. And because of my father, I did not have a loving family to go back home to. Also, I realized the Citadel was going to be my only chance at a college education. So I had to survive the plebe system.

One of the unhappiest parts about being a cadet is that it was noticed that I didn't participate in the system when I was an upperclassman. It shocked me that my classmates did. When I got to be a sophomore, I thought my classmates wouldn't do the same thing to the freshmen coming in. Boy, was I wrong. I thought, Okay, you didn't learn much. But in the groupthink of the Citadel, you got rank because the harder you were on the plebes, the greater you were proving your belief in the system. And they would tell me they believed in the system. They would say it's making men out of us. I would go, "Fuck. You. It's making us beasts of burden." The fact that I could openly hate it so early got me in trouble with my classmates. It ruined me with them, because they would go, "Let's show them. Let's go out there and show them we're the best class that ever came to the Citadel." "Fuck you"—that was me. So I was never really embraced by my company guys, although the word "classmate" is a holy one for me. One of the reasons I love my classmates—some of those poor guys, I don't know how they did it. I just don't know how they did it. Some were skinny guys, some were fat guys, and they were humiliated beyond anybody's capacity to believe. And yet they stayed, they showed courage, they made it, and those guys—those guys have always amazed me. The guys who went through the plebe system with you, who survived with you—these guys become untouchable.

And here is the cunning of things like the Marine Corps or the plebe system. Once you get out of that trial by fire, it makes you think you're better than the guys who didn't make it. They were not man enough to make it, to last through it as I was. Because I went through the plebe system, I am a whole man. And now you're part of this group, this fellowship, this brotherhood, and there's enormous power in this feeling. So afterward, everybody says they loved it, and that's how propaganda works. There's a whole male psychology and philosophy that goes along with it that you see everywhere. Since they went through it, it's the best. Because it's the hardest, they're the best. Because it's the meanest, they're the strongest.

I used to hear that "Conroy doesn't believe in the plebe system," and I would go, "I certainly don't. Torture? Degradation? Humiliation? No, gosh, count me out." I'm sure my reaction was partly a reaction against my father. Maybe I would have taken it a lot differently had I come at it from a different family. I knew I was taking the plebe system differently from everybody else at the Citadel.

But I never raised my voice to a plebe. I never said anything except "Hi. How are you doing smackhead? What a great choice of college you made. Aren't you happy? Isn't it great to be tortured from the time you get up until the time you go to bed? Isn't this just wonderful? It's making a whole man out of you, I can tell." They would be sitting there miserable, with their shaved heads. "Ah, yes, young smackhead. It's 6:15 in the morning in February. It's dark; it's freezing. Isn't it great to wake up and see the stars? Now all over America young men will be waking up just like you, only they will be waking up six hours later, they will be hung over from the night before, and they will turn over, and there will be something soft and warm and lovely beside them, and that will be called a *girl*. Can you imagine such a nightmare, turning over to find a girl in the same bed with you? Good God, not us Citadel men."

One of the reasons I did not get rank at the Citadel was I did not participate in the plebe system. And Dad, "Hey son, you need to get involved in that. I'd give them a hell they'll remember the rest of their lives." I'd go, "Yes sir, I'll do it. I'll do it starting next year, sir." Dad would have gotten through the plebe system easily and I think would have been extraordinarily mean when he got to be an upperclassman.

I enjoyed it thoroughly, Dad's despair: a colonel's son being a private at the Citadel, never an officer. It drove him crazy. It was one of my great victories over Dad. I was the best senior private in the class of '66–'67 at the Citadel, an award which humiliated my father. "You're the best of the shits? What an honor, son. You're the best of the non-leaders. Gosh, will you charge that hill for me, son? And make sure you take your men with you."

I hated every single part of that school, except for the teachers. My professors were good men. They didn't have their doctorates; they had no ambition; they published nothing. They were there for the students. While I was running around campus in platoons singing "I want a life of constant danger, I want to be an airborne ranger, I want to go to Vietnam, I want to kill some Viet Cong," I was afraid that God had not arranged for me to get a good education. But my English teachers were sweethearts to me. They knew I wanted to be a writer, and they did everything they could to encourage that.

Colonel Doyle was fabulous to me. The first week we had to write an essay, and I wrote one about a freshman who goes out in the middle of the night and takes a shit on the quadrangle to show what he thinks about that school, their ways of raising soldiers, their ways of discipline. I could have been kicked out of school, but Colonel Doyle called me to his class afterward. He said, "You're having a very difficult time, Mr. Conroy. I hope you can last." I said, "I hate this place." Then he puts up the grades by our serial number. Mine was 16407, thank you; they taught me that under torture. Anyway, A+ for me, F for the entire class. So I knew I had been spotted.

And Colonel Doyle got me through the program. He would choose the best teachers for me, the best teachers the college had. He was wonderful. "Mr. Conroy, I think you are going to find many subtle pleasures as we tackle modern fiction together." I wrote poems for him, and he'd sit beside me in his little study and circle words. "Now, now, there are too many 'poignant' moments already in English literature, don't you think? Let's not add another one to it." He'd strike the word, and we'd go on. He was as loving as he could be. Fat Jack Martin told me, "Mr. Conroy, I am absolutely positive you do not know a single fact of English history, but you write about your ignorance so beautifully." My classmates had a different way of encouraging me: "I saw your poem, faggot."

My only gratitude to the Citadel is that I was spotted early. An upperclassman named Clark Martin told me, "The English faculty thinks they've never had a writer like you in their history. They're watching you." I wrote for the literary magazine, the *Shako,* three or four short stories, innumerable dog-shit poems. I look at it now; I'm horrified. It's no-good crap. But I looked Miltonian compared to the other cadets; I looked titanic in my powers. It looked like a literary god had been unleashed. My senior year I won the literary award, and the guy who gave it to me, Major Alexander, as he shook my hand, said, "Mr. Conroy, we're expecting to hear from you again." I found that thrilling, because he had never even taught me.

~

When I graduated from high school, I believed I was going to be a Marine Corps fighter pilot. I never told anybody. I just wanted to suddenly appear as a fighter pilot, and I wanted to take Dad up in the air and kick his ass in one-on-one combat. I wanted to beat him in a dogfight. My image of myself and my ambition for myself was to be a better fighter pilot than he was.

I was shocked when they tested my eyes at the Citadel and learned I had no chance whatsoever of being a pilot. I was color-blind and had no depth perception. They could never allow me to fly. It was one of the worst moments of my life. There wasn't a thing about my father I admired except him being a fighter pilot, and I couldn't follow him in that. Also, it ended my military career. Otherwise, I think I would have done the exact same thing Dad did. I didn't know a military brat who'd ever done anything except enter the military.

When I had to think about going into the infantry and getting myself killed in Vietnam, I started studying the war. Why are we there? I couldn't quite figure that out: we were fighting against their George Washington, Ho Chi Minh, who ran the French out. I quickly realized that nobody knows what they're doing over there, and I've got no fight against those people. If the United States cannot explain to me, with my background, why we're going to war against a nation, who can they explain it to? I thought it seemed like the worst war we could get into, supporting the worst people.

Dad was surprisingly good about it and told me "Don't get yourself killed in a politician's war." All the way during the Citadel, he would say things to me like "I fought in three wars. My sons ain't got to fight in any of them. I paid our dues." That surprised me a great deal, that he never put any pressure on us to go into the military. And there's not one day served in the military by a Conroy kid in my generation. It was probably Dad's way of loving us. It certainly wasn't something he could say. He never told me he loved me once in his life. That was a deflected conversation. So I dodged the war for what I thought were very good, legitimate reasons, although I'm sure there was some direct rebellion against my father and the Citadel too.

～

Right before I graduated, they awarded me the first Citadel Development Foundation scholarship, and what they were going to do was send me to get my master's degree in English and then require me for two years to come back and teach at the Citadel. I was accepted to Virginia, Emory, Vanderbilt, and one other. The Citadel was going to pay tuition and books. I thought I'd go live with Stanny in her apartment, which is near Emory. I would have loved two years after the Citadel to write and talk about books, where the girls were pretty, the boys were handsome, and we all partied. It sounded great to me and sounded even better two years later after getting fired from Daufuskie Island. But I did not have the money to cover my monthly expenses. What I had never heard of was an assistantship. No one told me about it; no one told me I was eligible to apply for it; nobody told me it was a way to get through graduate school. I was in despair because I did not have the money to go.

Then Mr. Randel said, "Boy, what are you going to do next year?" Mr. Randel was the deputy superintendent of schools in Beaufort. His son had died right in front of me on the baseball field, and I became friends with the Randels for the rest of my life. "I thought I was going to graduate school, Mr. Randel, but that just didn't work out for me." He said, "You don't want to go in the service." I said, "No, I really don't." He said, "I got two jobs opening at Beaufort High School. One's teaching and the other's coaching football, basketball, and baseball." I said, "No kiddin'?" He said, "You get paid $4,700 a year. You get a little more, $200 for each sport you coach, and you won't get a better deal in South Carolina." So I shook hands on it, and suddenly, my fate was launched.

⌒

Because I came from nothing, it looked like I would live a pretty normal life and not do much. I thought I would teach at Beaufort High School forever and write poetry on the side. That was my dream of life, and I thought it was a good one. It did not work out very well, but that was my original plan. I did not plan on getting fired. The guy who fired me, on the school board, is still alive, and now he says, "I gave Pat his career. I started him out."

Because my writing career was a total accident of fate. With my background, with my inferior childhood and my inferior education coming from a military college, the chances of me becoming a writer seemed about none. It just did not seem possible, and I knew that. But luck and fortune played a part. I would not be able to get published today. If I had not been able to get my books published back then, I don't know what I would have done with my life. And it never occurred to me that someone would make movies out of my books. That was a world I never had any ambition to enter; it's been one of the great surprises of my career. The movies took me by complete surprise. That was not part of any plan I'd had in my life. Whatever fantasies I had, they did not include what happened to me.

And whatever success I've had, I've had trouble processing. I don't think I've enjoyed any of the good things that happened. The first of my books were controversial, and I was always embroiled in warfare. The Citadel banned *The Boo*. The state of South Carolina went berserk with *The Water Is Wide*. *The Great Santini*—my family explodes. *The*

Lords of Discipline—the Citadel went out of their minds. I always seem to irritate somebody every time I write a book. With each one, I had no time to think what a pleasant achievement this was. There was too much going on, and my life was always coming apart. It wasn't a time of enjoyment or satisfaction. So the first part of my career I was in this defense mode of trying to keep people away and fight people off. That was one reason I could not quite enjoy what was happening, and it didn't feel all that successful to me.

Also, Dad made it where I could not enjoy anything I accomplished at all, ever. He ruined something for me by denigrating any success I had as a kid and made it impossible for me to enjoy any success I ever had as an adult. There will never be any feeling of achievement for me, because that's not part of my makeup. I can enjoy other people, and enjoy giving joy to other people, but joy over something that happens to me directly is beyond me.

I am cautious about happiness. I have no trust of the good times, no trust of the happy times. I never trust success. When it comes, Conroy looks around and behind and over his shoulder to see what kind of bestial, inhuman thing is gaining momentum on him and will hurt him, beat him up, savage him, hate him, and pull him down. I think I never learned to trust life because I could not trust my father. I learned to distrust. A birthday party, like Carol's in our house on Culpeper, can turn in a second into the worst nightmare you've ever seen. I set a record in some gym, and I'm screamed at the whole way back. I scored thirty-six points against Chicora, and Dad slapped me for walking a kid who hurt his ankle off the court. Wham. "Never do that again!" Anything could turn. You could be walking along, laughing with your teammates, and Dad would slap you. You didn't know it was coming. This probably happened five or six times, where I'm laughing with my teammates and all of a sudden—BAM.

I think Dad killed my capacity for joy. I never know when I'm having a good time; that is part of the malady I bring to my life. I wish I could actually know that I'm enjoying something while it happens. I wish I had a part of me that was not so damaged I could enjoy my success. But I have never been able to feel good or take pleasure in anything that happens to me that is good. What I have been able to do is to accept as my due, as my lot and my fate, things that were bad. The only thing I have total trust in is utter failure, debacle, disgrace. Then I think I'm living what God wanted me to live. I forget everything good that happens to me. I only remember the things that leave wounds, extract organs, and create a trail of blood that follows me from room to room. Something good happens, and I will feel good for a day. Then I'll wake up the next morning and all the other things that feast upon the liver, that nibble at the edges of the soul, will be there as they always are when we wake up.

My deepest living is in the imagination of others, when I take that magic carpet ride of being a reader. When I enter into a world that is not mine, I find such happiness, such completion, such totality. I love it when a book does that for me. The happiness that reading gives me has been one of the greatest pleasures of my life. I read with joy, I take great pleasure in it, and I think it has saved my life. I have to get a certain amount of reading in each day; I've got to have those words coming at me. God, I love what it does. When I'm into a book that I love, it is a form of perfect happiness on earth for me. I don't need any more.

I think that's why I want to write, to make others feel that way. When literature is magical, it is life changing, and that's why the writer does it. And in my case, writing has been a lifesaving act. I don't understand when people ask, "Is your writing therapeutic?" I should hope so. Writing has provided that craft where I find myself. I had things I had to get out somehow. I do not know if I was blessed or cursed with being the rememberer. But we writers forget nothing. Every one of those guys who went to the Citadel took it and left it behind. I left nothing behind. I remembered every instant, every guy who yelled at me, every guy who humiliated me. Just like I remember the utter horror which I grew up with. If I did not let these things out, something was going to kill me. Also, I wanted to be a writer, and a writer who matters, because I wanted to prove that my life was not worthless, that it was leading toward something.

ONE

Beaufort, South Carolina

1967–1973

Here's this guy who loved being a hero and saving people's lives. He's supposed to be the hero in the situation, but he didn't save anybody. . . . It fed into his guilt that he wasn't good enough. . . . And he didn't understand his confusion about his identity. He was always conflicted between being the good guy—the hero—and the bad guy.

MARION O'NEILL, Ph.D., ABPP, clinical psychologist

Anyone who knows me well must understand and be sympathetic to my genuine need to be my own greatest hero. It is not a flaw of character. It is a catastrophe.

PAT CONROY, *The Lords of Discipline*

My first two years of teaching at Beaufort High School were immensely happy to me, although I was incompetent to teach the courses I was teaching—psychology and American government—oh, yes, I knew a lot about both subjects. So that first day was terrifying. I felt ill prepared to teach, ill prepared to face those thirty students that first morning. It scared me to death; I was so afraid of public speaking. I'd once taken a public-speaking course at the Citadel to get over my abject fear of this, but I had not quite done it yet.

So I had written out every word I was going to say during this first class. I even had instructions for myself like "Walk to the window. Tug at belt. Let them know you're not nervous or intimidated. Walk back slowly to the podium." I followed my directions. It was a psychology class, so I played some song that had psychological meaning and was going to apply that to all of life. You know, "Psychology is everywhere.

It's all around us. You're living it right now. You're living it as I talk to you." So I'm doing all this horseshit. Then I read them "Richard Corey" by Edward Arlington Robinson, with that powerful ending. I look up, I'm completely finished with the five pages of instructions to myself, and I have forty-five minutes left. Sheer panic ran through me, sheer and utter panic.

Then I realized that bullshit can flow freely out of my mouth at any time. And these kids seemed to love everything that came out of my mouth; I could do no wrong with these kids. I never knew I had a good personality until I was in those classrooms and could barely say a word without those kids laughing their asses off. I didn't know I was funny, and those kids laughed at everything I said. These kids had no particular reason to like me, but they could not get enough of me, and they let me know that. I found out from the girls I taught in class that I was attractive, which I had never considered. The girls seemed crazy for me; the boys seemed to want to emulate me and follow me around. I did not know that people would like me like this, because at the Citadel I was a misfit. When I realized my students simply adored me, I found out I adored teaching. It was a great moment for me, a great two years of my life. And I found myself very happy teaching.

In psychology I ended up teaching these kids sex education, because I had six girls get pregnant the first semester, and they kicked them all out of school. These were some of the smartest girls I had. I was roaring down at the principal's office, Mr. Biddle. "Why did you kick them out? These are six of the smartest girls in class. I'd be happy to teach them."

"Well, we have a policy in the county, that if a girl gets pregnant she has to drop out immediately."

I said, "Did you ever think about changing the policy? It's a dumb policy."

He completely failed there, and then I surprised Mr. Biddle by saying, "What about the boys? Kick them out."

"Well, you know, we have the problem that we don't know who the boys are."

I said, "I'll be happy to tell you. I know all six of them, and I'll give you their names right now. You can kick them right out."

"Well, you know, that's not the way the policy works."

There was nothing bad about Lloyd Biddle, and I think he said something to the home ec teacher, who came up to me, said, "Pat, I've been wanting to teach girls about birth control in my home ec class, but they all told me I'd be fired."

"How can I help you?"

"You're so young and new here, why don't you teach sex education in your psychology course? No one would think you'd be doing it. I can't get away with it in home ec."

I said, "I don't know how to tell you this, but I'm a virgin."

She said, "That's no problem. I have a book."

She gives me the book; I tell the kids what I'm going to do, why I'm doing it. I said, "None of you girls are getting pregnant while you're in this class. If they do, boys, I'll make sure *you* get kicked out." And I told them, "If any of you tell your parents, they will kick *me* out. So if you're not interested, you can get out of the course. I'll write you a pass to home room."

All of them stayed. All of them ended up loving the course. I was never betrayed by them. When I first of all tell them I'm a virgin and don't know what I'm talking about, this caused high hilarity. I said, "You are not being taught this by a stud horse." But, I told them, we will learn together.

In my own family, I must have been in ninth grade when Mom said, "Son, isn't it beautiful the way the sperm meets the egg?" I had no idea what she was talking about. Then Dad one day at a gas station said, "If you ever get a girl pregnant I'll fucking kill you. Got it?" I said, "Yes, sir." That was sex education in the Conroy household in a nutshell.

And these kids knew nothing; they didn't know a thing. (We didn't have cable then.) I taught them every kind of birth control they could use, and how to use it. I avoided things like drawing a penis up on the board because I can't draw. But I did not lose a girl in the next two years. It would not surprise me if that class was the most remembered thing about me at Beaufort High School.

Later I found out that Mr. Biddle knew about it and was secretly in favor of me teaching it. As I look back on my career, that was a warning sign: that I was a pain in the ass and could certainly get myself in trouble.

I turned out to be a very bad coach. I love coaching and I love coaches, and it was easy for me to imagine myself as a coach for the rest of my life. But I found that I hated cutting kids. When I cut my first bunch from the JV basketball team, I went outside to my car and heard a lot of these kids crying. I couldn't take it. I went home, called them up, and asked them all to come back. I found out I liked playing a sport better than I liked coaching a sport, and then I realized what I really wanted to do was to be home reading and writing.

Then I got into the racial politics of coaching at Beaufort High School. I was supposed to be the head basketball coach the following year, and Frank Small, the athletic director, was a racist of the old order. He told me I favored the Negro student too much.

This was the first year of "freedom of choice," and we got a hundred black kids at the white school that year. The black community hand-selected these kids; they were smart as hell. I got to know them very well and would try to go visit the parents when I could. These black parents were stunned when I made a point of showing up at their houses. It was then I realized that I was part of the changing of the South—a small part, but a part. And I wanted to be a white part of that change. It was not significant, but it was something, and something I began trying to do.

I told Frank Small, "We're going to have a much better basketball team." Coach Small called me in and said if I was going to be unfair to white people and look out for the nigger all the time, I couldn't coach for him. I said, "Coach, watch my back as I leave through the door, because you'll never see it again."

I walked out, and that was it. I taught, and in the afternoons I'd read and write, and I got a lot done that year.

$\sim$

During this time I had these three friends, fellow teachers. Mike Jones, George Garbade, Bernie Schein, and I became a foursome that year. Mike Jones and George Garbade taught with me at the high school. Bernie was the principal in Yemasee, which is the smallest little town you've ever seen, about twenty miles from Beaufort. He'd drive in from Yemasee almost every night, so we saw him every day. The next year he took a job in town at Port Royal Elementary School. He knew nothing at all about being a principal; he was twenty-one years old. But this was South Carolina.

Nobody can believe Bernie has been my best friend since high school, and has probably been the most important friend I've had in my life. As a military brat, I'd come into these towns and wouldn't know anybody. When I went to a school, I was always new, so I had to figure out who needed friends instantly: effeminate boys, unpopular girls, Jews. I could make friends with the sissy boys because I'd see them getting pushed around and beat up, and I hated bullies. These boys needed protectors, and I was a tough kid so I could do that. The unpopular girls, they needed somebody to talk to. In the South there was usually a Jewish kid who needed a friend. By then I could recognize the outsiders, the kids who needed friends.

So I was this boy of solitude walking into Beaufort High School not knowing a human being in that school, when I hear this hyena laugh. The laugh made me laugh, so I thought I'd try to become friends with that guy. The school was in a horseshoe shape, and the laugh was in the cafeteria, which was far away. This laugh is so loud, so obnoxious and absolutely individual. I don't go to movies with Bernie anymore because this laugh is so overpowering that the audience ends up waiting for his laugh so they can laugh at the laugh. Anyway, I went looking for the kid with the laugh, and when I found him, he's Bernie.

Bernie is the first guy I met who loved ideas, who loved politics, who loved books, who loved talking, who read the newspaper. He was exactly like me in that; he had a million ideas, and he wanted to talk about them. But he was a year ahead of me, so the real friendship began when I first started teaching at Beaufort High School out of the Citadel. From the very beginning when we were teaching, we were both interested in education, we were both interested in writing. We now look back and see we were both alive. We were alive and excited. This was '67, '68, '69. I look upon that as being very good for me, or very bad if you're looking at another angle.

What these guys all did for me is they liberated me from myself. I was coming from this spiritual chain gang of Catholicism, then I was at the Citadel, then I'd been raised by a Marine. It is a stern church, and

I had a stern father, and I went to a stern school. There is an uptightness in me which still is there. Even now, there's something basically conservative about me. I've been an old man since I was about ten. I know this deeply inside me, even though I've been what passes for a communist in South Carolina for a good twenty years.

Here is how uptight and Catholic I still was at that time: I was in a prayer group with Gene Norris and three old ladies. We met once a week and prayed for world peace, prayed that Mr. Thornton would quit drinking, that kind of shit. It was the most boring thing I've ever done, but Gene thought it was wonderful that I was such a spiritual young man.

Anyway, Mike and George started giving parties on the weekend at their apartment. I'd never show up because I was going to that prayer group. They came over the day after a party and said, "Hey, Pat, why didn't you come?" I said I didn't have a date. Bernie said, "Pat, has it ever occurred to you that you might meet a girl at a party?" I said, "There were girls there without dates?" He said, "Yeah, there always are." Then they said, "We're gonna have another party next week," and I didn't show up for that one.

What it was: in the Catholic culture you do not go toward near occasions of sin. To go to a party to hunt for girls, that's a near occasion of sin. So I was just uptight. I didn't drink, so I was uncomfortable with parties, and I had no experience with women, so I was uncomfortable with them. In this world of sex I just never did very well. The Catholic thing held me back; my mother held me back. The Catholic Church did a real number on me. I missed quite a bit of the American sexual experience.

⁓

When I was in high school, there was a girl I liked, Terry Leite, who came out to the graduation hop my freshman year at the Citadel. I was smitten with her, and she seemed smitten with me. Mom sends me her usual five bucks for the date. Here is what saved me: I win the journalism award from the *Brigadier* for the best article, and I'm given $50, the most money I've ever seen in my life. So I take her to dinner. I don't have to order water and a bean sprout. I'm so relieved.

We went to the hop. It was great. She stayed in the Charleston Inn, which I could walk to from the Citadel. We walked everywhere. We walked South of Broad. It was just beautiful, wonderful. We enjoyed each other. We liked kissing each other, and holding hands with each other. So anyway, I walk her back to the Charleston Inn after the hop. I said, "I'll see you tomorrow morning for breakfast."

I walk back to the Citadel and go to open the barracks gate. It is locked. There's not a light on anywhere. I walk down to the gym trying to figure out how to get in. The gym's locked, no lights, so I can't get in the gym. I think I tried the visiting team room, couldn't get in there. The whole campus was locked down. I try to figure out what to say to Terry because she's this little virginal Catholic girl.

I go back to the Charleston Inn. I knock on her door. She's got curlers in her hair.

She says, "Pat, what are you doing here? You're not here for what I think you are?"

I said, "No, no." I explained what had happened.

She was in her PJs, so she goes and puts Bermuda shorts on and this jacket she zipped up tight to her neck. Then she put her socks and tennis shoes on. She slept in her tennis shoes. So there was no point of entry, no point of sight that could arouse anything at all. A perfect Catholic girl.

I am horrified. She thinks I'm a rapist. She thinks I arranged this: "Aha, now I have you where I want you. I've fooled you, stupid little thing. Come into my trap." Well, I'm dying. I'm utterly dying. I slept either on the floor or the couch, I cannot remember which one.

I took her to a nice breakfast; I think we went to the Francis Marion Hotel. It's Sunday; we went to the cathedral, and we again walked around the city, making plans to live there someday. We pass by the house that she and her second husband would live in one day.

Then she had to go back to Atlanta. She said, "Where are you going for the summer, Pat?"

I said, "I don't know. I hadn't thought of it yet. My parents are in Omaha, Nebraska, but they haven't sent me a way home."

She said, "Why don't you come home with me?"

I said, "Would your parents mind?"

"Oh, they'd love it."

So one of the great sexual nights of my life was that train ride through the night to Atlanta. We were Catholic: our hands did not wander. She's a good Catholic girl, I'm a good Catholic boy, and it's a murderous combination. So we just kissed. But it seemed like heaven to me.

We get to the next day. Her boyfriend in Atlanta is waiting to take us home. It was the most uncomfortable ride I think I've ever had in my life. She forgot to tell me about the boyfriend. Terry called me a couple years ago to tell me he had died. I said, "Finally, my guilt is resolved." So he takes us to her home in Atlanta, at 1988 Timothy Street, and I stayed there about two or three days until Mom and Dad finally sent me a ticket by train to Omaha.

I wrote her all summer, every day from Omaha. They are the most hilarious, obnoxious, boy-in-love, boy-trying-to-be-a-writer letters you've ever seen in your life. Overwritten does not even begin to describe it. They were awful, awful, awful, but I now look at them as a treasure trove of a young man trying to become a writer and impress a girl with his writing ability, of which I had none. All I had was sperm-filled emotions and fantasies of making it out of this uptight Catholic-riddled body. I did not have proof that she was even alive during that time because she never wrote back once. But she saved all the letters, because she thought I was going to be a writer, and she still has them.

Every time I came through the Atlanta airport on the Christmas road trip for the basketball team, I'd call Terry. That was basically the entire sexual history of my life at the Citadel, those Christmas phone calls. I never dated anyone seriously.

My one serious relationship in college was Mary Alice, who I went out with one time in high school. I've dated every girl in the world once. She was wonderful, but Dad controlled that one. I didn't have a driver's license, so I had to double date; if I couldn't double date I couldn't date. And of course, I had no money. It costs money to go to the movies. "Why don't you go on base? It's only a dime." "Mom, I can't go on base. I'm doubling with the guys. They're going downtown." "Well, I think it's a waste of money." So Mary Alice, I just dated her one time.

Well, I'm a sophomore at the Citadel, not a very happy one, but I was playing pretty good basketball my sophomore year. And I get this letter from Gene Norris: "Pat, Mary Alice got pregnant," by a redneck, our class redneck. "And we don't know where she is. We think she's in West Virginia because that's where her family is from. You're going to play the University of West Virginia next week. Could you look up these names in the telephone book and call?"

So when I got up there, I looked it up, called, found out from one of them that Mary Alice was living on Sullivan's Island in South Carolina, which is outside Charleston. So when I got back, I wrote her a note. "Dear Mary Alice, we were in Miss Baumgartner's geometry class together. We even dated once, and I thought you might need some help, thought you might need some company." At that time, getting pregnant was the ultimate humiliation and nightmare for a girl.

I went out after a game. There are these two women staying in a shack on Sullivan's Island with nothing, no money. Mary Alice and her mother. I loved her mother, but she was a nutcase. Mary Alice was obviously very unhappy. So I started going out there each weekend, and I was a goner. I had never been in love with anybody, never dated. Of course, I'm not dating her, because she's pregnant. But I just thought, my God, this is it. She would drive me back to the barracks sometimes, and on one of these trips she leaned over and kissed me. That was as far as it went. I was such a good little Catholic boy, I cannot tell you. It never even occurred to me that anything else should go on. My friends can't believe I did not make love with her, but I didn't because I thought she'd be hurt by that. She didn't need that. She didn't need me in that particular way.

But we made plans that I was going to quit the Citadel, we were going to get married. I had some other schools interested in me for basketball at that time. So I was going to write them and see if I could transfer. I was going to work in the summer, work at night, and I thought we could do it.

We were playing Furman when she was getting ready to have that baby. Away at Furman, I get an emergency phone call from her mother that she'd just taken Mary Alice to the hospital. The baby was born dead with the cord wrapped around her throat. At least, that's what they told me. Now, I must have known twenty-five kids born in Charleston around that time who have come to see if they were Mary

Alice's child. One was not long ago, in fact. "I used to dream you were my father." And I said, "Well, if you were Mary Alice's child, I would not have been your father. But I would have raised you." I have no idea if the baby died or made it into Catholic Services.

When I returned to the Citadel, I couldn't go until that weekend to see Mary Alice. As soon as I walked in the door, it was different. Boom. She wouldn't look at me, wouldn't talk to me, wouldn't talk to me on the phone, wouldn't answer my letters. A couple weeks later, I get a letter from her. It said, "Dear Pat, you were so sweet to me during this. But the two people who remind me of the worst time in my life are my mother and you. You were here and you saw me at my worst, my lowest. I'm very sorry about this, I regret this."

Oh, Christ, Jesus. It completely shattered me. It had never occurred to me they could fall out of love with you. I thought once you fell in love, that was it, and I was going to love Mary Alice for the rest of my life; she was going to love me for the rest of her life. We were going to spend our life together, it was going to be great, and that was it. It never occurred to me that the girl or boy could say no. I didn't know that. It had never occurred to me you could love somebody that much and then have it flung back in your face, not because you're an asshole, but because you weren't. I could not get it. And, I was like, my gosh, she *needs* to like me. What it was, I now realize: I took advantage of this girl's complete, abominable loneliness.

I also think my mother probably got to Mary Alice in some way, although I do not know that. This could be just my ego: my male ego was so badly hurt that it still hasn't recovered. But I do know Mom had caught wind of it and was not pleased. "I hear you're dating a pregnant woman. I will never accept her." You know, "We've put all our dreams and hopes on you."

I said, "Mom, I'm so sorry. I fell in love with this girl."

And she said, "This will never ever be something that we can approve of. We'll never speak to you or your wife or her child."

Gene told me this much later. He said, "Your mother called me a lot during that time, Pat, and she was highly disapproving." But Gene would always take Mom's side. "She wanted better for you. She didn't want you to marry a used car."

Notice: I married used cars all the way down the line. I only married used cars. I never married an unused car. For one thing, I was not interested in sleeping with a virgin, ever. I did not want that on my plate at all.

Mary Alice was the great Nagasaki at the beginning of my life. My junior year is a lost year; I just remember being in pain the whole year. I didn't date after her, didn't meet girls when I was at the Citadel. Except for Mary Alice, I'd never dated anybody seriously, and you can't say I dated Mary Alice seriously since I took care of her during the last five months of her pregnancy. But that was my one serious relationship in college.

Then, the first woman I asked to marry me turned me down. I met her when I went to get a summer job after I graduated from the Citadel. She was also getting a job. In the summers, migrant workers came to work at the farms on the islands, and in Charleston there was a school for their kids. I was the athletic director in charge of sports.

Marnie was a beautiful, golden-haired Charleston girl with an impeccable name: Huger. But they had moved out of South of Broad, because when you run out of money, you're run out of the house South of Broad. Aristocrats can forgive anything except when you run out of money. Still, her name could not have been more glorious. We were together all summer; I met her family, and they sort of took me in.

Then I went to teach in Beaufort, and she went back to a tiny little Protestant college in North Carolina. In one of the first letters I wrote her, I said, "Dear Marnie, It's obvious I love you, and I think we ought to plan to get married." I go on in my florid, overheated style, offering myself, my life, my love.

She writes back a very nice letter rejecting the proposal, and giving me some advice. "Pat, with the next girl you want to marry, I would suggest you might want to hold hands with her, or even kiss her before you make the proposal."

So Conroy's sex life sailed on, a battleship fully armed and loaded, ready for action, entering the South China Sea.

⌢

Anyway, Bernie and them, they just could not take this, the stupid way I was living my life, so they came over and grabbed me for the next party. And of course it was fun. I ended up dating a series of girls. But at the point where we were about to make love, I would think of some reason to break up with them, because I thought if you made love you had to get married. And I'm thinking this is gonna be hard with Mom: "I'm married. This girl's Methodist." It was scaring me.

Anytime I would date somebody, Mom would find out from someone in Beaufort, and I'd get a phone call. "Son, I hear you're dating a young woman. Is she Catholic?" Or "She will not do. She's a Southern Baptist," giving her heavy disapproval of the convert.

I'd say, "Mom, give me a break. Weren't you a Baptist when you married Dad?" In her innocence, Mom thought she had taken a step up socially by becoming a Catholic and didn't know she'd taken a step down. In the South, being Catholic was weirder than being Jewish.

Anyway, I dated two Baptist preachers' daughters so I could date them more than once, because I thought they wouldn't expect anything, wouldn't want anything. A few years ago I met the daughters of one of these Baptist girls, and one said, "Mr. Conroy, Mom was always trying to get us to date boys like you." I said, "Could you tell me why?" She said, "You were a perfect gentleman and never tried to do anything."

I mean, I used to call my dates "ma'am." "Would you like some dessert ma'am?"

But that was when my road to perdition began with those three guys. Mike, George Garbade, and Bernie take full credit for the wild middle years of Conroy's misspent youth.

Bernie has always been very good about liberating the uptight Catholic boy in me. He planted a flag of liberation for me and gave me a way of coming out of this terrible shell I had built up. He showed me outrageousness; he showed me boldness that had never occurred to me. He would say anything to anybody. He was screamingly funny. Bernie set me free, where anything can be thought, anything can be said. Growing up, I had a million things I wanted to say but was afraid to. Bernie taught me that it was possible to say and think anything. I got to see a personality who was completely out there, and it was very freeing for me to see a personality let himself go. My uptight background needed a Bernie with no restrictions on what you could say or do. There's something about Bernie that has expanded everything about me.

One time we went to a party, and there was a girl there so fabulous, so wonderful, so sophisticated, beautiful, smart as hell. She was visiting relatives; I think it must've been Christmas. She started talking, and the four of us, George Garbade, Mike Jones, Bernie, and I were standing in radiant attendance around her, completely lost in her wonderfulness.

Then she started telling us why she hated Southern men. We were stupid; we were redneck; we were Nazis; we hated black people; we were against women. I naturally was agreeing with everything she said because she was gorgeous. She could've dipped my head in the toilet, and I would've let her flush it as many times as she'd like. I loved her. I had just met her, but that's the way I am. I was thinking, Gosh, how do you ask a girl like this for a date when you're a Southern man? Then she said she would never date a Southern man, and I'm thinking, what a shame. I'd love to have married her; I'd love to have children with her. I would love to grow old with her and die in her arms. I'm going through my fantasy life together with her while she's blasting Southern men.

As I was standing openmouthed with wonderment, I see her eyes, her beautiful eyes, lock onto something. I see a look of shock cross her face. She is silenced. I follow her eyes, and they are looking at the midsection of Bernie Schein. In the middle of this girl's diatribe against Southern men, Bernie has taken his penis out of his pants and put his horn-rimmed glasses on top of it, where the penis is now the nose. It looked like this deformed human being coming out of his crotch. This poor woman is looking down at these horn-rimmed glasses with this penis nose sticking out of Bernie's pants.

And Bernie says, "Oh! I need to introduce you to Mortimer. I'm so sorry; how rude of me. This is Mortimer. I love Mortimer more than I like myself. He goes with me wherever I go. And he's the life of every party."

She storms out of the house. I wanted to marry her and die in her arms, but when she leaves, I scream laughing. Bernie always affects me that way. I had never met anybody like this in my life who would say these things, and I am divinely grateful to him for showing me a different way of being. Bernie would pull his dick out almost anywhere. The other day he came into my house, and here we are ninety-year-old men, and he screams, "Pussy! The only subject in the world!" I would never think anything like that; I would never say anything like that. But he has played a great part in my life by doing things like that.

Also, Bernie and I discovered that we were both boiling over with this need for literature, this desire to write. And where Bernie has always been great for me—I'd give him something I'd written, and Bernie would call back and say, "God! Damn! God!! Damn!! God!!! Damn!!! How did you write this? This is so fucking great!" He would then tell me, "I guarantee you, somebody else is going to like this. It ain't just me."

I did not take it seriously, but that's a good reader to have in your early life, a rare thing to find when you're a kid starting out. You know how you think you're nothing when you start out. Bernie has always been my head cheerleader, my hallelujah chorus.

After I got to Beaufort High, I was on the Point, living in a beautiful house for $50 a month, on the water, with a very pretty view. I was writing as seriously as I could, concentrating on being a poet. I was convinced that I was going to be a poet. Now I realize that was my way of hiding from myself, hiding from my subjects. It's the worst poetry you've ever read. It is simply dreadful in the way that only poetry can be dreadful. It just wasn't any good. These poems were beyond redemption; they showed no promise of anything. There was not one salvageable word, not one interesting idea, not one original turn of phrase. Nothing. Still I was writing constantly, searching desperately for what I was meant to write.

One of my English teachers from high school, Millen Ellis, knew I was writing, knew I didn't type, so he came over one night and gathered all the poems I had done, took them to his house, and the next day he had typed a whole manuscript of about thirty poems, which I then read. I read them and realized, in one swift moment, that I was not going to be a poet, that something was hideously wrong with what I was trying to do. It came as a great disappointment. The poems were inert. They were dead in the water. I could look beneath the surface; there was nothing alive. It was sort of a bad *Waste Land* meets Robert Frost through *Howl,* that kind of shit. It just did not work at all. It was derivative; it was a waste of time; it was ill–thought out; it was ill-considered; it would look back from the page at me with fisheyes. All the poems were about nothing. They were subject-less. They were simply the moanings of sperm cells locked away too long in scrotums. It was just angst ridden. There was no point to them.

Then, for about a month I wandered around, knowing I can't write poetry so I'm trying to write a book. To me, writing a novel was simply the most overwhelming idea on earth. I go back to these novels I loved, I open them up, and I'm thinking, "I would look like a fool if I tried this."

Also, I did not realize that I had not yet begun telling myself the truth about even my own life, so there was no reason for me to write about anything. If that process had not begun, I should not be sitting down at a desk. But I had that image of myself.

George Garbade thought it was hilarious. He would say, "That boy's goin' home. He's gonna whip himself up some poetry. That boy's got this habit of thinkin', and he don't need to hear about women for a long, long time because he's gonna write some fucking poetry you gonna read someday in one of them textbooks." I had him tickling the shit out of me about this.

Then I went back to the Citadel for homecoming that first year. I went to see Colonel Doyle, my English teacher, but he wasn't there, gone for the weekend. I'm walking back to my car, and Colonel Courvoisie—the Boo—comes out of his house. I said, "Colonel, how are you doing? How's it going up in the commandant's department?" because he was in charge of discipline. In a military college, that's the guy who gives punishment. That's all he does.

He said, "You didn't hear about it? They fired me."

I said, "Fired you? For what?"

"They said I was bad for discipline."

I said, "Boo, you *were* discipline." And I'm thinking, holy God. At that time, the Boo was legendary. Saying the Boo was bad for discipline wasn't even possible. That was not possible.

He said, "They sent me down to the warehouse, Bubba. I order toilet paper for the campus now."

He called everybody Bubba because he couldn't remember cadets' names. It became a term of great endearment in the corps. If the Boo called you Bubba, you could not get higher than that. At Harvard you go for Phi Beta Kappa; at the Citadel, if you got called Bubba your life was good from then on.

But the Boo was this terrifying creature in my life. He was a godlike figure walking around on campus. He was loud, and he was scary. God, he was tough. I was scared of him all through college.

I remember when I was a freshman, I went over to Ashley Hall one weekend to see Molly Hoyler. This terrifying old harridan of a woman meets me at the door, "What are you doing here, cadet?"

"I came over to meet Miss Molly Hoyler."

"Does she know you're coming?"

I said, "No, ma'am, she's never met me before, but I just got a letter from her aunt."

She said, "You mean you don't even have a date with Miss Hoyler? I don't care if you got a letter from her aunt, and I can assure you, Miss Hoyler doesn't care that you got a letter from her aunt." She says, "Cadet, get off my campus. Don't come back, or I'm going to call the Boo."

Which is the first time I ever heard the Boo's name. Later, he tried to kick me out of school twice.

The first time was when, my God, I was the poetry editor for the literary magazine, the *Shako*. So I am going around, shaking down poetry. You talk about a hard job: poetry editor for the Citadel. I'm begging anybody who knows how to write a word on a piece of paper.

I was sitting at my desk at the Citadel, and this kind of snaky guy comes in. I didn't know him at all. He said, "Are you the poetry editor?"

I said, "Yes, I am."

"I got some poems."

I said, "They will be printed, I promise, no matter how horrible they are. I can't thank you enough. We needed two more."

So he gives me the poems. I'm reading them, they're shit, but that's okay. It was my duty to fill up a poetry section. This guy is looking at me with sort of a wolfish grin on his face. I'm reading the first poem, he said, "You don't see it do you?"

I said, "See what?"

He said, "Okay, get the first letter of each line."

He had arranged it like a modern poem with lines beginning in different places, back and forth across the page, as though that deepened anything. But if you put the first lines together, the first letter of each line going down read out to say, "Webb and Tucker suck." Colonel Webb ran the Army ROTC, was meaner than hell, and the cadets were terrified of him. General Tucker was the general commandant of cadets, and he would always give rules that we couldn't go out or we couldn't do this, so the cadets were always mad with him. So "Webb and Tucker suck."

This is right before the end of the school year, and I think, okay, this is good, light-hearted, humorous. Nobody will know. I won't let anybody tell anybody, and later on, after we graduate, people will find out, and they'll yuck it up at what hell-raisers we were and what shit-kickers we were, and we will loom in everlasting fame in Citadel lore.

But several things happened that were not in our favor. We were pledged to secrecy, but you cannot keep a secret in a corps of cadets. This is a well-known fact. Also, when they sent it off to the printer, the printer thought he was being helpful: "My God, those lines are starting all over the page, let me just even this up." So he evened it up, and of course, after he did, you could open it up, read straight down and see "Webb and Tucker suck."

It comes out, and all the cadets are waiting for it, that's how big a secret it was. They turn instantly to the thing, "Webb and Tucker suck," they roar. Anyway, I heard that the Boo and a tactical officer were seen reading it and roaring laughing before lunch.

But, of course then the Boo, being in charge of discipline, that night he's on the hunt. He spots me in the mess. He comes up to me, smoking a nauseating cigar. He said, "Just start writing, Bubba." It was an ERW, which is what you fill out to make excuses for what you've done, or what crime you committed at the Citadel. An Explanation of Report, Written. He says, "I got you, Bubba. You're going. Your name is on every ERW I've gotten from all the rest of your pansies down at the *Shako*. I'll be removing more gay cadets than at any time in the history of the Citadel, and you look like the main one, the big guy."

So I'm thinking, "Oh my God, this was my only chance at a college degree, and this is over." I'm thinking of my mother. Dad's in Vietnam.

So I'm like, "Colonel, there must be some mistake. I thought I was contributing to literature."

And he, "Ha-ha-ha, oh Bubba, that's so good. I like that. Even Clemson won't take you."

I go all summer thinking I've been kicked out, but nothing comes in the mail, so I go back. I go right to the Boo's office, and he said, "Bubba, we got a new president. If General Mark Clark was still president, you'd have been gone that night." And later Boo told me, he said, "General Harris laughed his ass off." So nothing happened to us.

I tried to put a much lower profile on myself. I was almost kicked out of school, so I took a lesson, I thought, from this. But toward the end of my senior year, there began a series of incidents between the cadet officers and the privates, of which I was one. There were a couple of incidents where the private gets nailed and the officer gets nothing. Then there was a huge incident.

Around March of each year, you go from those horrible wool pants of winter, which everybody hates, to your cotton field uniform. This last night in mess you're wearing your old wool things you've worn for four years, and if you're a senior they're starting to fade from dry cleaning. So there was a tradition of tearing the seniors' pants off. You're sitting there, and the underclassmen tore your pants off. Many times they would tear your underwear off too, in the pure deliriousness of ripping the pants off your body. It's some primal rape thing that military schools must love.

But this year they had forbidden it. It was a waste of material, some shit like that, so they had forbidden it. For a while it held—about two seconds. We march into mess, a signal goes up, next thing we're all on the floor and everybody ripped all of our pants off. So I get my pants ripped off; I'm sitting in my underwear.

All of a sudden we look up, and regimental staff is there. Regimental staff is looking stern, and they're looking mean like they're really going to take names here and everybody will get in trouble, and fourth battalion's going to have to sit in for several weekends in a row, and we will be punished. So, they come down, they look tough, because in a military school you have to look tough.

So, the regimental commander is Jim Probsdorfer—he's still a good friend of mine—Jim is eyeing it; they take this very seriously. Well, he is the only one who walks bravely down, staring us down, and he's going to call the company commanders together and demand what has happened. We've gotten quiet because we know, in the phrase, we're about to get jacked up our asses for our intemperate behavior and our lack of discipline. So he's staring at us meanly, and we know he's going to talk to all the company commanders and issue a command, and we will be in pain.

So there's complete silence as he's walking down, but of course, it's hard to take it completely seriously when you're in your underwear. Okay, I see a huge behind in his underwear moving surreptitiously between the seats. It's my friend John Bowditch, a huge guy, played tackle on the football team. He was the wild man of our class. So I saw his behind kind of low crawling, like we're doing maneuvers in the Army, and he's low crawling, setting himself up. So Probsdorfer is standing there, he's got his hands on his hips, very military. Probs always looked the part, beautifully dressed and coifed and wore a uniform well, as opposed to Conroy who wore it like a piece of badly put on wallpaper.

The next thing I know, Bowditch, who is huge, leaps and tackles a very surprised regimental commander, and he drives and drives him through the swinging doors of the kitchen and disappears. So there was about thirty seconds of silence, and then Bowditch comes out in his underwear with a huge, triumphant grin on his face, and he is waving Jim Probsdorfer's pants to the crowd like a flag. There was such jubilation, and the next thing, there's chicken bones flying through the air, mounds of potatoes flying through the air hitting guys. That was the second biggest no-no in mess, to have a food fight.

Bowditch got the worst punishment order. I would have killed myself. I would have shot my dick off. It means you're restricted and cannot go off campus. It means you walk tours, and walking a tour is doing fifty minutes with your rifle walking in military precision back and forth across the quadrangle, then rest for ten minutes. So you do that all Friday night, all Saturday and all Sunday until six, and it ain't fun. It can really do damage to a guy's psyche. It means you can't date, you can't go out and drink, you can't do anything. So, it's not one that I ever wanted applied to me. Now this was, once again, Bowditch was a private doing this to an officer.

If we were talking about college life at Harvard we'd be talking about, my God, should I take this professor who won the Pulitzer Prize for his seminal book on the works of T. S. Eliot, or should I take creative writing with Bernard Malamud? Those are the great decisions of life at Harvard. My college life was to participate in a food fight that breaks out because a guy's pants get ripped off and he's standing in his underwear.

Anyway, the next thing that happened, we had a guy in our battalion, a nice guy, who had a very unfortunate name. Nobody from the North has ever believed me when I told them what his name was: Jim Crow. Can you believe his poor dimwitted parents named him Jim Crow? Poor Jim Crow, he is a company commander of N Company. I was in R Company, so we were in the same battalion, in the same building, basically. Lovely, lovely building that I served four years in. Goddamn, you gotta love that Moorish architecture. It looked like a fucking prison.

So, Jim did not have what is necessary in a corps of cadets: a leavening sense of humor, a sense of the absurd. Now, Jim Crow is driven absolutely fucking crazy by something that happened. Somebody told me I did this first, but I don't believe it. You'd see Jim on campus and you'd go, "Caw, caw." Everybody knew he hated it. Finally, when he would take his place as the commander of N Company, we'd see him coming, and we'd start a crow call, just because there's nothing else to do. You saw him walking, and so we'd, "Caw, caw, caw." It started out about four guys doing it.

If he'd let it go it would've been nothing, but he rushed to the edge of the quad and shook his fist at us, said he was going to jack it up our ass, give us demerits if he found out who was doing it. Of course, this encouraged it. It got louder and louder every day he'd come down, until finally the whole battalion of about five hundred guys, when he came down every single lunch, did a crow call. It was deafening, "Caw, caw."

He'd be on the third battalion, looking like Mussolini shaking his fist at us, which just made it louder and louder. Well, that really drove poor Jim Crow crazy. Jim was marching out on a Friday, I think it was right after Probsdorfer had his pants torn off by a private, and so he was leading his guys out to parade. And he's head of the whole company, he's standing there watching these guys go out, and he's about to join them, when a little private from O Company sees him march past and goes, "Caw, caw." Crow evidently had been driven crazy by this experience; he has his sword out ready for the parade, and in this sudden and helpless gesture, stabs the poor sophomore in the thigh.

We still have to get through parade. So this sophomore marches out to parade, and all of a sudden somebody next to him says, "My God, what happened to your leg?" Everybody looks. His leg is covered with blood. So he has to post out of the parade and go to the infirmary, and I think he had three or four stitches. It was not a serious wound, but it hit a blood vessel so there was a lot of blood. They give that kid a punishment order for making the crow call; they did nothing to Crow for stabbing the kid with a sword. So by this time, the privates have gone about crazy.

I end up writing an underground letter about why the blood of privates counts for nothing, but if an upperclassman is touched, the private gets kicked out of school or gets the worst punishment order. A guy stabbing a guy and getting nothing for it? There's something unfair here.

We spread these letters out before mess one night. By the time I got back to the barracks and marched into the R Company, a riot was going on in the mess hall. I had listed all the things that had happened during the year where the privates got nailed, nothing happened to the officers, and almost always they were responsible for the incident.

Well, I did not think any more about it, except I heard the Boo was on my tail. My friend Scott Graber was on the regimental staff, and he said there was a meeting that night, and somebody started the meeting out and says, "We know Conroy did it. We just have to prove it." How did they know I did it? was a question someone asked, and the answer was, "Because no one else gives a shit. And no one else can write." So they said they'd hunt me down.

I was trying to get weekend leave, and I went over to the Boo's house. Boo's sitting there with a bunch of cadets around him. He has a wicked smile and a scary voice. He looks up, sees me and says, "Caw, caw."

I said, "Excuse me, Colonel?"

He says, "Bubba, I know it's you. Every sign points back to you. I'm gonna get you. It's only two weeks before graduation, and I'm hunting you down, and I will bet you don't walk across that stage at graduation because even the general says if I catch you I get to kick you out this time." And he gets this grin. He says, "I've already checked with Clemson; they don't want to have a thing to do with you."

I knew he was serious, because he took his job seriously. He said, "I'm going to crucify you without nails, Bubba."

I was very worried, and I knew that they were on my tail, but what saved me: the next day, three freshman cadets got lost at sea on a fishing trip, and I volunteered to be among those brave cadets who scoured the ocean for them. We were praised for doing it. I nearly got sunburned to death, but I was escaping campus legally, searching for my beloved brothers in peril on the high seas. They found them after four days, and it was the first time I've ever heard of this place: Daufuskie Island. When I got back, it was the day before graduation. When I went up to the Boo at graduation to shake hands with him, I said, "Colonel, caw, caw."

He said, "I knew it was you, Bubba. If I'd had one more day, I had you. I had you."

The Boo was just doing his job. He was good at what he did, but he did it all with great good humor. He took his military role very seriously, but he remained a human being. He was feared and loved both for the right reasons. If you ever needed him for real help, he was always there. We knew he'd help us if we needed it. You could always go to him, and he was the only one on campus like that. He had a beautiful heart. He'd discipline, and he'd rack us, he'd yell, he'd scream at us, but if we needed help, the law of the corps was good as Boo. That was the law, the iron law. They taught me that the first day I was there. You're ever really in trouble, go to the Boo. If your girlfriend got pregnant, for example, the Boo is where you went. He knew a doctor he could trust who was a Citadel graduate.

In my senior year a revolt started to develop against the Boo because some thought he had too much power and that he was usurping authority he did not have. The truth is they were jealous of the Boo because the cadets adored him. I mean, they worshipped him.

But his enemies said he was going in the barracks and taking things; they called it stealing. What it was—when he found contraband, like a TV, he'd take it and give it to charity. He'd find waffle irons or hot dog cookers or some piece of clothing that was unmilitary, he'd take it and give it to the Salvation Army. That was his job. But when they took it to the new president, he had no idea what the Citadel traditions were. He was a West Pointer.

After I graduated, they fired the Boo and put him in the warehouse where he took care of the luggage and ordered pens and pencils and toilet paper for the campus. A humiliating job from the one he held, and he held that the rest of his life; he never got out of there. He also was told he could never ever talk to cadets, except in an official capacity, at the warehouse. His genius was his connection with cadets. He could not quit because he needed the pension; he had a crippled wife. She was a nurse in a V-1 attack in Belgium during the Battle of the Bulge and got her knee blown off.

When I ran into him at homecoming, he had this look on his face as he's standing there talking to me, and I realize he had been totally humiliated.

I said, "Well, Colonel, if you ever want to write down your story, please let me know."

The Boo says, "Ah, yes, I forgot you were one of those girls who majored in English."

So when I got back to Beaufort I wrote the Boo a letter. It's now hanging above my computer. "Dear Colonel Boo, it was great to see you at homecoming. Sorry to hear what they did. You don't know this, but I want to become a writer, and I thought maybe if we got together, you could tell me your stories, we could put them together and do a book."

About a month later, I got a letter from the Boo. "Are you serious, Bubba? The only thing is, if it ever gets published, all proceeds have to go to the Citadel."

Of course I agreed blithely, not thinking there would be a book, not thinking there would be anything, just taking this on so it would force me to write. And of course, it did, because I was still afraid of the Boo.

So I'd go up on the weekends, spend the night up there. The Boo would tell stories, and I'd just sit there and write them down while he smoked a cigar. He'd go through the yearbooks, some cadet's face would remind him of something, and he'd tell me the story. "Oh, I remember this lamb. I should have shipped him to Clemson, but he got away from me." So I'd write those stories down.

It turned out to be a very good discipline for me. At that time, all I knew is I wanted to be a writer. I didn't know what to write about. The hardest thing I think for a writer is—God, the whole world is there. What do I choose to write about? I didn't have any choice with this book. I was writing about him; I was writing about what happened to him. And once again—always look for this with me—I saw the injustice. That always triggers something in me. This guy was called bad for discipline? I was terrified of him. He represented what discipline was at the Citadel. That part of me that hates injustice got nicked, and I had to do my little thing of correcting a wrong. Anyway, the subject was set. And it was repair work: I wrote about the dad I wanted to have. *The Boo* was my attempt at another father. Most of it was just his funny tales from college; the firing took place at the end of the book.

I wrote it too fast, and of course Boo would say, "Hurry up, Bubba, taps may be coming anytime," like he's gonna die. When I told him I had finished, it felt like a major achievement just to finish 250 pages of handwritten stuff.

The Boo said, "Bubba, you're my Boswell."

I said, "Colonel, I'm amazed that you even know who Boswell is."

It was such an innocent, stupid, badly written book, the worst book ever written by an American, but it was the first thrust toward art for me. And what you don't know when you first start writing is if you'll even finish the book. What I was most afraid of was not being able to finish a long project like that. Before you've done it, you just don't know that you can do it. It's a terrifying mountain for a writer to climb. So I learned in that first book that I could write a book.

∼

At the end of that first year, we all went to Europe together during the summer for two months—George, Mike, Bernie, and me. That was a magically happy time for me. That was just the best, the best, the best. I was dying to see Europe because at this time I felt completely uneducated. I'm living in Beaufort, South Carolina, and I've been to the Citadel. That rings a lot of intellectual bells in America. I found a special deal for teachers in the National Council of Teachers of English, really cheap flights, go see Europe on Air India, which I didn't know existed. If you were a teacher you got a special rate of—I want to say—$150 roundtrip. So I went racing around after school, finally got George and Mike and Bernie to go with me, thinking this will be a trip that would change all of our lives.

We took off from Kennedy, landed in London. On the way over to Europe, George taps me on the shoulder. I didn't know George well, but he was a riot. He grew up in Ridgeland, South Carolina, a little town about twenty miles from Beaufort, much more rural, much more hick, much more redneck. George was about six-four, six-five. He had an Olympian sexual nature. His nickname was the Daddy Rabbit, which he earned by going after every girl living and breathing before him, and sleeping with a lot of them. He was the most intellectually uninterested of all of us, because the Daddy Rabbit was interested in one thing: a willing young woman. Bunnies, he called them. And he would tell them anything to get their clothes off. "Honey, honey. I don't wanna do anything, I promise. I just wanna lay down there beside it." That's the kind of line I could never deliver to a girl. If I ever told a girl that, I'd have to fling myself out of a car going eighty miles an hour just out of self-hatred.

Anyway we're flying over there to Europe, and the Daddy Rabbit taps me on the shoulder and says, "Now boy." He was always calling me boy. "I want you to know somethin.' I know you're goin' to Europe because you wanna look at museums, you wanna visit sites where great writers lived, you're goin' to literally improve yourself, and you will buy books that the Daddy Rabbit wouldn't wipe his butt on. All that's fine, Pat. You can see all those cathedrals. But Daddy Rabbit is going over there 'cause he read how they believe in Europe in something called free loooove. In free loooove, the woman likes to—she wants to do it as much as a man does. And you ain't gotta get married after you do; you just do it for the personal enjoyment of it, if you know what I mean." So he said, "I been lookin' for a philosophy my whole life, and I finally found one that I can live with, one that I can believe in, one that I can dedicate my life to, and it's called free loooove." He said, "You go to all those museums, but the Daddy Rabbit's going to be spending a lot of time explorin' the limits of free loooove, if you know what I mean."

So I said, "Well, yeah, George, I think I do," and he says, "The Daddy Rabbit's not like you, Pat. The Daddy Rabbit needs a woman every couple of nights or Daddy Rabbit don't function right, you know what I mean? I know you ain't never had it in your life, so you don't know what you're missing, but the Rabbit, he's got to have it, so I ain't going to none of your fuckin' museums. I ain't going to none of your fuckin' things where you better yourself. You ain't gonna see the Daddy Rabbit too much around the museums. Now, you go to all those museums and give me a report."

I said, "George, let me help you with this. You may need to know one thing that you don't seem to understand."

He said, "What's that?"

And I said to him, "American girls come to Europe to study art, to see the museums. A lot of them are junior year abroad, and they're going to try and get cultured. So the women are going to be in the art museums and palaces and churches."

And he's, "Well, Goddamn, boy. Are you tellin' me that's where the Daddy Rabbit has to lay his trap?"

I said it might be where you'll have most success in laying your trap. And when George heard that, he said, "My God, I just became a museum lovah!" I end up loving George. He later said, "You know, Conroy is the greatest pussy hound I've ever known." He says, "Instinctively, Conroy knew these girls were gonna be at museums."

I got to watch Daddy Rabbit at work in these museums. I'd hear George go, "Well, that's a mighty fine picture if I do say so myself," and the girls would roar laughing at George's accent and collapse. George of course would use that, and he'd have a date that night. I was amazed. I'd never done that in my life.

That trip to Europe was a life-changing trip. That was absolutely wonderful for me; first of all seeing everything I wanted to see in London.

I went on some literary tour, saw the Old Curiosity Shop, went to Westminster, saw all the writers buried that I wanted to see, plus others I didn't know about. I went down to Shakespeare's home and saw his grave. Had a magnificent trip to Cambridge, where I just went crazy. I saw the admissions office at Cambridge University and met an emeritus professor with leather sleeves on his jacket, which I've always seen in movies. I came busting into this office, and I see him sitting there, and I say, "Sir, I have got to come to this university. I don't care what I have to do, how I have to do it, I gotta get in here. I would love this. You know, I've been all over this campus, I wanna eat a book, I don't wanna study a book, I wanna eat one."

So my typical, stupid personality is ablaze with my effusive overreaction to everything. He has this fabulous English voice; when he spoke it's like the pouring of extra virgin olive oil. And he's, "I say, young man, are you always this enthusiastic?"

I said, "Yes, sir, it's one of the things you'll hate the most about me, but this is just too fabulous to miss. And, you know, I'm young now; I'm not married; I'll move over here; I'll do anything."

He said, "Where'd you go to college?"

I said, "Okay, now comes the hard part. Have your sense of humor." And when I said the Citadel, he said, "I've never heard of it." I said, "Of course you've never heard of it."

Now, you know, the next question is, "Is it accredited?"

"Yes, it is."

"Is it four years?"

"Yes, it is."

And he said, "Will anything you tell me about it ever impress me?"

And I said, "Probably not, except you'll find a lot of Citadel guys buried on Normandy Beach and all throughout Europe."

So anyway, he and I had a great time, we go out to lunch, and at the end of it he told me he thought I'd be perfect for Cambridge. He said, "I think this can be worked out." And we wrote for about two years afterward. He could not have encouraged me more. I told him I wanted to be a writer, and he said that's a great thing to want to be. I have no idea his name now; I regret that. But for some reason he gave me a great belief in myself. That I could throw myself up against something like this and actually talk my way into this guy's wanting me to go to his university. It's just typical Conroy trying to claw his way up the social ladder.

Anyway, Mike Jones and Bernie wanted to see Ireland. I did not. I said, "I'm not going to Ireland." I didn't want to go to Ireland because of my father and his family. Nothing Irish appealed to me. That was part of my complete rejection of Dad and everything he stood for. My dream was the Greek Islands, and George wanted to go to Greece because he heard Greek girls love to fuck. He didn't think they were Christian, and the non-Christian girls had no morals whatsoever. So we split up.

When Daddy Rabbit and I were in our first hotel in Amsterdam, traveling together after Bernie and Mike went to Ireland, I said, "George, what are you doing?"

He said, "They've got the worst toilets here. I can't get this Goddamn thing to flush."

He'd taken a shit in the bidet.

He said, "You know, these people, you'd think with all these cathedrals and shit, they could do a little bit of personal toiletry. These may be the most cultured people in the world, but they can't make a toilet worth a shit."

We're in Zurich, and he hasn't had a woman in a day or two, and Daddy Rabbit says, "Now boy, I have not had my pipes cleaned out since we've been here, and the Daddy Rabbit's just like a car, needs his pipes cleaned out, his system greased and oiled."

We're at this little hotel, and he hears these two girls laughing next door. They're speaking English, they're American girls, so George puts on the love cry of the Daddy Rabbit, and he goes *ah-ow, ah-ow, ah-ow.* He grabs a cup, goes next door, and says, "Hello girls, I could not help but overhear that you speak American, which means you're my kind of people. Could we borrow a cup of sugar?"

Not surprisingly, they didn't have any sugar, but they were our dates that night, and they traveled with us for about five days. I was just stunned by the whole thing. The Daddy Rabbit said that was my first taste of traveling "with a live woman." The older one hooked up with the Daddy Rabbit. The younger girl, we got in the bedroom together, and she says, "You know, I'm not like my sister."

I said, "Don't worry about it. You hit the right guy."

It's all weirdness, it's all Catholicism, it's all stupid, and it is also my strange, byzantine attitude toward sex. I'd much rather have been like the Daddy Rabbit than Pat Conroy, but I wasn't.

Still, it was one great trip. We saw everything. We saw Rhodes and Cyprus and Lebanon, and oh my God, Crete. On a cruise ship for twelve days in the Greek Islands, we were with five other guys in the cabin. They were complete strangers, but they were from Sweden. I said, "Rabbit, you're going to learn something about free love from the originators."

I went to English tea during the day, and there was a girl who liked me, so we danced. She was pretty, and her parents liked me. So I'm dancing with her, and I said, "Lily, there's a few questions I need to ask. How old are you?"

She looks up at me and says, "Does age make any difference?"

I said, "Sometimes it does. How old are you?"

She says, "I was twelve my last birthday."

I back up. Now, we still had high tea, but we no longer danced.

So I came back unscathed for the summer with my poor unused penis. But it was a great sex education for me, watching these other guys. In the red-light district in Amsterdam, Bernie sees a whore. "Oh my, gosh, she's beautiful. I want to marry her."

The Daddy Rabbit said, "Well, you can marry her for about a half hour, boy, if you just go on in there." And the Daddy Rabbit's saying, "I've never had to pay for it; it always just came to me freestyle, if you know what I mean."

We truly had one of the great times of my life that summer.

～

So we get back to South Carolina, back to teaching. There were girls the second year I was at Beaufort climbing in the window of my house. Ex-students, making bets with each other, daring each other, that kind of thing.

I said, "Ah, you were a student of mine."

"Doesn't make any difference. I'm not your student now."

A few of those girls—we performed the black act together. The nuns who taught me sex education were hiding something terrific. But that was basically the extent of my experience.

What I did to shield myself—and I've done this more than once—I fell in love with a woman married to a friend of mine. It was very common for me. There was a safety in that. And this woman was fabulous. We were all in love with her, from Daddy Rabbit to Bernie to Mike. She married the son of Big John Trask. Freddie. Freddie's the richest kid in town, from the richest family in town. Lindsay was sort of our first hippie, but also the first one married, so she took care of us. We'd go over to her house, and Lindsay was always there, funny, low-key, pretty, you know, made life comfortable, made life possible. We could use her washer-dryer. I just went nuts over her. So because of her, I didn't date the next year. I just wanted to be around Lindsay.

Now that summer, I agreed to go to Scotland and England with Freddie and Lindsay. By this time, Lindsay and I were great friends, but nothing else was even suggested. So I go on this stupid trip. They had a surprise for me. They get their room, I'm getting ready to get my room, and they said, "No, no, Pat. Let's all sleep together. It's cheaper."

I said, "You know, I thought maybe . . . "

And she says, "No, we don't do that anymore."

"But I'd feel really uncomfortable."

"You'll get used to it."

So Lindsay sleeps in the middle, I sleep to the left, Freddie sleeps to the right. I wouldn't have gone near that trip had I known. But I saw Scotland, lots of sheep, and I'm lying there with an erection the entire time I'm in bed with Lindsay, the girl I love beside me, and I couldn't do a thing.

Finally we fly back. It's about this time I got serious with Barbara Jones, and two months later we were married. I had known Barbara— she lived next door to me. Propinquity seemed to be the main thing in my life. People had to be nearby. Barbara was a teacher at Beaufort Elementary School and was pregnant the first time I saw her. This didn't put me off; I thought it was nice, probably because of my experience with Mary Alice, and my experience in being the oldest of seven children: Mom was always pregnant.

I never met Wes, her husband, because he had been deployed before I met Barbara. In 1968, he was shot down in Vietnam. After his death, I was at a party one night, and Barbara came in, this pretty girl. I heard someone say, "That poor woman. What a shame she has two kids. No one will want to marry her now," which struck me as hideously unfair. Somebody dies for his country, and his wife can't get remarried because she's got his two children? Husband fights for his country, gets shot down, his wife is doomed? A guy dying for his country—that was my background. Guys from the Citadel were dying. A lot of guys were dying from my class at that time. In the deep subconscious, that had a big effect on me. Anyway, I felt bad for her; she seemed in a very bad place to me.

I don't think I thought it out, but we started dating. I liked her a lot, great personality, smart as shit. And I was comfortable with the children. I've always liked kids, got along with kids, like having them around. They tickle the shit out of me. I'm a Conroy. As the oldest of seven, I don't even hear a baby cry. And I wanted the full life. I wanted to be married; I wanted to raise kids. So we got married soon after that, much too soon. Without putting too much thought into it at all, I said, "Let's get married." She said yes to my great surprise, and so we did. When Barbara and I first got married and started going out to dinner, I felt like I was dating for the first time in my life. I had never really done that, and found I liked going out to restaurants and meals. That was delightful and fun.

But I think I got married for all the wrong reasons. I had not dated much; I think I married the first girl who seemed to like to kiss me a lot. And marrying the widow of a Marine fighter pilot was obviously part of some circle with my father. But I didn't think much about getting married; I just did it. I really didn't know Barbara at all. Nowadays Conroy is against first marriages; I think first marriages ought to be banned. They are dangerous. You don't know what you're doing.

Everything I seemed to have done in my whole life has been based on emotion, not thought. Emotion more than thought has ruled my life, and this is how I have screwed up my life. I have let myself be swept along by emotion. If I'd had more response of the brain instead of response of the emotions, it would have helped me with everything I did.

Mom and Dad disapproved because I was marrying not only a used car, but a used Protestant car. It meant I was kicked out of the church. When Dad found out she had two children: "You dumb son of a bitch."

They refused to come to the wedding and would not even tell the children I was getting married because they were too young to see someone abandon the church. Nothing I do is without battalions lining up to face each other.

But I was ready to leave the church. It seemed like all these codes, all these sets of laws were trying to control me: what it means to be a Citadel man, what it means to be a Catholic. I thought if I was ever going to become a real writer, I had to break away from these and come up with codes and laws of my own. And I had already lost my faith when I was a senior in college. "Father Hopwood, I am losing my faith." He said, "No, you're not." I said, "Yeah, I am. And to fight against this, I'm going to communion every day of the year." He said, "We only have it on Sunday." I said, "Yeah, but I'd like to come up here and meet you every day for communion so I can fight this thing." "I don't want to do it. I'm not going to do it. You can't force me to." I said, "I'll make the bishop do it." "Oh, Goddamn it, okay, come on." So I go up there every day, and very reluctantly, he'd give me communion, but he was there. He said something crappy every time, but he was there. At the end, though, he says, "How's it going?" I said, "I lost my faith." "After I was up here every day? Good God Almighty, are you crazy? I was just wasting my time giving you communion every day." I said, "It's not your fault. I thought I'd give it a try, but it just didn't work."

So by the time I married Barbara, leaving the church seemed like the right thing to do. Then Mom arrived with Carol and Stanny the day before the wedding. That night, the boys gave me a party, which was a sort of barbecue. Here is the explosiveness of my life: Barbara's parents hated me. Her father, Colonel Bolling, asked me, "How'd you get out of the war?"

I said, "Colonel, I'm a draft dodger, and I'm proud of it. I don't believe in this war, and I'm not going to fight a war I don't believe in."

He said, "We call that cowardice where I come from."

I said, "I don't mind a guy like you calling me a coward."

"She was married to someone who knew how to serve his country."

I said, "Yes, and you will note he's no longer here. He's dead, and his country needed that, but your daughter did not need it that much, and his kids certainly didn't need it that much. Now it's my job to love his wife and raise his children. I am trying to do that as best I can." I had never met with such disapproval.

Then, Barbara's maid of honor was her sister-in-law, Wes Jones's sister, who lay on the bed in this very small house and simply screamed in agony over her brother getting killed and the remarriage of the wife. I'm thinking: What have I done to myself?

Daddy Rabbit goes, "Hey Pat, my boy, you should have put a little more thought in your maid of honor, if you don't mind me saying so, you know what I mean?"

I said, "Yes, I know, George. I want to thank you for that."

He said, "That girl is bat-shit crazy, and she's not doing my party much good."

It was a bad omen, this woman screaming and crying and wailing the night before the wedding.

Bernie was keeping bar out in the yard, and Stanny found a window from the house to the yard where she put her glass when it was empty, and whenever Bernie would see it, he'd fill it up again. I didn't know any of this until my mother says, "Oh my God, somebody's feeding Stanny drinks."

I said, "How do you know?"

She said, "Look."

And Stanny is reaching for a glass, as unsteady on her feet as she can be, grabs her glass, puts it to her lips, stumbles and tumbles out into a huge bush, from which Bernie and Mike Jones have to retrieve my completely drunk grandmother. I think by then a bottle of Scotch had been consumed. She is completely blotto, so much so I don't think she made the wedding.

Afterward, there was so much pressure on Barbara and me instantly. I was teaching on Daufuskie Island by then, married to a woman with two children who would not even think about living on Daufuskie with her two babies. I'm going by boat, forty-five minutes across the water and back each day.

I come back from Daufuskie one night, and Barbara's weeping. Her parents, the Bollings, are getting ready to call the Joneses. The Bollings are going to take Jessica and Melissa away from us as unfit parents. This is the typical melodrama that always follows me, or I draw it out. I can't do anything without something like this happening. It was not good for our first two months of marriage.

I said, "Why is he taking the kids away?"

"You're a hippie."

I said, "You've got to be shitting me."

Hippie? In Beaufort, South Carolina? I was not a hippie; I can just tell you that. I have never been a hippie in my life. But Barbara had put up posters all over the house of Marlon Brando and Steve McQueen on a motorcycle. She had these ugly little mobiles saying "Make Love Not War." Her father thought it was hippie shit.

Barbara is terrified by the Joneses, and I feared them very much. Their kid did what I was supposed to do. Their kid was a Marine fighter pilot, as I was supposed to be. But his parents were utterly magnificent people. I call the Joneses. Said, "Colonel and Mrs. Jones, we've only met once, and I just want to tell you what's going to happen. I want to warn you about this. I have no idea what you're going to do about it, but the Bollings are going to call you."

They were fabulous. "Pat, we cannot thank you enough for taking care of our son's children. We have been worried about it since he was killed."

So the next day, unknown to Barbara, I went down and started adoption proceedings. Didn't tell Barbara, didn't tell anybody. Adoption papers came, showed them to Barbara, signed them; in less than a month they're my kids, Conroys. Her parents couldn't do anything once the adoption came through.

Over the years I became really good friends with the Joneses, and especially with the Colonel. He had been a Marine fighter pilot in World War II, shot down in Germany, badly wounded. What he did is he made it to a church, rested there for a couple days until he recovered some of his health, then started on his way. He dressed as a farmer and walked with a pitchfork, and the truckload of soldiers would wave to him and he'd wave back. He had to kill a woman in a farm who discovered him. That was the rule. You did anything you could to escape, to come back. Finally he got to Switzerland.

Anyway, the Colonel was very open and intellectual, he loved to read, was interested in everything, president of the Tennessee Library

Association. In the summer when the girls were older I'd take them to their farm in west Tennessee near the Mississippi River, and we would stay for two weeks. They had a finished basement; I'd stay down there, and they had a 120-acre farm and a pond we'd swim in. He'd drive me all around the county.

One of the last times I was up there, he drove me past the monument where his son's name had just been carved with the other guys in the county who had been killed in Vietnam. Colonel Jones tells me that when he lost Wes, it was the worst moment of his life. He then, rather intellectually, says, "You know, Pat, this is wonderful, you coming in to my life. It almost killed me when I lost my son. And then God gave me another son when you walked into my life."

I had to walk back to the car swiftly I was so moved. It must be rare for a man who lost a son in Vietnam to say that to a draft dodger. But I always found them grateful about me taking care of those girls, and they became as close as parents to me.

When they came to visit me once in Beaufort, I took them to the cemetery to visit their son's grave. Colonel Jones walks up to the grave, leans down, and starts pulling weeds up from around it. Then he stands at attention, military attention, salutes the grave, and says, "Well done, son."

I about fucking collapse. Mrs. Jones is weeping against my Buick.

"We've never been here, Pat. Not since the burial. It's too painful. Thanks for knowing where it is."

Anyway, I had to adopt those girls very quickly because of Barbara's stupid parents, the Bollings, who were not worth a damn. There was all kinds of shit like that going on. I don't think our marriage had a chance. And I don't think any relationship could have survived what happened with Daufuskie Island.

～

While I was in my first year of teaching, I wanted to serve my country some way without going into the military. I was feeling guilty about not doing anything for my country during the Vietnam War. I did not want to be a soldier, and I did not believe in that war, but I wanted to give two years to my country.

This embittered shell of a man I have now become, this empty husk, this spent cartridge, was not always like this. There was a time when I had blood surging through my veins, when I was young and could not do enough good for the world.

So Bernie and I applied to the Peace Corps. When we never heard from that, Bernie found out about this job on Daufuskie Island. It was the first year of teacher integration, and the county was in a bind. They needed some white schoolteachers on this all-black island, which had two black teachers there already. So Bernie said, "Pat, why don't you and I go over, rent a house and live there? I'll be the principal and you'll teach grades five through eight, and we can use that as our Peace Corps." I said that sounds great. So Bernie applies for both of us to have a job. Naturally we get it since we're the only applicants on earth.

The superintendent told me, "You're a godsend, because HEW demanded there be at least one white schoolteacher on the island."

But when I go tell Bernie we got it, he said, "It ain't we. I ain't going over there." He had found out that the place we were going to live had no indoor toilets.

At a party not too long ago, this very serious journalist-reporter came up and said, "Bernie, I heard you got Pat his job on Daufuskie and you were going over there with him. What happened? Why didn't you go to Daufuskie Island?"

He told her, "I, Bernie Schein, a Jew, would have had to take a shit in an outhouse. You may not know my religion very well, but Jews do not shit in outhouses. My people are an anxious people, a nervous people, and we all have fixations on our digestive tracts from the beginning to the very end caused by centuries of being pursued like dogs through Europe by your people. If you are Christian, if you're part of the goyim, you can actually take a shit on a toilet in a gas station on the interstate. If, however, you're a Jew, you could not take a shit anywhere but your own bathroom, with the possible exception of a Ritz-Carlton. Now, I can beat off joyously anywhere. I can beat off on that table; I can beat off on that chair; I can beat off in that chandelier; I can beat off on top of a car. But I cannot take a shit in an outhouse. Pat Conroy, a dumb Southern boy, can take a shit anywhere on earth, and it doesn't make any difference because his IQ is so low. So that is why Pat went to Daufuskie Island and I did not."

Anyway, Bernie did not go to Daufuskie, and I'd already told them I'd go, and that was it. My fate had taken over. So in 1969 I went to teach on an all-black Gullah sea island. I thought I had discovered one of the moons of Pluto, when all I had discovered was America. I spent nine months of the best years of my life being called "the white school-teacher." I became integration. The kids had no idea they were sending a white boy over to teach, and they were terrified when they saw me. They said, "We never met any white teachers, and what's a man teacher? We've never heard of it." There was a lot they'd never heard of. All their tests were below the first-grade reading level.

I gathered them together and said, "We've got to work hard, it's going to be a great year, let's get enthusiastic, let's get fired up, because I want to promise you something—they sent the right guy."

That night, I wrote a letter to the superintendent, Walt Trammell. "Dear Sir, I'm teaching fifth grade through eighth grade, and I've got kids who can't write their names, kids who can't count to ten. You told me their schools were separate but equal. It's the biggest lie ever told in the South."

I was not in my diplomatic best in my younger days—I was a fire-eater type person—and I pissed that superintendent off. He was not one of the worst racists in the world, but he still had this racist quality, and I got under his skin. He hated my guts from that day forward. Anyway, I fucked it up; I screwed it up; I screwed my life up, the life of my family. And now here I am, an old man, beaten by life, savaged by fate.

The guy I played guard with at the Citadel, John DeBrosse, said I deserved everything that happened to me. "Conroy, you are mischievous; you are devilish; you get yourself into trouble. You've got an incredibly big mouth. It must have enraged your father. You enraged the Citadel. Everything that happened to you at the Citadel was your fault if you go back and look at it honestly."

He quoted a little poem I published in the *Shako:* "Last night, I dreamt I was a dog who found an upperclassman tree." And he said,

"I heard they came from four battalions to eat you alive, to make your life miserable, to torture you. But you wrote that. You knew what was going to happen. You knew that you were going out of bounds. You did it anyway, because that's your nature. And so don't whine to me that the Citadel picked on you. You were picking on the Citadel, and they taught you a lesson."

There's no question I have pissed off an enormous range of people. I can barely work with anybody or anything without ending up fighting with it, which I consider a tremendous embarrassment now that I'm in my dotage and wonder what the hell that was all about. In retrospect I wish I'd kept my mouth shut a little more, because when I opened it, it seemed to get me in trouble. I was such a young asshole; I now realize that. Pat, why didn't you shut your mouth? Pat, why didn't you just keep quiet? What was the reason, Pat, you had to say that then? Why type of Tourette's syndrome mauled your youth and made it untenable for anyone to be around you?

So at the end of the year, my school board was trying to take the boat away I used to get to Daufuskie because it was too expensive. At that time there was a woman who came through town named Betsy Fancher, who must have had the most boring job in the world. She was going around the South during the summer covering school board meetings for *South Today.* That was the house newspaper of the Southern Regional Council. She stumbled onto me when I was arguing before the school board just for the gas in the boat. Now I'm an ancient, withered warrior, but back then I was an impetuous little cocksucker, and I fought them and won. The board voted gas. That was a rare victory of mine with the school board. Betsy wrote an article about it, and the article went, as they say, nationwide, right before the school year started. She made me sound like the most heroic figure since Apollo, trying to get gas to teach these black kids who didn't know anything. That enraged the superintendent. I got fired almost immediately. Betsy and I met in June, and I was fired by the end of September.

I think it was two days later I got my greetings from the president of the United States. They drafted me. I'd had a deferral because I was teaching. When they fired me, I lost that, and evidently, the superintendent just called the draft board and said, "He's not teaching anymore."

Zach Sklar had been an antiwar activist and done draft counseling in California, and he hears of this and comes flying back, stayed with us for the next month, I think, and was a great, great help. Zach was one of the California boys who came to take a sociology class on Daufuskie Island taught by a charismatic black guy named Herman Blake. Zach's father, George Sklar, was a playwright who got blacklisted as a communist in the '30s. Anyway, Zach sent a telegram to the head of the Selective Service protesting my being drafted for political reasons. That stopped it right there. I had ten days to report, and the telegram stopped that process. I had no idea you could send a telegram like that. So he was a terrific consigliore in these days. Later he and I had a great thing happen to us. The year I was nominated for an Academy Award for the *Prince of Tides* screenplay, he was nominated for the *JFK* screenplay, and we got to sit in the same row together. That was a magical sort of thing that you don't think of when you're young.

After I got out of the draft, then there was the fear how was I going to make a living? I had three kids under five years old, I had three or four black kids from Daufuskie Island living with me, I had a wife who wasn't working because she had just had our baby Megan, and I did not know how I was going to make it in the world. I look back and wonder how the hell Barbara did all this. I can't figure that out at all.

After I was fired in September, Megan was born November fifth. The night she was born, I was terrified. Dr. Keyserling was my doctor and Barbara's doctor and everybody in town's doctor, and he birthed every child in town. He was a great curmudgeon. This is 1970, and I go in to the hospital, say, "Doc, do you know men are watching the birth of their children now?"

He looks at me, says, "That's the most disgusting thing I've ever heard in my entire life. What kind of pervert would want to see that kind of mess? Good God, Conroy. Get the hell out of my hospital. I don't even want you in my waiting room."

He kicked me out, so I went down to some friends who lived near the hospital. They fed me drinks, and we waited until Dr. Keyserling called and said that Megan had been born. I went back and saw her through the window, and that was Meggie-Poo.

The two girls, Jessica and Melissa, seemed very upset about Megan coming on board. When we got home, both of them came out to ask me, "Do you like her better?"

I said, "Nah, I like y'all better."

"But she's yours."

"Yeah, but I've known you longer. That's how it works."

Since Megan didn't know anything, my main concern at that time was that I not make these other kids feel rejected by being too gleeful over the birth of my own. Now I think I may have screwed poor Megan by not showing enough. But there was so much going on, and I am not sure I was good at anything at that particular time, because I'd really messed my life up.

I was going I think fairly crazy, trying to get a job, not getting a job, knowing I wasn't going to get a job. I was getting turned down for every job I was applying to, and it did not look good. I think there was some kind of check that came for Jessica and Melissa. Gene Norris sent $100 a month; Bill Dufford sent me $100 a month; the Boo sent me $100 a month.

That was a tough period of my life. After what happened with the Beaufort County school system, I could not get a job teaching anywhere in the state. I went to Savannah, another state, and I'm sitting there with the assistant superintendent, thinking I'm having a good interview, when the phone rings. It's the superintendent of Beaufort, Walt Trammell, one of the guys who got me fired. They talk, and then this guy says, "Mr. Conroy, you're exactly the kind of person we don't want teaching our students in Savannah."

This demonstrates my ability to make psychodrama out of anything. Millions of people become teachers and don't end up like I did, where they can't teach again forever. I never taught again. It takes a special thwarted personality to arrange that kind of fate, which I found myself fully capable of doing.

It was painful to lose teaching so early in my life. Success I considered teaching in high school. I thought I was going to teach high school and write poetry my entire life. I would have had a lovely life, I thought, because I think teaching is the highest profession one can enter. I love what teachers do for you: they give you the world; they give you a way to live in the world; they give you a way to operate in the world; they give you a way to live above and beyond yourself. I had a cheering section of English teachers in my life, I admired what they did for me, and I wanted to be that kind of teacher. Gene Norris, Joseph Monte, Millen Ellis—I wanted to be a teacher because of those teachers in my life. I loved the way people thought of them in their community. I thought it was a good life; it held great appeal to me. I don't think you can do much better in life than the way these teachers did it. So the teaching wound remains and will always remain. I didn't get back to it. By not teaching, I lost something from my life.

I applied for a job at a chicken farm up in Hampton County, one of these horrible places where they raise chickens. It was a long ride, but I figured I could do it. I was going to be taking care of the chickens; I might have to kill them. So, the guy likes me. I told him I didn't have any experience with farm work, but I'm telling him that my whole family were farmers, and I'm trying to make the best case I can. So anyway, he likes me; he says he's going to hire me.

Then he thought about it and said, "Son, you're not the teacher they fired in Beaufort are you?"

I said, "Yes, sir, I am."

He says, "Well, I can't hire you."

I said, "Can you tell me why not? You know, it's a different thing, taking care of chickens."

He says, "Son, I got to hire somebody I can trust with my chickens."

I saw one job advertised paying $50 every five seconds, and I thought, Now this is a job old Conroy can get into. You know, $50, five seconds, just work a couple hours a day. What the job was: fighting an orangutan in a county fair. You got $50 for every five seconds you stayed in the ring with the orangutan. I went up to see it, this county fair. But these were big, strong, redneck boys in the ring with that orangutan. It would just pick the guy up and simply hurl him through the air into the audience. I didn't know orangutans were so strong, but they were strong, and they're a lot bigger than I thought, so that job didn't work out.

At one interview I found out that the deputy superintendent, Emmett McCracken, was on the board of this economic development company I was trying to get a job from, and I saw him there. He said, "You should know not even to apply." Yes I do. Good to see you, Mr. McCracken. Then I went to a job interview in Florence, South Carolina, and on the way back from that, I had a complete physical breakdown where I could not control my body. I was jackknifing in the car. I had to put my hands in front of me to keep my head from hitting the steering wheel, and I was crying uncontrollably.

This was not my first breakdown. The first breakdown I ever had occurred at the Citadel, when the plebe system broke me one night. It broke me completely, surprising the shit out of me. For some reason, they caught me by surprise. They came at me. When the pack goes after you, it's hard. There can be ten of them on you, each giving you different orders and screaming at you as loud as they can right by your ear. The officer in front of you may be spitting in your face; another may be pounding on your chest with his fist. It's an arena of chaos, a screaming horror. The pack came at me when I was not expecting it, and I had not prepared myself at all for it, and boy, I just broke. I just bawled, snot coming out of my nose, down my face.

I was about to say I was going to quit when the seniors next door came roaring in, grabbed me, and pulled me out of there. Then they told me: "They're coming for you tomorrow morning; they'll be coming for you. Are you broke?" That was the phrase: "Are you broke?" Now they see the opening, they can get rid of you. They can get you out of school. Because once they know you'll break, they'll come back to you and try again and again and again. You're finally going to say, I can't take it, I'm going to leave.

After the seniors got me collected, calmed down, I went back in to the room. My roommate had already gone to sleep, and I remember looking in the mirror, and I said, You can't leave. Your only college education is here, whether you like it or not. So what I tried to do is kill off anything soft in me that I saw in that face. Dad used to say, "You're like your mother; you're soft; you're weak; you're a pussy." I killed all that off as I was watching in the mirror. And when I went to bed, I knew the Red Army could not run me out of that school. I just knew it. But I wonder at what cost that comes to you.

They came to me all the next day; they came to me that afternoon; they came to me that night. And I was fine. Yes, sir, no, sir, no excuse, sir, and whatever they told me to do, fifty push-ups, a hundred push-ups, I did them. Jumped back up and somebody else would tell me to do something. What they try to do is confuse you. They're all screaming at once. I would choose one to answer. I'd answer him fully; I'd ignore the others. You didn't hear me, dumbass? You ignoring me, dumbass?

I got through that just by a decision, and so I made it through. But that was a crisis. And looking back, I considered that a breakdown. That was the first time. The second time was coming back from that interview in Florence when I lost control of my body. I lost muscular control and was shaking and twisting around. I knew I was going to crash if I did not get to the side of the road. So I pulled over to the side, tried to get control of myself, and looked for the nearest person who loved me.

It was Bill Dufford, my beloved high school principal. Bill was one of those guys—like Gene Norris—who found me. Bill was splendid to me, and I cannot thank Bill enough. So I drove to Dufford's apartment in Columbia, where he was then the head of the Desegregation Center of South Carolina. He opened the door; I said, "Bill, I need you." He was scared to death, so I must have looked terrible. Whatever hit me had gone on for fifteen minutes on the side of the road. Finally it slowed down, it stopped, and whatever control I had came back. Then I drove immediately to Bill Dufford's house and spent the night. When I woke up the next day, I felt better. I drove home.

I knew something horrible was wrong, and I had a feeling it was the pressure. I'd been drafted. Dad's in Vietnam. I have three kids; I have a wife, three black kids living with us on the Point. It was a madhouse. Barbara was freaking out, and okay, I was too. I knew that I was in a really, really desperate situation. Also, I was writing *The Water Is Wide*. I now look back; that was just too much. My life was overexposed. I could not take it. I just did not do well with it. It was overwhelming, what was happening, and when I got overwhelmed is when I broke down. I'm sure it scared Barbara.

The one job I did have during that time was working on a shrimping boat as a striker, the guy at the back of the boat. When the nets came in, I undid them and sorted the shrimp and fish. It's dangerous work, and it's heavy work when you bring in those nets; then you have the magic moment when you uncover the nets, and every once in a while, tremendous amounts of seafood go flying onto the deck. Everything's flopping and flapping and quivering with life. My job was to scoop it up, collect the fish they could sell, head the shrimp, and ice it down. I got paid in seafood, so that's what my family ate a lot of that summer.

It was a world I'd never seen, and it had great beauty to it. I fell in love with those creeks and rivers. I loved the complete dependence on the seas, the rivers, the bays, and the outside world. It seemed like a wonderful way to make a living to me. You're outdoors; you're your own man. It was exhilarating to me after worrying about being fired and what I was going to do.

I used to love hearing the shrimpers talk to each other on the radio. They'd give their latitude and longitude and say, "Ain't nothin' here but ants"—that meant the shrimp were really little—just ants. "Catch anything over there?" "Ants; it's all ants." They were always lying to each other. Shrimping was never going well; it was horrible; they wouldn't be here next season; they were going to sell their boat. It was a world I really liked. I got to watch the shrimpers that year, and they got used to me. I'd pass other shrimp boats and wave. I met a lot of these shrimpers' families and liked them all. They were all good people, and there was great respect for shrimpers because of how hard their work was. These guys did not get rich, and they'd have good years and bad years. I'd pass the oyster fishermen, old black men. On two or three occasions their boats would break down, they'd wave me down, and I'd haul them in, take them up to the oyster factory. I loved that world out there on the ocean, the rivers, the bays. It was a tough world, but I thought a good world. It felt safe after being fired from Daufuskie, and it was getting away from the world of assholes, which was wonderful.

I was writing the book seriously that summer also. I'd come home and write in the afternoon. I started writing *The Water Is Wide* in a fury, trying to explain to myself as much as anyone else, what had happened to me on that island. I was so pissed off, had so much guilt over letting these kids down. And I kept meeting people around Beaufort: "What happened to you, Pat? You're a nice boy." I could not explain to them what had happened to me. So I wrote this book quickly, and I think sort of unartfully, in about three or four months in an absolute blaze of fury.

I learned early that a good day for me was five handwritten pages a day on a yellow legal pad. Occasionally I'd get six or seven, but when I got to five I could quit, knowing I had worked hard that day, because there was usually about three hundred words on one legal page. The five pages a day has been what I've tried to do every time I sit down to write.

My mother would come up behind me as I was writing *The Water Is Wide* and say, "Now son, I don't mean this as criticism, but most men your age have jobs. Most men with three children have jobs."

I had no job, no prospects, nothing except I was trying to write this book, *The Water Is Wide,* and normally that would not have worked. A fired teacher writing a book—oh yeah, that works out well all the time. It worked out for me like most things have in my life: totally by accident.

⌒

When *The Boo* came out, I was in court trying to get my job back. I got fired in maybe late September. *The Boo* came out the first week of December at a time when I was headline news in South Carolina, being fired from Daufuskie Island for, of all things, supporting black people and liking black people. The trial where I sued to get my job back was that same week, and my mother's book party for *The Boo* was the same night as I lost the trial. I had ruined my life in a very short time, I was looking at a lifetime of doom, and things did not look good. So my first book party was in this funereal atmosphere.

After I had finished writing the book, the Boo says, "While you guys were down there fixing your panties and putting on your bras in the English department, did you ever talk about getting a book published?"

I said, "Colonel, I have no idea how to get a book published."

So the colonel, of course he says, and I always loved this, "Well, let's look in the Yellow Pages."

So we did. We looked in the Yellow Pages, and under printing, we saw the R. L. Bryan Company that said "Business cards, invitations, books."

I put on a coat and tie the next day and go down there and talk to the guy, a vice president, you know, and I said I've got a book I'd like to be published. And he said great.

I said, "That can't be."

He said, "We'd be happy to publish it. The Citadel is wonderful. We're a South Carolina company."

I said, "I heard it was hard to get a book published."

He said, "Not for a smart guy like you."

So I said, "How does it work?"

He said, "Two thousand books, $4,000."

I said, "Is that how it works for everybody?"

He said, "What, do you think it's done for free?"

I had met five million generals at the Citadel, but no writers, and the one writer I had met who had taught me at Beaufort High School had died, so I couldn't go to her.

Anyway, I go to Peoples Bank in Beaufort. Willie Shepherd was a banker, and Willie is a Citadel graduate. I knew Willie because everybody knew everybody in Beaufort. So I tell Willie about my project, and he says, "A book about the Citadel? We've never had a book about the Citadel. How much do you need?"

I said, "I think we'll need about two thousand, Willie."

This is the way banking was then. He says, "Two thousand? I'll give you three thousand." He wrote me a check at his desk.

I said, "Do I have to fill out any papers?" He said, "We'll do that later. Don't worry about it."

Jim Bowditch, the guy who ripped the pants off the regimental commander, was dating a woman, Peggy Reynolds, first family of Virginia. Her family owned a printing company, the McClure Press in Weyers Cave, Virginia. Jim brought her down for a homecoming weekend. I met her, the Boo met her, and she offered us the best deal to print our book. We all shook on it, so that's how McClure Press became our company.

Another Citadel classmate, Joe Riley, was our lawyer. Joe Riley was a senior when I was a freshman, a senior I admired and loved, which was a rarity. Boo had liked him a lot too. He's been the mayor of Charleston for twenty-seven years, but Joe was just starting out as a lawyer then. He's been a great friend of mine throughout my life, and I send money for him when he runs for mayor. He ran for governor once; I supported him, gave speeches for him. He's been the best mayor the country's ever had; almost everybody says that. He's a wonderful man and a wonderful mayor. I don't think there's ever been another American mayor like him.

Well, in the book I had used real names, so Joe was the one who made me change all the names of the cadets, and I had a night to do it in. I made up the dumbest names you have ever heard of. I just made them up one night. You have never seen stupider names in your life; God they were dumb. I'm going through and throwing any name I could think of in there. Peter Doorframe and this kind of crap. Some of them were not even names, they were just things I made up. They were silly beyond human belief. It's one reason I cannot look at that book again. But I learned the importance of names. I've always thought there was a genius in the naming of things, and I love it when somebody comes up with the perfect name.

I think it was very good for me to have to publish *The Boo* and learn things like the commerce of book publishing: going in to borrow money, going to a publisher, asking him to print my book. As innocent as I was, I had no idea what a vanity press was. The Boo was as innocent as I was, but we actually made money. We presold enough to pay for the book before it came out, then sold out our first printing and went back to press. But I was a rookie then. I had no idea the storm this book would stir up.

When *The Boo* came out in 1970, it was controversial, banned on campus as soon as it's written, I think simply because the Citadel thought it made them look bad for firing this wonderful, fabulous, life-affirming champion of cadets and putting him in exile where he ordered the toilet paper. I emphasized the toilet paper and said something like "lesser men got rid of a greater man." There was nothing in there that was really critical of the Citadel except they got rid of this guy. But I think there was a punishment order if they found the book in your room, so of course the sales shot up among the cadets.

Now, I was not allowed to have any of the money, because Boo insisted all money we made go to Citadel scholarships. Of course, they never thanked us for it. The Boo and I took it to the president, gave him a signed copy, and he treats us like shit.

We walk out, and Boo says, "Bubba, that didn't seem like a high point in literary history to me. That was my impression. What was your impression?"

I said, "I imagine we can see the smoke over his fireplace tonight." We were both laughing about it, although we could not have been treated more shabbily.

At the book signing in Beaufort for *The Boo,* nobody came. I was there for three hours, and nobody came to the Beaufort book shop, including my mother and my wife. They both said, Well, we already had books. All of us were rookies then, so I don't hold this against them.

I was sitting there in the shop with the *High Sheriff of the Low Country,* Sheriff McTeer. Lots of people are coming to see Sheriff McTeer and buy his book. He had learned about the Gullah people, because Dr. Buzzard was putting hexes on people the sheriff had coming in to court. So the sheriff had learned how to de-hex, and he wrote about that in his book. He says, "Pat, I'm famous all over the world. I get letters from Australia, China." That's great, Sheriff McTeer. And he said, "Isn't it wonderful? I have so much fun being famous." Sounds great, Sheriff.

I came across my own copy of *The Boo* not long ago; the Boo said this was the first one he ever signed. I didn't know what to sign when I first did a book. I only did best wishes, some oily little greasy meaningless statement like that, and I try to do it better now; I try to think about it more now. The Boo doesn't say to Pat Conroy, he doesn't mention my name. He simply says, "To the lamb who made me. The Boo."

He sent out to all his lambs these little cards he had printed up which are worth money themselves now, these little business cards saying you could order *The Boo* for $4.50. McClure Press couldn't believe it: they had checks from over five hundred people before they went to press, so we paid for the book long before it even came out. By the time we published it, it was almost sold out. I think the first printing was fifteen hundred, then it went into a second printing.

If I ever allowed anything to excite me, I'm sure that would have been exciting. But the book came out the same week I was in court trying to get my job back at Daufuskie, which I lost, so I was jobless. There was stark terror in light of my future, or my lack of one.

~

After I got fired from Daufuskie, the *Charleston Evening Post* did a full-page article about it. This was rare for them; this was 1970. I was controversial shit then, being a white boy raising this ruckus about black people. I didn't even think I was going to get a fair shake in South Carolina newspapers, some of the most racist newspapers in the world. But the times were changing, and I think this was one of the first times this paper got to prove it. Also, I think they had known me at the Citadel because of basketball, and I was known as a good kid. They sent down a very good reporter named Jack Leland, whom I had read all through college. Jack even said he'd seen me play ball a couple of times, and I did not look like a revolutionary.

So Jack came down, and I took him everywhere. I took him out to Daufuskie, showed him the kids, told my story. He wrote a great article about my being fired and how he thought it was unjust. He played it up. Then, to everybody's shock, the *Evening Post* came out with an editorial in my favor, supporting getting my job back. They were saying, "He's discovered something, he's trying to tell us something, and nobody's listening." That was unheard-of at the time, but it was certainly a great boost for me. That went on the wire and got picked up.

Next, Joe Cumming came down from *Newsweek* magazine out of Atlanta. He wrote a very nice article about the firing, and it went out on the wire all over the place. The trial where I sued to get my job back was covered by the state newspapers, and some of these articles went out on the AP. After one of those, a guy came through town who made film-strips about teachers for an education company. He did a filmstrip about my getting fired. I think he thought I was either some kind of apparition or new evolutionary strain of Southerner. Every person I met from the North at that time thought every white Southerner was a White Citizens Council member or worse. They didn't believe there were Southerners possible who could think right about integration and civil rights.

I told him I was writing a book about my experience on the island. At that time I had no idea that *The Water Is Wide* was going to be any different from *The Boo*. I just had no idea when I started that out. I was glad that Willie Shepherd at Peoples Bank had agreed to give me the money to have it printed. I thought I was going to pay for it myself, McClure Press was going to publish it, and I would schlep it around like I did *The Boo*.

But this guy asked me, "Who's your agent?"

I said, "I don't have an agent. I'm not an actor."

That's the first time I'd heard of an agent representing writers. I thought when you got to be Hemingway or Thomas Wolfe, somehow an agent appeared out of nowhere to guide you, but I didn't know as an unknown, you could get an agent. And of course, you can't.

He said, "Let me give you the name of my agent. You can call and tell him I referred you. Make sure you very quickly tell him I referred you."

So I took the name of his agent: Julian Bach. And I thought, "God-damn, his mother knew he was going to be an agent." You know, this name: Julian Bach.

I have not had a job now for four months, five months. I can't get a job. They won't even give me a job on a chicken farm because they need somebody they can trust with the chickens. So this is not going well. There's a little panic in the household going on. All of a sudden, Pat's got himself a chance at a New York agent. I remember Barbara telling her family that. Well, of course I'm terrified. I've got to call the son of a bitch.

When I'm nervous I write things down, so I had written this whole speech down. First of all, I had to beg his secretary. I think she was still called a secretary then. She became an assistant several years later. I said, "You don't know me; I don't know you, but—"

She said, "He'll kill me if I put you on. He'll kill me."

I said, "You don't know this, but I'm his first cousin, and his favorite uncle died, and Julian didn't even know. It happened so suddenly." I'm just lying my ass off.

And she says, "Well, for that I'll put you on."

Julian's famous for a bad phone personality, and he goes, "Who is this? How did you get my secretary to put you on the phone? I'll fire her for this."

So I started reading. "Hello, Mr. Bach. My name is Pat Conroy. I'm from Beaufort, South Carolina. I have written a book that I think you will enjoy."

He goes, "South Carolina? I've barely heard of South Carolina; I've never heard of Beaufort. Who gave you this number? Where did you get this number?"

I merely mentioned the man's name, and by then I'm hysterical. He's yelling at me. I did not make it through that first phone conversation. He said, "I have losers like you call me every single day of my life. I don't know how you got my phone number. Don't call me again." And then, bam, he hangs up. He's famous for hanging up without saying good-bye.

I wrote him a letter: "Dear Mr. Bach, obviously your soul has withered in the canyons of New York City, in the alleys and darknesses that you walk through to get to your office each day." Having no idea he did that, but he did that. And so I said, "Whatever your mother thought when you were born, when you were suckling at her breast, she did not know what a small demon she was making. Such rudeness and such discourtesy I have never encountered in my life before, and hope I never do again."

Apparently my letter hit home. He called to apologize. He told me, "I don't have any clients from the South at all, and I'm kind of proud of it."

I said, "In the book, I taught for a year on an island with black children." He told me later when I said "island with black children," that got his attention.

He says, "You're a loser, but I will look at your book. It's Monday now; get it here for the weekend read."

I said, "What's the weekend read?"

He says, "Figure it out."

I hang up the phone. Barbara and my mother are there, and I said, "He says he wants it for the weekend read." I'm tossing these terms around. My first publishing term. They scream with joy.

Then my mother says, "Oh my God, it's not typed."

I said, "You think he'd mind if I send it up handwritten?"

So we call every friend of ours who's still talking to me in Beaufort, which wasn't that many, and Mom stands at the front door, Barbara stands at the back, and people came up; they got a chapter apiece. "When does it have to be back?" "Tomorrow." And then I hear, "It's got to be in for the weekend read."

I'm a wreck. Everybody in the family's a wreck. Well, the next day, the chapters started coming back. One chapter came in on onion skin. Another came in on long yellow sheets. Another came in on little blue sheets. Then there was pica, elite, and fonts I'd never heard of in my life. One font looked like handwriting, and for some reason she typed it on her personal stationery. So we gather it all together. Mom typed chapter 1, and the pages were 1 to 16. Tina Calhoun: chapter 2, pages 1 to 25. Barbara: chapter 3, 1 to 13. It was paginated that way all through the book. The last one came in, and we just stuck it together, and Jack Calhoun held the post office open past six so that in two days it would get to New York for the weekend read. We all cheer; we come back; we drink wine.

Okay, the thing gets there. Julian Bach calls me the next week and says, "Pat, I must tell you, I have not read a single word of your manuscript, but the girls in the office have fallen in love with you. We think it's the cutest thing we've ever seen in our lives." He howls with laughter and hangs up. I go, "Oh, Christ." I'm beyond humiliation. Julian later told me it was the dumbest thing he had ever experienced as an agent.

So finally, in about three weeks, I get a letter on this stationery that just—I mean, Turtle Bay, New York. And I'm thinking, holy Christ, Turtle-fucking-Bay, New York. So I got this thing. I am so nervous, I take it out on this island this friend of mine owned, terrified to open it. Finally opened it, and Julian was great. He said, "Dear Mr. Conroy, whom we fondly call Conrack around the office, I think you're a natural writer, and I think this is the first of many books. I hope our association is a long one."

Well, I was absolutely thrilled, but then of course my nature kicks in. I was in that state of not trusting good fortune. I remain in that state. It goes back to my inability to enjoy much that happens to me. My brothers have this pantomime of pretending they're me when something good happens. Something good will happen to Pat, and all of a sudden you see him wheel around behind to see what's sneaking up on him, to see who's going to put the shiv in his back. This comes from my childhood, where I had to be cautious. If you caught Dad's attention doing anything and you saw his eyes light on you, you were in trouble. So you learned to go inconspicuously, not to be noticed. My theory of the universe is if God sees you enjoying yourself, he will fuck up the next week of your life completely.

When Joe Cumming's article was published in the *Boston Globe,* who was it who saw it? A Charleston girl, Shannon Ravenel, then a young editor at Houghton Mifflin. She wrote Julian and said they'd be interested in seeing the manuscript. And in the courtesy of publishing, because she expressed interest, she saw it. They bought it.

Julian calls me up and says, "Pat?" in his elegant voice.

"Yes, Mr. Bach?"

"I have good news for us both. Houghton Mifflin has called, and they have accepted your book for publication. They are the publishers of Henry James, Edith Wharton, Henry David Thoreau, Ralph Waldo Emerson, Emily Dickinson, and now Pat Conroy. And here is the great news: $7,500."

I said, "I can get it done a lot cheaper down here."

Julian says, "Excuse me?"

I said, "Julian, I can get the book done a lot cheaper down here. Let me just do it."

And Julian—he's shocked, says, "Pat, you do understand it is they who pay you?"

He never let me forget this, as long as he lived.

I think I had been out of work for almost a year. And so that saved my life. And of course Julian thinks, once again, my God, what a horseshit client. Later I learned Julian had been a classmate of James Agee, and he hated Agee. Agee was a slob. Julian was, you know, very proper and elegant. Agee was not a good Harvard man, to Julian. Agee was a bum. And I said, "That boy sure could write his ass off though, couldn't he, Julian?" He said, "He certainly could." And he said, "That is what I thought about you."

Then he calls me up and says *Life* magazine wants an excerpt. I say, "That's great," and my mother's particularly excited. *Life* magazine, you know, even though it was on its dying days. But *Life* had just gone through a crisis with Clifford Irving, who sold a biography that he said he had done with full cooperation of Howard Hughes. *Life* has spent hundreds of thousands of dollars getting an excerpt from him. Well, Howard Hughes comes out in his weird paranoid fear of the world and says he's never heard of Clifford Irving in his life, he's never met the guy, and this book is completely made up. *Life* magazine backs Clifford Irving; they go to court. It ends up Clifford Irving is a complete and utter fraud, and *Life* is burned; they are humiliated journalistically. All the stuff you can be, they are.

In comes this thing by this kid from South Carolina right after this. So by now they are paranoid. They see I've taught on Yamacraw Island; there ain't no Yamacraw Island. They look all over the maps, and they cannot find Yamacraw Island. And if there ain't no Yamacraw Island, how do they know any of it is true? This South Carolina kid who looks like a bumpkin and acts like a bumpkin has pulled another one on *Life* magazine. They were panic-stricken. They fly a Southern writer, Marshall Frady, down to Beaufort, South Carolina, to make sure I was not lying my ass off. Marshall later became a friend in Atlanta, but at that time I just knew his work; he had cut a wide swath as a journalist. He interviews the superintendent, who is not named Henry Piedmont but named Walter Trammell. Ezra Bennington is Emmett McCracken. I had changed all the names. So when they looked this up, I looked like a liar.

So Marshall goes over to Daufuskie, interviews the kids. Marshall comes back, writes a great letter, says it's all legitimate. "It's exactly as Pat described. He's even got the ospreys' nests on the telephone poles going over." Only then do they tell Julian that they almost cancelled the whole thing. Julian told me, "My God, this is one of the most embarrassing moments of my career." But after the *Life* magazine piece came out, Hollywood bought the book.

Then Julian called me to come to New York, so I drove up in my yellow '68 Volkswagen, leisurely stopping on the way to visit guys I'd known from the Citadel. Julian calls Barbara and says, "Where is he? I told him to come to New York."

Barbara says, "He's on his way."

"What do you mean, he's on his way? What time does his plane get in?"

"Oh, he's driving."

"He's driving? Is he crazy? I needed to see him immediately."

I didn't know where to stay, but I always heard the YMCA was a good place to stay cheap. So I call Julian from the Y. He said, "What? You'll be raped! You've got to get out of there! Hurry!"

I didn't know where else to go. I got a cab and went to the Chelsea Hotel, which I'd read about, not knowing it had descended into a drug den. And he says, "They take heroin."

I said "Julian, I've read about the Chelsea my whole life. Dylan Thomas, Thomas Wolfe, they all stayed here. This will be fine."

That first night Julian said, "Now Pat, tonight I am taking you to something called an o-per-a."

I said, "An o-per-a?"

He said, "Yes. I know you don't know about o-per-as, but to put it in your terms, it is like a play sung in a foreign language."

He took me to all these restaurants where I got collard greens and fried chicken. Julian would look at it, he'd say, "So this is how you eat down there?"

Finally I said, "Julian, you know, I've read the biographies of Hemingway and Fitzgerald, and didn't their agents take them to some of the finest restaurants in New York?"

He said, "Yes, but Pat, I wouldn't want to embarrass you. Their menus are written in languages you've never heard of."

I said, "But you're taking me to these shit shops that serve Southern food, and you won't eat it."

He said, "I wouldn't put that stuff in my mouth." So then he took me to this French restaurant where he had a table, and he satisfied my need for that.

But he thought I was an idiot, a complete L'il Abner figure. He said, "Now, the Citadel. Is that a college?"

"Yes it is."

"I've never heard of it. Is it accredited?"

"Yes it is."

"And it goes four years?"

"Yes it does. It's a full four years."

"Isn't it wonderful they have four-year colleges in South Carolina now?" he said. "It's a good idea that's spreading across the land. What do you major in at a place like that?"

"English."

And he said, "Oh, bravo for them."

Since this four-year education I got was the only education I was ever going to get, I had some pride in it. Julian treats it like a skunk pelt hanging from my belt. With everything he asked me, I would feel like I was failing some test. Ah, yes, how they do the Southerners; or, how they undo the Southerners. I became a lifelong project of self-improvement for Julian.

When Barbara got up there, Julian gave a party. God, he lived in a place. Turtle Bay. It's these beautiful brownstones on Forty-Eighth, near the East River, down in that United Nations area. Let's see. Who lived next door? Somebody lived next door. *The Best and the Brightest,* David Halberstam. You have your own garden, then you walk into a common garden, and it goes for a whole block.

Julian walked me down there and said, "The woman to the right is Katharine Hepburn. She is watering her yard." He comes to the next yard, and he said, "I know this is going to mean a lot to you. This is where Maxwell Perkins lived. Every writer you told me you love was in that garden at one time or another."

So Julian did a great job. It was glorious, it was beautiful, and it satisfied a million fantasies I had. Because you know that's what keeps us going is fantasies.

But that first time up in New York, I noticed I'd walk into a room filled with writers, and everybody's looking over my head. They're looking all around. It drives me crazy when I see these writers who don't look at people, don't talk to people. I'm Southern; I can't imagine anything ruder than that. And I like being nice to people. I like how people react when I'm nice to them. It drives me crazy when I see these writers who don't look at people, who don't talk to people, because I'm a friendly man. I think this has to do with my being a military brat, not knowing anybody, being a friendless boy. But whatever that is, that seems like a good thing to me. I just take people as they come to me. They're nice to me, I'm going to be nice to them.

In New York, it seemed very competitive. This is when I learned to loathe other writers and hate hanging around them. They're the weirdest people. They are geeky; they're unpopular in high school; they didn't go to the prom. All the things that make their lives lonely and miserable make them want to be writers. So I have not liked the breed much. It did not seem part of any scene I wanted to be around very much. And ergo, I wasn't. My nightmare has always been the McDowell Colony, where the point is going to dinner at night with the other writers, which seems to me like the worse thing a human being can do. I saw danger at that evening meal. You walk in, and the scorpion eyes of writers fix you in the malice of their glittering green eyes. If they don't recognize you, they hate you; if they do recognize you, they hate you even more. I'm sure you make friends and associations for life that help you later on if you hang around other writers, but it did not appeal to me. I don't want to be good at that, and I don't want to be one of them. It's not something that holds any appeal or value to me at all. All I want is to be unnoticed, walk through a room, survive the evil looks, the looks of jealousy and horror, and "How the fuck did it happen to that fat boy? Why didn't it happen to me? I am better; I'm more worthy; I'm more deserving."

Now, I know kids who go to New York and never look back. Some of the gay kids who go up there and have found themselves, found their dream, they would never look back except with utter contempt. But New York did not have that kind of liberating force on me, and I'm sure it's because of my own provincialism, the unconfident Southerner in me, and my own inability to stare straight in the eye of the big time.

Then when Julian came to Beaufort, I took him around, and he says, "My God, this wasteland created you." And he says, "This is bleak beyond belief!" Of course, Beaufort is simply out-of-this-world gorgeous. But later my editor Nan Talese said the same thing: "What on earth do you do here?" Anybody who comes to visit from New York is always asking, "What do you do down here? How do you entertain yourself?"

But Julian warmed to me, especially when I said, "Julian, I'm sorry I didn't make you much money on this, but I hope to make you some someday."

I was with him until he retired. But to tell you the truth, I don't know if Julian ever read a word I wrote. He would call me up. *The Great Santini,* he called me up. *The Lords of Discipline,* he called me up. *Prince of Tides,* he called me up. *Beach Music,* he called me up. All the books. And he would say, "Pat? On the second page, the first tear came, and I knew Conroy was at it again. I know when I cry that you've got me again and will have the reader again. This is just marvelous stuff."

I said, "Did you read the last page, Julian?"

And Julian would go, "Very witty, very witty."

But I don't know. I do not know if he even read my books. But he turned out to be a great force in my life, a great influence in my life.

The business was brutal later on; I mean it was just brutal. When Julian was getting to be an old man, people told me I needed to change agency, I needed to go to this asshole. But Julian was, for me, what I needed. I needed a gentleman. Julian was part of that gentleman's art of publishing that I guess isn't there anymore. I remember when he took the phone call from me, and I wouldn't say he was gracious about it, but he took the phone call and he changed my life. And I am a loyalist.

But when Julian got old, his reputation faded, and he got humiliated, which I didn't know, over and over again. Here's one way. I was represented in the movies by an agent at CAA, and like all CAA agents, he was the hot thing. There was this attitude, you know, we're the best. You're lucky to be here. I mean, give me a break.

So when I was completing *Beach Music,* this agent was looking forward to taking that around Hollywood. I called Julian Bach up and said, "Could you call him and ask him some questions for me about logistics?"

Julian says, "Well, Pat, I would be happy to do that for you. I would be happy to do anything for you. You know that, I hope, by now. But he hasn't returned my phone calls in years."

I said, "Julian, why didn't you tell me?"

He said, "Well, there was no reason. He's done a good job professionally for you and there's no reason to interfere with that. But I'm embarrassed and deeply humiliated to tell you, he will not call me back, Pat."

I said, "I'm going to give you a way for him to call you back, Julian. Call him up and fire him for me."

Several days later, I get a phone call. Julian gets on the phone, says, "Pat, this is Julian Bach, your agent."

"I knew that, Julian."

He said, "I wanted to share this moment with you. Your film agent has been waiting in my office for over an hour to see me. I need your advice on something, Pat, if you do not mind giving it to me."

I said, "No, Julian, I'll be happy to give you advice."

He said, "How much longer should I make him wait?"

I said, "I think another hour would be appropriate."

"You know, I was thinking along those same lines, Pat. You and I have started thinking alike over the years. I don't know if you have noticed this."

I said, "I pray that's not true, Julian. But who knows? It may have snuck up on me without me knowing it."

On the night of his retirement there were eight people at his party, and I spoke. Walking out to get a cab, Julian said, "Now, Pat, you know that you will be delivering my eulogy."

I said, "And I'll give you a good one, Julian. You don't have to worry about that."

"I know you will."

And I said, "Julian, thanks for taking that telephone call all those years ago."

Julian says, bowing, "Pat, I've never told you this: Thanks for making it."

Actually, he told me that all the time. He'd say, "Pat, you remember when you told me you wanted to make me some money? You have made far more money for me than any client I've ever had."

But who would have thought that unexpected encounter with Daufuskie Island would assure me of being published the rest of my life? I had no idea then. I had just been fired; I didn't have any work; I didn't have any money; I had a house; I had three kids; I had three black kids living in it. Dad was in Vietnam. I had almost gotten drafted. It was not a good time for me basically, so then this just seemed like the universe evening things out a little bit with this book I didn't even know what to title until finally I came up with *The Water Is Wide*. Which gave me my best lesson in how titling is one of the most important things to do. People have screwed that title up like you wouldn't believe, and that's exactly what you don't want. I have the funniest letters from people who say they loved *How Wide Was My River*, or *The Water Is Wine*, and my own favorite: *The Water Is Wet*. But I don't like that book and can't look at it now. It feels so young and immature to me, and I'm thinking, I'm twenty-four years old when I'm writing that book: fuck you, kid. Who cares what a twenty-four-year-old thinks? And, you know, fuck you, you liberal ass know-it-all bastard; no wonder they fired you.

~

James Dickey was the first big writer I knew, the first one I sought out. I learned about him from Tim Belk, who was teaching English at the University of South Carolina in Beaufort. Ann Head, who taught the writing class my senior year at the high school, had us over for dinner together. She was divine to me. Very cold, impervious, but great. She wrote me at the Citadel, loving, wonderful letters. I'd send her short stories and poems. She'd critique them and send them back. She introduced me to Tim Belk, and he became friends with Bernie, George Garbade, Mike Jones, and me. He was our first gay guy. He came from the piss-poor Belks, but he had style. He always had style.

Tim Belk was a great influence in my life and Bernie's. He taught us music, he taught us film, and he taught us about literature we'd never heard of. He first gave me Walker Percy; he first gave me Flannery O'Connor; he first gave me Dylan Thomas. He went to a poetry reading of James Dickey and said, "This guy's got it."

So in 1971, I commuted up to Columbia to take two courses with James Dickey at the University of South Carolina. I loved his poetry more than anyone else's, and I still wanted to see if I could be a poet. Dickey told me I was not a poet in that class. He broke the news by saying: "You're not a poet." He said, "Mr. Conroy, I do not think poetry is your realm." His sister-in-law, Patsy Dickey, always told me later that Jim was jealous and did not want me writing poetry because that's where he was in the world and he liked to discourage everybody else. But I couldn't imagine Dickey being jealous, not the way he wrote. And poetry has not lost one single thing by me heading in other directions.

At that time I thought that poetry was the greatest thing a writer could do, and I still do. Poetry is the highest form language can take. I always start off my day with poetry. Before I get going every morning, I try to read an hour of poetry. I like starting out the day with poetry; I like what it does, how it constructs your language. Poetry seems to say the most in the fewest possible words. With poetry, you take the stock and boil it down to where it's a glaze. It is the elixir of language.

But in that class I realized I wasn't a very good poet. I remember we were supposed to do something just based on observation, and I did something so stupid I can't even remember what it was now. It was mediocre; I remember that. But I'll never forget what this other kid said in his first sentence about watching a great blue heron. He wrote, "His task is stillness," and I thought, now that is a great fucking line. That is powerfully observed. That's what Dickey means by observation.

It was terrifying when I got there, because Dickey was one of these awe-inspiring guys, and I met him right when his career was at its apex. He was a giant; he carried himself like a colossus. He acted like I thought a great writer was going to act, and was fully in the game from the first day I met him to the last. There is no oxygen or even hydrogen left in the room once they pass out of it or come into it. And they sweep into it. They always sweep in, and there's always an entourage following wherever they go. And he never broke character.

I was completely intimidated; I would not say a word in his class. I did not have this enormous insight I have as a 120-year-old man today. I had just written *The Water Is Wide,* and was glad it was going to be published. I didn't know what that meant or was going to mean in my life, so I was still overwhelmed by Dickey's talent. I couldn't say a word in his class, and I don't think he remembered my being in there.

What he did not know was that *The Water Is Wide* had been accepted by Houghton Mifflin, which also published his novel *Deliverance.* I never told him, and he did not find out until my book was published in 1972. Then, of course, Jim being Jim, he claimed that he and I sat down beside each other. I came to him and said, "Jim, I'm having a tough time writing this book," and he said, "Come here, Pat. Let's sit down and whip that motherfucker together."

But I loved him as a teacher. He was a great, great teacher. Every day I used to drive back home excited about his class, excited about the poems he read. He could make you fall in love with a poem and see the absolute essentialness of poetry. And he was a flamboyant reader. I learned a lot about just the simple passion for the beauty of language. He had that like few people I've ever known. He had this generous gift of reading other poets as though he loved them, and he gave their poems his best shot. And Jim, like almost all writers, had trouble with the success of other writers. He was one of those guys who could not get enough of fame, believed there was not enough to go around, not enough of a world to absorb any other writers besides himself. But reading them aloud, he gave them his full measure. He had great respect for that poem when he was reading it aloud, like he was entering into holy territory because of the poem.

He taught me this level of perfectionism that you should always strive for. He told us: "I judge your poetry against the greatest poetry ever written in the language." He gave me one line I've never forgotten. He said, "The two most dangerous words in the English language are 'like' and 'as.' If you do not have something interesting to say after you write down those two words, cross them out, because you've entered into the country of cliché. Make sure you have something to say that is new or fresh or in a different way; otherwise, leave them alone."

And he taught us to make language precise. To have it be read like you want it to read and have it spoken like you want it to be spoken is the hardest thing, and he made the effort sound like a spiritual quest. He was remarkable for making me want to write better than I ever could write, and for making me want to read everything. He seemed to be one of those men who had read everything, especially in the field of poetry. There was nothing he had not considered, nothing he was not familiar with. That complete devouring of his world gave him an authenticity I wanted to have.

James Dickey also taught me everything I did not want to do as a human being. This writer whose work I simply adored was just a cocksucker. *Deliverance* had come out in 1970, and they were making the movie when I was in his class. I think I was an eyewitness to one of the first victims of our celebrity culture. I witnessed the change that was taking place in him as the movie was being made. The bragging. When he came into class he would spend the first part of the hour talking about what he'd said to Jon Voight and Burt Reynolds. You know: "I was up with Jon and Burt this weekend, up in the mountains, teaching them how to get out of the rapids, and I can teach better than the experts they have up there. I showed them some things, showed Burt some things about the bow and arrow that he couldn't learn in twenty years if he didn't have someone like me to show him." I was thinking, okay, Jim, none of us need to know this. But it just got worse and worse. His reports horrified me, of him grabbing Burt Reynolds by the collar and saying, "Are you man enough to play my character? Are you man enough, Burt?" Of course, Dickey's drunk, Burt's furious, and they hate him.

He gave me much to fear about fame during the year he was becoming famous. Fame did something to him, and it was disturbing to me because I just adored his poetry and did not like seeing this happen to him. I don't think it did his work any good, and I know it didn't do his life any good. I think fame is the one thing in life you can be absolutely sure will fuck you up, that if you get some, it becomes something you want more of. You need more important people; you're put in a limelight that when you're not there you miss it. You get attention you would normally not get. Everything about it is dangerous. Everything about it seems soul damaging to me. There's nothing I have found that's particularly good about it. "Oh hi, yes, I'm famous because you're not. Oh yes, my, my, my, of course you're making a fuss over me, because I am a great big man and you are a small, small insignificant person." You start being dissatisfied with hanging around normal people. You must hang around somebody more and more famous. The main thing fame seems to do is inflate your ego to Hindenburg-like proportions.

Dickey was probably one of the great monster narcissists of his time. He reminded me so much of my dad I cannot even tell you. My father could take a jet up and annihilate New York City, and that's an amazing power to have. He did not wear it well. So I was raised by the most egotistical man, a fighter pilot who had that fighter pilot's ego, which is not just a fighter pilot's ego. You see it in neurosurgeons; you see it in lawyers. You meet it in men all the time. The Citadel was full of it, I mean full of it. There is a certain look they have to them; there is a strut to their walk, a jut of the jaw, a pulling back of the shoulders, and a way of entering the room.

I don't think fame is good for anybody; it changes everybody. There are so many ways fame goes askew and doesn't do you any good at all. Dickey already had enough cockiness in him because he was a very, very good high school athlete. But the poet had never been treated the way Jim was treated after that movie came out. And no one ever played into it the way Jim did.

Later, when Jon Voight was cast as Conrack in the movie of my book, he would not talk to me on the set. I did not know why until Dickey's son came out with the book *Summer of Deliverance.* His father enraged all the Hollywood actors with his Southern writer routine, and John Voight was expecting the same thing from me. Voight hated Dickey; he'd had all he was ever going to have of Southern writers and wanted nothing to do with me.

One day when I was signing *The Great Santini* in Columbia, new in my career, I think my brothers were the only people there in the store. This attractive woman comes in and said, "I'm James Dickey's wife, Pat. I knew you were in his class. I'd like you to sign a book for me." I was so grateful to her. Conroy is always pathetically grateful and ass kissing when people treat him like a human being. She said, "Pat, my husband is so proud of you, but you'll never know it. He'll never tell you, and he'll always be jealous of you no matter what. He can't help that. He would never ever come to your signing, but he's well aware you come to his."

As I watched Dickey's fame growing exponentially, it taught me to be careful of the perils of fame, to not let it in as much as he seemed to be letting it affect him. I watched the other students following Dickey around like a small colony of little turtles trailing the loggerhead around campus. The girls sort of lined up according to their status. There was the girl he was having an affair with, then the one he had just broken up with. It didn't seem to do him much good. The sycophantic student or the worshipful student who adores you brings nothing good to you. In Jim's case, it solidified all his worst tendencies. He could not open his mouth without people swooning with the utter pleasure of wisdom flowing over them like honey.

Then I heard the story of Dickey coming in the year before and announcing: "As of last night, I have slept with every female student in this class." I'm sure Jim must have been drunk when he did it, but he did it. This struck me as ego in a runaway train. I thought: fame is bad for the soul. It is destructive to human nature. I did not see why he had to wear a cowboy hat and carry a guitar around. I did not like that he needed acolytes and ducklings and goslings following him around. The greatest threat I saw to writing was this gathering of camp followers.

I also found it a danger when famous poets would come on campus and Dickey was with them. It seemed like the warring of screaming egos flashing thunderbolts across the sky at each other. Also, fame seems to take up more time than it gives inspiration, or gives time for writing. But Dickey was not seeing the signs of what was happening to him. He was not treating fame as something to beware of, something that could harm his art.

I found the whole thing not for me. I did not wish to be like that. I promised myself at the time I would not have this if I ever became successful. I would not be walking along on a college campus with a trail of duckling undergraduates behind me. Also, I noticed that a lot of older professors were married to women my age, and I was in my twenties. I decided that I did not want to be sixty-five chasing rug rats if I could possibly avoid it in my life.

Dickey got caught up not only in the maze and jungle of fame with *Deliverance;* he got caught up with becoming poet of the nation. Also, alcohol made him do things that I'm sure he must have regretted horribly later. When his wife died he said on television "I saw her lifeless, soulless body lying in state and I thought no more about her when I stared upon her body than I do when I stare at a dead dog killed on the Carolina highway." I said, Okay, Pat, you need to learn from this. Never compare your dead wife to a dead dog on a Carolina highway.

When *Deliverance* came out, I went to see it with one of my brothers in Columbia. I didn't know Dickey was in the movie theater until he appeared on-screen as the sheriff. Suddenly a man gets up in the back of the theater and applauds the whole time the sheriff is on-screen. I look back; Dickey is giving himself a standing ovation the whole time he's on-screen. I said, "Okay, Pat. Try not to do that."

I thought, well, greatness has its requirements. And great individuals sometimes are not understandable to the normal human mind. Genius comes in strange packages. Genius shows itself in some utterly undivine ways. I think you can be a cocksucker and write like a prince or a princess. But, I know writers who are not famous who are also jerks. There's something about the gift that is given equally to bastards, probably more to bastards. With great writers, often it's best just to enjoy their work and not meet them.

When his complete works came out, I was slowly reading it all, and for the first time I could see flaws in Dickey's poetry which I could not see before. They were almost all in poems that came out after *Deliverance*. His *Poems '57 to '67* is as great as anything I know in the language, and it still holds up. I reread that almost every year. The power, the perfection gets to me every time; the movement of it, the magnetism still excites. Those poems rank with anything in literature, including T. S. Eliot. But I started seeing the weakening in his later poetry, and whether it was age, drinking, or too much going on, I don't know. His mind got too scattered. I worried that he fell in love with the lights too much, which is a deadly disease in this country. I think his poetry got weaker in his later years because he was trying more and more desperately to be accepted by the masses. He tried to become more modern in a way that did not fit his talent. And it is death when a writer tries to be hip.

Every once in a while I would see James Dickey over the years. People told me he used to talk about me a lot, but to me personally he never said much. One night at my friends Alex and Zoe Sanders's house, they had me to dinner and invited Dickey and his very young wife. Dickey got me in a corner of the hallway and grabbed me by the lapels. He's a huge man, much taller than I am. He grabs me, says, "Conroy, you and I are going to write a screenplay together." He had both my shoulders.

"We're going to write it together. James Dickey and Pat Conroy. We're going to tear Hollywood apart. They won't believe what we can do." I was going "Yeah-yeah-yeah," but you know, he'd been drinking. He did not remember the next day. I did not remind him of it. After I was in his class, one of my decisions was to stay away from Jim. Hanging around him did not seem like a good idea to me.

But I love his writing more than that of anybody else I've ever met. Jim did not have a good heart; Jim was a great artist. There is integrity with those people when they sit down to write. I am grateful to him beyond belief, and I still have the letter where he accepts me into his class.

~

I never wanted to move from Beaufort. I could have taught there the rest of my life, but that did not work out, and I had put my family in a perilous spot in Beaufort, and I knew it. Now I've gotten to be an avuncular sort of elder, but I was a polarizing figure in the state for a long, long time.

I grew up with this indefensible South: slavery, Jim Crow. So I became a liberal out of self-defense, and when *The Water Is Wide* came out, there was an explosion in Beaufort. Southerners reacted like you were afraid Southerners would. I wasn't invited to have a book signing in the stores, so Mom and Barbara arranged for the store owners to have one at our house on Hancock Street. But we had the Daufuskie kids there, and the owners of the book shop would not come into the house that had an integrated party going on. I was going to throw them off the porch, but then my mother, the great diplomat, comes out, and they agreed to sell books at the door because they would not go inside the house where there were blacks being entertained.

Then, when they wanted to film the movie in Beaufort, the town wouldn't let them do it. That would have been the first movie ever made in Beaufort, but Beaufort didn't realize its mistake until the movie got made on St. Simon's Island. I started to realize that Beaufort was not a place where my family was going to be comfortable. It made Barbara really uncomfortable, and she wanted to get out of there. We were both military brats, so who knows if the reaction to the book didn't set off something in both of us—it's time to move on; it's time to go somewhere.

Also, I think Barbara was having her first stirrings of wanting to go back to school, and she really wanted to get out of Beaufort, get to a big city. Mom and Dad were retiring to Beaufort, and Mom was putting pressure on me to sell our house to her and Dad. We lived in a remarkable house on the Point; we paid $26,000 for what still looks to me like a mansion. I could not get over it. I owned a house before my parents did. And I'm so proud of that house, I can barely say. Nobody encouraged us to move more than my mother did. No one encouraged Barbara going to law school more than she did. I think Mom was already planning to get out of that marriage and saw the nice life she could have in Beaufort, so she plotted to get that house away from Barbara and me. I did not know she was planning to dropkick my father through the front door and send him on his way out. The mistake Mom made, and it was a fatal one, was she didn't realize she would be cut out of almost all Dad's retirement. They corrected that later on, but it was too late for Mom. So Dad got this terrific retirement; Mom got nothing. That was to come.

We chose Atlanta because that is the city I knew best of all growing up, and it was where Stanny lived. Moving is one of the skill sets I have brought to my life; I know how to get out of a place. Then the military brat optimism kicks in: let me make the best out of this I can. I have found that to be the greatest gift of the military brat's childhood: let me do the best I can with what has been handed to me. And often you didn't like what was handed to you, didn't like it at all.

But Atlanta, I ended up loving Atlanta, loving my time there. Another writer would have moved to New York or started teaching writing. I probably should have done something like that, but I did not know how.

Atlanta

1973–1981

I had no experience in writing down the graffiti left along the
margins of a boy's ruined heart. . . . As I wrote, the child of the
military in me began to fall apart. I came apart at the seams. For
one thing a military brat is not allowed to do is commit an act of
treason. I learned the hard way that truth is a capital offense . . .

PAT CONROY, *My Reading Life*

Pat keeps talking about my saving his life. I really didn't save his
life. He saved his own life. What I helped him do is to see that
his life is worth living.

MARION O'NEILL, Ph.D., ABPP, clinical psychologist

We moved to Atlanta in 1973. *Conrack* came out in 1974, in a small theater on Peachtree up toward Buckhead. It was a fundraiser for Paideia,
the school my kids went to. The kids were all young then; they didn't
know what the hell was going on except there was somebody running
around with my name up there on the screen who looked a lot better
than I did. It absolutely creeped me out to hear the name Conroy being
called out over and over again. I cannot see that movie now because he
goes around with my name. I cannot even look at that movie.

I did have some wonderful moments with it. When it came out later
at the Fox Theater, I got to take my children there to see *Conrack*,
which I loved doing because I had been to the Fox to see *Gone with the
Wind* with my mother. I've always loved the Fox since I was a kid, and
that seemed like a great moment.

My mother *l-o-o-o-ved* it. *L-l-l-o-o-ved* it. She loved the public part of
it and the status it gave her. There's a picture of Mom talking on the

same stage as then governor Jimmy Carter. She went down to where they made the film in Brunswick for its opening, and Carter was down there. He and Mom were sort of the masters of ceremony, and my mother, never looking more beautiful, is there with the future president, and she looks like she was born to be on that stage. It's a great picture. I love that picture. She adored it. She loved every bit of it.

It was somewhere during this time that she told a newspaper reporter that she always knew Pat was going to be a writer, and she said "When the nurse brought his naked body to me the first time and laid him into my arms, I knew a writer had been born."

I said, "No kiddin' Mom, you knew that then?"

"Oh yes, son, mothers have this instinct."

So I said, "And in that motherly instinct, why didn't you choose to name me Rutledge Ravenel Conroy? Why do I sound like an Irish bus driver from the fucking Bronx?"

And she said, "He's never understood the elegance of simplicity."

That I'd made my mother proud meant a lot to me. It gave me some enjoyment. We can all deny it, but it will make you proud if your parents are proud. I don't remember Dad much in that period because he was still going through the divorce and in denial about the divorce. Dad did not go to the opening because Mom was going to be there, although by then he'd moved to Atlanta.

Then I went around the country traveling with the movie in the role of the good Southern white person. I knew nothing about teaching. I knew nothing about anything. They were pointing me to places, and I would go and talk after the movie was shown. Usually it would be teachers I talked to. This moment I always loved is Jon Voight's head is the last thing you see on the movie screen. They're playing Beethoven's Fifth Symphony in the scene between Jon and his students; he's leaving by boat, and he wants to cry, but he's a Hollywood star; he can't cry. So his beautiful blue eyes are trembling and shimmering as he says farewell. There's been progress made, but the horrible authorities have won again. So anyway, he's going off. Okay, the screen would flicker off and the fifty-foot beautiful head of Jon Voight would disappear, and then suddenly, the lights would come on; there's reality; there's day; there are your lights. At that exact moment after Jon Voight's beautiful head disappears from the screen, the lights come on, and Conroy rises like a toad out of the audience. And to my mind there's a gasp of horror. An actual physical repulsion takes place in the crowd that I can feel, or at least vividly imagine. I even thought that somehow Jon Voight had stolen my soul. Later, when I was writing *The Great Santini,* I put a small character in there named Johnny Voight, and what I wanted to do, if they ever made a movie of *The Great Santini,* was have a bit part where I played Johnny Voight so I could retrieve myself.

I was also on *Sesame Street* as the godlike teacher of the century, beloved by children. Of course, these kids had no idea who the fuck I was. I just walked out there, and then I learned that, oh yes, there's a baby tiger, the hell with you. The kids don't care about anything else, nor did I care about the kids, so it was a line about a tiger.

I'm about twenty-five, twenty-six when all this is going on, and it was much too early to have success. Okay, I'm twenty-five years old; I'm in *Life* magazine. A movie has been made about me. I was not expecting that. And I think nothing screws you up like early success. Sudden fame like that does nothing but fuck you up. I had learned early to keep my head down with Dad, and he did not allow me to develop an ego. I found it best to keep low, hide in the grass, know where the shrubbery is, get out fast.

But it was overwhelming having all that happen when I was that young, especially because it was something I simply had never considered would ever happen to me. And all of this happened after I was brought low to the earth and a herd of elephants had trampled me in my front yard and my body had been used to fertilize the gardenias. I couldn't get a job anywhere in the world teaching. My teaching career was over. I tried to get other jobs; I couldn't get them. I just didn't know what I was going to do. I did not know how it would ever turn around. Things were not looking good for the old kid. My life had been so bleak, so dark; it was so impossible to look forward to anything, and then suddenly my fate seems to change on a dime. I had a chance at an actual real life. I did not seem as doomed as I was right after I got fired.

I don't think I was prepared for it. It seemed like it all happened at once, and I did not have time to process any of it. I was fired; I was desperate; I'm looking for jobs; I write *The Water Is Wide* in a three-month white heat. A man comes by, tells me about his agent; I call his agent; I have that ridiculous scene with Julian and his secretary, then he sells the book to Houghton Mifflin. Holy God, it all seemed to take place at once, exploding around me. It all just seemed to happen rapidly without me being in control of any of it. I think too much happened to me in too little time, and I simply did not bear up under it all very well. It seems like I processed nothing. I let events swallow me up, eat me alive, tear me apart as I broke down.

First of all, I was still in a state of shock about being published. That shocked me; that process shocked me; how inept I was going through that process shocked me; my going to New York to visit Julian was full of surprises. But in America, you know, a book is nothing. A movie is something. And that does a number on everyone around you. Every single person around you becomes aware of that, from your children, to your spouse, to your mother and father, to your brothers, to your friends in high school, to everyone. It changes every single one of your relationships instantly. I went up to some kind of event at the kids' school, and one of my daughters said to her friend, "I'd like you to meet Pat Conroy."

I said, "Daddy. You'd like her to meet your daddy."

"Yes, this is my daddy, Pat Conroy."

And I thought my God, it's gotten to the kids. It must have been overwhelming for Barbara. But as far as I could tell, it just made her more ambitious, made her want to go to law school, and got her in to law school. That seemed like a good response to it. She found something solid, and it led her into a very, very good career.

But this is where I think early fame hurt me, interfered with my life and fucked it up: I had no idea that my being a writer would attract women to me. It just never occurred to me. And since I'd never dated, I think this ended up breaking my marriage up and screwing me up. I was a good Catholic boy, a nice Catholic boy; so this screwed me up. I tried not to make it hunting season, but I was simply responding to the testosterone God put in my body. But if not for fame, I would not have had women coming at me. It wasn't because of my ebullience, my life force and charm. It wasn't as if my personality had improved that much or I'd had a dick implant. It was simply because fame is an aphrodisiac that I had not really understood until it happened to me. So if not for fame and my lack of dating in high school and college, I would not have had affairs.

It was always shocking, women coming on to me. It just shocked me. I should have been protecting the marriage with Barbara and these kids, and I have always regretted that I did not. Basically, I was just your common, dreary asshole new at fame who was too big for my britches, and my marriage with Barbara did not have a chance because I did not handle the first incoming of fame very well. I became an asshole because this came to me way too early. I think I could have handled it better if I'd been older. But I was a kid. I went to Daufuskie when I was twenty-three; I was fired when I was twenty-four; I started writing *The Water Is Wide,* which came out in 1972. My generation had not quite gotten started, and I have Jon Voight playing me in a movie. I was early, and that will kill you. This is where I think fame fucked me up, and I saw that it fucked me up, and I tried to fight against it after this. I see fame doing no one any good at all, so I try to draw back and not let those forces in. There's some shield that I put up where that cannot penetrate, and I choose for it not to penetrate.

~

The Water Is Wide sold five or six thousand copies in hardback. But after the movie, I think the paperback rights went for $125,000, shocking Houghton Mifflin. Julian Bach was shocked, but happy. Everybody was shocked but happy. During this period, the mid-'70s, selling six thousand hardbacks was considered successful. Nowadays if I only sold six thousand hardbacks, the publisher would drop me. They would not wait for my career to build. They don't wait anymore.

But Houghton Mifflin thought my book was a success and wanted me to write another one about education, which I did not have in me. And I was not interested in writing nonfiction at all. I had the Thomas Wolfe, Faulkner, Fitzgerald dream. I don't think it made them very happy that I wanted to write a novel. They wanted me to write teacher books for the rest of my life; they thought it was a natural direction to keep going. But I didn't even know anything about teaching when I wrote *The Water Is Wide.* So I said, I'm not teaching anywhere, I'm not going to teach anywhere, and I'd like to write the novel. And of course when I told them what the novel was about, they had never heard of a novel about a military brat. That did not excite them. Then when I was going to write about the Citadel, none of them had ever heard of it, I can tell you that. Is that a college? Yes, it is. Is it accredited? Yes, it is. Four-year? Yes, it is. Does it have active alumni? Yes, it does. Why haven't I ever heard of it? Because it's completely unknown in the real world. There's always a problem with every book I write. A shrimper—who gives a flying fuck about a shrimper? Luckily, the paperback sale was always high enough to encourage them to get me to write something else. I think *The Great Santini* sold seventy-five hundred in hardback, and *The Lords of Discipline* I believe sold ten thousand. So the paperback saved my early career.

Now with *The Boo,* I was writing about the good dad. *The Water Is Wide,* that was the good teacher; I wanted to be the good teacher. I wanted to be Gene Norris. Afterward, I was starting to face the reality of what Dad was, what our lives were, and what a lie we grew up under. That's what drove me crazy, the lie that we all fell prey to, that we all paid lip service to: the happy family, the happy Conroy family, Dad calling us the magnificent seven.

I remember having a one-two moment, a snap-to moment in Oliver Bowman's wonderful psychology classes at the Citadel. He was a magnificent teacher; this guy was unbelievable to me; dynamite. In his class I was getting jolted all over the place. He hit us with some statistics: "When you have seen your mother being beaten by your father as a child, you have 64 percent more of a chance of becoming a wife beater when you are a husband." Okay, I snapped to attention at that. "If you were beaten as a child, it goes up to 70 percent that you will probably beat your own children when they are born." He goes all over this study that was done. I'm sitting there absolutely shocked. I've never told a soul what Dad did. Oliver Bowman made it sound like this is just a fact of life, and I have a feeling a lot of Citadel guys had fathers like mine.

And I'm sitting there thinking okay, there is some poor girl running around out there that I have not even met who I will be beating someday because I had an asshole as a father. And not only that, if we're lucky enough to have children, good God, what luck for them, I'll be beating the shit out of them like Dad beat me, and it horrified me. It just absolutely struck me with horror that this is even a possibility. I'd never even considered such a thing. It repelled me more than I can tell you, and I'm sitting there feeling complete and utter sorrow for some girl who has not even fallen in love with me or I with her yet, because she's got a reason to fear that I'm going to be pounding her face in. She doesn't know, wherever she's sitting right now, and I don't know it, but now I do. That was one of the moments of clearest distinction for me, where I would start looking at things, watching things, making decisions about things, and changing whatever it was inside of me that I *did* know about that would cause me to beat a wife or a child.

What it led into is Oliver Bowman wanted us to write something personal about our family that we'd never told before. I think he figured that a lot of his students had something like this they were hiding. And he was gay, so he knew about secrets. I got plaudits for writing the bravest article, as naturally I would at the Citadel. I wrote about Stanny's alcoholism. The other guys wrote about how they once stole three records from Sammy's Music Shop on Main Street. One had gone joyriding in his uncle's car and crashed it. It was all that kind of stuff. So when I wrote about Stanny getting drunk and falling downstairs, it looked like the real thing to him, but I knew it was fake. Even then I knew I was avoiding the big subject. I don't think I had articulated it that well to myself at that time, but it was a very important part in my transition of what I had to write about. He got me thinking.

Later I was burning with all that, seething with all that. Then, the summer before I got fired from Daufuskie, Dad was going to Vietnam. The family came back from the movies, and I went up to bed with Barbara in our house on Hancock Street. I hear Dad hitting Mom downstairs, and I go down to stop it. That night, I beat Dad up.

Barbara's yelling from upstairs, "What's going on in my house?"

"Nothing, dear."

"Oh, there's something horrible going on in my house. I demand to know at once."

"It's nothing, dear."

When Barbara comes down, I realize I have never told her a thing. I'd never told anybody anything about the abuse I'd gone through as a kid, or my family had gone through. That was the hidden self that I had kept really hidden because we feared if Dad were ever arrested for child abuse or wife beating, that would be the end of his career. Mom used to say, "None of you will go to college." Not that the Ivy League was waiting for the seven Conroys out there, but we would not even have gone to chiropractor or beauty school. I grew up in one of those households where the problems were not acknowledged or talked about, so there was always a festering, there was always a geyser exploding from inside. It was going to come out somehow.

After I settled people down that night, I then go out looking for Dad, who's not in the house, and find him passed out on the Green. Get him up—he's drunk—and walk him back. Out of nowhere, I say, "I love you, Dad." He looks at me and starts running. It tickled me so much that I'd finally found the words he could not take. I'd finally found the phrase that could drive the Great Santini away. So I started saying, "I love you, Dad. I love you." He would turn each time I said it, stumbling, and turn, stumbling. I suddenly realized I had discovered a power that I had no idea I had. I had words that were more powerful than anything he had, more powerful than his fists, more powerful than his beating up of his wife and kids. I had discovered something that was beyond anything he could put up against us, anything he could throw against us. Any sort of armament he could fire at us; I had found some shield. That shield had developed in this secret place in me, and I didn't know it was there. It took me years to figure out where that came from. And I think my writing life has been dependent on where that came from, how it was in there, how it developed in there, how it survived in there.

Then when I went into the bedroom that night, I told Barbara everything. That and beating up Dad broke something. That night broke something where, okay, the truth is out now. It's fair game now. I think I began writing *The Great Santini* that night, not literally, but it certainly began things in my head.

Later, after *The Water Is Wide,* I was invited to the Marine Corps Officers' Wives Club in Beaufort to talk about the book. The officers' wives were very proud to have an officer's wife's son address them. It was a nice day, and I get up there to the Officers' Club, where I've been innumerable times, I'm surrounded by these pretty women who reminded me of my mother, my mother is there, and something got set off. Something was actually set off in my then feverish, now addled, now calcium-deposited brain.

Nowadays I am famous for never talking about the book I'm trying to sell. I have driven the book reps nuts in every company that's ever published me. I just go and tell stories and have fun, and I want the audience to have fun. If there's a funny story about the book, I'll tell them, but otherwise it's boring to talk about your own book. It is boring to me. I've listened to writers, and God, I've listened to more writers trying to sell their own books than anything in the world, and it bores me; it's a boring form of human speech. And I've always told the reps, "Look, here's my theory. If they like me and enjoy me, they'll buy the book. If I bore them to death about the book, they're not going to buy a book. That's my theory, so let's see how it goes."

That day, I was supposed to talk about *The Water Is Wide*. That's what they asked me to do. I got triggered, I wasn't expecting it, and I ruined the day by talking about Dad knocking me around, knocking Mom around. I just wanted to tell them for your kids, that shouldn't be, that should not have any place in a Marine Corps life or heart. That should not happen to you; it should not happen to your kids; your husband should not do that. Well, some women in there went crazy with fury. I can always piss off half the known world whenever I want to. But Mom and I noticed that other people loved my ass for it. It turned out for me to be the absolute beginnings of *The Great Santini* because of the emotion it raised.

~

At this time in Atlanta I started breaking down from the pressure of writing *Santini* because I knew as I was writing it that I was entering territory I was going to pay a great price for. I was diving too deep for where I was at the time, and it all just simply came apart for me. As I look back on it, I put immense pressure on the young boy I was. I just put huge pressure on that kid, and obviously I was not equipped to handle it. It was the pressure of taking on *The Boo* as a project, writing *The Boo,* which was banned immediately at the Citadel, marrying a

woman with two children, taking in three kids from Daufuskie who
didn't have a place to live on the mainland, having a child of my own,
and then getting fired from Daufuskie Island, which I did not know but
would take me out of teaching forever and what I thought was going to
be my profession. A movie comes out about me in 1974, and all this is
in my twenties. Thinking that *The Water Is Wide* is just beginner's luck,
and then starting to write *The Great Santini,* starting to tell the stories
I knew I was not supposed to tell, the stories I was not quite ready to
tell. When I was writing that novel I was starting to face the reality of
what Dad was and what our lives were, what unhappiness and what a
lie we grew up under. I was not psychologically prepared to handle it.
That was too much on me, and it brought me to my knees. It was just
too much for me. I was taking in too much. Barbara had started law
school, and that put on added pressure. My life seemed overfull, brim-
ming, spilling out, too much of everything. I was not equipped to handle any of it. And that pattern continues through my whole life.

Writing the book was having a horrible effect on me, and I was crack-
ing up because in the background there was a sense of betrayal, that I
was playing the role of Judas Iscariot to my family when I knew the rule
of omertà as well as anyone on earth. I was picking a subject where I
knew there would be an explosion in the tunnel. And I saw it continu-
ing. If I kept writing I knew I was going to do it to the Citadel; I was
going to do it to everything, because the only thing I thought could
actually keep me alive was telling the truth about all that stuff. At the
same time, I was so worried deep down inside that what I was dragging
up was what was going to kill me. Then I realized that I wasn't telling
everything, I was suppressing, I was in the act of not telling the truth.
I also had an anger to deal with, a fury I could not hold back coming
through. All of this drove me crazy.

Also, I was having trouble with Anne Barrett, who became my editor
after Shannon Ravenel left Houghton Mifflin. Anne Barrett was this
motherly, sweethearted, kind woman, and I was like a barbarian to her.
She rejected the manuscript the first time because it was too violent and
she did not believe in the character of the Great Santini. She thought
fathers were fonts of wisdom; no father would ever treat his son that
badly.

"We don't believe a father like this can exist," my little New England editors were telling me.

I said, "Anne, not everybody comes up like you, I promise."

"People like this don't exist."

I said, "Anne, say it this way: 'I don't know people like this who exist.'"

I had not even begun to tell the whole truth about Dad in that book, and already I was shocking people. When Bernie went through the manuscript with me, he came to a part where the father is beating the shit out of the entire family, which Anne had struck out. He saw that and said, "I wouldn't cut that."

"Bernie, *they* cut it. Anne says it's not believable. She says, 'America is not ready for that story yet.'"

Now, what my head cheerleader says when he tells that story: "Pat Conroy made America ready for it." By now we have enough reports of men and women who are brutalized by mom, by dad, by Joan Crawford, by men beating their children with their dicks, but at that time guys like my dad hid from their own cruelty because it was not well known. They could hide behind the whole idea of Father's Day and the happy American family, which people believed in during the '50s when I was growing up.

In the middle of writing it as I was having a very difficult time holding it together, it was also tough for me to find a place to write in Atlanta. When Barbara went up to buy a house she asked what I wanted, and I said—we laugh about this now—I said, "All I need is a place to write, I don't want it on a busy road, and I like a wood-burning fireplace." Okay, she calls me up, we bought the house; it is on Briarcliff Road. If I took a left out of Briarcliff Road and kept going, I could get to Miami. If I took a right out of Briarcliff Road, I could have gone to Michigan. So, I considered that a busy street, and there was no fireplace, wood burning or not, and there was no place to write. So I had to find places. I do not have this ability to write on trains, buses, or sitting on park benches. I wish I had that more than anything, but that has never been available to me. So I had to go off and write in these places of retreat and solitude, and I usually needed a clear space ahead where I would not be bothered for months.

I would sometimes come to Beaufort, rent, or somebody would often give me a cabin on a beach, and I would write down there. Norman Berg, a book rep, gave me a farmhouse in Dunwoody. That was a great place. I had a whole house to myself on his property of about forty acres in Dunwoody. I could go home at night if I wanted to.

But sometimes I would just go away for two or three weeks to Charleston. Mayor Joe Riley would go with his family to the beach for a month. I think it was the whole month of August, maybe even six weeks, including some of July. They had a beach house on the Isle of Palms. They offered their house South of Broad in Charleston, and I was delighted. How I almost paid them back: I went into a depression and then tried to kill myself in his house. That must have been '74 or '75.

I don't remember great thought going into it; I remember great agony going into it. It didn't seem there was much rationality in it. I was in such pain all the time. You can't sleep, you drink, you're bent double in anxiety, and what can you do? What can possibly bring you out of this? I'm not like my brother Tom; heights are out. I can't do that, because I have a vivid imagination, and I could imagine this six seconds where I'm mumbling to myself, "My God, I didn't really want to do this. Holy shit, what do I do now? Good God, it's coming up fast. My God, the earth, it's almost here. Lord, here I come." This wasn't for me; I found that out. That was out. Now, guns I don't like because that's the soldier's death. I'd read about drowning, how you struggle your ass off and you're dying to breathe, your body's going into convulsions, then your final breath comes, and your body is in complete agony and goes into rigor mortis before you even die. Then my daughters' faces would all come in a triumvirate before me, and I would see them reduced to prostitution, drug addiction, and marrying people who are on the Most Wanted list by the FBI. And I personally did not want to feel any pain.

So the one I chose is the debutante's death, the death that involves no pain whatsoever, just drinking a dry martini, falling asleep, and never waking up again as you slip off into dreams and then ultimately annihilation. I was a pill and liquor guy. That's the way I chose because, one, I'm a coward, and it's totally painless; two, I'm a coward, and I wouldn't be aware of the actual moment; and three, my father could laugh his ass off that there was something so wimpy about me. "Pat took an overdose of something called Sominex."

I'd gotten together a lot of sleeping pills—what I thought was a lot—and a lot of Valium. I tried drinking liquor and taking what I felt was way more pills than I needed. The one thing about suicide I learned is, when you're serious about it, it's the release you're after. That's what seems lovely about it. You cause no worries anymore, and whatever it is that is bothering you will go away. What suicide looked like to me was just blessed relief. I remember, in going to sleep, I remember the great burden being lifted, being happy when I started getting sleepy that I wouldn't have to deal with anything anymore.

I woke up two and a half days later, surprised that I was waking up. Obviously I didn't take enough pills, although I'd read about these things and thought I'd used enough. There was a reason I got a D in chemistry in both high school and college. I thought I'd taken quite enough pills, thanks. I thought I drank quite enough liquor to get those pills down. I don't know what went wrong, but I woke up many days later in terrible, terrible shape, puking in Joe Riley's bathtub, my guts heaving. I was surprised to be alive, but I felt like I was dead because I felt like shit. Then being shocked at what I had done, remorseful, guilt-ridden with survivor's guilt that I had survived my own suicide. Then the faces of my children coming up before me, the fear of the damage I would have done to the people around me, the kids, to Barbara, to my parents, my brothers and sisters. You don't think about yourself as part of a whole movement of people, but you are. Anytime I've known a suicide, I'm always staggered by the things they set off in a family. And that I almost caused that kind of agony, that distressed me as much as anything.

And what would it have done to young Joe Riley, his sweet wife, his two young boys if I had done that in their house? I was a young writer; it wasn't like I was much of a personage then. I thought what trauma to put these nice people through who have given me their house for the summer so I can be writing on my stupid book, *The Great Santini*, which depresses me so much that I try to kill myself in their house. And I thought, you've got to at least be nicer than that when you kill yourself. Guy gives me his house, comes by and finds me dead in his and his wife's bed that they so graciously gave me and, you know, I mark him and his family forever because I'm nuts? I was horrifically embarrassed by this. I had read enough biography to know that writers were often depressed and this was not unnatural. It never occurred to me this would be the kind of thing I would do, though. What I now realize: it was during the suicidal times in my life, when I tried to overdose on drugs, that my sense of humor failed me and I saw nothing funny or hopeful in anything.

After I woke up days later, Bernie checked in on me, and when he heard my voice on the phone, he got worried. My voice goes funny when this great sadness happens. I get weak voiced and whiny. My voice completely changes and becomes pathetic. Bernie heard this voice and rallied a posse. Mike Jones and Bernie came and got me out of Charleston, and we went down to George Garbade's cabin on the Chechessee River between Beaufort and Savannah. The guys rallied around me and sort of took care of me. We fished and crabbed, we told stories that made us all laugh, and George was hilarious because he is just a good old boy. He's the Daddy Rabbit, and he thought I just needed to get drunk and get laid.

He said, "You know what's wrong with you, boy? You're always depressed. You know why you're depressed? You think too fuckin' much. You're always thinkin' too fuckin' much. Now, be like the Daddy Rabbit, I don't think about nothin' at all. And you're too fuckin' sensitive. I just go along and one thing leads to another, that's fine, nothin' I can do about it. I ain't sensitive about it. And don't be readin' them fuckin' books. They're so depressing anybody would want to kill themselves. Just hunt up some pussy and it'll make you feel better."

We always loved the way George simplified the world for us. He'd say, "Pat, I know what's going to help you out of your depression, boy. You need a hobby. You've got to get yourself a hobby. Like, golf is my hobby. You know, I feel bad, I just say, Goddamn, Rabbit, why don't you just go out and play a little golf? And I do feel bad sometimes. I know you guys don't think I'm smart enough to feel bad, but I do sometimes. So you need a hobby, son, you gotta get yourself a hobby. And once you get yourself a hobby, you can concentrate on your hobby, and you don't have to worry about these weird little thoughts that run around your little head, your little writer's head. You gotta have a hobby. If you got a hobby, you're not gonna kill yourself. You're not gonna have time, because you're goin' to be busy with your hobby." He was hilarious. "It may not be a hobby that I like, maybe you like stamp collectin'. Maybe you like collectin' coins. The Daddy Rabbit, I love collectin' broads, always have. But there's all kinds of shit you can do for a hobby, go fishin', play chess or bridge."

That was good for me at the time. It got me laughing again. I told him, "Yeah, George, I got it. I'll just play some checkers."

Years later, when George's son went to the Citadel, George met the general who was in charge. My name was anathema to the Citadel at this time, and George would say, "Now, General, you don't understand my boy Pat. He had nothing against the Citadel. He had nothing at all against the Citadel. It's just he's always hated torture, and he's always hated brutality. And you got to admit—Pat is sensitive, he's just fucking sensitive. Pat would take everything seriously because he's so fucking sensitive." I always liked to see how George described me to the world, and there's something dead right about it: I'm too fucking sensitive.

I think I got out of Charleston almost immediately after that. I remember knowing I was back to something like my old self, because I tried to leave the Riley's house immaculate. I called Joe and told him I was leaving the key somewhere. Then when I got back to Atlanta, I knew I had to see somebody fast.

⁓

The writing of *The Great Santini* split me open, spilled me out on the floor, and threw me into Dr. Marion O'Neill's office. I cried uncontrollably when I wrote that last chapter, cried for days. I thought I was going to go crazy and kill myself. Also, Barbara and I were not doing well, and that depressed me. I was still living with Barbara, but I had a place to go write, Norman Berg's farmhouse. I would stay there—especially when I got to be so depressed—I would stay there sometimes for days at a time. I was only thinking of myself. I was not thinking of Barbara; I was not thinking of the kids; I was not thinking of family. I was trying to hold myself together and was having trouble doing so.

Then I met a woman at one of Cliff Graubert's book parties who'd written a couple of novels. Candace. I was talking to her, and she said she had this great shrink, and I said, okay, what is the name? She told me. Marion O'Neill. There was another woman at the same party who also saw Marion O'Neill. I liked Candace and could tell she wanted to have an affair. I slept with her twice, which I regret, but at least it got me to Marion O'Neill.

I had to have a female therapist. I couldn't stand these fucking guys I went to. I hated them. I had gone to a couple of shrinks who would just look at me. It drove me nuts. I said, hey pal, I'm paying you ninety million an hour for you to look at me? I want you to talk to me. I want you to say something to me. One psychoanalyst—I'm sitting there talking to him, and he stared at me, and I stared back at him, and finally I said, "Sir, are you ever going to talk to me?"

"Do you have a need for me to talk to you?"

"Yes, I do."

"Why do you have a need for me to talk to you?"

Fuck you, I'm outta here.

Marion was straight with me. I had to have straight answers. You've got to talk to me. Don't sit there like a shrink fruitcake and just stare at me. You got to give me some advice. I got to know how I'm doing. The first thing when I got in her office, she wanted to know, "How did you get my name?" I said, this woman mentioned you. And she said, "Are you having an affair with her?" I said not really, but I thought it might lead to one. And she said, "You've got shitty taste in women, pal."

I thought, "I found my girl." And I said, "Yes, this is one of the problems I've had in my life, Marion."

Then I said, "I think I might be crazy."

And she said, "Yes, I think you are. But I can help you."

I can't tell you the relief I felt. These were the greatest words I'd ever heard. At least somebody had finally named it. I was feeling crazy. I was, to me, acting crazy. I was feeling completely nuts, isolated, alienated; feeling so completely despondent, so on-the-floor sad, and when she said it, it at least gave it a name. At last I had a name. Okay, I'm going through a period that's crazy, but I can get out of it.

Marion thought I had a reason to be crazy. We went through my whole childhood, my whole life, and there were legitimate reasons why I had problems, problems that were going to pursue me my whole life. Because you cannot make up for that ruined childhood. You never can quite correct that. You can learn to live with it, you can explain it, you can understand its effect on you, but there is no cure for that. Childhood is a matrix of immense power, and it works on you in ways you cannot control.

She did not put me on medication. "Why would I put you on medication? You'd take it and kill yourself." So I had the talking cure, which I learned to believe in. The talking cure is going out of style? Not for me. I think it saved my life. I told Marion stuff I'd never told anybody. It all later came out in the books. I'm sure I talked out my books—*The Great Santini, The Lords of Discipline, The Prince of Tides, Beach Music*— I'm sure I talked those books out to her in that therapy. I first had to release it to her, in the privacy of her office, because it filled me with shame, and it filled me with disgrace, and it filled me with absolute horror, that I had seen my mother beat up and I couldn't help her, that I should have plunged a knife in my father's back, that I should have done this, I should have done that, but I wasn't strong enough to kill him. Her take was—considering my childhood and everything else it led to—her conclusion was: Why wouldn't you be crazy with that?

She was great for me: straight, direct, and honest. I learned things about myself I did not want to learn. But one day she told me, "I've never seen anybody under such stress and anxiety. I think you were raised to believe you could take stress. You can't. You're terrible at it. It kills you. She told me I am not good with friction, I am not good with high anxiety, I am not good with tension, and I am not good with stress. You just can't do it, she told me. This was like sticking a pin into the Hindenburg. I felt this huge release, because I had felt stress my entire life and didn't know it. I had been overstressed from the time I was I think a baby. And the thing about anxiety—it never leaves, it just moves elsewhere. It almost had you yesterday, but then you got away. So the forces of anxiety simply shifted, the troops are in movement, the infantries are on the go. They're on foot, and they're finding something else right now. They have their eye on things that you love.

Marion also told me, "Don't fall in love with every woman you meet." She said, "Pat, you have no taste in women whatsoever. You like them all. Be careful about that. That is hurting you."

I would have fallen in love with Marion had she not been so completely unapproachable in that way. It was an accident, a total, complete, and wonderful accident that she was so utterly impervious, unsusceptible, and bulletproof. I did not even try to flirt with her. She was no-nonsense. There was no bullshit. I could not fool her. I could not use my charm to deflect her. I could not use my stories to get away from her. Sometimes I hide behind stories and don't reveal myself. Marion let me get away with nothing. She simply stared at me like a buzzard, waiting for me to rot properly in the sun before she made her move.

At first I was embarrassed about actually going to a shrink, and she had to work through that with me: the Southern male of the nontherapeutic breed, the Citadel man, the son of a fighter pilot. I had to get through some of that. Therapy is what men say they won't do. I've had male writers boldly tell me they would never go to a shrink; their psyches are so attuned to literature that they put all of their demons into the writing itself. Of course, to a point guard, that sounds like macho bullshit. My father told me I should never say it out loud so nobody knew. It would hurt my reputation as a writer and everything else. And after my second breakdown years later, I have had people want to attack me for it. What has happened a lot is Citadel guys coming up to me at book signings. They'll say, "You admitted in the *Wall Street Journal* that you actually had a nervous breakdown and required psychiatric care."

"Yes, I did."

"Well, why would anybody give a shit what you have to say?"

"I don't know. A lot of people don't."

"But you admitted going to a psychologist."

"Yes, and here I am. I'm standing here and you're buying one of my books, so it seems to have worked out somewhat well."

Marion used to say that men were usually not open to talk about their emotional life; that was most of her work, getting men to talk about their emotions. And she said, "Pat, here's where you're going to be all right: you can talk about your emotional life." She said I had the kind of anxiety that would never lead to ulcers because I do not hold my feelings in. Somewhere I must have a hidden vagina or a female organ, because I can talk about my feelings, and I can cry. Marion assured me my anxiety had a way of getting out into the world, and I think she thought that was writing. What therapy is like is also what writing is like. Every book I've written has been called forth from a dark side of me. Marion told me: "A lot of your cure comes from your writing, and the deeper you go, the better it's going to be for you and your mental health. There are things you have not dug out yet. You've got to make sure you keep digging."

Everything I think I do and say and write is a huge Sisyphus-like rock that I got in childhood and struggled to push up a hill. The English would say I've only written misery memoirs, but what the English fear most is a book that can actually help you psychologically get through life by releasing the demons you keep inside. This terrifies the English; they cannot stand it. And some writers seem terrified that there could be any therapeutic aspect in their writing, because if it was therapeutic it would somehow take away from the literariness of their work. So they can't possibly admit there may be some psychological healing that can be done in the writing out of a novel. And that's always, to me, just seemed like fear of the critical establishment. I imagine Homer crafted his epic poetry because he was working out some kind of psychological issue—maybe his blindness—who knows?

When I write, I go to someplace that I don't know about to write, and I think I did that when Dad was beating me. Because when Dad would beat me, it was either so traumatic or painful, I simply had to go to this place, which was almost putting myself through a self-psychosis where I could not take in everything that was assaulting me but I could close it off. I could take myself out of the situation when Dad was beating me. I've even had dreams about going out of my body and looking down at what was happening, not believing it was me that it was happening to, but observing it. So when Dad beat me I would disappear into myself and go to this place inside me. I had to go somewhere when this took place. It's the same place I go when I write, because I have to go somewhere when I write.

Marion O'Neill thought it probably helped me survive without becoming psychotic like Carol. She said, "Pat, I think what happened is when you got beaten as a child, you had to withdraw or dissociate from what was happening to you, and you learned how to do that." And she said, "I think that goes with your writing. I think you do that same thing when you write. You go into this world of yours, and that's why you can't remember anything you've written afterward."

Anyway, therapy seemed to open up my life, which I liked a lot. Self is an unknown territory to many people. It ain't to me. I think the best country you can visit is that of self, and if you have never done that, you've missed a great part of life.

~

When they were desperately looking for blurbs for *The Great Santini*, I could tell there was some worry about the book, and finally this one publicist said, "Pat, we've sent your book to writers all over America. We can't get anybody to blurb your book. Do you have any other ideas?"

I said, "No, I don't."

It didn't upset me because I didn't even know what a blurb was then. And I never filled out this form that might get me blurbs, because I didn't know anybody. Anne Siddons had not made it yet; Terry Kay had not made it yet; Paul Darcy Boles was nobody, so I just didn't know anybody.

One day they told me, "Pat, we almost had a blurb for you." And they sent me a postcard by Ward Just, this journalist who started doing novels late in his life. So Ward writes Houghton Mifflin, "Dear," whoever the editor was, "I couldn't possibly use my name to further such a poorly written book. But tell the author when that sister appeared on stage, the book took on something that seemed like life. Ward Just."

I remember it hurt my feelings. But as publishing life goes on, years later I receive a book in the mail for a blurb. It's called something like *The Ambassador's Daughter*, by Ward Just, and I write back on a postcard, "Dear Editor, tell Mr. Just I could not possibly lend my name to such a poorly written novel. But tell him when that ambassador's daughter appeared on the page, it took on something that almost seemed like life, but not quite. Pat Conroy."

Okay, I thought about it. I didn't mail it. I didn't mail it. It was the bad me acting up. But I enjoyed the thought of mailing it.

Because I got pounced on when they tried to get blurbs for me, it's turned me into this Beast of Blurb Land. That's how I became a blurb slut, which is a phrase stolen from Josephine Humphreys, who told me, "Pat, you and I together are called the Blurb Sluts, because we'll give everybody blurbs." I did not want any new, young writer just starting out as I was once, not having a blurb from at least one writer. So I will give anybody a blurb.

Now, I did not realize for about ten years, Bernie Schein was giving blurbs out for me on a frequent basis. I've had people say to me, "Mr. Conroy, my God, I feel like putting a hickey on your neck because you gave my poor book the only blurb it got." And they tell me the book; I've never heard of it.

I've lied about it so many times, I just, "Oh, you're welcome."

Finally I called Bernie. "Is that you?"

He said, "Pat, you'd give them if they could get to you. They just can't get to you. So I do you a favor and do them a favor. They are so grateful to me for the rest of their life for getting you to do it. And frankly, Pat, I've become a lot better blurb writer than you are."

These people would give their books to Bernie and say, "Give it to Pat," and Bernie: "I'll give it to Pat. I promise." Or somebody will call Bernie and say, "You know Pat Conroy. Can you get me a blurb from Pat?" "I'll be happy to." And I never hear from the person.

I said, "Bernie, how many blurbs have you given for me?"

"Oh," he said. "Not many. Couple hundred."

A woman came up to me the other day, she has a self-published book, and she is in full adoration mode. She says, "Pat, I cannot thank you enough for giving me a blurb." And, you know, "It changed my life; it changed my husband's life; we're naming our first child after you; we named both of our dogs after you." She goes on in this moment, and I always know I shouldn't ask what the book's called, and it was something like, you know, *Full Dancing Bobos* or something. She said, "You don't remember the book?"

"I remember it, yeah, it's great. I loved it, I couldn't put it down."

But I have never seen, never heard of the book; the book was never sent to me. And yet, there's my name with this elaborate blurb. And I called Bernie, I said, "Bernie, you cocksucker, you've done it again." And I said, "Bernie, I wish you'd quit doing that. It's so unprofessional. It makes me look like an idiot. But of course you don't mind looking like an idiot."

And he said, "No, when I think about it, Pat, it makes you look much more like an idiot than it does me. And I like you to look like an idiot, and I like to make you look like an idiot."

Now this is appalling to all human beings except Bernie. Once he did it to our friend Terry Kay, and Terry won't stand for it. As Terry says, "Conroy, I have some principles and dignity which I can fall back on. You have nothing."

What he did with Terry is, Bernie wanted to get a short story published in the *Georgia Review*. Stanley Lindberg was the very distinguished editor of the *Review*, so what Bernie does is he writes a letter from Terry Kay to Stanley Lindberg. "Dear Stan, the next great short story writer in America is an undiscovered writer named Bernie Schein, living in Atlanta. I've read some of his stuff and it deserves to be in anthologies and compared to the best in literature. I think *Georgia Review* should publish him. Terry Kay."

Terry knows nothing about it until he gets a call from Stanley Lindberg, "Who's this guy Bernie Schein?" Terry Kay goes nuts. He goes crazy. He explodes with rage. He tells me he will cut Bernie's dick off and feed it to a trout if Bernie ever does that to him again. He calls Bernie up and screams at him. Bernie just laughed.

Bernie's daughter Maggie was a very good ballerina, and he was fund-raising for her school, writing up a fund-raising letter. So I get a letter in the mail that says, "Dear Atlantans, I believe that everybody who truly believes in the arts in Atlanta, Georgia, should sit down right now and make out a check for a million dollars to Patsy Bromley of Terpsichore Dance Studio." I'm thinking that's the dumbest fucking thing I've read in my life. I'm quite amazed to find my name on the next page: signed, Pat Conroy. I'm so pissed off I run over to Cliff Graubert's bookstore. As I run in—fuming, furious—Cliff hands me a check for $1,000,000 made out to Troupe de Terpsichore and Patsy Bromley.

He said, "I certainly believe in the arts, Pat. And I want you to know that." Then, of course, he falls down on the floor laughing and, "What an asshole you are. Why do you let him do it?"

I said, "I can't quite figure how not to let him do it."

I've never quite figured it out, I still don't know. And people always wondered why I put up with it. All I can tell you is that most of it tickles me, and it tickles the shy boy in me who would never say or do any of the things Bernie does.

Terry Kay cannot believe that I give Bernie this leeway. "Excuse me, Terry. Will you please explain to me exactly what I can do about it?"

"Goddamn it, Conroy. You can protest."

"Oh, yeah, Terry, protest to Bernie? 'Bernie, I'd like to issue a protest about your overuse of my name'? Okay, I can beat Bernie up, I can take a tire iron to him and beat him into the ground. Do you think it would stop him? No! He'd still do it, he'd do it more."

Because that's Bernie's nature. He would continue to do it. What can I do? You know, arrest his mailman? Do I put an alert out: "Bernie Schein is sometimes writing blurbs for me"? The hardest thing to do is protect the integrity of your signature. And tell me how you stop Bernie Schein. I don't know how.

Someday, it's going to happen with Bernie. I know that. "This book sucks." But so far, it's been okay.

~

When *The Great Santini* came out, it just exploded all over the place. Even I underestimated the fury it would unleash when you begin that little journey of telling things about a family they don't want to hear, are not prepared to hear, are completely prepared to deny. I got called the name of every traitor in history. I was Judas Iscariot; I was Benedict Arnold. I knew when I wrote the book I was going to be called a liar, but my God, I didn't realize how much I was going to be called a liar. I did not know how many people would side with my father. I did not know Mom would go crazy, and it was Mom who said I was messing up her life. For a redneck girl from the Alabama and Georgia hills, Mom had done what she felt was extraordinarily well, and to have that sullied, to have that damaged by me . . . I didn't realize she had kept it totally quiet and nobody else knew it. She'd never told any girlfriends; she'd never told her sisters; she'd never told her brother; she'd never told anybody that this had been going on.

Stanny was one of the biggest pains in the asses of all. "I never saw your father once hit anybody. He was a wonderful man. A great provider."

And I'd have to say "Gosh, Stanny, I can't remember him ever doing it around you, but I can't remember him ever doing it around anybody."

Of course Dad had turned on the charm around everyone else. He was Mr. Snake Boy pretending he was a human being. I never felt anything when he did it except contempt, but it evidently worked very well. I had no idea he had been this ambassador of goodwill and the rest of the family saw him as a great guy with a great personality. We found out he had been going to see the cousins, the Harper boys, and taking them all to get ice cream. We were shocked by this, because we can't remember him ever taking us to get ice cream. I think there is something about men like my dad who want to be recognized throughout the family as a kind of nobility, and in their own household they take it for granted they are nobility and are not answerable to anyone. They're not responsible to anyone; it is their business how they treat their children; *my* children. It's a sense of ownership, but they don't own the nieces and nephews, so they have to woo them.

Then Mom came up to Atlanta to tell me I wasn't a very good writer. And, you know, thanks, Mom, it's great to hear it from the woman I love the best in the world. She said, "You gave the book to him. I was the leader of that house. I was central. I directed everything that happened, and everything that happened in that house happened because of me. I was so much smarter than he was. I was so much smarter." She was more of a warrior, she told me, and she could plan her battles. Dad couldn't; he just exploded. But she'd prepare her wars in the field against him and do them properly. "You missed it. You weren't a good enough writer to see it."

I simply said, "Mom, I saw it too late, but I saw it. I wrote about what I needed at that time. It was a perfect mother, like I thought you were. That is the woman I included in *The Great Santini*. And it weakens the book, but that's all right, that's how that kid made it through that horrible family." And I said, "Mom, I'll get you the next time out." But when *The Prince of Tides* came out, thank God she was dead. I'm not sure I would have had the guts to publish that with her still alive.

Dad did me that great favor of disappearing; everybody thought he had committed suicide. But he came back with a letter that was terrific, letting his family know that they could be as mad as they wanted, but his son wrote this book. Even if the book is critical of him and hurt his feelings, he was proving that he was going to back me up. I appreciated that, and our beginning started with that.

When they had the book party for *The Great Santini* and somebody came up and had Dad sign it, something changed in Dad. He started accompanying me to signings where he'd sit beside me, and he started having a ball. He developed a sense of humor that I never knew he had. I don't think he knew he had it. And he played off the character. I gave him a role where he could be the opposite of the one I presented in the book, and he said, "I'm going to make a liar out of you the rest of your life, son." He made all this stuff up about this wonderful, fabulous man who was sitting beside me.

When the movie came out, then the glitz of Hollywood took over, and they both adored it. They both loved it. It took the pressure off the book. Beaufort of course went crazy, and Mom's living there. Her son brought these people there, and they're renting all the motels, and all the restaurants are filled. She's calling me up, "Robert Duvall gets here next week; they've rented this house for him. Oh, Blythe Danner, they've rented a house right beside the one we lived in." It totally thrilled my mother. Dad I had to bring down from Atlanta, and we watched the basketball scene of the movie being filmed.

During all this, I never had a family life that seemed stable. I had made it unstable. Everything in my life seemed like a mess. Then I hooked up with Maria Margarita in the Dominican Republic. This makes it more of a mess. That was the affair that broke, I think, the marriage up. I was smitten with her, and that was the final straw in the marriage. You know, I have found that the other woman does not please the woman you're married to.

The *Atlanta Sunday Magazine* had run an article about *The Water Is Wide*. One of the things that ended up happening from that: the

University of Georgia calls me up and asks me to go for a USIS thing in the Dominican Republic where I talk about literature. So I said, da-da-da, Conroy's getting around. This'll be the rest of my life. I'll be traveling to foreign countries; I'll be meeting presidents, prime ministers, ambassadors. "Hello, Mr. Ambassador, how are you? I'm Pat Conroy. It's good to meet you, sir. Oh, no, no, I can't serve as your assistant. It's the wrong time." You know the fantasies you go through.

I think I had just finished *The Great Santini,* my first breakdown had occurred, and I'm coming back from this breakdown. So I go to the Dominican Republic. I'm excited; I've never been to a Latin American country. I go there and talk, and I've got a translator, gay guy; God, he was a sweetheart. Miguel. Everybody's named what they should be: Miguel, Maria.

I get this class, this lovely class, and the first question that comes up: "Are you working for the CIA?" I said, "No, are any of y'all? Because it's much more likely y'all are than I am." It turned out to be a magical week. Maria's in there, but I did not notice her being in there particularly. Everybody was smart; everybody was communist. I never met a bright person from a Latin American country who was not a communist during that era.

I've never had such a nice week, and at the end, they gave me a party. I said, "Let me invite this class to America. You all come to Atlanta, and I'll take you on a tour of Southern literature," and so about seven of them did. We piled into a car, and I took them to Flannery O'Connor's house, to Thomas Wolfe's house, to James Agee's little school. Then I went and introduced them to the kids from Daufuskie. We stayed with Mom and had a great time.

Driving them back to Miami, I realize I'm falling in love with this girl, and I was like, oh great, let me fuck my life up in another entirely different way. But I thought she was just magnificent. Her father once ran for the president of the Dominican Republic. He was imprisoned by Trujillo for a thousand years. He's one of *those* guys. Maria Margarita was as radical as anybody in the world. She said what she most hated about me was my love of freedom. Because I must cement myself to the party and to the party rule, and she said, "We would have to keel you the first day of the revolution." I said what a shame. And she said, "We must put you on *la pared*." I said, "What's *la pared*?" She said, "That's the wall."

Anyway, she was exciting. She had gone to the Sorbonne. She had her master's, loved film. And Latin America is intense. I've still got the letters she wrote me, the most passionate love letters. "Gringo, I love you. Gringo, I tear you with my teeth like you are the meat that I chew." I'm thinking, holy God. "I love you so much, even though I think you're a pig, like all Americans are pigs, and because you're an hombre, you has to be a pig."

But also, because she was intellectual, she introduced me in 1977, '78 to Gabriel Garcia Marquez, to Vargas Llosa, to all of Latin American literature, which was a great find at that time. I was early to that parade and loved it. This is writing that I just adored. Latin American literature, what I know of it, and I know a lot of it, was fostered in me by Maria Margarita. Where she got her master's degree and undergraduate had magic for me the way Harvard's got magic for me, and the Sorbonne makes my heart sing.

When Barbara and I were separated, I went down to live with her for about a month, in her house, where Maria would sneak in the room at night and say, "Gringo, if my father catches me in here with you, he will be honor bound to keel you."

And I said, "Well, get out of here, beat it."

"He must keel you, or he must keel himself."

I said, "Well, I have a solution for that. You go back to your little bedroom."

And she said, "No, gringo, you don't understand. I love to fock too much. I never love to fock until I meet my gringo."

So I said, "Maria, you say I'm going to be killed, you're going to be killed, your father's going to have to kill himself. This is too complicated, okay? This is too complicated. Stay in your own fucking room."

She was hilarious to me. I mean, "Gringo, I luff you." She says, "I luff you more than these American ee-diots you have dated before, these blonde ee-diots. This is the love of a Dominican woman. Passione grande; this is love that cannot be duplicated by the American ee-diots. And even though I may not do the filthy tricks gringos know and practice as they watch porno, you will have the love that will last forever."

I found this all hilarious. And, "Even though I must keel you after the revolution, I will love focking you until the revolution comes." I used to scream laughing at this. And I think it appealed to a romantic view of love that I had. Foreign countries, and who knows what fantasies I developed in the stupid world I grew up in.

Well, she went to New York to get her master's degree in film at the New School. She had one from the Sorbonne in something else, but she wanted one in film. So I would go visit her. God, one-room apartments in New York: this was the smallest thing I'd ever seen in my life. But that was our love nest in New York.

We finally broke up one day. "Oh, gringo, you have such American sensibilities, it makes me seek. It makes me seek."

She had a real temper and threw me out of her apartment, hurled my suitcase into the street, which I found very Dominican. I was crying, so I get a cab, I go home, and then of course there's a telegram waiting, "Gringo, I love you with my heart," you know. "I'll come to Atlanta to live with you. We'll get married. I will have gringo children."

And at that time there was just too much coming down, so I did not write her back. And I've regretted that. I thought I would marry Maria Margarita. But I just don't know what that would have been like. I have no idea if we had gotten married what it would have been like on a daily basis. I figured this would be kind of tough to live with. And I knew if I married her, there would be this tension with the kids. I worried about that, and I should have. Also, I couldn't quite figure this one out either: the Santo Domingo novels of Pat Conroy.

~

The Great Santini came out in '76. Barbara and I may have gotten divorced in '77, '78. This happened in my little crazy period where I have trouble with remembering time for this period.

There was no good reason for me to leave Barbara at all. I gave her plenty of reasons to leave me. I don't remember a great fight to keep me. But I can't think of any reason that would have been legitimate for us to get divorced without these other women coming in. She was also impatient with my craziness. Barbara is one of these girls: I want to get my life straight. If this guy can't do it, I'll find somebody else. She always used to say, "Crazy scares me. I don't like it." So she was pretty rapid about calling it quits. And I don't think she had any regrets—none that she expressed at the time or has expressed since then. I was taking my family on a walk down the *Via Negativa* every single day, and it was hard on all of us.

We went several times together to Marion to save our marriage kind of thing. And I think Barbara walked out of the session. "He's the one that's crazy. You fix him. I don't need you." I have never blamed her for that. I had the first of my great depressions when I wrote *The Great Santini,* and I'm sure it scared her. I feel bad for getting Barbara into that. I still feel bad. It was not my thinking that things were broken; I thought *I* was broken.

When I look back on it, I realize Barbara had never had freedom. Wes, her first husband, was pretty controlling, a Marine. In Atlanta, she was in law school. That was a good time in her life. I think she enjoyed it. She loved her friends. She had a healthy ego, and she was finding out how smart she was. She was almost a pioneer at Emory Law School. She was among the first women who were going through, one of the first women graduates, one of three in her class. Then she became an assistant district attorney in DeKalb County.

Barbara ended up having a marvelous career. When she retired a couple of years ago, she had this big retirement ceremony. One of the chief justices of the Georgia Supreme Court came and read an appreciation of Barbara, said that Barbara Conroy changed the way briefs were written to the appellate and supreme courts of Georgia, and she set a standard that will probably never be met again. He said it will never be the same in the appellate court or the supreme court after Barbara Conroy. And of course, our kids went crazy and loved this.

But before the ceremony was going to happen, all three of the girls said, "Dad, what time are you going to get there? What time are you coming up?"

I said, "Girls, let me teach you a little lesson in life: I have not been invited."

And they said, "Oh, you know Mom, it's an oversight."

I said, "I don't think so. I think Mom, this is her big day, she wants to play it out as her big day, so let's let her do it."

I was right. Barbara told me, "Pat, you would have taken away some of my glory that day, and I just thought I would keep it all to myself." It pleased the shit out of Barbara. And she has always been grateful that I put her through law school. Nowadays Barbara and I call each other quite a bit to talk about the girls. She comes to Fripp and vacations there, so our relationship is very strong now.

One of the worst days of my life is when I had to tell those three girls Barbara and I were getting divorced. It almost killed me. I'm thinking I am fucking these three girls' lives up for no reason except I'm an asshole. I remember the little-girl heads in that house on Briarcliff Road in Atlanta, Georgia. I think Megan was about five, and the complete lack of understanding, the complete lack of knowing what's going to happen. I hated the looks on their faces. It was awful. It was just a terrible, terrible moment in my life. I thought, here I am, fucking these little kids' lives up before their lives have even begun. For what, I have no idea. I was a womanizer for a while. I'm thinking of me, a one-night stander. What the hell was that all about? That did not lead to much happiness. I still loved their mother, and she was sick of me. She had a need for me to take the blame, which I can do because I come from the ancient Catholic tradition of guilt, penance, and hair shirts. But I take all the guilt onto myself because that's where it belongs.

I didn't know divorce would affect me as long as it did. It seemed like a great failure, divorce. There was a drag down on the spirit, an anchor weighed against me of thinking I could never be made right. One moment after I had just gotten divorced nearly killed me. Every divorced father takes the kids to Disney World, so I took mine to Disney World one summer. I wrote an article about it so I got it all free. On the way back, Megan is riding in the front seat. She's the littlest, and she must have been six or seven then, and she said, "Daddy, I need to ask you a question." I said, go ahead, kid. And she said, "Melissa and Jessica are worried that you're not going to be their daddy anymore now that you and Mommy are divorced."

I pulled over and said, "Girls, sometimes adults don't remember to say everything. But let me tell you: You're always going to be my girls." I just had not thought of it. They were adopted, and they were worried. I said, "You're always going to be my girls."

And, "We were worried that Megan was your only real daughter."

I said, "Nah, I adopted you all, it's on paper, it's official, I've got to have you; I can't even throw you back if I wanted to. It's me and you, girls, and that's it." I told them I was just trying to do the best I could. I was never going to be their real dad, but I was going to be their dad. They could make of that anything they wanted. I was gonna love their ass, that was my job.

Children—they ride like gargoyles of guilt on your shoulders your entire life. They're sitting up there like rain spouts, only blood is pouring out of their mouths. They have dreadful lives, and you try to comfort them and give them joy, but you can do nothing. They go out into the world unprotected, and there's nothing you can do. The child is always what gets you, what makes you tremble before the world's judgment. You think what you're doing is best for your children; otherwise you wouldn't do it. But I would tell my children, "Girls, I'm fucking up. I'm fucking you all up all the time. I don't know how. If I did I'd stop, but I don't know how I'm doing it. Just kind of grow up and get by me the best you can."

~

When I sit down and think about it, I can see my time in Atlanta was a very happy time for me in many, many ways. It wasn't perfect, but it was really good.

I always have this need to form some group of people, and Cliff Graubert was one of the first people I met in Atlanta because he had a sign outside his Old New York Book Shop, "Hardbacks 25 cents," and I thought, my God. I didn't own any hardbacks, and I thought, that's incredibly cheap. Of course they were all crap, but it got me into the store, and I started going through the stacks thinking, good God almighty. I realized I was going to use that bookstore like no one had before or since, and I really did. I thought, I can get another college education out of this bookstore. When I saw the books that came through, I really thought that I had found some undiscovered gold mine that would feed me the rest of my life. I plundered that bookstore for the next thirty years.

Cliff had sold furs before he sold books. I said, "Why did you choose books—for the love reading?"

Fuck no. He said, "My father had a friend who had a bookstore in New York; he said he wanted to get rid of it, wanted to retire, so I said, "Hey, books, it's like anything else you sell."

I said, "What a beautiful story of conversion."

Eventually he learned the business, learned what a book was worth. Heirs would come to the shop and say I've got some books to sell; there'd be like a thousand books, and Cliff would give them $300, go through them, and find really great books.

But Cliff was always complaining about not making any money. "I can't make a fucking shekel in this town."

By then I had met a black writer named Vern Smith, who had a novel coming out about Detroit, so I said, "Cliff, why don't we give him a book party?"

He says, "A book fucking party? It ain't his birthday."

I said no. Just give a party celebrating the book coming out. So that began the parties at the Old New York Book Shop, which became something big on the Atlanta scene, kind of an institution, and now they're legendary. At the time it was a new thing for Atlanta, some new order. *Cosmopolitan* magazine said that the parties at the Old New York Book Shop were the best and safest places for young women to meet young men in Atlanta. And I said "Cliff, this is genius at work."

Every time Cliff got his name in the paper because of the book parties, they would misspell it, so one time he was Cliff Graubarf, another he was Cliff Graufarts. And when he got interviewed, they'd say, "This is like Paris in the '20s." And Cliff would always say immediately, "It wasn't a Goddamn thing like Paris in the '20s. These writers didn't buy books. Except for Conroy, they didn't even read."

So I called him up and said, "Cliff, would you give me some insight into the wisdom of telling people your store was not Paris in the '20s when that's what they want to write?"

He said, "Oh, it's all bullshit. It's all horseshit."

I said, "Well, it may be Cliff, I agree with you, but I don't think that's a bad thing to be throwing around about your bookshop. Do you get it?"

He goes, "Oh my God, I just fucking got it. How did you figure that out?"

I said, "Well, unlike you, I'm not an idiot."

"Fuck you."

But it was a nice group, a great democratic thing. Now one group that did not come to the parties, because they were expected to buy a book, were the college professors. They are the most impossible people on earth. Professors never bought books from Cliff's store. When he was bitching about not making any money, I couldn't understand it because there were so many colleges and universities in Atlanta. He said, "College professors are the cheapest sons of bitches who ever lived."

I said, "What are you talking about?"

He said, "You count them."

What Cliff told me turned out to be totally true. I remember there was one book collector from Morehouse who looked exactly like James Baldwin, and he used to come, but that's the only professor I remember coming on a frequent basis. Cliff said he knew when a college professor walked into his bookstore that he wouldn't eat that night.

In Atlanta, the academic community would not admit that a writing community existed. If they had writers at Emory or Agnes Scott, they did not make themselves known to anybody that we knew, and we always noticed that the people connected to the universities kept to themselves. I think they're terrified of their own insecurity with the institution, and they don't want to dare interest anybody that might threaten their position. I met one Emory professor, guy I didn't like, Floyd Watkins. Supposedly the expert on Southern literature. And I'd always get this, "You sure aren't no Faulkner, are you?"

"No, I'm not."

"You sure aren't any Robert Penn Warren."

"No, I'm not that either, Floyd." I said, "But Floyd, here's one great thing you don't know. You and I don't know who I am, and it's for me to find out."

"Are you presuming?"

"I don't know. We'll find out."

Floyd used to tell me that I was wrong to come to Atlanta. That Faulkner had to be from a small town and live in a small town. Floyd was always put down, put down, put down, and I didn't like him. He was an asshole.

⌒

In Beaufort I used to get the Sunday *New York Times* and the *Atlanta Journal-Constitution* to make me think that I was actually keeping up with the culture. Terry Kay was the film critic for the *Atlanta Journal-Constitution,* and I thought he was a good one. Tim Belk and I used to read him in Beaufort, and we'd all go down to see movies that Terry recommended. I met Terry when he was sent down to do an article for *Georgia* magazine on the making of *Conrack* in 1974. So I came into a bar on St. Simons Island, and I saw a man trying to put his arm around my mother's shoulder. I walk over and recognize Terry from his pictures. I said, "Mr. Kay, I see that you've met my mother," and I see this look on his face like he's been electrocuted.

My mother said, "Pat, Terry and I are having an intellectual conversation. We've just been talking about books and literature."

I said, "Ah, yes."

We became friends that day and started seeing each other a whole lot, seeing each other at parties. He saw right away my country hick aspect, even though I thought I was sophisticated. He was the entertainment editor also and said, "Why don't you ride along with me? We'll go see the entertainment in the city."

We did go to a play at the Alliance Theater. But the other part was, he wrote up all the strip shows in Atlanta. He would walk in, and all the strippers would be, "Terry, how are you doing?" This one woman had this amazing trick. She could twirl her little tassels, and she could twirl one this way, and the other one she could twirl that way, and then reverse. Well, she comes over, and she's doing this, and I'm dying, and she's putting them near my face, and I'm thinking, holy Christ. Then she goes over to Terry and does the same thing. And she leans down and she says, "Hey Terry, sweetie, how's the kids?"

"They're doing fine."

She said, "Did the little one, did she do all right? Did she get over the flu?"

"Oh yeah, she got over it. It only lasted a couple days."

Terry showed me Atlanta in this way I would never have seen. Then he started telling these stories about growing up in the mountains of Georgia without electricity, and I said, "Terry, have you ever written any of this?"

He said, "Conroy,"—he always had this voice of God—"Conroy, I'm a journalist. I can do 250 words about any subject on the earth, but I can't do 251."

But he wrote a short story that I thought was hilarious, and I got him an advance for his first novel, *The Year the Lights Came On.* Terry did well with that book. It started his career. Eventually he made enough money where he quit journalism and just wrote novels.

I've tried to encourage novelists wherever I found them. All writers I've ever met need that voice, not only to console, but that can encourage, that can drive them on. You know, the good coach, the teacher. I've always liked the cheerleader role. I like encouraging people. I enjoyed it when my teachers were cheerleading me, and there's something about being around me that makes it seem easy for other people. If a doofus like me can write a novel, anybody can. I have a sort of sad sack, lackadaisical movement into the current of life of anybody I meet; everybody thinks they can write if such a doofus like me can write. I've had this effect on people; I truly have. They look at me, I'm dressed in a Mr. Hefty bag, and my shoes are made from the pelts of rats. I stumble around and tell a lot of jokes, I make people laugh, and no one can truly take me seriously when they meet me. So what they do is say, my God, if he can write books, what about me?

❧

Governor Carter gave a party at his mansion on West Paces Ferry for all the writers and journalists in town, and there weren't that many of us. He didn't permit drinking, you know, so he was watching all these writers go into delirium tremens. This is when I heard high heels clicking down the marble hall, and I turned around, and a beautiful, luscious Anne Rivers Siddons turned the corner with her Princeton husband, the very dapper Heyward Siddons, wearing his little bowtie. I met them that night. I remember those heels clicking down the hall, and there she was, in full flower. She was from outside of Atlanta—Fairburn, Georgia. Her father was with one of the big law firms, Hansel, Post, Something, and Rivers. He was the Rivers, and you know what that means. High cotton. It was rare for a lawyer like this not to raise his child in Atlanta. He wanted to raise Anne in a small town.

And talk about a good-looking woman. Goddamn, Annie Lou was a doll baby.

Annie has been great since the day I saw her turn the corner at the governor's mansion until today. She has not said, that I know of, one mean thing to anyone. She was a magnificent cook, fed us all, lived in a beautiful house, which none of us did then. Annie and Heyward's was this post of civilization that we could always go to, were always invited to. They were an adult couple who were running a household that looked like a household, as opposed to the rest of us who lived in the inside of potato chip bags. If they ever had arguments, I never saw it. If they ever got mad at me, I never knew it. Those two people brought great kindness, great times of happiness into my life.

Paul Hemphill, the journalist from Birmingham—I met him that night. I met all the writers. Jim Townsend was there, who became very important in my life. He was the founder of *Atlanta* magazine, a mill town boy from Lanett, Alabama, and a brilliant mill town boy, had to drop out of the University of Alabama because he did not have the money to go there; came to Atlanta, founded *Atlanta* magazine, and founded the concept of a city magazine. He was an extraordinary drunk, but a fabulous personality, died at forty-seven; one of my first eulogies.

Annie was mostly writing stuff for *Atlanta* magazine when I met her. Jim Townsend said, "Annie only writes frou-frou." That's how women were treated. I told her, "Annie, it ain't frou-frou; it's terrific writing. You need to let me put a hickey on your neck, but you also need to start writing novels, because you are good." Annie and I grew up together as writers; we all kind of helped each other. We were nice to each other; we weren't mean. We weren't trying to hurt each other much, or trying to kill each other much.

There were certainly jealousies that developed. Paul Darcy Boles was the one novelist in town when I got there, and we were all friends with each other. Now, Paul had some unfortunate affectations, like wearing an ascot, smoking cigarettes in what looked like a French film director's cigarette holder, and he wore a beret sometimes. He played the writer role great, and it was colorful for me. He was generous to all of us. I came across a book of interviews of young writers on the way up; it had one of Saul Bellow, and Paul Darcy Boles is one of the eight writers interviewed. He must have been hot as a firecracker at one time, and something must have happened to Paul's career. It all seemed tragic by the time we got to Atlanta. With a literary career, there are few ways to go right, and a million ways to go wrong.

Then Annie and I sort of made it. I came out with *The Great Santini;* her first book was terrific, *Heartbreak Hotel.* Suddenly we were pulling up a little bit from Paul. No, we were pulling way up from Paul. And when Paul saw good things happening to the rest of us, he had trouble with it.

So one night Annie gave a dinner for a book of Paul's that had just come out. Annie had just signed a big contract, had recently been in the newspapers. She got extraordinary book money for her time and place; she really did. But Annie was so nice we all loved it when good things happened to her. One thing I *can* do is be happy for other people, and she could not have been nicer about it or prettier or just fun to be around. She is a completely loving woman. She never played the bitch goddess once. So Paul is sitting there smoking his little cigarette in a cigarette holder, wearing his beret at the dinner table. Cliff and whatever stupid girlfriend he had at that time were there; we were all celebrating Paul's book.

We had just started eating this wonderful meal, and Dorothy, Paul's wife, looks over and says, "Pat, have you read Annie's new book yet?" And I said yeah, I did. "Well, what did you think?" I enjoyed the hell out of it. She says, "My colleagues thought it was trash. Thought it wasn't worth the paper it was printed on."

Okay, Annie is a sensitive soul, and she's now getting weepy over there. So I look over, I see her, and I said, "We've all got our opinions, Dorothy, but a lot of times we don't share them with a woman who is feeding us dinner. That's just an old rule of humanity, you know what I mean?"

Annie leaps up, crying, races out of the room, into the yard to kill herself in Peachtree Creek. Paul is doggedly smoking a cigarette. Dorothy couldn't stop. She is the mouthpiece that night, and she said, "Pat? My Paulie, he doesn't understand how you and Annie can just sell yourselves out for the most money, how you cheapen your art by being for sale to the highest bidder. And you know what they call a woman who sells herself for the best price."

I said, "My God, Dorothy, you must mean a whore, that Annie and I are whores."

She said, "Paulie writes literature, but y'all know that. What he and I both just don't understand is how you and Annie can sell out to the highest bidder of your work, when what is important is literature. Can you give me an answer, Pat? Why do you sell out to the highest bidder?"

I said, "Look, Annie and I got together one night, got drunk, and before we made love, I said, 'Annie, Annie, should we write works of literature? Should we write works that will never die or should we write trash so we can make money and feed our friends, our friends who write literature, and get them drunk with our liquor? Which would you rather do?' Annie looks at me and says, 'Pat, trash. Pure trash.' I said, 'Should we sell out for countless millions?' And we both came to the conclusion we didn't want to be a loser like Paul Darcy Boles. We wanted to be rich losers."

"Well, my Paulie has too much integrity."

I said, "We discovered that we had no integrity whatsoever. We lacked integrity. We're simply whores. And we admitted that, we drank to it, we got drunk based on the fact that we're whores out for the money. Fuck literature in all its forms."

We were great friends with Paul Darcy Boles, but your friends are the ones you need to fear with your body and soul from the time you get up in the morning until the time you go to bed at night. This is a rule. It's a rule of life and one that I have gotten very used to. Another rule of human existence: If you ever lend anybody money they hate you for the rest of your life. Paul borrowed a zillion dollars from Annie and me. What we both found out tickled us: if you loan somebody money, they not only don't pay it back; they hate your guts. That was a surprise to me. Whenever I lend people money they never pay me back and hate me for the rest of my life.

Paul was sued for plagiarism, and he had a two- or three-year trial in which I appeared over and over again. He was hired by a rich woman named Hazel Cartin with an Indian background to ghostwrite a novel for her. He did it. Then when he came out with his next novel, she sued him for plagiarism. Like there was a fat sheriff in the book he wrote for her, he has a fat sheriff in his book, so it was a mess. Paul had no money, and he was the worst witness that ever lived: a proud, vain man. But I was in and out of court and giving depositions for I think about three years for that.

The issue was: If you ghostwrite a book for someone else, can you later be sued for plagiarizing your own style? For resemblances between the book you wrote for hire and those under your own name? My role as a professional writer was just saying that Paul was innocent, that there wasn't anything to the charge of plagiarism. Anytime in Atlanta there was a freedom of speech case or a book being banned, I would be called. I would testify sometimes in federal court, sometimes in state court, with my typical liberal bullshit with which Conroy could knee-jerk his way from home all the way to the courthouse. I was willing to do it, and the lawyers got to know that.

Paul got to be so poor during that trial trying to pay his lawyers, that's when I ended up giving him money; Annie gave him money. Okay, Paul wins the case. But what does a rich woman do when she loses in court? She appeals. This dragged on, and Hazel Cartin and her lawyers were upset at the time it was taking, so they started this legal procedure to get the judge who had heard the case removed and replaced by another judge. By then, Paul and Dorothy Boles, after three years in court, are impoverished—I mean utterly, completely, totally. They have nothing. They had a hearing coming up, and their lawyer who hadn't been paid wouldn't go in with them. They had no one to speak for them, they were desperate, she was crying, Paul was near tears, and they begged me just to go with them. So I said sure, I'll be glad to do it. I said, "As long as you two promise me one thing; you'll shut your fucking mouths and not open them," because they were the type of people who had a tendency to race over and nah-nah-nah-nah at people, and strut and dance.

So anyway, I go downtown, Hazel Cartin is there, and she's got a very good law firm representing her. I think they had two of the law firm's founders, and I seemed to notice a lot of assistants. Like, three people, one of them was a young woman working feverishly, and everybody's writing down something.

Well, the judge who was accused of not doing his job fast enough, not coming to judgment quick enough, he has to come out and sit in a witness stand. You did not have be a novelist to know that this was one very pissed-off judge. He is looking at Hazel Cartin and her lawyers with a hatred he didn't even try to hide. This is embarrassing him in front of his colleagues, embarrassing him in front of the stenographer he knew very well, the officers who ran the court. This just humiliated him. So I notice this; I take this in. Meanwhile, another judge who I knew from just being around Atlanta came out to preside over the hearing.

Hazel Cartin's lawyers have an hour presentation: The judge is incompetent; the judge did not understand the importance of the case; the judge has had plenty of time; the judge had plenty of input. They've put in so many hours of legal work; they've sent him documents; they've sent him proof; they've sent him legal briefs. They make a huge, huge deal. I'm just watching. I have no role, I'm just observing this, and it's interesting to me. It's an important case because if Paul loses, writers everywhere who get jobs ghostwriting are going to be troubled.

It goes on, it goes on, and finally they rest. The judge looks out and says, "Mr. Conroy, do you have anything to add to that?"

Well, it surprised me, but since the judge asked me I stood up and said, "Your Honor, the writers of Georgia and the writers of America understand how important this case is, and we are very happy that the judge who heard it is taking his time because we understand that his decision is going to be important for writers all over this country. So the more time he takes, we feel the more he's studying the case, familiarizing himself with the legal background, and especially with plagiarism. The American Authors Guild has sent money to Mr. Boles, PEN has sent money to Mr. Boles to support his legal case, and we are in disagreement with our esteemed opponent. We have no problem with the amount of time it's taking, because of the importance of this case to the writing community of America."

Well, I sit down. This judge immediately rules for us. I don't even think my behind scraped the seat before he ruled for us. Okay, my two idiots, Paul and Dorothy, get up, and they both scream out loud, *ah-hah-hah-hah,* and then they go racing over to Hazel Cartin's lawyers, and they're sticking their fingers in their faces, you lost, you bastards lost, you motherfuckers lost, you lost, did you see it, you lost, we showed you. And I'm going shut up, shut up, will you shut the hell up?

Then I'm walking out with the Boleses, who are just so horrible. They could not have reacted worse, and they're still talking over my shoulder as I push them out the door, when one of the other lawyers comes up to me. "We had no idea that you were a lawyer, Conroy; no idea that you went to law school. We could have you arrested for impersonating a lawyer."

I said "You can't do that. I didn't impersonate an asshole."

~

All this time I was trying to get Bernie and his wife, Martha Schein, to move to Atlanta. Bernie had gone to Mississippi and did valiant work there during desegregation. He was the first white principal of this school in Clarksdale, Mississippi. One of the guys he admires most is Mel Leventhal, who desegregated Mississippi schools and gets no credit for it now because he's a white boy. He was also married to Alice Walker. Anyway, Bernie got fired from his school in Mississippi like I did from Daufuskie, because he believes in integration and he tried to make it work, and those people ate him alive. Bernie actually did heroic work there, and then he came to Atlanta about a year later when I got him a job at Paideia. I got Bernie and Martha both a job at Paideia, the hippie liberal school where my kids went.

Cliff Graubert was a bachelor then, and I was a cook, so we had boys' night out in Atlanta. Bernie would come, and Terry Kay, and the two California boys, Zach Sklar and Frank Smith, who had taken Herman Blake's sociology class on Daufuskie Island. We would meet once a month, we'd talk, we'd laugh, we'd have fun. Cliff would not let us talk about any of our children. That was the only rule, because he didn't have children. So Terry Kay would start, he'd talk about his son scoring thirty points in a basketball game, and Cliff would say, "Who gives a shit? It's boring. I don't care. I don't care that you have kids. Fuck it. That's off-limits. We're not talking about your fucking children." Naturally, we all have children, and Cliff doesn't get married till he's ninety-eight. Then he has two children, and of course, I know their report cards each semester. Anyway, we would run our mouths, and I would cook.

I got into cooking when Barbara goes to law school, then she turns to me, I think her first day or something, and says, "By the way, you're responsible for the evening meal. I'm not going to have time; I'm going to be studying." I'd never cooked an egg. I had not. But I said okay. It was the time of women's lib and *Ms.* magazine. We had just come through the civil rights movement in the South; I believed in everything that represented and had a small, small part in it. When I heard about women's liberation, it seemed like the next phase of modern life, and I found it interesting as hell. So I was one of the first subscribers to *Ms.* Magazine, reading these very bright, pissed-off women. Everything they complained of men doing, I did; everything they complained of men thinking, I thought. Everything they are talking about, I am guilty of. I didn't help out with anything in the house, didn't help out much with the children. I thought that was a woman's job. Mom had raised us where the boys mowed the lawn and took out the garbage; the girls washed the dishes. Then the Catholic Church was very one-sided for the boys. So the magazine had a great effect on me, and I said, "Uh, oh." I was all for women's lib, and I had to prove I was all for it, which I hated. Barbara knew I didn't know how to cook, and she had that little Barbara mischievous look on her face. She got a lot out of that change in the '60s. I didn't become the house cleaner of the month or anything like that, but I became the cook eventually. I certainly thought it was a fair thing for Barbara to ask, so I became a good cook. But whether it made me a better human being I'll never know.

My mother had been the worst cook on earth. We had Italian night once a week, and I used to hate spaghetti and pasta. Obviously she did not know how to make pasta because she would boil it up, possibly for hours, put it in the colander and the colander would look like an octopus. It was in a hunk with arms hanging out of it. She would tell me or Carol, "cut the pasta." So we would take this huge thing out, put it on a cutting board, and we'd slice it into nine, ten, however many kids we had. We'd throw wedges of pasta on our plate, and Mom would have warmed up whatever crap spaghetti sauce was going around, and that was Italian night.

What I did was I went down to Cliff's bookstore; I said, "Cliff, I got to cook meals now, and I don't know how to cook. Do you have a cookbook section?" He says sure. I said, "You know any cookbooks I could get?"

He said, "Yeah, I hear Escoffier's good." So I go to this thing, I find Escoffier. He says, "I hear that's the best there is." I think, great.

So I went home and started reading Escoffier. And Escoffier says, in the first pages, if you do not make proper stock, you should not eat, so I call Cliff and said, "What's stock?"

"How the fuck do I know?"

I call Bernie, "What's stock?"

"I have no fucking idea."

I call Annie Siddons, and she told me. I said, "You've got me breaking bones, roasting bones before I even begin?"

She said, "Well he's teaching you how to make the best stock."

So I spend days. I'm breaking bones with hammers and axes out of the basement. I'm roasting the fucking bones. I'm doing all this bullshit. Anyway, I started making soups and sauces and these chicken dishes and lamb dishes and veal dishes. I had access to that because I lived in Atlanta. Barbara goes ape shit. She thinks this is the best fucking food she's ever eaten, thinks I'm a natural. I never received such praise for anything in my life. So that was how I first got interested in it.

And of course, I did not know I had started out in the hardest cookbook on earth. I finally, later on, took my first cooking class. Nathalie Dupree had become famous in Atlanta because she started a restaurant in Covington. I had gone out there to eat a couple of times, and it was a really good restaurant. I heard she was doing a cooking class, so I ended up taking that. She was eccentric, neurotic, but so is everybody, and I thought she was a good cooking teacher. I enjoyed her stories; I always love it if somebody can tell me stories.

Cynthia became Nathalie's first producer of her public television show about cooking. It was very big in Atlanta and Georgia, and I think it started Nathalie's career. Nathalie knew Cliff by then, and would come to all the parties at Cliff's store. Cynthia was young, maybe twenty-four, and somehow fell in love with the ancient Cliff Graubert. They got married in Rome after I moved there. Nathalie was the matron of honor, and I was the best man. Annie and Heyward came over and went on the honeymoon with Cliff and Cynthia through the hill towns of Italy. That's where Annie wrote her book *Hill Towns,* which everybody had great problems with except me, because I didn't mind her writing about me. I thought it was great. Anne's got this wicked part of her that I love.

Nathalie Dupree called me up and wanted to sue Annie. She's crying and said, "Have you read her new book?" Yes, I have. And she said, "Did you see what she did to me?" Yes, obviously you were Yolanda. She said, "My lawyer wants me to sue her." I said, well, have fun. "He wants you to go into it with me."

I said, "Nathalie, if I sued a fiction writer for using the quirks of other people, who would be the greatest hypocrite in the history of the world? Yes, you're right, it would be me."

Then I told her, "I didn't know it was me at first, Nathalie," but here's how good Annie is. I started reading it, and I said, "You know, I know this son of a bitch. I've met this son of a bitch somewhere, somehow. I know who this cocksucker is, and if I just concentrate, I'll figure it out." I kept reading and I said, "My God, it's me."

When Annie got a Lifetime Achievement Award at the Hoover Library in Alabama, I introduced her for that, and I told them about *Hill Towns.* "I'm Sam Forrest," I said. "There's no question about it." I said, "And in it, I am a fat drunkard who does not bathe. But I'm an artist. Annie herself is a beautiful, winsome ingénue, and naturally, the old, unbathed drunkard wants to have carnal relations with her as my character tries to do. And as he is fumbling and mumbling and cartwheeling his fat body over the lithe, beautiful body of this maiden from the South, he finally passes out on top of her. Poor Conroy, in his one lustful appearance in world literature, cannot get the job done."

Years later after I published my cookbook, I get the phone call from Nathalie, she's crying, she's weeping, and she's going to sue me. I said, "You're always suing people."

And, "You wouldn't sue with Anne."

I says, "Wouldn't I be the biggest hypocrite if I sued somebody for basing a character on a real human being?"

You know, "You used my real name."

She was upset about the whole thing. She thought I had pilloried her, mocked her, made fun of her. She didn't understand that I was making her into a character. There's always an element of elegy anytime I put somebody into a book. Because you have noticed someone; they have distinguished themselves in the world you are creating. Whether good or bad, whether foul or fair, they are somebody. I also know that when I write about people, I have a large capacity for love for whatever reason, and that is also part of why I'm writing because I love them and they are part of my canticle, whatever that is. They are a part of my litany to the saints, however that comes out, and I try to be true and follow that wherever it takes me.

I said, "Nathalie, it's the nicest thing anybody will ever write about you."

Well, she started getting phone calls from people who'd loved it, and she has forgiven me. Now she simply tells my wife, "I must give you the name of my plastic surgeon. You've got to do something with those eyes before you go out on the road again."

Cynthia and Nathalie did several cookbooks together, and I wrote an introduction for the one that won the James Beard award. When they won, Cynthia said, "Now I know what it means to feel like Pat Conroy."

I said, "You mean, suicidal?"

～

When I was a young writer in Atlanta I wanted to meet Jim Townsend because—if I had been younger I would have met the great editor Ralph McGill, but Ralph was dead, so Townsend is what was left, and we meet for drinks after work, and Townsend says, "You know, Pat, you're going to hear some rumors about me," and I said "What's that, Jim?" He said, "A lot of people are going to tell you I'm an alcoholic."

I said, "Jim, a lot of people told me that already."

He said, "Well yeah, I know, but I used to be an alcoholic."

I said, "What happened?"

He says, "I found out that if I just drank Brandy Alexanders it wouldn't happen."

I said, "What wouldn't happen?"

He says, "I don't get drunk. It's the milk, it absorbs the alcohol, and you don't get drunk. It's amazing."

I said, "Jim, you ought to write an article about that. That could save a lot of people a lot of trouble."

He said, "Yeah, I may do that." Then he said, "Conroy, let's get down to business. I don't want to talk to you about your writing; I only want to talk to you about one thing." And then he asked me this question, "How many Miss Americas have you slept with?" I looked at him like he was crazy. He says, "Well, don't answer that, it may be a private thing. I've only slept with three."

He was usually too drunk to edit, but when he was sober he was good. Jim's achievement, it wasn't that great, but it seemed to be at that time, because Atlanta seemed to have almost nothing on the literary landscape when he started *Atlanta* magazine.

I knew he was troubled because I'd have to pull him out of bars. His wife would call me, "Jim's drunk." I'd say, "What bar?" She'd tell me the bar, I'd go, ask for his bill, and sometimes it would be for thirty drinks, and the bill would be hundreds of dollars. I was actually carrying him out on my shoulder. I was younger then. And he'd be telling the women as he passed by which one of them he was going to come back and fuck, and of course their boyfriends were leaping up, and it was a nightmare. It was just a nightmare. He was bad, but like many drunks, he could also be utterly fucking charming. He could call you the next day and charm you. He had a series of people like me; I mean there were hundreds of us. So Townsend got away with it.

I was friends with two journalists in Atlanta, Joe Cumming and Bill Emerson. Joe is the one who interviewed me for the Daufuskie story for *Newsweek.* He became one of my best friends in Atlanta, and through him I met Bill Emerson. They had sort of grown up together as journalists. These two guys were going to be writers, they were going to get out of journalism and write novels, and of course it never happens.

Bill was the editor of the *Saturday Evening Post* at about that time, and one of the funniest sons of bitches I have ever met. He was also an infamous womanizer. He would say, "My God, Conroy, there are muffins in that room. We must go in, and we must warm them as they deserve." At one party, the women's bathroom was so crowded they sent a couple of women into the men's. Emerson comes in and goes, "My God, there are muffins in this bathroom." He chased secretaries, and they would run away from him. He would shout out, "My God, have they never encountered heroes before?"

As he was getting old, he would say, "Conroy, my dick's not working very well, but I read about this amazing breakthrough where you get this operation and you can pump your dick up like a tire and you get a hard-on that lasts for as long as you want. You just keep pumping that little thing up. Since you're the only one I know making any money writing, I said I'm gonna go to Conroy and have him pay to give me this operation. Then I said, nah, I'm not doing that. I'm not an idiot."

I said, "Why not, Bill? I'd love to pay for it."

And he said, "Nah, you're the type of son of a bitch that would go around saying I paid for Bill Emerson's dick."

Once a year we would have a writers' party up at Tate Mountain, Georgia. It's a private enclave, kind of where Buckhead would go to these cabins around this lake. No one knew about it, hard to crack, you had to be a real insider to get there, and both the Emersons and the Cummings came from very good Atlanta families, very good. I, of course, was an Irishman from the Bronx, trying to make my way driving a bus in downtown Atlanta.

Marshall Frady was another journalist I knew in Atlanta. He was dark and contemplative, and he spoke polysyllabically, which I've always liked. We were good friends on the face of it, but it was never a great friendship. It was locational more than anything else. We'd see each other every summer when Joe and Emily Cumming had their house party; we'd meet at Cliff's bookstore for parties. He liked me when I was an acolyte and needed him to vouch for *The Water Is Wide* with *Life* magazine. But when I started writing novels, Marshall had a bit of trouble. His girlfriend Gudrun had read *The Great Santini* and loved it, but she said, "Pat, when I told Marshall how much I loved your book, I thought he would be happy for you. But he took *The Great Santini* out into our backyard and threw it across the lawn."

My career remained unremarked upon by him after *The Water Is Wide,* which he was sent to verify. One of the things I've had to learn about is jealousy in friends, this whole lightning bolt of jealousy going through someone's entire body when they hear of something good happening in my career.

Marshall was always trying to write a novel himself; this is the great and dirty secret of many journalists. One day they're going to sit down for the big one. I encouraged him to write fiction; I thought he had great talent and an eye for the telling detail. I think he tried hard, but it just did not come to him. For the real journalist, it's a difficult step. That journalist's code is hard to break. When you've got a voice you know is not real, and you start quoting people that you're making up or imagining, it's hard for them. It ain't for everybody; it's a hard thing to do. I imagine journalists assume it's going to be easy.

My friend Sonny Rawls, another journalist, used to say, "Conroy, you make up shit."

I said, "Yeah, I do, Sonny, that's why it's called fiction."

And he said, "Well, I'm a journalist. We don't make up shit."

I'm sorry: every kind of writing is hard and difficult to master. When I was in Hollywood people would say, "I'm not a real writer; I'm a screenwriter."

I would say, "Why does everyone shit on screenwriting here? It is an art form. It is hard to do well."

And every man I've ever met has told me they don't read fiction, they read real stuff. "I'm a man of the world. I don't have time for frivolous things like women do, frivolous things like—ha-ha-ha-ha—reading a novel. My God, they also paint their toenails, if you've noticed. This is not the real world of men. This is not the real world of business, or soldiery, or this is not the high practice of law. When we read, we read biographies of great men, great men like us. And when we read, we read about war or experiences in war. We read about politics and what is really going on in Washington."

I read a lot of nonfiction and enjoy every moment of it, but when I hear fiction thrown out like that, when I hear these third-rate minds dismissing it as something that serious people would not even consider doing, it irritates me. It seems to me that fiction is a place you can look for truth that you cannot find in nonfiction. Often you can use real life in fiction like you cannot use it in nonfiction. I think the most honest book written about the Clintons has been *Primary Colors,* and the reason is the author had the benefit of fiction to hide behind.

~

Larry Woods became one of my best friends in Atlanta; a poor kid out of Tennessee. He was a reporter for *Atlanta* magazine, classical reporter, smart, asked great questions. Larry and Dee Woods, when I get to Atlanta, are a married couple when I meet them. Larry was hysterical and witty and attractive and fun to be with, and so was Dee. They had a bunch of kids I adored.

Larry also slept around as much as anybody I have ever met, and eventually he'd be coming to my apartment or my house with his new girlfriend. She was always cute and kind of dumb, but I thought, you know, I was up from Beaufort; this is how the big city guys do it. But Dee was cute as hell and a lot of fun, and I always enjoyed their children. They had four beautiful children, and I got to know the kids as they were growing up.

Then Dee calls me up one time and says, "I got a job offer as secretary to a guy that's trying to start a movie company," and she was a school secretary at the time. So she took the job with Ted Turner, and by the time she died she was a millionaire many times over. She started out with Ted when he was headed up, and she went right along. And what she did for Ted that I eventually found out is I think she was one of the most important people in raising his children, and I think all of them know that.

Larry left her eventually, and I think he went to Colorado, or some job took him to Colorado, and during that year he'd call me. I'd go check up on Dee and the kids; the kids were in high school, and the kids were beautiful, and Dee was doing great. Ted Turner by this time owned the Braves and was hotter than shit.

I was working on *The Lords of Discipline* when I get a knock at the door, and I open it, it's the middle of the day, I don't expect anybody, and Dee is in tears and agony, and she gets hysterical. I know just what to say in cases with women like that. I said, "Dee, what's wrong?" She tells me there's a warrant out for her son Larry's arrest. $50,000 worth of stereo and music equipment had been stolen from Radio Shack, and someone in a photo lineup picked out young Larry and his best friend.

So, she was just, you know, "I can't do this; I can't raise kids alone and work."

I said, "You're doing a great job. Don't worry about it. I don't think Larry did it; he ain't that type of kid."

So I said let's go see him. We jump into my car and drive to Dee and what was Larry's house, and he's down in the basement asleep; he and his best friend are sleeping, so I wake him up. And there's Dee, and she's been crying, it's obvious she's upset, so I told the two kids, I said, "Okay, Larry, all you got to do is tell me and Dee you didn't do it, and we're going to believe you, and we're going to have a lawyer who will fight for you, but the important thing is you got to tell us the truth, because the lawyer's going to cost a lot of money, and we're going to testify for you, but I got to know you're telling me the truth because I don't want to deal with liars, and I don't particularly want to deal with thieves. So right now I need you to tell the truth."

Oh, they were innocent, they were innocent, they were innocent, they were innocent, and I said, "Okay, I believe you." Dee didn't believe them worth a shit; she told them that. And so I said, "Dee, I'll go down and hire the lawyer right now."

I started walking out the door, and young Larry said, "Pat, I got something to tell you."

They had stolen every bit of it, and Dee goes crazy, "You're humiliating me in front of my employer; that's the best job I've ever had."

I said, "Dee, please try not to kill Larry. We can't have child abuse added to this."

We were sort of laughing somewhat, but I said, "First of all I've got to take this shit back." So, I had the ugliest car on earth, which I am famous for, and this is a Datsun station wagon. Anyway, it was about buried underneath this material when they finally loaded it all on there and strapped it to the top. It looked like they were going to set up Radio Free Europe with this shit.

So I drive it back to Radio Shack, and I go to the manager, "Sir, I've brought back some material that was stolen from you." They have a cop there, and the next thing I know, I'm arrested. I'm saying, "Sir, I have a reasonable explanation for this, but it's not going to appear so right now, not with handcuffs."

Before he could take me to book me at the station, Ted Turner calls, and Dee calls, and all of a sudden Dee shows up, and I've become a heroic figure in the Radio Shack people's eyes. I am released from the handcuffs and sent off to my home, where I was on probation for the next ten years.

That was one of the ways Ted Turner and I had dealings with each other, but Turner is not a guy who gets close to people, I don't think. Later, accidentally, this is how accidental the world is, I'm staying in Rome, and this is years later. This is three years after *The Lords of Discipline*, and I get a phone call from the Citadel Alumni Foundation. I am the only person who was a Citadel graduate living in Italy that they could find, and they said, "Mr. Conroy, we would not have called you."

You know what I said? "Believe me, I know better than you, pal."

And, "But we have a freshman cadet who has gotten sick in Rome, and we need a Citadel man to go over there and offer comfort to him and the family."

So I said I'll be glad to do it, and it was the hospital where my daughter was born, so I knew it perfectly. I go over there, and there is this poor, sickly kid, and said, "What's your name?" and he said, "Hey, Mr. Conroy, my name is Beau Turner."

I said, "How have you heard of me?"

"Dee Woods works for my father."

Aha, Ted's son. So anyway, I went over to see that kid every day, nice boy. Meanwhile, Ted Turner's second wife almost drove me crazy. She would take me out to dinner, pick us up in a limo—it was embarrassing beyond human belief—and we'd go to some tiny little restaurant. Anyway, she told me every affair Ted had, every humiliation she'd gone through in her life, and she wanted to write a book. She says, "Pat, I want you to write these books with me," and I said, "Yeah, well, I'll have to think about that."

This obnoxious publicist who was traveling with her would grab my arm and say, "I see it now, a shelf of books, Janie Turner in big letters, and with little letters, 'with help from Pat Conroy.'"

I kind of enjoyed all that. And when I got back to Atlanta, Dee called me up; Ted wanted to thank me for helping his kid. So I went up there, and Ted was as uncomfortable in his skin as any man I've ever met. He is also one of the most boring men I've ever spent time around.

Ted was telling me, "I hear you took care of Beau, thanks."

I said, "Well, it was fun, I like the kid a lot, and how's he doing in the plebe system?" because he was just going in his freshman year.

Ted says, "Ah, the plebe system's nothing."

Yeah, I saw it, it's nothing.

He said, "Yeah, people complain about it, but it's nothing at all to go through."

I said, "You know, I'm always hearing that from people who didn't go through it."

~

There were some writers I didn't like. Lewis Grizzard and I did not like each other. He had started writing a sports column for the *Atlanta Constitution*. He's good, and I heard he's interested in coming out with some books. So I invited him over to my apartment and introduced him to a young agent who was visiting from New York. He could not have acted shittier, could not have acted more pompous. I thought he was an asshole. He hadn't taken off at all; he hadn't published a book yet. I caught a gunfighter vibe from him, which I do with males quite easily. There are certain guys who draw back like a gunfighter. A gunfighter walks into town alone. He was the kind of guy who picked up sycophants but couldn't have an equal or a guy he looked up to. Lewis was the first with me who did that. This competitive type is worm ridden with jealously, and they cannot hide it.

Anyway, Lewis started writing these books which were enormously successful among the rednecks of the Western world, and he was always yipping at me. Every once in a while he'd call me up, "Conroy, Conroy, you got to come on down; I got you a date with a stripper at the Gold Club. She's got the biggest tits in Atlanta, and she's waiting here for you."

I said, "Thanks, Lewis, but there's something you don't know about me. I went to college so I wouldn't have to date strippers."

So he said, "Are you turning this down?"

I said, "Yeah, I think I will."

"You're shitting on me; you think you're better than I am."

I said, "Lewis, you got me there; I really do think I'm better."

"You don't fool me Conroy. You don't fool me at all."

He loved that redneck role; he appealed to rednecks in his writings. He really was a redneck, but not as much as he pretended. I wrote a letter to the editor one time saying, "Gosh, Lewis, what a brave man in the South, going after gay people, lesbians, blacks. Such courage. Such a gift for stereotype." And I don't like it when people write gimmicks and pass them off as books.

We had a conflict when Bill Kovach got fired from the *Atlanta Constitution,* which had hired him to make the paper world class. He had been the Washington bureau chief for the *New York Times,* and he was considered to take over the editorship of the *New York Times* when Max Frankel got the job, so as a booby prize he took over the *Atlanta Journal-Constitution.* He was going to make it one of the nation's great papers, and he was doing it. I don't think they'd won a Pulitzer Prize in twenty years; they won two the first year he was there. One of the Pulitzer Prizes was for articles about the Atlanta banks redlining loans—not loaning to black people in the ghetto but loaning to all white people who walked through the door. That didn't go over with the white power structure in Atlanta at all. Ultimately Kovach quit, because they would not let him do what they promised him he could do, to make it a great, great newspaper, not only in the South, but in America. That's what he came down to do. Lewis Grizzard was on the side of the newspaper, and I was on the side of Kovach and people trying to change the paper.

I've got to admit I did love Lewis's titles: *Shoot Low, Boys—They're Riding Shetland Ponies,* and *My Daddy Was a Pistol and I'm a Son of a Gun.* When I did the screenplay about Bill Kovach getting fired, I did a parody of Lewis and had him write a book called *Don't Light a Match around Mama—She's Been Eatin' Navy Beans.*

When Lewis died early of a heart attack, the paper called me up for a comment, and I was at my meanest. I should have been nicer, as my father told me. And I said, "Yes, Dad, I learned nice sitting on your knee, and you're right, I should have been a lot nicer, but gosh, I wasn't." They didn't print what I said, so it didn't make any difference.

A woman called me, said, "This is horrible news. Did you hear the great Atlanta writer Lewis Grizzard died?"

I said, "Yes, I just heard that." She would love to get a quote for the newspaper. I said, "Sure, be happy to."

She says, "What did you think when you first heard that Mr. Grizzard had died?"

I said, "The first thing that went through my mind was *Lewis Grizzard Is Dead, and It Couldn't Happen to a Better Guy.*"

She was shocked. "Mr. Conroy, I can't print that."

I said, "Fine, how about *Lewis Grizzard Is Dead, and I'm Feeling Like a Million Bucks?*"

"I can't say that either."

I said, "My gosh, you seem to be having trouble."

So I gave her a few more ridiculous things like that, but none of them made it. My father was appalled. He loved Lewis. He would see him at bars, and Dad would say, "Lewis, I love you way more than I love my boy. I just don't know why." Then Dad would race over to tell me that and laugh his ass off about it.

Howell Raines also wrote for the *Atlanta Constitution* and was my age. I thought we would have a rivalry, which I think we did have, but I thought it would be a healthy one, I thought it would be a good one, I thought we'd be friends for life, and it didn't work out that way. Howell was one of these full-of-himself guys.

His talent as a journalist, which was immense, took him to the top of journalism. What I admired about Howell that I admire about anybody is ambition. I've always liked that, when people wanted to do better, and certainly Howell wanted to do better and did better than most of his generation and left a thousand journalists behind him. I always admired that, he knew I admired it, but he also knew that I had something he wanted.

Howell resented me a great deal because I went to Daufuskie. I had an active role in civil rights, where he had just reported on civil rights. I could never recover from this one. That was such a blow to him. He was supposed to be the chosen one of our generation in the South. He always wished he'd done what I had done, and that struck me as the oddest thing, as though I'd had a plan.

Then I had become a novelist, and I'm not sure one he even liked because he was not the type to ever let me know he liked something. Journalists have that problem. I saw him in England one time, and he took me to a place called Santini's, which I thought was his way of acknowledging something.

I thought Howell had an extraordinary beginning with a novel and a nonfiction book coming out at the same time, and I thought his novel showed real promise. Then the *New York Times* took him away from that. I know he has somewhat always regretted that he gave up to journalism what he thought could have been a career as a novelist. I do not know whether that would have happened. We never know, but he made that choice. He came to me saying he didn't know whether he wanted to be a novelist or stay in journalism. I said, "If you want to write novels, you'll write them."

But the *New York Times* called; they hire him. It was the power; it was the prestige. I'm over at the Old New York Bookshop with Cliff when Howell comes in; he wants to share his good news with his friends. And he is dressed to the nines. I mean he is dressed beautifully. So.

He said, "Pat, Cliff, I've just been hired by the *New York Times*. I've got to tell you, it's different. They just took me out shopping, took me to Brooks Brothers, and bought me this suit, these shoes, these socks, this tie, shirt, cufflinks. They wanted to show me how the *Times* dresses. I've already done several interviews for the *Times,* and I've got to admit, going in there and putting my card on the table and saying, 'Howell Raines, *New York Times,*' is one of the most powerful feelings I've ever had. You can feel the guy collapse in front of you."

I shouldn't have done this, but I did it. Cliff and I are quick. We do this imitation about four or five times until we've perfected it, in front of Howell. I walked into the store where Cliff's sitting down. I staggered into the store, throw down my card, look up at Cliff and said, "I'm Howell Raines, the *New York-fucking-Times.*" And Cliff perfectly goes, "Oh my God, the *New York Times*? I'm fucked. I better give up my business. I've got to move out of town." Howell was not amused. Now, later I would do this every time I saw him. His wife Susan, after their divorce, said nothing killed Howell in the world more than Cliff and me doing this scene of him. "Howell Raines, the *New York-fucking-Times*." And he just, he would die. I mean, you'd see his face crumble.

Howell is one of these people who let fame interfere with their personalities and interfere with their way of dealing with the world. He let himself become a bully. He was a real great reporter, I thought, in some ways a great writer, but that ego was overwhelming. It got him in terrible trouble at the *Times*. It cost him his job at the *Times*. I told him when I last saw him, I said, "Howell, I would drop the pith helmet." When he became editor, he wore what looked like a pith helmet. I said, "Unless you're hunting a rhinoceros somewhere on Broadway, I would not wear a pith helmet. That's just my advice."

He said "It's my style. You know, you have no style."

I said, "That's true, but then I look at your pith helmet, and I don't want to have no style, Howell."

But he got in so much ego trouble. He was such a harrumph-harrumph guy, a pronouncement guy, and I've always hated pronouncing guys. "Well, I talked to Ho Chi Minh only this morning." He was always doing that.

I'd say, "Hey, Howell, what does Ho Chi Minh say to you he's not saying to anybody else?"

And "Ralph Abernathy and I went to lunch today, and I told Dr. Abernathy . . . ," and he's wagging his finger.

It was self-importance and pomposity and flatulence. I would simply tease the shit out of him, and he couldn't figure out why people laughed.

~

When I moved out of Barbara and the girls' house, I was living in an apartment in Ansley Park, 71 Maddox Drive. I began writing *The Lords of Discipline* there. Anne Barrett had retired from Houghton Mifflin, and when she retired, I got this editor named Jonathan Galassi. I called him up, said, "Can you explain what an Italian kid is doing with a Southern boy? How did they arrange this?"

He said, "I've really liked your work, Pat."

I said, "Great answer." He couldn't have had a better answer.

Jonathan had Phillips Exeter; he had Harvard; he had Oxford. He may have had a double major at Oxford. He had everything. He spoke Italian; he spoke French. I envied his education like nothing else. That was the education I would have paid to have. And he was the nicest guy in the world; also an excellent editor with excellent taste. We really enjoyed working with each other, and then I get a phone call from Jonathan that he was accepting a Fulbright fellowship, taking a year's leave of absence from Houghton Mifflin to translate the Italian poet Montale, and he was going for six months to Paris, six months in Rome. I went berserk. I said, "You can't go. You can't do this. What do I do?"

He said, "We'll get you another editor."

I said, "That's not the way I work, pal. I don't like this at all."

I'm yelling and irritated, and so he says, "Pat, why don't you go with us?"

I said, "I can't go with you."

Then I thought, why not? I was divorced by this time, and Maria Margarita and I had broken up, so I went to Barbara, told her I'd be gone for about five months, and promised to do something for her. Later I sent her and her boyfriend on a cruise.

So that's when I went to Paris and had one of the best times I've ever had in my life. I got a hotel room for $7 a night on the Left Bank. Jonathan and his wife got a much nicer hotel than I because he was on a fellowship, and we were there for I think four months, then they went down to Rome. I finished the book up and drove to Rome with Cliff and Frank Smith, who came over, and I gave him the finished manuscript of *The Lords of Discipline* in Rome.

That may have been the happiest time of my writing life, being with Jonathan and Susan. They seemed a very happy couple; his wife, Susan, was wonderful. I had a great time, because they made it that way. I wrote all day every day, and we met for dinner. We ate dinner together two or three times, sometimes more, a week. Susan was doing her dissertation—I think it was on Picasso—and I'd go to museums with her. It was just wonderful to go to a museum with someone writing her dissertation on art, taking me through the Louvre, giving me the history of art. I mean, I couldn't believe my luck. Here I am, poor redneck fucking Citadel-educated Conroy, with two people who both spoke

French, both spoke Italian. I'm thinking, nice education, Citadel. Thanks tons. Susan and Jonathan seemed to be really enjoying themselves then and enjoying Paris together, and I envied that in a lot of ways. As I look back, I envied it too much and gave away my hard-won freedom much too soon when I got back to Atlanta.

Each day I was writing, and with *The Lords of Discipline,* I thought I had finally gotten control of my style. *The Great Santini,* I didn't think I had it then, but when I was writing *The Lords of Discipline,* there were times where I thought, okay, this is good. Life feels great when that happens. I was in Paris when I felt that happen, and it was magical to me. I had a balcony on the sixth floor, an accordion player playing next door. We were the artistes on the balcony. That's where the artistes were put. I've never had such a good time in my life. Paris just lit me up. I had never imagined something like that happening to me, and every Hemingway, Fitzgerald wish fulfillment came true on that trip.

That book came as easily as any book I've ever written. It felt terrific, because these things usually don't come easily. I started with that sentence I've always loved. I'll never write a better one: "I wear the ring." I thought, okay, pal, now you've started to say things like you want to say them. I just absolutely loved that line, and I ended up loving the last line. I loved the lines in between. And I thought, okay, this is under control. I can do things other people can't do, and I can try things that other people won't try. It was a book where I finally felt the writing sounded like what I wanted it to mean. I could finally tell a reader what was on my mind, and I thought it had a completeness that I had lacked before. I thought I could tell a reader what I wanted to tell them in a completeness and an articulateness I had lacked before. I didn't have it, and I couldn't do it, and I struggled to do it, and I would only see flashes of it.

When I first started writing, I didn't have the story, but I was writing as my protest about the plebe system. I did not like the cruelty or abuse that was rampant at the Citadel when I went there. I did not like the fact they lied about it. The whole school lied; the state lied. It didn't happen. They denied it. It was group denial. It all seemed like a conspiracy to me. I was trying to tell the truth of the place and what it is like to go through a system that is unmoored by the cult of masculinity.

When I finished, I then had to prepare for the ram. I had to prepare for the reaction. It was always much worse than I had anticipated. Whenever I'm writing, a form of idiocy takes over me. I say good-bye, I depart from this world, and whatever I write seems to belong only to this other world I go into. So I don't fully understand the impact my work will have until it's too late. I didn't know the Citadel would go absolutely ape-shit crazy when that book came out, but they did. *The Lords of Discipline* was immediately banned from campus at the Citadel. Of course, that meant every cadet would read it. That's all it ever means. It means they made sure that it was read by every single cadet who was alive. But my world exploded around me when that book came out. Instantly I was in a fight with my college. They came out roaring against me, and of course, I had to roar back. I wrote several letters in defense of my sorry ass; I had a great letter-writing career. I'd have to look it up in the *Post and Courier,* what I wrote to them, but it was back in my fiery early days, not like now when I'm this empty husk of a katydid clinging to a tree and waiting for the wind to come carry me off to Jesus.

The best place to write a letter to the editor in the United States is the *Charleston Post and Courier.* They put your whole letter. They do not fuck with you. I remember once I wrote the *New York Times* a letter, which they told me they didn't censor. I said yeah, you censored it, guys. And they said, you know, we reserve the right to edit. I said yeah, here's what I can tell you. If you make it better, you're a good editor. If you make it worse you're a bad editor. If you take out stuff that's important, you're a censor.

My letters to the Charleston paper about the Citadel were funny, and I could always kick their ass, because the Citadel wasn't funny, they weren't witty, they had no answer, their answer was an institutional answer of denial, which never can hold up. Generally the Citadel found out they did not want to go up against Conroy in the press too much. The Citadel said I exaggerated, and I said I exaggerated nothing. I described exactly what happened to my classmates and me in R Company, and we could tell you the names of all the upperclassmen who tortured us. I was once on the Citadel honor court, and I kicked guys out for lying. If the Citadel tells me I'm lying about the plebe system, I will charge them before their own honor court.

When I was interviewed, the reporter would tell me the Citadel said I was a lousy cadet. I'd say, no, look it up. I was a very good cadet who did not make rank because I would not torture freshmen. The Boo told me, "They're looking for somebody that you tortured, that you were hard on when he was a freshmen, and they got frustrated they couldn't find anybody." I said, "That's because there's nobody." He said, "That's what I told them, Bubba. You didn't do that."

Then the Citadel put out that I was a wild man, against all authority, against the military. That is something they were projecting onto me after the fact. I wasn't a rebel at the Citadel. A rebel at the Citadel walked tours their entire time there; they bucked the system; they found ways to go out after taps; they went drinking; they went to spend the night with their girlfriend and sneak back in at reveille. I never walked a tour my entire life at the Citadel, because I had enough trouble just getting through the school. I didn't want to be punished by the school as I was going through it, too.

I believe I lit into some innermost sanctum by displaying the plebe system for everyone to see. I exposed the lie that was told by the Citadel, that there was no hazing allowed, it was against the law, it's strictly forbidden to haze the freshmen. They said they didn't do it or didn't stand for that or would not tolerate it. This was patent bullshit. But we knew intuitively that we could not break the silence about what really happened in the plebe system. There is something with men and their rituals, men in ritualistic organizations. Skull and Bones at Yale, the plebe system at the Citadel, fraternities everywhere, it's the same. You go through it, and you don't tell what went on. A serious part of the military code is that the worst thing you can do is whine or complain. It's the same with athletics. You play hurt; you don't complain about being hurt. So I broke the code of silence, and they went nuts. I broke a taboo that had never been broken. And the whole system worked on us remaining silent about it. I did not anticipate the power of exposing that.

When *The Lords of Discipline* came out, was it true or was it not was the question. When any newspaper called the Citadel, they would renounce the book and say that is not the Citadel as we know it. Now, the Boo explained to me then that the Citadel wasn't like what I experienced when he came through as a cadet. Mostly the upperclassmen just ignored the plebes as if they were not human beings. I said, "Oh, the agony of that, Colonel. How did you stand it? Oh, what pain. That must have been awful, to be ignored by the upperclassmen. I would love to have been ignored by the upperclassmen." But he said it changed. When he came back to teach, he was absolutely in a state of shock. He could not believe the cruelty that had taken over the plebe system. He was stunned by it.

What happened was, when General Mark Clark became president of the Citadel, they had a problem with American G.I.s during the Korean War being broken by various forms of torture in the concentration camps in North Korea. So he decided to make the plebe system at the Citadel the toughest in the world so we would not break if the North Koreans got a hold of us. He wanted to make the whiners quit, to get rid of those guys. The Citadel couldn't be like West Point, where they had the smartest cadets in the world, so his claim to fame was going to be the Citadel had the toughest men that came out of it. And here's also how the ego of the Citadel answered Harvard and Yale and Princeton: they're a lot smarter than we are, but we can beat the shit out of them. If you survived the plebe system at the Citadel, that was going to be a mark of honor and glory that you would get from nowhere else. That was our way of making it through the world. We can kick the shit out of them. It all came down to the mystique of the Citadel man: We are tough; we can take anything; we can do anything. Of course, young men loved going along with it; you know, we're going to be the toughest. The tragedy of it is, once that cruelty begins, then the next test of the plebe system is putting the next kid through something worse than what you went through. That's how it built up into something absolutely ferocious. When I went through it, it was out of control, and it continued to be out of control.

General Clark came in I think about 1954 and left when I was entering my senior year, so I was there in the full blossom of his plebe system. Naturally, when Conroy went, it was at its worst. It was just my great good luck and God watching out for his favorite child. But the older graduates, who had not gone through anything like that when they were there, they thought I was some kind of psychopathic liar that made this stuff up to hurt the school. They thought I was a lunatic who had completely invented this nightmarish world, this bizarro theme park where cruelty ran rampant. They said what I wrote about the plebe system was all lies. It wasn't lies; I was writing journalism when I wrote about the plebe system.

What that was to every Citadel graduate when I wrote that: a betrayal. What was *The Great Santini* when I wrote that: a betrayal. When I wrote *The Water Is Wide,* that was a betrayal of these Southern values I felt were horseshit from the time I was a little boy. When they say betrayal, I always recognize the sham words, the made-up words used to silence. It can come from anywhere, but it's always to silence. So whenever I hear the word betrayal, I hear censorship; I hear do not write; I hear you are breaking rules; I hear the Catholic Church; I hear the Jim Crow South; I hear the Citadel; I hear the Marine Corps rules on base. What I hear is you cannot write this, this is sacred, and when it is sacred you cannot enter that cathedral; it is forbidden. And everything in my body revolts against that; everything in my soul is completely repelled. I've always fought that kind of censorship. "You can't write about this. You can't write about that." Anytime I hear that, it irritates me badly enough to make me want to write about it. When people say don't, something in me says full speed ahead.

One time my sister Carol said, "I hear you're writing about me in this new book." Yes, I am. "You can't write about me; I forbid it." Fuck you, I'll write anything I want. I don't ask people's permission, I'm sorry. "I refuse to give you permission to ever write about me in any way, shape, or form." I said oh, I didn't hear myself asking for permission.

And I said, "Carol, no one tells me what I can write about, and I don't care who it is. They do not tell me that."

She said, "Well, I demand that you take out whatever you based on me."

I said, "You can demand all you want. But I'll write what I want."

I said the same thing to Joyce Maynard, when I met her. She always asked me if she should write about her relationship with J. D. Salinger. I said, "Write about anything you want to. Never let anyone tell you what you have to write, what you should write, what you can't write, or what they'll read, otherwise you'll drive yourself crazy."

In the world of literature I don't like bindings; I don't like handcuffs; I don't like readers who point and say you cannot go there; you are not allowed to go there; you're not free to go there; that is off limits. I hate the limitations anybody tries to put on the world of literature. I imagine this came from great English teachers; I imagine this came from literature itself as a lesson I picked up. And then of course my natural sense of rebellion. The Catholic Church told what movies you could not go to, books you could not read; they had lists of banned books. This is the old military brat, the old son of a Marine, the old Citadeler: when I hear the gates crank shut, something in me goes nuts. When I hear censorship coming down, I just don't like it. At the Citadel, I got censored all the time. No, you can't write that, and sometimes it was even no, you can't think that. And over the years and over the thousands of books, I think there are some truths you come up with for yourself, especially if you have the desire to become a writer.

With everything I've tried to write about, my relationship with Mom and Dad, my relationship with Carol, my relationship with the South, my life at the Citadel, I wanted to say something about it, and I couldn't ask them what they thought. Your service is to your art, and nothing else makes any difference in the world, not your love of your mother, not your love of your children. It simply doesn't. When it comes down to writing a book, you are at service to art. And if you're not, do something else. What you always want to be serving is that thing that called you in the first place, that thing that was there in the room with you when you were reading in bed as a teenager, that thing coming off a book, that thing that was stirring, and you could not read this stuff without it stirring something inside you, and it's still stirring, and that's why you're writing.

There is no room for timid souls on our high dive. My writing life would be worthless if I did not write about the things I wasn't supposed to. Telling the truth trumps every single thing. Politicians can talk for hours and not say one thing. This is also true of most people—there's this giant conspiracy of silence to protect your own nest, which is always under attack. So it is the writer's job to say something, to tell the truth. And I am a writer. That's the only thing I've ever been or ever could do well, and I try to tell the truth in my writing.

The Shannon Faulkner story is another highlight in my poor relationship with the Citadel. It began in about 1988 when I was living in San Francisco. My wife used to set up talks; that was her business deal. She would set up the talks and send me off. So I'm going around; I'm talking. She sent me off to one at the Rhode Island School of Design, where my daughter Melissa was a student, and I was talking to a few other schools in New England. I come to one on my itinerary, and it says the Coast Guard Academy. *The Lords of Discipline* had been published in 1980. It was not a big hit with military academies.

I call my wife. "There's been some mistake. You have the Coast Guard Academy for me to speak to."

She said, "Not a mistake. They really want you to come. This captain is dying to have you there."

I said, "Are you sure?" She knew no more about military colleges than I know about fashion schools, but I said okay.

The guy that meets me is in hysterics. He said, "My God, I never knew you were so controversial. I never would have invited you here had I known my job and my livelihood would be in jeopardy."

I said, "Don't worry about it, Captain." I think he was a captain.

This guy told me in agony that the commandant of the Coast Guard heard I was coming, called him up, and said if I said anything controversial he would fire this guy. Even though the guy had tenure, he'd figure out a way to get rid of him. I say, "Relax, pal. We'll have a ball."

He had three cadets with him, this young woman and these two handsome guys, and they were my military attachés guiding me around. I said, "Yes, yes, I always wanted an entourage, and now I have one. I feel like MacArthur."

I didn't have rank at the Citadel, so I said, "Do you all have to do anything I want you to?" They said, "Yes, yes, sir." I said, "Good. I want to march you around campus, because you're very high ranks." So I stood them in line. I would yell left, right, left, right; I did about-faces. I had a ball with them. So then we went to the first thing, which was, I was talking to the plebes. They're all these miserable freshmen going through the plebe system.

And I see girls all over the place. I see about 30 percent of the class is girls, and I am shocked. These boys clubs are hard to break into. I'm going, "My God, let me ask a question. What are you young women doing here?" And they look up, and of course they can't answer me. They're plebes. I said, "Let me just ask you this one question. Is it as miserable and unhappy and hellacious and stupid for you as it was for me when I was a freshman at the Citadel?" Okay, they can't answer, but I saw these imperceptible nods of their heads, going up and down. I said, "Well, I'll be damned. I did not know this would happen."

The woman taking me around was a Chinese American who'd been adopted. Her parents had been hippies in San Francisco, and both died of drug overdoses, so this girl was adopted by another hippie family. And here she is one of the top-ranked kids in the Coast Guard Academy. She was sharp as hell. She said a national law was passed that women were allowed in the service academies, I think it was like '76 or '77, so it happened a while back. Great; I was delighted.

So that night the commandant of the Coast Guard is sitting in the front seat right in front of me. That was one of the best times in my life. I had those kids rocking and rolling, telling stories about the plebe system. It was one of the great times. The commandant comes up to me right after, shaking my hand. He wants to take me down in his helicopter to Washington, D.C., to introduce me to his staff, and he wants me to come back once a year to talk to the Coast Guard Academy. It turned out to be as nice as it could be.

The next day, I have four women from the Coast Guard taking me to the airport, back to San Francisco. So we were talking, and I said to the driver, "What do you want to be when you get out of the Coast Guard Academy?"

She shocked me by saying, "I want to captain a destroyer ship."

I go, "No kidding."

Another girl in the backseat, "I want to captain a submarine, sir."

One wanted to be a Coast Guard pilot. One wanted to be a helicopter attack pilot. I'm thinking I have not met women like this too much in my life. This is amazing.

So before I get on the plane, these women said, "Mr. Conroy, can we ask you a question, sir?" I said sure. They said, "We loved your talk about the Citadel last night. Could we ask you, when the first girl applies at the Citadel, that you support her? She's not going to have much support, and she's going to need all she can get."

I always love being the idiot male. So I said, "Oh, excuse me, girls. You do not understand the Citadel. That will never, ever happen in my lifetime. There are many miracles that could take place in this country; that does not happen to be one. That will never happen because of South Carolina; it won't happen because it's the Citadel. You don't know the Citadel."

And one of them answered me, rather brilliantly I thought, "I beg to differ with you, Mr. Conroy, but you don't understand women."

Now, tell me I did not just fall in love with that particular young woman right then. I was thrilled. I was absolutely thrilled with it. I said, "You know, I can't imagine it happening, but I promise I'll help that girl."

Well, about—Goddamn—six years later or seven years later, I get a letter from those four girls. Said, "Mr. Conroy, we remember your time at the academy. It was one of the best things that happened to us during our cadet years"—or our midshipman years, I think they called it. "And we remember especially your very moving talk about your work on the honor court and how the honor court affected you deeply and how seriously you took it, and we believed every word you said. The first woman, Shannon Faulkner, has applied to the Citadel. You promised us you would help her, and we know as a member of the Citadel honor court, you will keep that promise."

Screams erupted in the house; those Goddamn women will get me killed. But that day I called Shannon and said, "Hi, Shannon Faulkner. I'm Pat Conroy. I'm about to become your best friend."

She had already applied, so I was pretty late on the scene. I had not heard of it, I think because I was living in San Francisco. I got to her too late. I really did. I think if I'd gotten to her earlier, I could have helped her. But already she had learned to throw her own press conferences. The people helping her navigate the very rough shoals of the Citadel were the National Organization for Women and the ACLU, and they just were not the ones to prepare a young girl to go to that school.

They were certainly helping her and bulldogging her all the way. She couldn't have done a legal thing at all without them. But they were making her say and do things that were good for Joan of Arc, not good for getting a girl through the Citadel. Anyway, I call Shannon and give her advice. My advice was, "I would keep my name out of the newspaper any time you can. I would not give press conferences." But by this time, it had taken off where she could not control it. I couldn't even give her advice on it; it was just a free-floating disaster going on.

I fought in the paper with General Claudius Watts, the Citadel president, who wrote a letter saying it wasn't appropriate for women to go there considering the mission of the Citadel. I am not a quiet man, and I got into the fight. In my usual shy, retiring manner, I wrote a letter to the *Columbia State* paper, where the legislature is, coming out for women going there. I got more death threats over that than over anything *The Lords of Discipline* ever brought me. It was a pain in the ass.

The Citadel called me and said, "Please don't come to the campus. It's dangerous for you here."

I said, "Don't worry. I have no plans to come whatsoever."

My life has been explosive this way, with constant explosions going off, many of them self-made, many caused by my reactions to things which I did not have to have. I did not have to react this way. Other people seem to have fairly good lives, and these things don't bother them at all. They don't even think about it. They go to work, go home, go along. I too could have not given a shit. But as Cliff Graubert once told me, "You give a shit. Nobody else gives a shit. But you always give a shit." My friend Mike Jones used to say, "If I ever get in trouble, I'd call Pat. Why? Because he gives a shit." That could be my epitaph: "He Gave a Shit," although I'd like to be the Marlboro Man, leaning against fences, smoking cigarettes, not giving a shit about anything. The writers I admire are the ones who never get quoted in the newspaper, the laconic western type. They say, "Yup" and "Nope" to reporters, and there's a part of me that wishes that had been my lot in life, but unfortunately, God made me a mouthy creature. And I always believed in stuff. It's because I'm the son of a warrior; I'm the son of someone whose whole life was to be sent into battle, waiting to be sent into battle, waiting to take flight upon the bad, the enemy, the corrupt. I'm simply doing what my bloodline has told me to do. Usually it's an instant defense of the underdog, because I grew up hating bullies. But it can be anybody.

So I have a great ability to piss people off. I have noticed this. Until I became the very shy, retiring man I am today in a body cast after he's been brutalized by life, I always kind of said what was on my mind. I've not been one to hold it in much. It's been part of what I've had to deal with. I've told more people in my life to get fucked than I'm comfortable with. In my later years I've tried to shape it more delicately like a Lalique vase, but it is a tough thing. If I see something that's obviously wrong, I will say it out loud, which a lot of people just don't like. A lot of people in high positions just don't like it. But it's always been part of my thinking that I don't care what anybody thinks. I truly don't. It's America.

During all this, the questions kept coming, "Does it bother you that you're hated by Citadel graduates?" No, it doesn't. "All Citadel men say you're not a typical Citadel man. Every one of them says you're not typical, that you don't represent them. You have nothing to do with this school except you graduated from there. Can you tell us the difference between you and other Citadel men?"

I said, "Yes, I can, very easily. I'm richer, I'm smarter, I'm more successful, and I'm nicer."

And they would say, "What makes you think you're so much better than the average Citadel guy?"

"I don't, but there is this: I can out-write all ten thousand Citadel graduates whenever I would like to, every minute of every hour of every day for the rest of my life, and there's simply nothing they can do about it."

I used to love saying things I knew would piss them off, and the school went berserk. They went absolutely berserk. Now, why did I say that? I don't quite know, but it usually comes out when somebody asked me a question that irritates me and they deserve an answer quickly. I call it the Santini part of me. Once I was interviewed by a snot-nosed Ivy-Leaguer who was asking, "What are your ambitions, Conroy?"

I said, "I want to write better than anybody who went to the Ivy League in my generation."

Then he says, "Well, how do you think you're doing?"

I said, "I'm doing a lot better than you."

Now that strikes me as particularly obnoxious and unnecessary and warlike. I don't like that part of me, because I know that comes directly from the fighter pilot, the uncensored Santini underneath.

So I got involved in the Shannon Faulkner controversy and wrote some stinging letters. In this one little letter to the *Beaufort Gazette* I said, "The thing I've noticed about South Carolina, not one South Carolina woman that I know of has stepped forward publicly to say they're behind Shannon Faulkner's entrance to the Citadel. And it occurred to me, South Carolina women would not even be able to vote if it had not been for Northern women. The people who fought for women's rights, it's never the women in the South. And once you get here, you get this poor Southern girl hanging out to dry by the Citadel, being humiliated by this corps of cadets, and you do not hear a single woman's voice raised. There has not been one thing to support her, not one meeting, not one rally to support her in this entire state." Feminism down South, that's always been something that has not stood up to poor loudmouth Conroy's high, high standards.

Good God almighty, I pissed off the girls of the state. I was dog shit with Citadel graduates. I have rarely pissed off people like I did with this one. I got a lot of letters to the editor saying I was an asshole. I was called so many things by so many people. But no one is more used to that. At book signings the Citadel guys would come up and say, "Where's your fucking ring? The Citadel made you return it, didn't they?" and I said no. They said, "We heard you had to return it. They forced you to return it."

I said, "They can't send guys big enough to make me return it. I earned that ring. I keep it on my writing table."

There was a line of Citadel grads at a wedding reception I went to just waiting to tell me in what ways they thought I was full of shit, not a real Citadel man, because I went weak in my soul over humanoids like women.

I'd say, "Thank you very much, sir. I appreciate it. Nice talking to you."

"I just think you're fulla shit, Conroy."

"Thank you very much, sir. It's a pleasure talking to you."

Then all of a sudden younger grads were coming up saying the same thing as the older grads, but here's where I wouldn't take it. The black guys were coming up, and they would tell me I was full of shit. I said, "Oh, please, please let me tell you how the white boys reacted when you guys came to the school. I was there; I was an eyewitness; I knew the first kid. Martin Luther King wasn't called 'nigger' as many times as this kid was. They went crazy when you guys came. And this is the same thing, perhaps worse." I thought it was worse; I did.

But I got calls from Fritz Hollings, who was our senator, and Joe Riley, who was the mayor of Charleston, thanking me for coming out for the women. They had come out for women and caught unmitigated hell from the Citadel alumni, which they both were, and I had taken all the heat away from them. No one even spoke to them anymore about it because everybody forgot that they had actually come out for it, so they could hide behind me. And they were both grateful. Governor John West wrote me and said, "Pat, thank God, you got the pack off our back. And now we never hear about it again because you're taking all the flak. We feel kind of bad about it, but not real bad about it."

It ended up with some women from Beaufort wanting to do something, so they had a rally for Shannon Faulkner which we got about 250 people to attend. TV came in, Shannon and her family came down, stayed at my house. She liked it; it was nice; she got some positive publicity. But I did not get to teach Shannon how to act like someone who is going to the Citadel. The ACLU had gotten to Shannon before I did. I was up signing *Beach Music* the day before she was going in, so I went to a party for her in Greenville, South Carolina, the day before she was going to start at the Citadel. Her father was taking her down. It was like a wake to me. I'd heard Shannon telling her cousins and her friends, "I will not submit to the plebe system. No one makes me submit to anything."

So I take my drink and I walk out into the night air thinking, okay, this will not last long. And I'm followed by her grandparents; all four of them were alive then. They said, "Mr. Conroy, you're upset about something."

I said, "Nah, I'm okay."

And one of them said, "You don't think Shannon's going to make it?"

I said, "Don't tell her that, but no, I don't, because when she said she would not submit. . . . The plebe system *is* submission. It is a complete, absolute submission of self to a system. I don't happen to believe in the system, but I had to submit if I was going to survive. So I did submit. I submitted utterly. I made no attempts to change an ancient culture. And I just worry about Shannon's approach. Also she has no other woman going in with her. I don't know how she's going to survive."

The Citadel was vicious. They even criticized the way she looked. They had sweatshirts with this caricature of Shannon in the background and the Citadel bulldogs crying and saying, "You'd cry too if the only girl on campus looked like this." Or it would say, "The Citadel: 2000 cadets and one bitch."

I think she lasted five days. There was one girl's toilet for her. I'm sure they mocked her when she went into the toilet. The whole thing was not going to work. They didn't even get a chance to work on her, but what they did, they scared her so badly. It's terrifying. It is absolutely terrifying. They scare you to death. I can't imagine being in her situation. She got sick, and I'm sure that was emotional, and went to the hospital.

There was footage on national TV of cadets celebrating, leaping up and down, cheering, and hugging each other when she left campus. They had a riot of happiness which the knobs and the upperclassmen participated in. That they let the knobs celebrate with upperclassmen was simply unheard of. They were cheering the car her father drove when she left campus. It was like a pep rally, cheering the car as it drove slowly through campus with a poor broken-down girl being taken away by her dad in humiliation. It was awful. I went crazy when I saw this.

Shannon was a chunky girl, so all the women reporters said she had let women down because she was chunky. I had to join in that fray, too. This one woman interviewed me, I think she was from Atlanta TV, and you know how these girl reporters are all good-looking and they're in great shape. This woman is saying to me, please explain to us why Shannon Faulkner did not let all women down by going into the Citadel out of shape.

I said, "Ma'am, it doesn't make any difference if you go in shape or not." I said, "One thing I noticed is that fat boys from all over the South were sent there by their parents, and I promise you the Citadel has the best weight reduction system on earth. I knew one guy who weighed 300 pounds when we started out, and he weighed 170 when his mother saw him the next summer. So weight has never been a problem or condition has never been a problem; they handle that extremely well."

And so this pretty young thing said, "Oh, c'mon, if she had been in shape she'd have had a chance. We can be in as good a shape as these boys," obviously indicating her lovely body.

I said, "Oh, you're talking about yourself, ma'am." She said, yes I am. And I said, "Do you know I could break you physically in less than thirty seconds?"

She says, "I doubt that very seriously."

I said, "I'd have to have you get down in push-up position."

So she does it, and she's showing off for her audience, and she said, "How many pushups do you want me to do?"

I said, "Okay, we're going to do this a little differently. You go halfway down," so she goes halfway down, and I said, "Hold it."

In about ten seconds—I don't know if you've ever done this—ten seconds, your muscles start to spasm. By twenty seconds you really start to spasm, and about thirty you fall to the floor.

I said, "Ma'am, you just proved to me you can't even do one pushup, and you're talking about Shannon Faulkner not being in shape?"

She said, "That wasn't fair."

I said, "Oh, do you expect the plebe system to be fair? Where do you think I learned that trick? One thing I know, pick any muscle of your body, I can work on that muscle, only that muscle, and I can have you screaming very soon after we start to work." It's a culture that is not widely understood, and not many people want to understand it.

When Shannon drove off, I drove from Beaufort to her house outside Greenville and met her that day to tell her that her life was not over. She was devastated; I tried to talk her down. I just hugged her and told her she did the best job she could and try not to worry about it. I stayed that night at the house with them and left the next day. And then she found out she was deserted by all those people who had been her champions before. They left her in the lurch with nothing. That's when her mother called me and asked if I would give them a loan for Shannon's education, because they had spent all their money on lawyers. So I said I would pay for it outright, and the reason I'm doing it is I want to tell you all this: the Citadel I believe is a better place than they showed you, so when the story is written I want it said that Shannon Faulkner's education was paid for by a Citadel man, and he did so with pride.

Of course she went to expensive colleges, very expensive colleges. The first two years to Furman, and then switched over to Anderson College in Anderson, South Carolina, where she graduated. Now she's a teacher and a coach.

I wrote a letter blasting the Citadel when she left. They never showed any ability to plan ahead to get ready for something, to even prepare for something. The women caught them off guard, and they had no idea what to do once the court said they had to let them in. They had no clue. I think it took two years for the case to be decided. Wouldn't you think somebody would say, "What if we lose? What is our plan if we don't win in the courts?" There was no plan. So I said, "For a military college, the Citadel shows a surprising lack of strategic planning. Wouldn't the Citadel be great if it could think ahead; if it could come up with a strategy? And where was the sense of honor among any of you? Couldn't the Citadel admire this young South Carolina girl, who for years fought in the courts to get women to enter there? Why couldn't you have lined the campus with cadets and saluted this girl on her way off campus for her courage? Wouldn't it be fabulous if on the day she left, an honor guard of the Citadel lined the streets and Citadel cadets saluted that girl as she left the campus, saluted her for her courage, for changing her school forever? If they'd lined the streets and saluted her as she made her way out of campus, and saluted her for her courage and her bravery and fighting for the rights of women, in a state which does not care much for them. What would that have cost? Instead of making yourself the laughingstock of America, loathed by women in America? What woman wants to send her kid to a school where he becomes a man like that?"

Oh, and I said, "They will keep coming." I said, "If you think this will stop them, think again. They are on their way."

And of course the girls started coming. Here's another thing that shocked the Citadel. There's a little section in our alumni magazine that's been a tradition for a long, long time: when your son is born, on that day you provisionally enroll your son in his class eighteen years from his birthday, and they accept a son that day provisionally. As soon as Shannon Faulkner gets there, and is driven off, the next issue of the magazine came out, and every daughter who had been born in that time was provisionally enrolled by their fathers. It caught the Citadel by shock. They were absolutely stunned by the number of alumni who started provisionally enrolling their daughters. It's now my favorite part of the magazine. They used to have blue flags for provisional enrollments, and with the girls they now put pink ones.

And here's what always happens when places go coed. They always fall in love with the girls. Always. And the Citadel has fallen in love with their girls. They are a real part of the school now, and everybody I talk to says it's improved everything. The teachers say it's gotten a hundred times better, made the school better; everybody says that. And it pleases me; I can't tell you how much, every time I see a woman on the Citadel campus in uniform, it pleases the shit out of me. One of them came up to me at a basketball game, "Mr. Conroy, the women of the Citadel want to thank you for what you did, sir."

I said, "That's great. I'd never do it again, it was a pain in the ass, all these people were going to kill me, but I'm glad you're having fun."

She said, "Mr. Conroy, you don't understand, sir." I said what don't I understand? She said, "You'd be proud of us, sir. We're fucking kicking ass, sir."

But that blasting letter was one of the low points in my relationship with the Citadel. By the time the next set of girls came in September, following Shannon, I went on a cruise. I am away from this; I'm glad to be away from it; I'm sick of it. I just wanted to get away from it all, so I went to China. I had never seen that part of the world, so I did it. Well, I'm walking through the Hong Kong airport, never have been in China in my life, and I look up at a Chinese/English language newspaper. By this time, the next set of girls have come in to the Citadel. I read a headline that says, "**Citadel Sets Girls on Fire.**"

I'm thinking this time the boys have gone too far, so I buy the paper, and what it was, it's an old hazing trick they do where they put some kind of crap on your shoes, then light it, and it flares up. The blaze scares the shit out of you because it goes all the way up. It comes off your shoe and blazes straight up almost to your eyeballs, then goes right down. I remember when it happened to me. It startled me, and I said, "Sir, my feet seem to be on fire, sir." It was done to all freshmen. It was stupid, it was fraternity-boy bullshit, but it doesn't kill you.

So I called the acting president from China. General Poole was the interim president because no one wanted to be president of the Citadel after the girl failed. Watts had said he would never be president of the Citadel when a girl walked through the gates, so he left. He quit, and they had to do the interim thing. I said, "General, I got it. I know the trick. I will tell the newspaper this, it's an old trick, they did it to me, they did it to everybody in my class. But let's get some of these girls through. We've got to get some through this time. That seems to be what we should do. Nobody's going to like you, particularly, General, but at least they're not setting the girls on fire."

This General Poole is grateful to me for the rest of his life. He was replaced that year by General Grinalds, who'd been a West Pointer, a Marine, and a Rhodes Scholar. He was not an idiot, and he was not a Citadel grad, which always bodes better for change. He was a great force in the reconciliation between the Citadel and me, which began about three or four years after that. Registration was down; it became hard for the Citadel to get people to apply there for the next five years because the women in America didn't like it much. The Citadel, like the rest of us, were learning the power of video, and in the late '90s it had not quite gotten to all of us, what we were dealing with. That footage went everywhere, these dumbo boys leaping up and down hugging each other because the first girl had been driven off campus. It didn't go down well with mothers trying to decide where their sons should go to college. My reconciliation with the Citadel began about then. They had screwed up public relations so badly they didn't know what to do. And I didn't know what to do when they called me down there to help.

Then something came up where I defended the Citadel; it was even in a mocking way. They were talking about ending it as a military college and getting rid of the corps of cadets like they did at Clemson, like they did at all these schools. So I wrote a letter and said great, the only thing they have going for them is that they're a military college. Take that away from the Citadel, you have nothing, not that you have a whole lot now, but you at least have that. And I said it seems like the Citadel lost some of its vigor and manhood in its fight against women, and what a shame it has lost all ability to defend itself. Let's figure out what the Citadel does well. So I gave them a defense they could use.

Now, Sandra and I had just gotten married, and I was hated, I got people shooting me birds in the streets in Charleston, and I said just get used to it, they don't mean anything; they just like the Citadel. Annie and Heyward had moved there about this time, to Charleston, and we went up to their house to spend a night, and one of Annie's surprises for us, she had a horse carriage come by her house and take us all on a horse tour through Charleston.

So we're riding down the streets South of Broad when all of a sudden Sandra laughs her ass off. She has a great laugh, and it's uncontrollable; she almost fell off the carriage. Annie and Heyward said what are you laughing about? You know, because we were in this beautiful street, tree lined, and it's a gorgeous golden afternoon, and Sandra's pointing to a newspaper box. They had the headlines and a special thing above the box that said—even I had to laugh—it says, "Conroy defends Citadel."

General Grinalds called me up, and Grinalds used me well. He used me very, very well. He is the one who eased the Boo and me back into the school. He got us honorary doctorate degrees and got me to speak at graduation. They had a parade for us, and I saluted when R Company came by. The company commander was a woman, Rosie Gonzales, who saluted me as she walked by. Then she winked at me. I loved that gesture. Even jaundiced, no-joy Conroy could take some pleasure in that. It all did something important for me. I did not want to be eighty years old and still in a fight with my college. I just did not want that to happen to me if I could personally help it. Nothing looks stupider than an eighty-year-old man fighting with his college.

Then Grinalds suddenly does things like invite me to the president's house on campus. I walk in and say, "Boy, nice house."

He said, "You've never been here before?"

I said not in my whole life, and I was about fifty-something then. I said, "No, never have. Never been invited." This is about 2002, I think, or something like that.

He goes, "My, God."

And I said, "Yes, there's been a bit of a rift."

The Citadel had become a symbol of women-hating, and their drop in applications alarmed them a great deal. In the middle of that uproar, I got Gloria Steinem to go talk to them. Somehow she and I were both getting awards from the Charleston Women's Society. She was getting the major one and I was getting a minor one, for nicest guy of the year with a dick. Gloria's always been nice to me; I'd met her a couple of times before, once at a screening for *The Prince of Tides* in New York. She came up and said she adored the book. I said, "Thanks a lot, delighted you read it. I had no idea you read it. And that's terrific."

And so then she said, "There's one part in your background, Pat, that feminists do not understand at all about you."

I was curious about that, and I said, "Would you please tell me? I can't wait to hear it."

And she said, "In your books, and it seems in your life, you have never once identified with the aggressor."

When she came to Charleston I found out where she was staying and called to ask if she would go over to the Citadel to speak to the cadets. "My God!" she said. "In my world, Pat, that is like speaking to Nazi Germany." She agreed to do it, but she was only going to spend fifteen minutes there at the most, the women had to be there, and the Citadel could never advertise that she went there. General Grinalds saw the value of it immediately and agreed to the rules.

I said, "She wants those women in there," and he said, "Well, you know, they're freshmen, they're knobs and they're plebes," and I said, "They've got to come, or she's not going near there."

He agreed, and she spent two hours talking to the cadets. When I saw her that night she said, "They were wonderful! Those kids were wonderful. They asked the best questions; they were interested; they asked hard questions that were sincere." She actually loved it. And I saw her a couple years after that, and she said, "Pat, how did I never hear anything about the Citadel thing?"

I said, "Now you know the Citadel knows how to keep a promise."

They were dying to advertise that, and I told them they could not because Gloria, you know, she got criticized by the feminists just for getting married.

The cadets told me, the ones I saw later, that she was one of the most wonderful women they'd ever met. She was smart as she could be; she understood their points of view; she tried to show them where she thought they were wrong and might consider something else. Evidently she was just terrific, and General Grinalds was impressed as hell. She's an impressive woman. I mean, she really is, and a beautiful woman, you know, lovely.

After the Citadel made a horse's ass out of themselves in front of the world and Grinalds had me up to give advice, I hadn't talked to them in thirty years, and now I'm now the advice giver. He said, "Well, Pat, what advice can you give the Citadel?"

I said, "For a military school, y'all ain't very good at planning. You'd think a military college would plan for the future, plan strategies. You'd think in a military college one thing a military man could do is make plans for the future. Okay, how does the Citadel need to change for the future? This women-in-the military issue is all over America, and the Citadel is totally stunned when women apply. No one even considered the possibility women could come here and were going to get in. No one seemed smart enough to know what the Constitution says. Oh! And fighting this is going to cost a lot of money for nothing." Then I told General Grinalds, I said, "Here's the next thing I would look out for. Some gay kid—young man, young woman—is going to come into the office and say, 'Hey General, I'm gay as shit and I don't care if you know about it or not.' And General, you may not like that, you may not like hearing it, but it's coming, and you need to prepare for it." Before, they used to get kicked out of school, kicked out that day.

So this poor president says, "Well, I don't think things will go that far."

I said, "I guarantee you you're going to be going that far, or you're going to be back in court against a lawsuit, $16 million in legal fees."

And I mentioned transgender, and he said, "Well this will never," and I said, "Oh yes, it will."

John DeBrosse about five years later called and says, "Conroy, you're responsible for this. I don't give a shit how you try to get out of it, you are the cause of this somehow." There was an ad in the *Charleston Post and Courier* for an invitation to a gay/lesbian/transgender ball they were going to have on the Citadel campus. They invited all alumni, all interested students, all interested cadets. And DeBrosse: "It's you. You did this." I told him about my discussion with General Grinalds, so he says, "I knew it! Conroy, you make me wanna puke."

I said, "Well, John, I was going to invite you to the ball."

"You make me sick."

I said, "And by the way, I'll give you a choice: you wear the prom dress or I will. It depends on, you know, what you're most comfortable with."

And he said, "Conroy, this is why you'll be hated and despised by the Citadel as long as you are alive." He hung up on me.

But there are two transgender Citadel alumni who are in touch with me. Sometimes it's hard to believe what I've lived through since I've been alive.

When I was totally accepted back into the fold was when *My Losing Season* came out. For some reason *My Losing Season* did not offend the sensibilities of Citadel graduates like *The Lords of Discipline* or *The Boo* had. I actually said things I liked about the Citadel in *My Losing Season*. It came across that I loved my team, loved those guys, and loved being part of that. And something happened among the alumni, where I'd go to signings and they'd come in to get a book signed and say, "Welcome back, brother." That was the password of the Citadel. "Welcome back, brother." That book got to them; they could finally see my love for the Citadel drifting through the cracks of that particular book. It totally healed the rift between the Citadel and me.

Then the librarian started calling me up to give speeches every week. I'd say, "Angie, I didn't speak on that campus for thirty years. Now you're calling every week. But I've got to wash my pantyhose; I've got to rotate my tires; I've got to put new strings on my guitar. And besides, you tortured me as a young man. I was brain damaged in the process."

One thing that's been interesting is that after they read *The Lords of Discipline,* a lot of Citadel graduates now feel guilty about how they treated freshmen, that they had run kids off and had gotten rid of kids. I've met a lot of guys who feel horrible about what they did to freshmen now they're adults and they've been out in the world. The question is: Why did I decide to run a kid out of school? How did I get that power, and why did I abuse that power like I did?

Recently I met a guy who tortured me when he was a senior. He goes "Pat, Pat, you won't remember me?"

I said, "Oh, au contraire, Dave, I'll remember you to the day I die. I've always hated your guts."

His poor wife is there, and he said, "Yeah, Pat, you know, I was bad when I was an upperclassman."

"You were not bad, Dave; you were a nightmare. You were horrible. But this is quite all right."

Then he talked about running two of my classmates out of school. Some of those guys would pick two or three plebes and decide they were not Citadel material and just proceed to torture them until they left. They could run you out anytime they wanted to if they decided you were not worthy to be a Citadel man. Dave mentioned two of them, and I remembered these kids' faces.

He said, "I hated the seniors when I was a freshman, and I was going to get back at every freshman I ever met."

I said, "Yeah, that's sort of the attitude. That doesn't make you the Lone Ranger. They fostered this, so you were doing exactly what they told you to do."

We had a nice talk. I sensed some remorse, as I always do with these guys. And he said, "Pat, I never felt bad about it until I read *The Lords of Discipline.*"

I said, "Well, what was interesting about *The Lords of Discipline,* Dave, is I was called a liar by the Citadel my entire life until recently, that I made all that up."

He said, "Pat, you didn't make anything up."

Now he can't understand why he did it and told me he feels bad. "Pat, I was twenty years old. What did I know? What gave me the right to run somebody out?"

Over the years there have been scandals with the plebe system, and *The Lords of Discipline* caused enough of a stir, so there were studies in the '80s and '90s about the plebe system, with recommendations on how to improve it. They formed committees that were trying to tone down the cruelty, put pressure on the upperclassmen not to let it get out of control.

General Grinalds told me, "Pat, we think we have it under control, but as you know, anything can happen at any time in the barracks. You and I both know that. Behind closed doors we can change the rules, but horrible things can still happen in the barracks. We can try to control it, but anything can happen in the plebe system anytime."

I got involved with one hazing scandal that took place in 1991, when I was living in California. The *Charleston Post and Courier* ran an article about four jocks leaving the Citadel in one weekend because they were being hazed beyond their ability to endure. I wrote a letter, "If the jocks are leaving, the plebe system is out of control. When the jocks leave, something is really wrong, because they are going to school for free. Their education is being paid for." And these were football players leaving. The *Post and Courier* named all the freshmen who had left on that particular weekend, but said they did not know the names of the people who allegedly abused them.

By noon that day I had talked to every one of the kids who left. And they told me this story that was horrible. People should have gone to jail. One jock had missed a field goal that would have beaten some big team, some big rival. If he had made the field goal at the end of the game, the Citadel would have won. This kid missed. Okay, he gets back to the barracks, and they come for him: You're too much of a pussy; you cracked under pressure; if you crack under pressure for games, we can make you crack under the plebe system. They spread his legs like a field goal, and two upperclassmen put his head through his legs into a bucket of water and held him there until this kid completely and utterly panicked. They tortured him all night, and he had serious psychological problems from this.

All these kids were traumatized, and they gave me the names of the guys who hazed them in a second. So I wrote this excoriating, red-hot letter and told them if anything happens like that again, go to the police and have these people arrested because every one of those incidents was assault and battery. And I said, "Oh, by the way, you said you couldn't get the names of the cadets who did the hazing. Here they are. I found them easily, and I'm in California. This didn't take great detective work."

The *Post and Courier* would not print the names. That's the protective Charleston society. I said, "That is a problem right there. You put their Goddamn names in the paper and it stops." It just infuriated me. It was awful what they did to these kids.

But they had got the plebe system pretty well under control they thought in the '90s. Then they discovered they were using *The Lords of Discipline* to institute the old plebe system. A guy who was a year behind me in T Company came back as a commandant at the Citadel, and he said what he could not believe is, "They thought they'd done a good job in curbing the plebe system, except there was one sort of underground movement of a group of cadets who were trying to bring back the plebe system as it used to be in the old corps, and they were using your book as an example of how to do it." I said, "Oh great!" They were actually finding out how to do it the old way by referring to my book, which became a kind of textbook to them. It never occurred to me somebody would want to do that. I think you'd read my book and decide never to have anything to do with the Citadel. At least you'd be repulsed by the plebe system. You would not want to be that nightmare in some poor guy's life.

Now the current Citadel president, General Rosa, is definitely serious about curbing the plebe system, because I picked up the paper this year and read where they expelled four or five kids for hazing, and they have now made it an honor violation if a freshman does not report hazing. This is a complete overturning of the honor system, and it means they're really serious about getting rid of hazing. When I was there, if a freshman had turned in an upperclassman for hazing, that freshman would have been gone that night, no questions asked—gone, disappeared. But I think there have been great changes in the military itself, and all these military colleges that used to have horrible plebe systems have changed.

Not too long ago when I had cataract surgery, the nurse asked me, "Are you from Beaufort?"

I said, "No, I got here when my dad was a Marine."

Then she says, "I met my husband when he was in the Army after he graduated from the Citadel."

I said, "My God! What a coincidence."

She said, "Are you a Citadel graduate?"

"Yes, I am."

"When did you graduate?"

"1967."

She says, "That's the same class Pat Conroy was in."

I said, "Yes, I am distinctly aware of that."

And before I could say anything, she says, "You know, my husband really had problems with his book."

I said, "Oh what a jerk that guy was. What a monster. To think he would treat our school like that."

Then she said, "I suddenly got it. You're Pat Conroy aren't you?"

Then the anesthesiologist comes in. He's sort of grumpy with me, and he said, "I just want you to know, Pat, that I am Citadel class of '78, and five of my brothers were also Citadel graduates."

I said, "There was a time I would have jumped out of here and run screaming from this hospital."

And he said, "There was a time when you should have." So we both roared with laughter, and I felt somewhat better as he eased me toward unconsciousness.

～

Cliff told me once, he said, "Pat, *The Lords of Discipline* comes out, and I thought you had it made like no one else. Lots of money, you were single, living in Atlanta. Then you marry she-devil, and you blew it all."

Something in my body must have said, "This is no way to live. You seem happy." Because I went from that to Lenore, something in me must have missed great trauma, great horror. I soon rid my life of that portrait of happiness and joy. What I did is I went from living a nice, unemotionally involved life to a life where every day was like living in the center of the battle of the Somme. What upsets me, of course, is there's something that was natural about all that to me. I seem able to accept more of that than most people can, and I bring disaster on myself. I am attracted to chaos. I move toward chaos. I can pull it out of the air and make it quite chaotic around me. I wanted chaos in some strange, weird way, connected to my childhood. When all hell is breaking loose, I grow calm in that. I can take something great and make sure it's not great. I can take something wonderful, I can damage it in mid-air as it's flying toward me. I can always do that. I can always manage to turn something nice into something hideous. I have an expertise for finding ruin in the midst of splendor. I am the toreador wearing the suit of lights who does all that work with the bull, and then instead of inserting the sword to sever the spine of the bull, at the moment of truth I put the sword in my own spine. I think that was a pattern that I got into my whole life.

Marion O'Neill helped me see that my comfort zone was chaos; I functioned best when I was looking over my shoulder, seeing Dad beating Mom. My instinct was to run into it. The problem is that I seemed to learn very little from having Marion point that out. Marion led to Lenore; that doesn't seem like what Marion was trying to instruct me about. I still made these stupid, impulsive decisions, and then had to live by them. It's a shame I could learn nothing from my former experiences, nothing at all. I will die wisdom-less. I don't think any wisdom has accrued to me yet. On my grave they'll say He Didn't Learn a Thing. The best you could say is I was living a life that gave me material for a writing life.

Anyway, I was dating a lot of different people then, and sleeping with them. I found myself popular with girls. This made me nervous, and I was sick of dating. I hated dating. I'd rather get married and divorced than go on dates.

"Hi. How are you?"

"What sign of the zodiac are you?"

What sign of the zodiac? I just hated dating. I wished I had liked it a little bit more than I did. Somewhere in here, Bernie Schein comes up to me and says, "I've got you a date with the woman you're going to marry. Her name is Lenore Fleischer."

I'd heard of Lenore because of an article I'd written on divorce for *Atlanta* magazine. I described these metaphors for broken marriages. One woman's husband was very proud of his salt water aquarium. A whole wall in the house was this aquarium with beautiful fish and healthy plants. A year after their divorce, it was a wasteland. It was like the Dead Sea. This was the metaphor I found for the death of their marriage. Everything had been allowed to die in this aquarium. Nothing was alive in that tank. Other women had shown me their wedding albums, where every picture of the groom had been cut out and flushed down the toilet.

When my marriage was breaking up with Barbara, our great little dachshund, Beauregard, runs out of the house and gets hit by a car right before I get there. I see it happen. I get out of my car and swoop the dog off to the vet's. We set the dog up on the table, and the vet takes x-rays. I am sitting there talking to Beau. I said, "Beau, you dumb son-of-a-bitch. I told you not to go out that door. You've never listened to me. I've never said one thing you've listened to."

The vet comes back with a picture of Beau's back. His spine is severed. I just crack up, and by crack up, I mean I'm bawling uncontrollably. Then I realized I was a man, and I was a Citadel man, and tears were inappropriate, and that a steely jaw was much more appropriate for the situation. I did not see when Beau crawls over on two legs that are still good. Suddenly I feel him licking my tears. I completely collapse. But when I saw that x-ray of the severed spine, I knew I was looking at my broken marriage that nothing could put back together. That was my metaphor.

Lenore and Alan Fleischer were in this article. I hadn't met her, but I'd heard this story about the time Lenore and Alan had been to family therapy. They were in marriage counseling because Alan was having an affair with a woman named Alice, whom he later married. Lenore and Alan come out, and they're in two cars. Alan always drove a Porsche convertible, so he's in his Porsche, and she's in whatever she's driving. They like cars. He's the type who'll beat her car in with a hammer. Alan does frontal attacks. He beat my car in with a hammer once. A bully, a small guy that's a bully, he'd always come up to me to fight me. My surprise of him approaching me with his fists every time he saw me was he was very small. He was a nice-looking man, but very small.

Their cars were parked in this porte cochere, his in front of hers. So she gets in her car, crying, and straps in the baby. He gets in his Porsche, but comes back out and says, "Lenore, you might as well get used to it. I'm going to marry Alice, and there's nothing you can do about it. She's going to be the mother of your children because I'm going to take them away from you. We're moving away from Atlanta; there's nothing you can do about that either. There's nothing you can do about anything, so you might as well give it up. And you're going to be living with no money."

She's crying, says get out of here, I'm getting out of here, and he said, "I'm not going to let you just drive out."

She said, "Just get out of my way."

He said, "I'm not going to let you just drive out."

So he goes and stands with his arms crossed in front of her car, which unfortunately is parked behind his car when he makes this stand. Lenore starts up the motor and says get out of my way. No, you're going to talk with me, we're going to talk this out. Lenore puts it in gear, guns the motor, and crushed him between her car and his car. He slumps to the ground, and she speeds off. He was in the hospital for a couple of days. I don't think she even damaged his car because his body protected it, but she damaged something internally in him, like one of his kidneys. I cannot remember precisely what it was, but she put him in the hospital for a couple of days. Conroy never got between his car and hers, let me tell you. I learned from that story. But I knew she was marriage material.

It makes no sense. You can make no sense out of it. And when you get to the funny part, raise your hand so I can enjoy the joke too. Every time I think of Bernie saying he's got me a date with the woman I'm going to marry, I want to kill him. Bernie will say, "I liked her tits." That's Bernie's deep assessment. "Great tits." I wish he had said, you know, "My God, she subscribes to the *New York Review of Books,*" something like that. But, Bernie Schein: he liked her tits. Bernie is somewhat defensive about this, but not totally. Bernie says, "Pat, I introduced you to her because I wanted to lie on her chest." And I thought, you enjoy lying on her chest. And so I fantasized lying on her chest while he's lying on her chest, and that's basically the whole story. Girls think of pedigrees and degrees, how your children will look, and how they'll be raised, what kind of houses they'll be raised in, what kind of cars you'll drive, what kind of pearls you'll wear. Conroy thinks of body parts.

When we went on our first date, a double date with Martha and Bernie Schein, Martha thought Lenore was nuts that night, because Lenore told her, "The strangest thing just happened. I looked in the mirror on my way out of the house, and I didn't see anybody in there. I didn't see anybody in my face." And Martha's thinking, "Uh-ho." But Martha didn't tell *me,* she told Bernie, who did not tell me.

Later, when I heard that she looked in the mirror and didn't see anybody, that seemed funny to me. Even later on—*beep, beep, beep*—warning signals flashed from all over the place. But I am sure my attraction to chaos, my attraction to dysfunction—everything was drawing me toward her. The whirlpools had begun, and I would always be dragged toward the center of the worst that is around me. What disturbs me is why did I not learn to control it? Why did I have to seek it out? Why did I have to find it? Even today, I can be at a party, and I'll walk up to the woman who is most troubled, and I will be attracted to her. I can do this anywhere I go. It is like something electric. This ill-led life will skitter across the room to attach itself, even for ten minutes, to another ill-led life. Show me the woman with the saddest story, and I will marry her. Point out a girl, give me a sad story, and I'll leave any woman I'm with and marry the girl with the sad story. Of course, it terrifies me. Marion O'Neill thought I did it because I found comfort in it. I found great comfort and satisfaction and relief whenever I got myself in the worst situation on earth. I can figure out ways to replay my childhood over and over again, no matter whether it's my writing, my relationships, my friendships.

And in a military brat childhood, I don't think we learn about people. You never get to know people in the way you get to know them when you go to school with them year after year. The military brat comes into town, doesn't know anybody, has to make friends quickly with whoever he can, and it doesn't matter anyway because he'll be gone after the end of the school year. With Lenore, I got in quickly, always thinking I could get myself out whenever I wanted, but then I got stuck.

I could tell she was neurotic, and she had a reputation for craziness, which of course would have thrown a normal guy off the track. But crazy—you called my name? Ah, I hear that bell in the beggar's alley, and Lenore was a beautiful girl. There was cleavage involved, and Conroy is a shallow, shallow, shallow shit of a man. Also, she was smart, and I've always liked smart girls. She was a red diaper baby, and I generally liked the communists of the '30s. The people who made *Conrack* were communist, blacklisted during the McCarthy era. I met a million in Hollywood. They seemed like better people than me. You know, the whole thing of mankind being equal.

Also, Lenore was from New York, she was Jewish, and I'd always loved Jews. That is always the group I drifted to because they always seemed smarter than anybody else. I'd go into their houses, and that was like culture to me as I had never seen it. There were real books, there was real music being played. There was a culture. There was almost always a piano, and the kids took lessons. When I took piano, my mother copied down on a piece of paper where the keys are and laid out this piece of fucking paper on the dining room table. She had darkened the black keys, and she said, "Now, practice for an hour."

I said, "Mom, I hit these little notes but I don't hear nothin'."

She said, "Use your imagination."

But in these Jewish homes, I would see real pianos, and the kids could really play them, and that's where I saw the most significant cultural life when I was growing up, within these homes of Jews around the South.

Bernie Schein's mother Sadie was the first Jewish graduate of Converse College in South Carolina, and she was a concert pianist. I used to love to go over there and hear her playing the Hungarian Rhapsody No. 3. Bernie's father was the nicest, the best, the kindest man, the opposite of Santini, sweetest guy, ran a grocery store in a black neighborhood. I fell in love with him for a million reasons. One was, when World War II was coming on, he ordered and stored butter and things he thought would be rationed. He had a warehouse full of it. So when the war came and the rationing started, the rich people came to his little store to buy the butter and stuff, and he said, "Oh no, no, that's for my customers."

He and Mrs. Schein used to come over to my house the year I was getting fired because they were worried about me. He would come over every year to do my tax returns. He would say, "Young man, I have noticed that you are like my son Bernard and do not seem very good at the mathematical part of life."

Then, my mother and my grandmother always told me, "Jews make great husbands. They're nice to their wives." And I know why I was hearing that. Stanny said, "They're even nice to their mistresses." I don't know if Stanny was speaking from experience or not, but she acted like she knew what she was talking about.

Unfortunately, Lenore's parents were the worst on earth. Gert and Herb Gurewitz. He was a communist organizer for most of his life, organized workers in New York City. Then when that fell apart I think they both were teachers. He must have been the worst English teacher ever to live. I do not know if he ever read one of my books. I think the only thing he ever said is, "You must think you're pretty big stuff down South, but nobody I know ever heard of you."

When he visited Atlanta, he'd see me saying hi to everybody. "You running for mayor? Why do you say hi to everybody? You don't know these people."

"Maybe it will make them have a nicer day, Herb."

"Why would saying hi to you make them have a nicer day?"

"I don't know, Herb. It's just a different culture."

"What a stupid culture you come from. God, what idiots. Saying hi to people you don't know."

Oh, he was lovely. He was a lovely man. I've missed him since his death. Part of my feeling bad for Lenore was I knew how terrible her parents were. My God in heaven, they were a sour pickle couple. He especially was the most unfeeling man, one of the most unfeeling men I've ever come across. When all the communists went underground because of the FBI, he just simply left one day, a Wednesday, and for a year. Lenore had fear of abandonment the rest of her life.

She did not have a chance, although Lenore was the first great beauty of the family. I think it shocked everyone that Lenore had turned out so pretty. But I never envy pretty girls. It's always a problem for pretty girls. They attract too much unwanted attention too fast and from a lot of the wrong people.

She met the evil Alan Fleischer when he was in medical school in New York. They married and came to Atlanta for his residency in the neurosurgery department at Emory. Two kids, and he started having an affair with another mother at Paedeia. It was a small community, so if you had an affair with anybody, it was well known very soon. Also, they were not quiet about it; they were very open about it. It was a public affair. Public humiliation for Lenore. He made no attempt to hide, made no attempt not to stick it down her throat. He was a prick; that's the technical term. And I don't give out that honorarium without meaning it. That is high praise from me indeed. Alan was a loathsome, spiderous, cancerous, scorpious son of a bitch. There are some people—I hate living in the world they live in. They draw air that could be used by a dying cockroach.

When Lenore started dating me, he goes crazy. Before their divorce, Alan had me in court for alienation of affection, which I think is not even a law anymore, but I had alienated his wife's affection from him and caused trauma between them. He was suing me I think for $100,000. That's as I remember it. Now, later he would sue me for millions, but I think it started out kind of low, where I would just have to write one book of pornography to pay off my debts to him. I'd been depositioned several times. The legal fees for me were enormous at that time. I was up against a neurosurgeon, and they make more money than I do on a natural basis.

Even after the divorce, Alan's one of these guys who—she was his forever; she belonged to him; he belonged to her. He's one of these ex-husbands—you've heard of this type—they can't let the ex-wife alone. They just can't do it. Some weird tango of the spirit would go on with them forever. He also became obsessed with me. His kids told me that he had a pristine set of all my books, signed first editions, in his house.

One day after I had just been spending thousands of dollars paying my very nice lawyer, I was waiting to go to a bar mitzvah for Royce Bemis's son. Royce was a great friend and one of the founders of SIBA; he was in charge of book sales for Houghton Mifflin in the Southeast. Cliff and I knew him well. I had been invited six months ago to this affair, so we're going to the temple downtown. Lenore as usual is late because dressing for her is not easy. It took her a long time to get dressed. This is in Lenore's condominium on Ponce de Leon, across the street from Paideia. Lions Gate I think was the name of it. All those housing developments and condo developments have ersatz poetic names. Martha Schein's daughter Lara Alexander is the babysitter, and she's brought over a friend from Paideia. Alan has the kids for the weekend, they're coming back, and the exchange will be made. I'd been waiting for about half an hour, and I'm sitting there talking with Lara and the other babysitter.

We were late for the bar mitzvah, so I was trying to get Lenore to leave before the children got there, but she wouldn't; she had to be there for her beloved children coming in. So I am waiting by the door, and I have a drink, which we used to call a traveler, in my hand. Lenore keeps saying, "I'll be right down, I'll be right down"; I'm still talking to Lara and her babysitter friend. The next thing I know, here comes Alan, and Alan's one of these guys, their car is everything, their car is emblematic, something about his car always was huge with him, and he wore leather driving gloves. In those days I was still driving my Datsun station wagon. It looked like I was driving hogs to the market. Alan used to look at it with obvious disgust when he was coming to pick up the children. I could look down and see him staring at it with his nose twisted in horror at why anybody would drive such a vehicle.

On this particular day he's driving with his brother, his brother is driving the supercool Porsche convertible, and the kids are in this little area behind the driver, so they jump out and run. I'm standing by the door in my coat and tie and my khaki pants, the best Conroy can do. I am dressed as I am usually dressed but nicer. So the kids come jumping out from the back of the Porsche and come running in. I think Alan's message was they had to appear happier than they had ever been, just spending time with him, and lost and bereft as soon as they entered her household.

So little Gregory runs by me, does not say a word, and Emily, who I adored, still a child, says something like "We just left my father's supercool Porsche convertible, and Mom will have to travel in that piece of shit Datsun station wagon of Pat's." She's about eight then, was very articulate from a young age. I like the pain-in-the-ass kids; I admit it. So I laugh, I enjoy that. The supercool Porsche pulls off. I hear a little beep on the horn, so I turn around and look, and Alan gives me this grin and this limp-wristed little "I got you" wave. So I shoot him the bird, didn't think much of it, just thought I'd answer the beep of the horn.

By this time Lenore's on the stairs with her kids, and they're telling her what a fabulous time they had. The next thing I know Alan is racing past me, screaming at his children, "Did you see what he did to your father?! He shot me the bird! That's means 'Fuck you!' He said 'Fuck you!' to your father! What do you think about that, kids?! Do you like your mother dating somebody who says 'Fuck you!' to your father?! Can you imagine him saying "Fuck you!" to your father in the house your father paid for?!"

Well, I was about to tell him "Fuck you!" right in front of the kids and everybody else, but it was purely out of control. I'm standing there with my drink kind of astonished, and the babysitters were completely astonished. They'd never seen anything like it; I had never quite seen anything like it.

He comes up to me screaming, grabs my arm, and says, "I thought you were a Southern gentleman, Conroy! I thought you were a Southern gentleman! Everybody's told me you're a Southern gentleman! They were completely wrong! You're nothing but a Southern redneck! I'm calling my lawyer right now! I'm getting the kids taken away!"

I look around, Lara is horrified, and the other little girl was, and they're looking like this guy is absolutely a madman. Then he comes up to me and grabs me by the tie.

He does not know me. I do not like to be grabbed by the tie.

He keeps screaming and screaming, out of control. "I thought you were a Southern gentleman, Conroy! I thought you were a Southern gentleman! I won't let somebody like you hang around my kids; I won't let you be a part of my children's lives that are precious to me."

He's screaming, out of control, and he then puts his hand beneath the glass I'm drinking from and throws the drink in my face. I had bourbon all over my face and eyeballs and the suit I was in, whatever that was.

Now. I went to the Citadel. That shit don't work for me. Okay?

I normally do not explode because that would remind me of my father. Long ago I told myself I would kill myself if I found I was like my father in any way. Of course you know how nature answers you back with that one. One of God's great cruelties is to make you exactly like the parent you like the least. When something snaps in me, Santini can bloom in my soul and come alive. Usually I control it. I don't let it out. I don't like it; I don't agree with it. I don't think that's how somebody should be. But this was one of these times I realized I was indeed related to the Great Santini. That night, Santini rose out of a very repressed interior, struck me in the scrotum, in the anus, and all the organs of disruption, the organs of despair. I don't go after people until they sally forth, but if you sally forth against me, then you must prepare.

All right, Alan runs.

He does not get far.

He was running fast, but Conroy was more youthful then, not the fat slob that sits Buddha-like today. Now there are no blood corpuscles left in my body, there is simply clear fluid swimming through my adrenal glands, keeping me barely alive, but there was much more blood pumping through my system then. You could run from me now, and I could not catch a fiddler crab, but at that moment I could have caught a greyhound. I go hauling out after him, grab him by the shoulders, and he turns around and says, "You touch me I will sue you for every cent you've ever made, and you'll be in jail for a long time."

I've had enough of this. I was enraged. I went nuts. I think first I tore his shirt off. Why I did that I cannot explain, but I did it. Then he told me I was going to be in jail for many years because this is assault, and that pissed me off so bad I picked him up, lifted him up over my head, walked him over to these boxwood bushes I think about six feet high, and holding him by the seat of his pants, I stuffed him head first into the bushes where his two legs were sticking out in a V.

All right, as I have stuffed Alan head first into this bush, the brother attacks me, tackles me from behind. I'm on the ground, and this guy's throwing fists at me, but I noticed when he tackled me, I'm also dealing with a smaller man than I am. I am a fat rhinoceros-like man, and I did not like being on the ground, so all of a sudden I get up. I rip his shirt off. I have never been in many fights, and I did not know my first instinct is to rip a man's shirt off. I still do not understand that particular beginning of a fight that I seem to have started. But these were expensive shirts and I ripped them off, so I'm facing this bare-chested man.

I said, "I'm gonna take your pants off, your underwear off, your shoes off, and I'm gonna take your car keys and throw them in the sewer. Now you do what you want, pal, but I'm telling you what I'm gonna do."

The guy puts up his fists, and I laugh and say, "Please, please, just the way you did your fists is so pathetic that I cannot hit you because I'd break every bone in your face, okay, so I'll walk you back, you get your brother, and you guys get out of here."

And he's saying, "You're a beast just like Alan said, you're a wild man, you shouldn't be around these children, and you've lived up to everything Alan told me you were."

I said, "Yes, but after I break your jaw, you're going to think even worse of me, so I would like you to keep backing up."

Anyway, Alan gets out of the shrubbery, shirtless. There was an indentation in the bushes for years. He's completely humiliated. The neighbors are everywhere. He comes out and says, "Now you're going to jail, Conroy. Now it's jail time."

I said, "But first you leave. Run back to that car, and when I tell you to run, you run."

So they race back to the car, and I heard, "I didn't know you were a Southern monster redneck, Conroy."

"Now you know."

Alan can't let it go. He rolls down the window and says, "I don't have to leave here."

I said, "Don't leave here. See this nice million-dollar rearview mirror? I will tear it off and I will make you eat it."

"That thing cost $1,000, Conroy."
I said, "I'll put it on my Datsun."

He says, "I want you to know that cunt in there has been well used by a great many people."

I said, "Please go home and tell Alice I wish her my best. She'll know what I mean."

And with that I removed the mirror from his Porsche and walked with it back into Lenore's house, trailing wires. This seemed to alarm him more than anything, and the next day I was in jail.

He had me arrested for assault and battery with intent to kill. That night the police came and arrested me. Arrested. My lawyer got where I could report the next morning, so I reported the next morning. They photographed me, handcuffed me, and I'm in jail all morning with about ten black guys, in this holding cell for four or five hours before my lawyer got bail. All of them but one were in for child support. I said, how much do you owe so you can get out of here? One guy said thirty-five, one guy said fifty, one guy forty-five, so I ended up paying all their child support while I was in there. I had nothing else to do. I got six guys out of jail. I think it was less than $200 to get all of them out. The other guy's in for murder, so I said, "Sir, I do not think I can write a check to get you out of this, I'm so sorry." He was scary too.

I said, "What are you in for?" He said murder. I said what do they say you did? He said they said I strangled my wife to death with my belt. I says "You do it?" Yup. I said, "Uh, good luck, sir." And I went back to all the guys who owed child support.

So that was my day in jail, and then when we had the trial, I hired a lawyer from the best defense firm in Atlanta. John Nuckolls is his name; I thought what a great name for a defense lawyer. I knew that John Nuckolls was a great lawyer when he walked into court, took off his beautiful suit coat, and hung it beside the judge's sport coat on the judge's coat rack. It was great style. Then he eats these Fleischer boys alive. He just savaged their story. He was superb. He made them look like the two biggest liars that ever lived. Alan, you know, has suffered irreparable damage to the arm he uses as a surgeon. So John Nuckolls takes these records, looks at them and says, "Oh, by the way, Dr. Fleischer operated last night, and the operation took three hours. The day before he operated for six hours. He charged $40,000 for this, $75,000 for that, even after these terrible injuries." And bang, it was gone. The case got tossed.

Now, here's the question: why did I marry this woman after that? What insanity was I following? Why didn't I walk away the next day? Of course, I was in jail the next day, so I couldn't walk away. That's the way Conroy's life goes: a cheap novel, a bad novel. It is embarrassing; my life is embarrassing; I live the life of a fool. The problem is, when we're young, we don't know any better. It's the first life we've ever lived, and since we've never lived a life, we have no idea how one is supposed to be lived. But I know exactly what happened to me: I was a fucking idiot. And when you're a fucking idiot, you make mistakes. My brothers and sisters have always wondered how somebody that seems so bright can fuck up so many, many times. But I've got a certain genius for it.

Although I have never sent naked pictures of myself to perfectly strange women.

Alan sued me for the rest of my life. This guy kept coming and coming, and being a brain surgeon, he knew he could murder a writer if he kept bringing these cases. He always knew he could find lawyers to bring them. That's how lawyers make their money. He sued for custody of the children, because Lenore had had sexual relations with me. It was a mess. When he married Alice, of course this gave him great legitimacy. "I can provide. I'm a neurosurgeon." He kept telling the court he drives a Porsche 280-Z or some shit like that. And I drove a '76 Datsun station wagon. He kept mentioning his Porsche as compared to the level of automotive transportation his poor kids would be exposed to if he didn't get custody.

Here's how weird he was: he used to come to depositions to watch, which is very rare. He had depositions; I didn't give a shit. But if Lenore or I had a deposition, he'd always come to watch us get uncomfortable under the questioning, and then he would snicker. Note that the fat boy does not like snickering, and the fat boy registers that in his darkest, darkest heart.

Alan came to one deposition that blew everything up. I started getting asked this series of questions about my sexual life with Mrs. Fleischer, and it was irritating me. Alan had sent a private eye to Fripp Island when I took Lenore and her kids down to meet my mother. A private eye had followed me to my mother's house. They had pictures of Mom. That irritated me. I am a mountain boy from the hills, like my mother, a Chicago Catholic boy like my father, and I don't like being deposed about my habits of either fucking or not fucking. So they're going on, and they say, "You took Mrs. Fleischer down to a resort spa called Fripp Island."

"Yes, sir, it is where my mother lives. I was introducing her to Lenore."

"But you slept in the same room with Mrs. Fleischer."

"Yes, I did."

"And her children were in the next room."

"Yes, they were, my God. To think what they must have heard, seen"—I was just irritated as shit by the whole thing.

So this thing went on and on, and then finally the lawyer sums it all up. Alan is sitting there grinning and smirking before me, about two feet from my face, and I am not enjoying myself.

The lawyer says, "Now, we can get out of here, Mr. Conroy, if you sum up a few things for me. You've been very honest with this, we all appreciate your honesty, and we'd like to thank you for that."

So I am like a flounder buried in the sand looking for the tide to come swimming in over my head. Alan is just giggling and enjoying himself.

And the lawyer said, "Let me sum it all up. You admit to the court, and you admit under oath, Mr. Conroy, that you smoked dope with Mrs. Fleischer. Is that correct?"

I said, yes, I smoked dope with Mrs. Fleischer.

"So we have it on the record; it's official that you smoked an illegal substance with Mrs. Fleischer?"

I said, yes, that's right.

"And you have made love with Mrs. Fleischer, and that's on the record also."

Yes.

He says, "Let's sum this up. We can say you have smoked dope and slept with Mrs. Fleischer."

I said, "Yes, that is very true. But we can go further than that. I admit that I have smoked dope and had sex with both Mrs. Fleischers."

Alan's cute little wife had not revealed that she had once come knocking on my door, and Conroy, at that time a young single man, found her cute as hell, and one thing led to another. Alan and his lawyers obviously did not know that, and it ruined the deposition for them. Alan goes out of his mind. He gets up screaming. He just went crazy. He stood up making motions like he's going to beat me up, put up his fists like he was going to fight me, and his lawyers had to hold him back. I looked at him, "Alan, pray they hold tight, just pray." He always made sure when he approached me with his fists there were people to hold him back, which I told him I had noticed. They had to jump on him. They had to grab him, and they dragged him out. You know, "I'll get you for this. I'll kill you for this. You're not a gentleman. You're not a Southern gentleman."

In the middle of all this, I'm not quite digging Lenore like I should have. No one else liked her either. They were all onto her except one—moi. Dad said to me, being as fatherly as Dad could, "Son, you don't realize that you got small town written all over you. You're not sophisticated, and you're not cultured."

"Well, excuse me, Noël Coward."

He said, "You can make fun of me all you want, but you can't see a big-city gold-digger going after you." Dad said a Chicago boy could spot those women, and he said, "That's what I get for raising you in the crazy fucking South."

From beginning to end he called Lenore Lenoinks—oinks for pig. Cliff called her a Neiman Marxist. They all said, Pat, she's bad news. She's after you for money. She's after you for what you can give. She does not love you.

I should have listened. I should have gotten out of it, but I felt something funny. I felt something odd over the whole thing. Certainly the woman in peril was one of the things I felt. This woman is in trouble, and this guy was coming after her, and this guy was mean. My loyalism had kicked in, and I couldn't leave her in the lurch where she found herself. It became a thing of her lawyer saying, "You can't sleep with him because you are not married. You're in danger of losing your kids." Lenore's about to lose her kids, and I felt responsible for that. My rescue impulse went into high gear when that happened. I find it very hard to explain Lenore to myself, except she seemed pathetic to me. A woman that seems pathetic I always seem to try to help, and that's an instinct that comes from seeing my mother getting the shit kicked out of her. Always I was a boy rescuing his mother. Anytime there's an underdog, I'm rushing into the breach. Now it seems like a cliché in my life. My brothers and sister say, "Just give Pat an underdog, and he'll be happy." Marion O'Neill pointed out that I always had to be the hero, the savior, because Mom required it of me, and then my father was the brave warrior, the war hero. There was something in me trying to live up to what both my parents expected of me, but it was ruining my life. Marion said, "Pat, every time you see an injustice, you throw yourself in, and you don't give a shit what happens to you." I think I got married twice because I felt a deep sorrow for these women I was dating. The seducer was never my role; my role was the rescuer. These women seemed to have gotten their lives messed up, and always I see myself in the role of the hero, the role of the rescuer. It is one of the most loathed roles one can play, and I think it should be loathed. It is a self-glorifying role, and that's the problem with it.

My sister Carol would say this need to be the hero has also ruined my writing. "The one thing Pat always has to be, he's always the hero of his own books." She says, "Pat, I know there'll be all these shitheads in your book, but they will be surrounded by a golden-haired youth of charm, wit, humor, and wisdom. He's the funniest guy you've ever met. You want to take him home. You want your parents to get to know him. That character will be based on you. There will be hideous people that the golden boy must encounter, as he makes his way to the Promised Land; that will be me, Mom, and Dad."

Carol is hilarious when she says it. But these characters will do things I don't think I would do. They show courage I don't think I have. They say things in situations I hope I would not say. But it certainly comes out of me; there's no question about that.

⁓

I should have written more in those years, but one main thing happened to me between *The Lords of Discipline* and *The Prince of Tides,* one very great thing. It is Lenoinks. What I did is I ruined my life in between those two books. I'd gotten myself into such a psychodrama of constantly being assaulted by Alan Fleischer, him trying to take his children back from her, lawsuits; very simply I think overwhelmed me. Going to Rome was a defensive mechanism to get myself away, to get myself out of there, get her out of there, get her kids out of there. He was such an asshole, such a control guy. And he had to have their children. When Houghton Mifflin sold the paperback rights to *The Lords of Discipline* for $695,000, they split that with me, and that's when we decided to move to Italy to get away from this guy.

Alan actually won one round in Atlanta because Lenore and I weren't married. That was it basically. He was; we weren't.

As we were walking to the elevator, Alan races over to me, says, "Conroy, prepare to be a loser for the rest of your life. I'm going to make you the loser, and you're going to get so used to losing it's going to become a part of who you are."

His brother wasn't there for this one, so I said, "Where's the other midget?"

He went crazy and started swinging at me, and his lawyer kind of grabbed his arms and pulled him off, and I said, "I'm praying for your sake now, those boys have a good grip." But it was always something; it was always confrontational. Alan came at me every time he saw me.

I'm in court constantly. One day I tell this judge, "This guy's driving me nuts, Your Honor. I've been in court since I started dating this woman. We talk about getting married and moving to Rome just to get away from all this. I hear that a terrific life is available outside this courtroom."

This sealed my marriage. Why did I do that? Will somebody tell me? Okay, my IQ wasn't that high; I wasn't that smart; my education was very, very iffy; I'm an autodidact, that most pathetic of all creatures. But what was I doing when I did that? And why, for God's sake, did I not do this differently?

The next time we're in court, the judge says he will grant permanent custody to Alan "unless Mr. Conroy actually marries Mrs. Fleischer and they actually do move to Rome." He had it in the court order. The only reason she keeps her children is we got married and moved to Rome. I owe it to the order of Judge Bell why Conroy the Rescuer got married. The next week we got married, and she kept her children. And that's how we moved off to Rome. Rome was Alan's accidental gift to me, and that was her accidental gift to me.

Rome/Atlanta/Rome

1981–1988

That was a turning point in his life, from sort of living an
ordinary life to getting involved in a psychological drama.

MARION O'NEILL, Ph.D., ABPP, clinical psychologist

Some people make an early acquaintance with a dark, disfiguring
anarchy so strong that they cannot consider a day complete
without the music of chaos roaring in their ears.

PAT CONROY, *South of Broad*

Rome worked out splendidly for me. It could have been ruination, but
it wasn't. I am even grateful to Lenore's incredible, extraordinary asshole
of a husband because he gave me the gift of Rome. Everything about
Rome made me happy. It makes me happy in memory.

The first place we lived was Olgiata, a compound for Mafia people in
a new suburb north of Rome with big mansions. Lenore had decided
this was the best place for the children; I was completely repulsed by it.
We were in this huge modern house, built in 1974, and it was 1980 when
we were there. This was not why I came to Italy. We eventually moved
into the historic district of Rome. I couldn't believe how beautiful this
apartment was we found. We shared a courtyard with the Belgian
ambassador. We had a great terrace that overlooked the Roman Forum
and the Colosseum; we saw the back of the Campidoglio from that terrace. It was beyond anything I ever imagined, and I was happy there. I
had a nice office for writing upstairs. I could sit up there and write and
watch the Forum and the Campidoglio; the view was magnificent.

Thomas Wolfe wrote something I loved about walking the streets of
Brooklyn relentlessly. He was trying to drink in the city; he gulped; he

swallowed. I bought into all that horseshit. I had three years in Rome, so I really got to walk that city and know that city, noticing everything, every detail, every single thing I passed, every smell I encountered, every taste, and finding myself alive like I thought Wolfe was. Rome was perfect for me in that because it was a walking city, and God, it was beautiful. Every place I turned, every alley I went, there was something so wonderful, so beautiful. And I knew I was walking over cities buried beneath me. Walking the streets, I thought this is as near to heaven as I'd ever get. Rome was about a hundred times more beautiful than I ever imagined it. I got to see the inner Rome; I got to see the private Rome. It was thrilling to me in every kind of way. It satisfied that itch I had to live overseas, and if possible, bring kids over there and give them that experience of being raised abroad. Now where I got this, why I got this, I don't know, but it was there.

Lenore's two children and Megan came over to live with us; Jessica and Melissa would come for the summer. Megan has always said that those were great years of her life. She became a teenager there, a young fourteen- and fifteen-year-old. I wanted to drop them in an Italian school, but Gregory and Megan went to an English-speaking Catholic high school in a gorgeous old monastery close to Circus Maximus, and Emily went to a different elementary school. I had always wanted to live in a foreign country, have my kids know what life in a foreign country was, and this was some sort of strange fantasy of mine I got from nothing else but literature.

But I realized quickly that I had screwed up with my marriage and made the most horrendous mistake of my life. Regret had entered my stomach and was crawling like termites. I had lots and lots of "Oh, shit, what have I done to myself?" moments. I had married this woman so she wouldn't lose her kids, and stupidly thought we could always get divorced if it didn't work out. But then Lenore got pregnant. Fate has this way of sneaking up on you. When you're being led in a cart past the jeering crowds on the way to the guillotine, only then do you realize you have fucked up badly. Lenore had not told me she was going off birth control, but once she got pregnant, I thought: You got yourself into it, so make the best of it, pal. And I gave it a try; I gave it a run. That is something a military brat can do: make the best of what you have. The Citadel certainly reinforced that too. You're given an assignment, and you carry it out. We military brats have our own sense of responsibility, our own sense of duty, our own sense of orders that were written by a higher power for us to carry out, and our mission was to do the best we could.

But Lenore was my father with tits. And she was a screamer. She and Emily yelled constantly. They had the worst relationship of two human beings on earth, and it used to drive me crazy, as my mother and Carol nearly drove me crazy when I was a kid. I think Lenore rejected Emily because of the way she looked; Emily was born with a wandering eye and was not the beautiful child that Gregory was. Eventually they corrected her eye, but there was still a problem there I never understood. Whatever it was, it was poisonous. I used to tell her, "Lenore, God will never forgive you for doing that. You better pray He does not exist. Quit doing that."

"I can't help it."

That was always her big excuse: "I can't help it." I could never stop her screaming at Emily.

But I am not much of an argument guy. Once I established that I was not a person to be yelled at, and that I could not put up with somebody who argued every day about everything, Lenore was never horrible to me like she was to Emily. I told her, "That may be you and Alan, that may be you and your children, but I cannot survive that way. I need harmony and tranquility." If she was screaming at me: "Excuse me, Lenore, wrong guy. I don't do this, and I hope you know that. That's not how I'm going to live, and I hope you know that too."

Lenore and I got along in my belief that I can get along with almost anybody. I always told her, "I have a theory about myself: I could be married to almost anybody," and she said, "That's because you make it such a point to be good-natured and try to be happy all the time and not argue." I said, "I've never looked upon that as a great central flaw of my character, that I try to be easy to get along with."

But I think Lenore knew she was dealing with an idiot. She felt she was in a chess game with me, and she knew when to castle. She hid herself enough from me to make it okay on most days, at least when we lived in Rome.

I think we might still be married if we had stayed in Italy. It was the best part of our whole marriage, because we were in a foreign country and we depended on each other. Lenore was much more competent in Italian than I was; she was competent at getting things done, which, in laissez-faire Italy, is the hardest thing. I made a rule for all of us: if we can get one thing done in Rome in a day, that's great. Do not try to get two things done; it will end in frustration and hatred. Lenore was good at that, and I completely depended on her. She seemed to blossom in that role. She kept a great house; she was a great cook; she could throw a great dinner party and be charming at other people's dinner parties. Lenore seemed to relax in a place where no one knew her, because she had a history in Atlanta. She'd been mean to people and burned many, many bridges. Rome seemed like a fresh start for her. I think she was pretty happy there.

Then Susannah was born at the Salvator Mundi Hospital, and I allowed myself to go nuts over this kid. It's amazing how women can have these masterpieces out of their own body. Susannah is the great gift of my middle age. I could feel a blossoming inside me, and I could welcome this child into the world in a way I was not in a position to do for Megan, because I'd had Megan in the most horrible circumstances, and with Susannah, I didn't have that pressure of my life falling apart.

She was a precocious little shit, talked early, walked early, did everything early, seemed like this little wonder child, smiled, was quiet, was not a pain in the ass in any way. What I loved is when I became responsible for the 3 A.M. feeding after Lenore quit breastfeeding her. Somebody had sent this little music box that sang "O, Susanna," and Susannah learned to click it so the song would play. When she woke up at three, she wouldn't cry; she'd click that music box, and I'd wake up hearing "O, Susanna." I'd walk over in the dark, and I don't know how this developed, but she would have her arm straight up, holding her bottle out. I would take the bottle, like in a relay race, say, "Be back in a couple of minutes," and she would keep clicking that box so I could hear music when I was warming her bottle up. There was something about hearing this Southern song with this kid with a Southern name.

I'd warm up the bottle, come back, she'd have her hand out, I'd pop it in her hand, she'd click the music box one more time, and that would be it. We did that every night. I got to hate it when she finally started sleeping through the night.

~

As soon as I got to Rome, I started writing *The Prince of Tides.* Jim Roe was my financial advisor, and Jim had this delightful little thing he would tell me in a frantic phone call every once in a while: that I had married a very expensive woman. I had no idea how much she was spending. I never kept up with money. I still don't. But because of Lenore and the lawsuits and everything, money needed to be made. That pressure was on me big.

I don't know how the book got written, except I saw something clearly when I was in Rome. I could see Beaufort clearly from Rome. I carry Beaufort with me wherever I go; I carry Charleston wherever I go. I missed Beaufort, and I missed the lowcountry. I realized that I had developed a deep devotion to that landscape on my way to and from Daufuskie Island every day. When I was in that boat, it was a forty-five minute trip, and I went through every kind of weather, every kind of condition you can imagine, and I learned to truly adore it. I'd always wanted a chance to go back and do the lowcountry, describe that landscape, and *The Prince of Tides* gave me that chance.

Just as I could see the lowcountry clearly in Rome, I could see the book coming together clearly. I've always wanted to write about a coach, especially one who loves to read. I know a lot of them. I always liked those guys. I was one of them at one time, so I felt comfortable with this character. I'd had the experience of being a coach. I'd had an experience of being fired. When Barbara started law school, I drove the carpools; I was the soccer mom. It was: "My daddy doesn't have a job," and all these little girls would look at me like I'm a loser. I'm driving to soccer practice, and they're staring at me, whispering, "He doesn't have a job at all?" "No, he's home all day." So I'd had the experience of kids looking at me like I'm a loser. I'd had the experience of divorce. By that time, I'd really had the experience of despair. So I could feel this book coming together.

I loved writing about New York and Tom and Lowenstein being from two different worlds and hating each other's guts at first, Tom being fragile enough not to want to take any bullshit from a Jewish psychiatrist in New York. Lowenstein was probably Lenore, Marion O'Neill, a fantasy shrink who did not exist, and the New York women I met when I first went up there. Lowenstein lived like I think Lenore thought she was supposed to live. The insight of Lowenstein certainly came from Marion O'Neill.

And one thing that had amazed me the first time I went to New York—I was unprepared for the beauty of New York women, and I was unprepared for how professional they were. I did not realize that had gone on. It was '72 when I first got up there. It seemed like these women were giants. They were all six feet tall; they all had Ivy League educations. They had terrific jobs, exciting jobs. That was a whole new exciting version of woman that had just started to come out, and the women's movement had just started, and there was excitement in the air. I thought these girls were otherworldly. I had just come up from Beaufort, where, "Hey Pat, how ya doin' honey? Let me put a hickey on your neck, will ya? You're so cute." In New York, I'm sitting there thinking, holy God, and talking about literature and history, current events. This was totally new for me. I was very excited to see women that educated and that accomplished. And it was interesting to be looked at like I was a hillbilly who somehow learned to use the D train. I thought for a guy in my circumstances, I was fairly sophisticated, but that's only because I read a lot. I did not realize that experience-wise, I was as rube as they got. I was amazed by all of it.

Also, I wanted another crack at that family that was coming apart at the seams, that great unhappiness a family can produce. In *The Great Santini,* I thought I had let myself down by not being able to give a description of the full war the father waged against his family. My editors made me put in these charming scenes of flowers for the prom and flight jackets for the son's birthday, when Dad never did any of that stuff. I just did not see him ever do anything nice. In my life, gesture became very important to me, because I never saw Dad do a single one. He didn't do anything like the nice gestures they made me put in the book. It was just total war on the family, and what I did not get to put in that first novel was how you are afraid all the time. You're scared from the time you wake up to the time you go to bed. With *The Prince of Tides,* I could open up about the physical abuse because as I was writing, America was opening up about abuse too. It was becoming more and more commonly reported.

One question I'm trying to answer in the book is: What made Carol crazy? Why did my parents drive her nuts? Or why did all of us drive her nuts? With *The Boo,* it was: Why did they fire this guy that so many people adored? *The Water Is Wide:* Why did I get fired from that island when I thought I was doing some good for those kids? Then: Why do I hate my father?—*The Great Santini.* And *The Lords of Discipline:* This is why I do hate the Citadel. Usually what I've been doing is trying to explain my own life to myself. Every book has been about some overriding issue in my own heart.

There's a scene that occurs at the beginning of *The Prince of Tides* when the guy—whatever his name is—Tom—gets a phone call; it's his mother saying, "Your sister tried to commit suicide again,"—that simply was what happened, except Carol was in Minnesota, not New York. And, "Pat, try not to blame yourself."

"Oh, that will be easy, Mom. I haven't seen her in five years, and she blames you."

"We're having a party this weekend, John and I. I can't possibly break away to go up. You need to go up and see your sister. You're the only one who doesn't have a job."

No one in my family has ever thought I worked. None of them, not one of them, has ever considered the fact that I may work. In their entire lives that has not occurred to them. I have accepted it in the enormity and expansiveness of my generosity, and I understand that I am surrounded by idiots who do not understand the writing process, are not capable of understanding the writing process, and don't care to understand the writing process. I have no choice if I'm going to love my family.

But that was one of the scenes that I lifted from life, although all these great writers say you should never lift stuff from life.

So I had a mother figure I had not even touched the surface of. Marion O'Neill was always telling me, "The unexamined one for you,

Pat, is the mother. You've got to somehow figure her out or you're going to figure nothing out. Because one thing you do know, she chose Don; she stayed with Don; she saw you abused by Don; she saw her kids abused; she was abused by Don; she continued to stay there." I realized Mom was complex, and I had dealt with none of that complexity. Anytime Carol tried to kill herself or there was some crisis in Carol's life, Mom's reaction was, "Try not to blame yourself, Pat."

One time my mother and I had a fight; it was one of those scenes you only see in bad movies or bad lives. My mother told me that everybody knew from reading *The Great Santini* that I had sexually molested my sister when she was growing up, and that was why she was crazy. Now, there is nothing in that book remotely indicating any such thing, for the simple reason that I would have killed myself if I'd even thought of doing any such thing in my life. The only time the word sex even appears in the book is when Mary Anne talks about the "sicko sexual" relationship of the parents. I think Mom just needed to blame someone besides herself for what happened to Carol; she needed to explain Carol's craziness to other people. It was obvious something happened to Carol. I was surprised it was me that became the obvious, but then I wrote the book, and Mom did not like that sappy portrait of herself. I think she was protecting that one precious immaculate human being she was involved with, Peg Conroy.

In this fight, she came over to argue with me about *The Great Santini;* this is after I'd separated from Barbara and Mom had gotten her divorce. She came to stay with me in Atlanta in my apartment there; I was writing *The Lords of Discipline* then. She'd come up to let me know how hurt she was by *The Great Santini,* and disappointed by me personally in the writing of the book. This seemed to be the point of the visit. She'd never come to stay with me in my apartment before; this was a first. She got drunk, I think I got drunk, and she started on me about my lack of talent. She expected me to be a much better writer than I had become; I let her down; her belief in me and her support of me had been betrayed; she had been disappointed by the lack of gifts I brought to the game. Then she started with "You thought he was in charge of that house; I was in charge of that house. You thought he was a leader; he didn't have the insight. I ruled him with everything he did."

I was kind of in shock by this, because I certainly didn't know that. I wanted to say, "If you ruled, why didn't you stop that shit?" And I may have said that in the argument that followed. Dad was an emotional idiot, and he could be wrapped around her finger when she wanted it, but what she could not do, as I was happy to tell her, is when he exploded there was nothing in the world that could control that. He used his fists and his temper against a woman and a house full of kids, and there was nothing she could do to protect against that.

Then finally—and Mom never drank; this was a completely new mother to me—she started drinking when she started dating John Egan, and I had never dealt with her being drunk before. And she then said everybody in Beaufort knows the reason Carol is crazy is because of me. "It's in your book; you practically wrote it out yourself."

What's in the book is that my sister had a very precocious mind that my mother and father did not seem to appreciate, so part of my job was to make sure she didn't get murdered by Mom and Dad.

I am so enraged, I go to the wall—and of course this is where I just want to kill myself and slit my throat—I just punched the wall. I was younger then, I was stronger then, so I punch the wall; my fist doesn't go through the wall; it's the real shit; it's not sheetrock. It's the real shit. It doesn't go through; it just leaves a bloody fist print; it's my hand, with these five knuckle prints. Of course Mom always is waiting for a moment like that, and she says, "You're a beast just like him." Oh, pardon me, Mom. I never got to thank you for that lovely DNA you selected to be the father of your children. I go in to wash my hand off, it's bleeding copiously, and when I come out, she's gone. I go outside to find her. That night I did not find her, didn't know what happened to her. I called her cousins, her aunts; I called everybody, and it wasn't until later that I realized where she had gone: Dad's house. He was only a mile from me.

That was a big moment for Mom and me, when she's telling me something that worried me about myself: that I'm not a very good writer, that I'm not worth a shit. That's the echo writers like me hear their entire lives, and we don't need it coming from other people. We do it to ourselves. Part of my particular psyche that I've always had to deal with: I did not think I was smart, did not think I was talented. I don't today. I have great internal doubts about myself, like what am I doing in front of this page? Who am I fooling? This is nonsense. I'll be ridiculed as a fraud. Soon they will find out how phony a talent this is, that this is counterfeit, this is imaginary, and "How did this guy fool so many people?" Mom knew that about me, and she was trying to hit me with that. At least by then I had more sense of achievement behind me; I had more things I could actually point to. I could actually lift up a book and say, "I did that." For whatever reasons, no matter what fraudulent devices and magician's tricks I had to use—there it is. There's a book I fooled some of the people with some of the time.

So it was a terrible night, one of many terrible nights. I'll have many more of them until I slit my wrists and calmly sink into Battery Creek as the tide goes out. There will be a few minutes of grunting and groaning, huge bubbles coming to the surface, and then there'll be a long peaceful silence.

But Mom scared me by disappearing. She called me the next day to let me know she was all right and said she was sorry. She never mentioned it again, and I never did either. I thought cowardice was the better part of valor when it came to dealing with my mother. In the family I came from, what I knew is Mom was the best I got, and I was not going to jettison her. She was a protector from my father. When Dad went after me, she was right in the middle of it, trying to protect me, get between Dad and me, and of course I picked up the same habit, and so a bond of battle had developed between us. We are tied by blood and pain forever. We bled for each other; we fought for each other. We could actually say that: we fought for each other. Mom and I were a team. If he was slapping her, I'd be trying to kick him in the balls. And I paid for that. Dad hated me for it, that this little kid made him look very bad to his wife. What developed between Mom and me was solid and unbreakable. I've always thought that the supreme relationship is the one between mother and child, and the bond of mothers and sons can be devastatingly intimate like no other relationship on earth.

Notice I didn't ever use that scene.

But right away I start out thinking I'm on to something good in *The Prince of Tides,* and I threw myself into writing that.

⁓

When I was in Rome writing *The Prince of Tides,* Jonathan Galassi called me up and said he was leaving Houghton Mifflin for Random House and wanted me to go with him. I loved Houghton and thought I was going to be with them my entire life. I thought I'd be with Jonathan my whole life; there was nothing that was going to take that away. I like loyalty, and I like staying. I don't like change, so I was upset by it. I didn't have any realization that Jonathan was positioning himself in publishing. We made a lot of money with the paperback sales of *Lords of Discipline,* and that made him a hot young editor, I think. But he said, "Don't make any decision now. You're not going to be finished with your book for a while. The next time you're home, I want you to come up to Random House, just meet the people and see what you think."

About a year later, I had 250 pages written, so I sent those to Houghton Mifflin and to Jonathan at Random House, and then I go to see him in New York. The receptionist at Random House—she was a young black woman—could not have been shittier to me if she tried. Could not have been more nasty, more rude, no matter what I did to be nice. I'm thinking: Did somebody tell her I'm writing a book on the Klan? I couldn't figure out why in the hell she was treating me this way. I can be accused of many things with great credibility, but unfriendliness does not top the list much. As a military brat, I learned how to get along and be nice to everybody, because you get into town not knowing anybody, and you don't know where your next friend is coming from. This can be something obnoxious about me, but I have a need to instantly become friends with every cab driver, every cashier, and every grocery store clerk. Yet I could not get this receptionist even to look up at me when I said something. So I'm sitting there, and it's taking a long time for Jonathan to come out. Finally he comes into the waiting area and finds me there. "Oh, Pat. I didn't know you were out here." She had not even told him I was waiting.

Jonathan takes me back to his office and talks about how much he loves it at Random House. He says, "I want to take you around and introduce you to some of the editors."

I meet Robert Loomis. He could not have been a bigger shit bird. He can barely look up at me from his desk; he can barely look me in the eye. All of them were like that. Jonathan was interrupting them, and they were doing work of world-class importance. He was interfering with them doing the things that made Random House great in the world of publishing. I'm watching this, and I see Jonathan get real edgy.

Finally we went to see Jason Epstein, and Jonathan said, "Jason, I have somebody I want you to meet."

Jason does not even look up. He says, "Jonathan, I told you never to interrupt me when I'm editing a manuscript. I've told you several times now, and I hope I don't have to do it again."

Jonathan said, "Well, I just wanted you to meet—"

"I don't care who you want me to meet. I don't know how many times I've got to tell you this."

As we walk on, I said, "Jonathan, would you like me to walk back in and throw him through a plate glass window? I'll be happy to do it."

He said, "No, no. He must be in a bad mood."

Everybody seemed to be in a bad mood that day. We go in to Bob Bernstein, who was the president of Random House. Bob sits me down and says, "We read your manuscript, and none of us were impressed. But because of Jonathan, and out of courtesy to him, we're going to give you an advance. It won't be anywhere near the advance you'd get from Houghton Mifflin. But you will have the prestige of the Random House escutcheon on your book."

I said, "Bob, thanks for being so perfectly honest with me. You've just made this the easiest decision of my whole life. I'll see you guys later. Write me, don't call, stay the same as you are, love you."

Jonathan jumps up. "Pat, Pat. He didn't mean that."

Bob said, "I meant it exactly as it came out, Jonathan."

Jonathan is just completely, utterly humiliated. He is devastated by this; I am devastated by this. Jonathan Galassi is perhaps the greatest editor of our time. I thought that then, I think it now, and part of me grieved because I knew I was losing that. He did not beg—he's not that type—but he did everything to try to get me to stay with him. However, Conroy does not take humiliation well. And I just did not see a way to make it work with Random House.

Then a new editor named Nan Talese who had just come to Houghton Mifflin wants me for a writer, sends me a very nice letter, calls me up, and says, "We're going to offer twice as much as Random House would ever think of, because we're going to get you." I said, "That sounds nice. I like Houghton Mifflin, and I hope we can work something out." So that all sort of happened without me being a real player in it. I was one of the pawns moved around on that chessboard and did not even know it was taking place. But Nan Talese was my fate; for whatever that has meant, she was my fate.

Years later, when the Book of the Month Club took *Beach Music* as their selection, the guy who contacted me said, "Pat do you remember me?"

I said, "I don't believe so. Where did we meet?"

He said, "I was the new assistant for Jonathan Galassi when you came to Random House. They still talk about the time they humiliated Jonathan and you, the intellectual and the redneck. That was all a setup between the older editors to put Jonathan in his place and put you in your place: the intellectual and the redneck."

Of course, here I am, an uptight, overly sensitive Southern boy, who would like to be an urbane man of the world, and to be thought of as a redneck by those Goddamn Random House people . . .

I said, "That is very interesting. Does Jonathan know that?"

He said, "I'm not sure. We never talked about it."

Jonathan had been fired by Random House not too long after my visit there. So after I heard from this guy who'd been his assistant, I called him up and told him what he'd said. Jonathan said it didn't surprise him.

I said, "Jonathan, they didn't want it to work. And then you got fired."

He said, "Yes, Pat. But if you'd written *The Prince of Tides* for me, I never would have been fired."

I said, "Here's what I love, Jonathan. You went on to kick their asses. They are now part of the collective unknown who will be buried in the tomb of the unknown Random House editor, and you are the great Jonathan Galassi. I have enjoyed that. I have reveled in that."

When Nan Talese became my editor, she said to me—I think sort of good-naturedly, but she said it—"Now we're going to see if you can write a book worth a million dollars," and it paralyzed me. I got $7,500 for *The Water Is Wide,* I got I think $10,000 for *The Great Santini,* I got

$15,000 I believe for *Lords of Discipline,* and that seemed great to me. I was going up every time, it made me as happy as I could be, but I never asked, and I never paid attention much to that part of it. Here's what I look for: Are they going to ask me to write another book? If they're satisfied with the last book, or they were happy with the last book, if they want to sign me again, that is the great thing. I'm not sure my confidence ever got going as a writer, but they kept asking me to write another book, which was confidence making. Then this million-dollar business threw me. Anything connected with writing—success or failure—creates anxiety. I don't care what happens to you, if you become king of the world or your book slides down the toilet, it's still going to cause great anxiety, great stress.

⌒

When Lenore and I first got to Rome, we didn't know anybody in Italy. Jonathan Yardley, the critic for the *Washington Post,* had heard I was going over there, and he gave me the name of Michael Mewshaw. I had heard of him as a Catholic novelist and read one of his books; they're very Graham Greene-ish, expatriate novels. We had been in Rome about a week and were still way out in this Mafia-ridden suburb, so I called Michael Mewshaw and said, "Jonathan Yardley gave me your name. You and your wife, Linda—could you all come out for lunch this Saturday?"

He said, "I've got a friend named Steve Geller who's a writer and a screenwriter. I could bring him and his wife and kids, and my kids."

I said, "Certainly, bring everybody."

So they came out and thought I was Frank Conroy. I was so lonely, I pretended for the first hour that I *was* Frank Conroy. "Yes, *Stop-Time.* I knew I was onto something when I wrote that." I didn't quite know what else to do. But finally I said, "This is not going to work guys. I am not Frank Conroy; I'm Pat Conroy. I'm sorry I operated under false pretenses, but isn't this a great lunch? Aren't you enjoying it?"

Anyway, Michael Mewshaw became my best friend there. He's one of the funniest guys I've ever met; I love Michael. I just loved him. He would tell stories that made me laugh my ass off. But I learned very early that Mike was one of those people whose great joy in life was knowing famous writers, and almost always, famous male writers. He had a series of these guys: Anthony Burgess, Graham Greene, William Styron, Gore Vidal. Anybody who came to Rome looked Mike up. He and Linda would house-sit their villas in the summer. They would get great benefits out of this. It was big name, big name, big name.

I think repair was what Michael Mewshaw was doing by seeking out the greatest writers of his time. This excited the poor boy in him, and he was desperately trying to repair what he was born into. This was healing the wounds; it was curative. Mike's family was so poor that when he and his brother played basketball on the same team, they had to call timeout so Mike could take off his shoes and give them to his brother when he was put in the game for Mike. By surrounding himself with famous people, Mike was trying to cure the wounds of coming from nothing.

When we met, Mike had never heard of me in his life, and was surprised I'd done so well without entering his framework. After we met, I collected and read all his books, and I wished he'd taken my writing more seriously, but he didn't. He thought I was a small-timer who did not run with the big dogs. To him it was weird that I did not like to run with the big boys or even meet them.

At the University of Virginia, where Mike got his doctorate, he had the job of meeting all novelists who flew in to Charlottesville and driving them to their hotel. He used every one of those meetings in very career-enhancing ways. He would make the contact, and he would keep up with them, which he said I would never do, which I don't do very well. I've never done that well. He thinks it is a great, great weakness, not only in my writing career but in my character, that I cannot dance at the big dance; I cannot play with the big boys. That has been his theme. When I described all the friends in my life, the best friends I've made, Michael listened to me in appalled silence and finally said, "Pat, to be perfectly honest with you, I have never heard of a bigger bunch of losers in my entire life."

When two of my friends from Atlanta came to visit in Rome, I was taking them out to lunch the first day. Mike calls up and says, "Hey, Pat, can you go to lunch?"

I said, "No, I'm taking my friends from Atlanta out."

He said, "Well, I've got a little surprise for you. You're not going to be taking them out to lunch."

I said, "Why not?"

He said, "Cancel right now. I'm going out to lunch with Graham Greene, and I want you to come along. I bet you'll cancel your lunch plans now."

I said, "Mike, what kind of a human being would you think I was if I said 'fuck you' to my friends from Atlanta and went out with you and Graham Greene? I'm just curious. What would that say about me as a person?"

He said, "Well, it would say you are ambitious."

I said, "No, it would say I was a jerk. Tell Graham I said hi."

Michael Mewshaw thought this was part of my unnatural, totally false, good-natured shepherd-of-all-men routine. He found that an incredible loser quality about me. He thought there was something basically wrong with me when I had a chance to have lunch with Graham Greene but chose not to. He'd call my friends the midgets and say, "My God, it's the midgetry, the gathering of little people. You need to hang around with the giants of your age."

He never did understand why I didn't want to hang around writers of supernatural gifts as if they would pass that flame on to me. Another part of my loser-dom for Michael was that I would not ask a writer for anything. Mike sees opportunity that is not seized. He sees career enhancement which I throw away for no reason. He'll go, "Oh, you are too good to get your hands dirty, to grovel before the great."

I could tell him, "I don't want to meet those people. I want to *be* those people."

He used to say, "Conroy suffers from an irresistible attraction to the Lilliputians. He likes to be tied down by the little people, captive on the beach as they swarm all over him taking whatever bodily fluids they need."

I said, "Mike, that may be a truth about my personality that you are spotting. It's as good as any theory I have. But I do not have the need that you seem to have to hang around these people, be at their parties, be at their beck and call, house-sit for them. I don't want that. I just do not want it." I could ask him: "What did you get out of that Mike?" He thought it was going to rub off on him. He did.

"Oh, Mr. Big Man. Big Man. Go back to the little people who swarm around your ankles. Conroy is only happy when he's surrounded by Lilliputians."

That made me laugh my ass off. But I could never get him to understand why I don't seek out celebrities as friends. One thing watching James Dickey taught me about the danger of fame was wanting to hang around only with famous people, which I think is the death of it all. So I've always told myself to be careful of meeting famous people. Just be careful. It's fun to do, you can brag about it, you can drop their names, but you need to watch yourself getting caught up in it. Those people—they're not all out to be your friend, and some of them will be out to hurt you. They don't always come into your life to encourage you; some of them will make you feel bad, make you feel unworthy. And sometimes, one of the distractions from writing is the presence of other writers.

We had dinner one night with Bill Styron, the great man, who had been a friend of Mike's ever since Mike picked him up from the airport in Charlottesville. To me, he was as friendly as a turd. He was not the nicest guy I had ever run into in my lifetime. I did not feel any warmth emanating from him. All I remember is shaking his hand and him nodding at me. He looked at me like I was gum on the bottom of his shoe. I knew he couldn't have given a shit about meeting me, wanted nothing to do with me. He talked to Mike mostly; he didn't talk to me. But I thought he was rude to Mike and Linda too. He didn't care. He may have been getting drunk. I have no idea. But there was no interest. I knew I would never see or hear from him again, which I didn't. I knew he would never hear from me again, which he didn't. He seemed vesuvial to me, one of those tightly wound men that you never knew when he was going to go off or be displeased, yet you knew he was going to be displeased all the time, and it was going to be based on something you were responsible for, whether you knew it or not.

His wife, I would have married. Rose Styron was beautiful; she was witty; she was charming; she had personality. His daughters, I would have married. They were wonderful girls. Styron's daughter Susanna even stayed with us, and she was fabulous. But one thing she told me that was interesting as hell to me is they had met everybody in their world, and I wasn't sure that was good for children—celebrity worship beginning so early, so your worth becomes part of who you know. I just did not think that was such a great thing.

The main thing I remember from that meal was the great surprise on the Italian waiter's face when William Styron ordered a fifth of Scotch, not to be served to anyone else, but for him alone. Since I ended up paying for the meal, I remember this precisely. A bottle of Scotch costs more in an Italian restaurant than you can imagine. I'd never paid for a bottle of Scotch sold by a restaurant, and I felt like I owned part interest in the restaurant when I left that night. It was some billion-dollar Scotch. The reason I paid for the bill: it is part of my inferiority complex that comes from having no money in my childhood. It is a weakness of character, something pathetic that lives deep in my soul. My brothers and sisters—we all got wounded somehow about money. My wound was I never could pay for anything ever. It killed me when I started to become known as a mooch at the Citadel because I always borrowed money. I always paid it back, but I hated that reputation, so this was my repair work over the years. Much of what we do in life is repair work on our childhood. We try to make it better than it was when we were growing up. But usually our insecurities remain our insecurities.

Anyway, I thought Styron was a shit bird. I think fame killed something in that guy. You know, Jackie and Jack Kennedy would come to Styron's house on the Cape, so I can see why he looked at me like I was a toadstool. But this is why I don't like writers. I don't like hanging around them; I don't like being with them. I think they're shit birds. You know: "As the president was telling me," or "when the queen of England gave me a medal . . . " It bit my neck down. I really needed a chiropractor.

One of Mike's complaints about me was I never wrote a letter "Dear Mr. Styron, I really enjoyed meeting you and Rose when you were here in Rome." After Mike met him at the airport on his visit to the University of Virginia, he hands him this manuscript and says, "Will you read my novel, Mr. Styron?" Styron politely takes it and evidently does read it. Mike wrote him constantly after that, and every once in a while, Styron would write him back. I think Styron required sycophancy in the same way Dickey seemed to require it. I can think two ways about it: That's the way you get ahead, but I'd rather die.

Mike used to say, "Conroy knew no one; he wanted to know no one. When he met someone, he never called them back, followed up, got in touch, or gave a shit. He hung around people who dwelled in the valleys and ate goat cheese. Conroy was happy with his tribe of Lilliputians, the little people." He thought I was slumming. Mike thought Anne Rivers Siddons was nothing in the world he inhabited, and he would say, "Oh, Paul Darcy Boles. I'm so sorry, Big Man. I happen to know the real Paul Bowles. We went to Morocco, and I stayed with the real Paul Bowles. This Darcy I do not know and do not want to know." To him they were simply part of my exquisite collection of miniatures. I collected cameos where he collected Caravaggios.

Mike always complained that I never called Gore Vidal again, never called Anthony Burgess, never called Styron. I said, "What am I going to call them for? We're not friends. They obviously don't need me as their friend. They gave no indication they wanted me to call, so why would I do that?"

He said, "Well, you love your midgetry. What you can't take, Conroy, is the big time. You can't take being in the big time, playing with the heavyweights."

The one I got to know best was Gore Vidal, because I would see Gore on the street. We did not live far from each other. I took him to dinner several times with Mike and Linda. Gore liked me because I picked up checks. Everybody likes me because I pick up checks. There are people with a money shadow who could be billionaires, and it drives them crazy to lose a nickel. I've seen this over and over again. But I like to pick up checks, and Gore was a great conversationalist. I loved listening to him, which I think made him like me. I did not try to compete with him, which also made him like me. And he once told me he liked me because I asked nothing from him.

Gore liked *The Lords of Discipline* because he was attracted to military colleges; his father was one of the great football players at West Point. He told me *Lords of Discipline* could have been a good book if only I'd known that all those guys were gay. I said, "I can't wait to tell my roommates."

But basically, Gore showed no real interest in me at all until *The Prince of Tides* hit the best-seller list. I had no idea that he had even noticed; I had no idea it would mean a thing to him. But he wanted to know: How did you do it? How did you figure out what the American people wanted to read? Of course, I had no idea what the American people wanted to read. I still don't have any idea what the American people want to read. I write what I want to write, and you don't know if it's going to be of interest to anybody else at all. But Gore thought I had busted my way into a best-selling subject—the screwed-up American family—and he wanted to know how I'd discovered it. It may have been that night that something changed between Mike and me. I don't think Mike was ready for anybody of his generation to become a big name. And I use that advisedly, with a certain humor.

Gore was very aware of his place in literary history, and from the way he talked to me, I could tell he never thought he wrote very good novels, and it bothered him a lot. But Gore Vidal was unusual for this: he admitted he read my book. It seems to cost most writers a pound of flesh to admit they read your book. And withholding is much more natural to most people than praise. Giving praise seems to take something out of the human spirit of most writers. Now, I am a competitive male, but writing is one area where it doesn't seem to make sense to be competitive, because there are so many things that can go right or wrong that you have no control over in a writing career.

When I'd given Mike Mewshaw the first three or four hundred pages of *The Prince of Tides,* he read these pages as though I'd given him the directions for taking Tylenol. He said, "This should be ten novels, not one." That was his reading of the book. Cut it into several novels and publish them for the next ten years. And with no enthusiasm at all. This was over lunch. I can still show you the restaurant. I remember him walking out, and I'm thinking, "He didn't say one good thing about it." *The Prince of Tides* to him was like opening a can of tuna. I was terribly disappointed.

Then Cliff Graubert reads it and says it's the most anti-Semitic book he's ever read in his life. I said, "More than *Mein Kamf*?" He said, "It's obvious you hate Jews." Could you tell me, Mr. Graubert, how you got that out of reading? He said, "You say it's an art form to hate New York City. More Jews live in New York City than in Tel Aviv." But since Cliff has read only three books in his life—one of them was a Hardy Boys—this didn't bother me. And now I get to say, "Is this the man who hated *Prince of Tides*?"

~

We moved back to Atlanta when I was about halfway through *The Prince of Tides* because Mom was dying of cancer. I wanted to be there with her, and as my brothers and sisters all pointed out, I was the logical one to be there, because I was the only one who didn't have a job.

After her death, there was the coming back of Dad; that became a full conversion for Dad. By then he had been divorced and retired for some time, and when the colonel could no longer bark and everybody had to answer, he was really adrift. Life had trampled him for the first time. I think he realized he had really screwed up with us, we were really mad about it, and he needed to do something about it if he was going to have any kind of life with his children. He looked around and was horrified by what his family took him to be. I think he was absolutely shocked. My father thought he was a great father, a great husband, a great provider. For him that meant he provided for his kids, we went to church, we went to Catholic schools, we went to college. He'd done great. Everything a Depression kid was supposed to do for his family, my father had done. Dad was perfectly happy with the man he was, delighted in every way. And that he had inspired such loathing and contempt made him determined to prove us wrong. He really wanted his children to love him.

Dad did the best he could, but it was going to take years before I trusted him. I was not in my Good Shepherd forgiveness mode at that time. Many of the other kids let Dad in long before I did; I was the last to come around. There was no question I was hardest for Dad to convince. I was disgusted by him as a human being. I hated everything about him. And so I put Dad through an obstacle course.

He came by my house every day. I was terrible to him. I said hideous things to him. "Oh, good morning, Dad. How does it feel to be the worst fucking father that ever lived? Come on in, I'll fix you some coffee." "Oh, hey, Dad. What did it feel like to hit a three-year old baby? I'm curious. Come in and tell me, I'll fix you some coffee." "Oh, good morning Dad. Tell me how it feels to punch your fist across a pretty woman's jaw and make her nose bleed. I'm really curious about that; it must be fun. Come on in, I'll give you some coffee."

I would greet him with something like that every day. I don't know how Dad knocked on the door. I always had something waiting for him. This assault on him each morning—I had to do it. And I think, deep down in his amoeba soul, he knew I had to do it too, because he kept coming over. And some days I was just vicious with him. I said, "Dad, one thing, if you keep coming over here, I'm going to tell you every single thing I think about you as I think it, and I'm not going to hold anything back."

Dad would tickle me, because I'm finding out he has a sense of humor, which I never knew. I would say this to Dad, and he'd be reading the sports section, he'd put the paper down, he'd go, "Sheesh, Mr. Sensitivo." I started to see how Dad was one of those men who love by indirection, who love off-the-nose. His conversion wasn't perfect, because he was born an asshole and remained an asshole, but he was trying, which all his kids appreciated. Every one of us appreciated his attempt.

~

At some point Nan Talese calls me up to New York. She is the only editor I've ever had who needed me to stay in New York, and I think she did that because it showed her mastery of the personal touch; it showed her power in the publishing company that she could get that done. I stayed up there for about five months; I think the hotel was called the Roosevelt, and they must have spent a billion dollars on putting me up there. Houghton Mifflin was located near the Chrysler Building, and I would go over every morning. Nan and I would work side by side, eight hours a day, until the afternoon, when she would give me homework to bring the next morning. Then we'd do the same thing all over again. She repeated this process with *Beach Music*. Nan works hard; she works her ass off. It's a hardworking profession when people like Jonathan Galassi and Nan Talese practice it.

Nan can't write worth a lick, but she has a great literary mind, and she knows good writing. She knows what it is, what she wants to hear. I drive her crazy with my overwriting. Nan has always said I'm the hardest author for her to work with, because I like these bombastic, impetuous, impossible plots. That embarrasses Nan, because she mostly publishes books where if something happens, it's a glance between married couples when they both know they want to have an affair. It's a simple glance, or a man spilling his wine. He gets yelled at by his wife, and he looks over at another woman, who passes him her napkin, and they know they will be together the rest of their lives. Nan likes that. But in the overdose of imagination that I go into, and my overwrought, fever-brained thinking, I can't just have a rapist; I can't just kill a rapist; I have to have a rapist eaten by a fucking tiger. I always collect stories, and the story of the tiger at the gas station was one of those in *The Prince of Tides*. Nan thought it was ridiculous to have a tiger. She hates these stories and looks for them and tries to eradicate them when I've shoehorned them into my books, but I love them too much.

I am always overbaked, overdone, over everything. And you know, I do prefer that stiff upper lip, but I cannot do it—those British gentlemen in their clubs, perusing newspapers and smoking pipes, and getting quietly drunk in those great leather chairs in front of fires in the fireplace and portraits on the wall, before they return to their loveless lives and loveless marriages and unknown children. I went to England with some book I had written, and at one of the dinner parties, an Englishwoman sitting next to me said to her friend, "I say, did you hear that Penelope's son fell in the Tube and had both legs severed?" Her friend—I can't do English accents, I'd love to be able to—but her friend said, "Pity." And I'm going, "What the fuck are you saying?! Both legs severed?! My God!" Of course, then I realized I had my typical overreaction and was horrified by my overemotionalism at this legless child who lay in a hospital in a coma somewhere. But that's me.

And in my whole life, every teacher has mentioned my odd prose style. I don't know when this hit me, but it evidently hit me fairly early, because every time I wrote something, it sounded different from everybody else in the class. Sometimes a teacher would like it a lot; sometimes they'd hate it. I got a C in a creative writing class at the Citadel because

Colonel Carpenter hated the way I wrote and would mock it openly. You know, "Come on, there's simplicity, the elegance of simplicity." Everybody talks about "the elegance of simplicity" as if they made the phrase up; I've heard it more times than any writer in history. Even Gene Norris would say, "Cool your jets, Mr. Conroy. Just cool your jets."

I did come across people who absolutely loathed my writing, but I came across people who loved it. Fat Jack Martin, my fabulous history of England teacher: "Mr. Conroy, stand up and face the class. I want the class to get a close look at what these sewer pipes of Europe can produce, and its absolute perfection when it comes to the Irish. And yes, Mr. Conroy, of course is getting angry at me. Notice the red face, notice the flashing eyes. He is sitting there loathing me. In the Irish you get loathing, but Mr. Conroy I ask you, explain to me an island nation that has never, ever built up a navy. Explain to me a language-loving nation that only produces those harmless Irish ditties. Explain to me a warlike nation which has never won a single battle." He was hilarious with me, and he'd always write on my papers: "Dear Mr. Conroy, I do not believe you understand, or absorb, one fact of English history, but you write your ignorance down so beautifully," and he told me he loved my writing.

I remember this following me even before I'd written anything. When all the guys went to Europe, I would write postcards to Tim Belk, and Mike Jones would say, "Would y'all listen to this bullshit." He'd read something I'd written and have the whole place laughing their ass off because it was so flowery, pretentious, and stupid. I'd be sitting on Hadrian's Wall and getting moved by it, or sitting in some cathedral getting lost in describing it and sounding like a Hallmark card on steroids. But I get letters from readers all the time saying, "You're not writing for yourself. It's us that need the tiger. We need the tiger."

Nan says that I would fight her and disapprove of her suggestions. I will take her word for that. I don't feel like I've been overly combative, but who the hell knows? I have fought for things I've wanted very badly. To Nan, I was Southern, out of control, needed a bronco rider to break the stallion. When I started writing *The Prince of Tides*, I said, I'm going to write everything I want to write and then let Nan figure it out. I didn't want to hold back on anything. Unfortunately, I followed my own advice. But I think it pleased her that she had to be the lion tamer. And we had a great time working.

~

Back in Atlanta, once again it is a nightmare with custody of Lenore's kids. Alan has gone to the University of Arizona, where he is now chief of neurosurgery. I'm delighted he's out of Atlanta, but he keeps the kids one summer and would never send them back. We had to fly out to Tucson, Arizona, for a custody battle. He's put them in bar mitzvah school and in Jewish schools. It was a mess. Alan had also sent Emily and Gregory to a shrink who wrote to the court vouching for the reputation and character of Dr. Fleischer and saying how important it was for the kids to get a Jewish education. In his professional opinion, it was by far the best thing for those kids to be raised by Alan. Later, this shrink went to prison for life in Arizona for child abuse.

It took about a month to deal with this and cost thousands upon thousands upon thousands of dollars. We had to fly our lawyer out, put him up in this great hotel. We stayed in this great hotel, and it was just a nightmare.

On the stand, Alan made a mistake. Alan always makes a mistake. He gets on the stand and says, "I cannot allow my children to go home to live,"—and he points to me; he begins weeping—"with that crazy man, that crazy man." He's weeping. And as he's weeping, weeping, I turn to Lenore, I point to myself, and out loud I say, "Moi?" The court collapses. Now, what I had done since I'd been there a month, I'd made friends with everybody, the stenographer, the deputy. I was going to lunch with the guards. And when I said, "Moi?" they had to shut down the court.

Finally we win; we get them back. But I was worried about Gregory and Emily. I felt something in the air that was wrong, like there was a dark, dark secret in the corner.

We know we have to send them to Arizona for Christmas, and we know he will not send them back. Yet we're under court order to send them. Lenore's on the phone, screaming. I hate screaming. I can't stand it. And yes, this did come from my childhood. I can't handle it. I just told her not to scream at me or not when I was around. "You scream all you want. Scream out the window. Go on the roof, scream, do it all you want, but don't do it when I'm around."

But I hear him screaming at her on the phone. She screamed at him. They're screaming back and forth, fighting over custody for Christmas, when Emily, who's about eleven, comes in. And Emily, I adore. Emily was on a swimming team, and to show my stepfatherly love for her, I would go down to her meets, and I would see Emily plop into the pool in complete agony, and whether she was swimming the breast stroke or the crawl or the butterfly, it all looked like the same stroke; it looked like a pained animal had been wounded and was making her wounded way. Invariably she finished last. And in one of them, about fifteen minutes after the race was over, she was still struggling, and I would be sitting there, "Emily, it's important to finish." Sometimes she'd simply stop in the pool and tell everybody what agony she was in and how she could not go on another stroke, and then grab the rope and pull herself in. But I used to let Emily struggle with that, thinking that is what life is truly like. I see life as a great struggle for everybody.

She was funny to me; she'd make up songs, and I started making up songs. I'd sing "Don't cry for me, Arizona, the truth is I don't like tacos. I don't like nachos. That part of the nation, I only go there for visitation." I would sing this, and she would sing something back. But while her parents are on the phone screaming, Emily comes in, and I'm reading, as I always do, especially to shut myself out of this nightmare. So I'm reading. I'm sitting there reading, and we can hear the screaming going on downstairs with Alan and Lenore.

Emily comes in, gets in bed, "What you reading, Pat?" Told her. Would you rather talk to me? I said, "Sure, I'd rather talk to you."

She says, "What do you want to talk about?"

I said, "What do you want to talk about?"

She said, "I want to talk about something that you're going to hate me for, Pat, when I tell you this. You're going to just hate my guts."

I said, "Nah, no more than I do now, so don't worry."

She said, "Yeah, you will. It's so disgusting. I shouldn't have done it, but I did it."

So I said, "What are you going to tell me, kid?"

It was rape in all possible ways, committed by her father. I felt my heart sink to my left foot.

I said, "Emily, I'm sorry that happened. But let me tell you something. I'm telling you to your face, and you can take this to the bank. It'll never happen again."

She said, "Yeah, I've got to go back to visit."

I said, "You'll never go back there for visitation."

So we report to the lawyers. Alan, of course: we're making it up. She's making it up. She's dreaming it. Then it was me putting filthy thoughts into her mind. Alan's outraged. He's going to sue me. So he comes to Atlanta to argue for visitation. He's in court. He's weeping. He's always weeping. He's one of those guys who can weep on the stand. He's an egomaniac, so he loves the scene. He's wailing, telling his sad story, "They're trying to keep me from my children." Then he starts saying, "This crazy man, Your Honor, he's even accused me, falsely, of sexually abusing my own daughter. He's accused me of sexually abusing my own daughter. What kind of man would do that? This is outrageous."

He has just put this in the public record. Ah-ha, public record: I will one day use this.

We had an idiot Southern judge for this, and at the end he says, "Well, I'm not going to keep a daddy away from his children. He needs to see his children."

I walk over to Alan's attorneys, and say, "Here's what your good lawyering has done. You just got your boy arrested." I told Lenore, "When we get home, we start packing for Europe. Emily ain't going to Arizona again. I just want to tell you that. We should go back to Rome."

But going to Rome was against the court order; we'd be in contempt of court. I think it was either that night or the next night Emily and I went to the police and testified to what he did, gave them her whole story on film. They put a warrant out for his arrest, and we went back to Rome the second time just to protect this kid.

When we're in Rome I said to Emily, "If you have other stuff to tell me, tell me sometime, whenever you can."

Finally, in the first month we were in Rome, she said, "Pat, I think I can tell you some other stuff now."

I believe she was getting scared about him going to court, bringing her back home. That's when she told me the worst stuff that had happened, and I wrote it down word for word. I wrote for seventeen pages. You would not believe it.

It started when she was a little girl, the most savage rapes you ever heard of. It was awful. When you enter that world of child abuse, you enter a world where you've never been before, where there is a horrible breed of human beings, and any depravity is possible.

Emily lies about everything, and because she lies about everything, nobody believes her about this. I believed her because her description was just too graphic. Here's why I trusted it: she had described everything that happened—she was young when it started—and she knew details I didn't think a kid would know. She knew things I didn't know.

She's lied about everything in her life—everything—but it's also I think what happens to those girls who are threatened if they don't lie. They become liars, and then nobody believes them when they step forward with this truth. The one thing about Emily, she has never—since she told me this—she has never once told me it didn't happen, that she was lying to me. That's the one thing she has kept up as truth from the time she told me until now. And I always told her, if this is imagination, we need to know.

Anyway, I'm writing it down, writing it down, writing it down. Horrible—God, it was horrible to write down. She told me everything with her pillow over her face, and said after I married Lenore, she couldn't sleep because she waited for me to come in for her at night. She thought it was what fathers did to their daughters. And when you're little, you don't know that every father is not doing what he's doing to you to their own kids. There was a time I thought every kid was going home and getting the shit kicked out of them by their dad. I was raised to think, okay, that's part of it.

Finally Emily finished. I said, "That must have been incredibly hard for you, but it ain't happening again. I repeat, that ain't going to happen."

Lenore seemed as shocked as I was to learn that this all started when she and Alan were still married. It was hard to understand how she didn't know about it if she was there, but it was even harder to think she knew about it and did nothing. I give her the benefit of the doubt on this one.

I sent Alan a copy of the seventeen pages and a letter. "Dear Alan, Emily just told me everything you did to her, the multiple rapes, and I just want you to know something. If you ever touch her again I'm going to cut off your dick, I'm going to make a wallet out of it, and I'm going to carry it in my back pocket the rest of my life."

Of course, the DAs went crazy. "You're hurting our case." I didn't care. I told him what I was thinking. That's what I was thinking. Deal with it how you want.

There was a warrant out for Alan's arrest in Georgia, but the state of Georgia did not seek to extradite him from Arizona, so he was safe. But when I was in Atlanta doing an interview for *The Prince of Tides*, a reporter for the Associated Press asks me, "What's your next book?"

I said, "My next book is about the sexual abuse of my stepdaughter, Emily Fleischer, by her father, head of the neurosurgery department at the University of Arizona. His name is Doctor Alan Fleischer."

He said, "I can hardly believe that."

I said, "Check the public records."

He checked it. The story went out on the wire. What happened— and it was interesting—it went out everywhere on the wire, but the Arizona papers would not print it. However, we had entered the age of the fax machine, and faxes are moving AP articles into Arizona households and offices. It becomes a scandal that the papers don't print it. Then there's an article about why they didn't print it.

Then of course Alan, who is always good for this, about maybe less than a month later—he evidently had great pressure on him—a month later had several patients die on the operating table. Now, if I'd been a brain surgeon, there would have been a series of dead people. But the rumor was Alan was almost comatose with cocaine. He was let go by the University of Arizona from his position. After that, he had nothing to stand on then, and he disappeared from my life.

But Emily is a human tragedy. After she told me about the abuse, she would tell every cab driver she passed, every ticket attendant at a movie theater, "I was sexually abused by my father. I was sexually abused by my father." She had this need to put that out there. It drove us crazy; it drove Lenore nuts. I thought it was something she's working out, so I said okay, you know.

Then, Emily's at some Catholic school way out in bumfuck Rome. One day I come in from somewhere and Lenore's in a complete panic, "I won't do it; I can't do it; I can't take it." Same old.

"What happened?"

"The nuns called. Emily's been talking about how she was raped, said she was sexually molested. I'm not dealing with it. You have to go out there."

So I went out the next day, and there were about four or five nuns waiting as I walked in. I'm used to nuns. They looked like nuns; they acted like nuns; they talked like nuns.

They said to me, "Mr. Conroy, thank you for coming."

I said, "Oh, think nothing of it." You know, "I wish these were happier circumstances, but they're not."

"We need to ask you some questions, Mr. Conroy."

I said, "Feel free."

"Emily claims that she was sexually molested by her father."

"As far as I know," I said, "That's true."

"And does this include rape and anal rape?"

"Yes, yes, that's true also from what she's told me."

"This has been going on since she was three or four years old?"

I say, "Yeah, yeah, it's been going on a long time. It should have been caught earlier; it just wasn't."

So they're sitting there, and I'm looking at these nuns, and they're looking at me, and I suddenly get it. I said, "Sisters, oh my God! I just figured out what's going on! Do you realize I am Emily's stepfather, not her real father?"

And these four or five nuns simply collapse into their hands, and one of them was crying she had been so upset by my coldness in describing the way I had raped this child.

"Mr. Conroy, we're so sorry."

I said, "No, don't worry. You thought you were sitting in front of a child rapist, and I was acting so nonchalant about it I can understand your being upset. But allow me to assure you that this did not happen exactly the way you thought it had happened."

You know, that's my life. That is my life. An accusation often made against me—that I sometimes exaggerate in my stories—has always tickled me. It's not so much that I exaggerate in my stories; it's more like God has exaggerated in my life. When I learned that critics considered me melodramatic, I had to figure out what they meant. Then I got it: shit happens in my books. That's because shit happened in my life. All kinds of shit. My life has been one long melodrama.

~

Emily created drama anywhere she went, and I mean anywhere. Lenore was always trying to get rid of Emily for the summer—she would have sent Emily to the moon if she could have—so one summer in desperation, she sent Emily to the longest, boot camp-iest Outward Bound, somewhere in Maine. One of the things is Emily has to paddle her kayak out to an island that is uninhabited, and she has to live on this island for three days. Emily is not gifted at any of this: making fires, keeping dry, pitching tents, all this stuff. After two days, the authorities of Outward Bound have lost touch with her, Emily has called for a helicopter rescue, and Emily has been airlifted off this isolated island to a posh hospital in Bangor, Maine. It cost thousands of dollars. Emily is the only person I've ever heard of who was kicked out of Outward Bound. My God, the world explodes around her. Emily goes off to Outward Bound, and the next thing you know a helicopter is going over to pick her up. They send a guy risking his life, bounding down a ladder.

Another summer, Lenore sent Emily to Camp Blue Star, up in the mountains near Highlands—a Jewish camp, famous all over the South. All these Jewish families had sent their kids there for years. Bernie had been there, so I think Bernie talks Lenore into sending Emily to Blue Star. But nothing with Emily can end up correct. Nothing can end up actually helping. There is a melodrama around Emily that is absolutely unbelievable.

Well, Cliff's wedding is taking place in Rome; Annie and Heyward have come over; Nathalie Dupree has come over; we give a party on our rooftop terrace. This is about when Emily liked to strike, and Lenore gets a phone call. So I hear Lenore in agony, "Oh, my God! I don't know what to do. Holy Christ!" It was the director of Camp Blue Star.

Lenore's saying, "I can't deal with this. I just can't do it. I can't deal with this. I just can't deal with this."

I get so tired of it I said, "Look, let me deal with it. Whatever it is, let me deal with it."

I get a "Mr. Conroy, I'm the head of Camp Blue Star."

This guy's father and mother had founded it.

I said, "What is the trouble, sir?"

He says, "Well, your daughter, Emily."

I said, "You need to know this. And make a quick note of this. She is my stepdaughter."

He said, "Well, you know, she's had a rather unusual life."

"Yes, she has. What has she done now?"

Okay, well they have a ghost story–telling night with all the girls. They're up in this cabin, then they turn out all the lights, and the girls and the counselors take turns telling each other ghost stories to scare each other. I think it's pretty traditional at camp. But, you know, I didn't go to camp. My mother gave me used tuna fish cans to play with instead.

So I said, "Well, what could she have done?" waiting for the explosion that I knew would come hideously, and it did. What she did was, when it was her turn to tell the ghost story, she told how her father, a Jewish neurosurgeon, had raped her time and time again, held her down, starved her, beat her senseless. He wouldn't let her eat until she agreed to the rape. All these little Jewish girls are looking at her. And so Emily then brings out an audio-visual aide. She says, "But my stepfather, Pat Conroy, the writer"—she always used me in this kind of way—"When he took me to Rome to escape my father, he went out and bought me"—and I did not do this by the way—"He went out and bought me a rosary blessed by the Pope." She brings out this rosary, hangs it over her neck, gets the little crucifix and says, "This was blessed by Pope John Paul the II, and it offers special protection to girls who have been molested by their fathers, and my father looks like Satan." She raises the crucifix up in the air and says, "This will keep him away from me and all of you safe." And then she looks out the window and says, "Oh, my God! That's him in the window right now!" All of a sudden there are thirty-four screaming Jewish girls racing headlong into the night, down the mountain.

Well, you know, they've got to do something. What do I suggest?

I said, "Well, first of all I'd give her a medal for who told the best ghost story. Obviously, Emily won that hands down."

"This is not a joke, Mr. Conroy."

I said, "I didn't mean it as a joke. But, you know, that's the problem we're dealing with."

Anyway, we had a nice talk, I brown-nosed him, and he reluctantly kept her.

But Emily's had a terrible time, so she can do just about anything with me. I cut her a lot of slack and wish her well.

In most ways Rome was a magical time, and I'm very proud of what I accomplished over there. *The Prince of Tides* went on the best-seller list when I was in Rome, but one of my disciplines is I don't look at lists, I don't look at reviews. I did not realize that Lenore was showing Susannah where my book was listed in the *International Herald Tribune* every week. After fifty-one weeks, it dropped off. Susannah was down at the piazza where they bought the newspaper, and she burst into tears when my book was not on the best-seller list. I said, "Why did you do that, Lenore? What kind of values are we inculcating into Susannah?"

When I found out *The Prince of Tides* was on the *New York Times* best-seller list, I felt nothing. It doesn't make me happy in remembering it. I don't have "Pat's flooded with happiness at the memory when he first heard the words 'You're on the best-seller list.' And he walked the streets of Rome, considering himself a Caesar of the moment. He stood over the city, and he knew the city was his at last. He held up his arms in a Christlike pose above the Campidoglio and said, 'Yes, finally, the world is coming to me as I wished it, as I always knew it would. The earth is mine. It belongs to me. All women will soon be on their backs, all men will be on their stomachs, lying prostrate when I walk by them." Unfortunately, I don't have any of those moments in my life. I'm not a guy who can walk down the street and say, "Oh, I'm happy, happy, happy!"

It always astounds me when I hear people say things like: "When I first went on the best-seller list . . . " or "When I was number one on the best-seller list . . ." Then there's "I can't remember if that was before or after I won the Pulitzer," and "Life is different after you win the big one." I mean, I just can't even get my mouth to say those things.

I've seen other people moan and groan about not being on the best-seller list, but I have never looked at that part of my life. I never look at the best-seller list ever, and this includes the time before I was on it, the times I've been on it, and the times after I've been on it. When I started writing, I decided I was not writing for that reason. And I don't want that to become any reason why I write books. The way I grew up—Wolfe-obsessed, Faulkner-obsessed, writer-obsessed—that seemed to be not the way those guys I admired did it. Obviously they had to make a living, but I never came across that kind of obsession. I try not to worry or care if my books sell or not, because I don't think there's much I can do about it.

If I'm going through the newspaper and see my name in any article, I turn the page. I read no article where my name is in it. If I see my name—Bam—it's next page. And if I know my name is going to be in there, I don't read the paper or the magazine to begin with. This is part of a protective shield that I tried to develop early. I think it started when Dad caught me cutting out articles about myself playing basketball. He slapped me and said, "What is this? Cutting out Valentines to yourself? That's not what's important. It's how you play the game, win the game." So I thought, "Oh, my God, this is egomania. This should not be important to a real athlete." It may have started with that.

But I built this shield up, and it is strong. Now it protects every part of my writing life. When I publish a book, I never look at it again. I can never look at the book again even when it's sitting on the shelf. I don't go back and say, "God, what a dope I was," because if you reread, you will see every flaw. They will leap out at you; they will make you blind; they will drive you crazy. By the time it's published, it's set in stone, and there's nothing you can do about it. It will tie you in knots. So this protects me against something not being as good as I want. It protects the perfectionist in me that few people know about.

The shield means I don't remember one thing I've ever written. It always surprises me when somebody tells me they like something that's in one of my books. I'll say, "Oh, no kidding. That sounds great. I'm glad it's in there. I had no idea." I've had readers look at me like I'm nuts, because there are writers who can recite their whole book from memory.

When people hear I don't read reviews of my work, they don't believe me, but I do not listen to anything that might get in my way at all. As a writer, your own insecurity is enough of a thorn to be piercing your flesh for the rest of your life, and I was not going to add anything to it. So I tried to have the outside world have as little to do with what happened in the writing room as possible. Critics can cripple you; I've seen them tear into writers. I've heard writers talking about bad reviews and hideous reviews, and I don't want that to be part of my conversations. So I have my little disciplines that actually are very self-protective.

When I got a good review, it did nothing for me, sort of like the Barbra Streisand scene where she sings to a standing ovation, but she sees the one guy who doesn't like it. There's something like that in me. Then I got some bad reviews with *The Water Is Wide,* and I thought, "God, it hurts my feelings. That's horrible." But what did I get out of it? I don't see what the whole point is. If I could write a book better, I'd do it. I swear I would; I would do it. If I could please the critic, I would, but that seems impossible to me. If my books don't work, it's because of a lack of imagination and talent on my part, not a lack of desire. There's not much I can do with these flaws staring me in the face. So I quit reading reviews after one or two of *The Water Is Wide.* I did not want to let that stuff in where it could get to me. I don't need these people. They can say anything they want about my book, but I ain't got to read it. They don't get to hurt my feelings. All these little worthless shit-bird voices, however they flock together, in whatever chorus, are meaningless in the long run.

Gail Godwin gave me a horrible review for *The Prince of Tides* in the *New York Times.* When I first met her afterward, she almost died. I said, "Relax, Gail. Don't worry about that. Some people like it; some people don't." My attitude is they can say whatever they want to say—it's America—but I ain't got to read it. I've known a couple of writers who quit writing because they got bad reviews from the *New York Times.* I don't think I ever got a good review from the *Times.* Dad used to memorize them. He would say, "My, the *New York Times* really doesn't like my boy." He would start quoting it, which tickled me more than anything else. But I've seen people hurt; they said they couldn't write again.

The one thing you have to avoid when you're writing is being afraid, because everybody makes you afraid. The critics will make you afraid. Your professors will make you afraid. The writers who teach you will make you afraid. Your friends make you afraid. Your parents make you afraid. Society makes you afraid. Everybody has ways of putting you down as a writer. "Were you on the best-seller list? How many did you sell? Did you make a lot of money?" So everything is working against writers fully letting themselves flower unto themselves. I didn't want to be afraid of anything. I wanted to be able to attempt to do anything, or say anything.

It's tough finding your way, but I've never seen a critic in the *New York Times* I didn't think I could out-write. That critic hasn't shown his or her face yet, so I don't worry about what they think. I have never figured out why anybody who was reading great books in college would say, "By God, I'm going to become a critic," unless they could not write these books they were loving. I decided critics were not going to be a part of my creative life, and I decided early I was not going to be a critic. They'd send me books to review; I just said no thanks. I did not want to be a part of some writer opening up the *New York Times* or the *Atlanta Journal-Constitution* in the morning and seeing my review of their book as they're drinking coffee and them getting sick to their stomach and hating me, as of course they should, for their whole lives. Now, critics will tell you they have a higher calling, you know: we need to keep the measurements high. Well, good, let them do it. I don't need to.

⌢

In about 1988, they tell me they're not going to pursue Emily's case in Atlanta because she's living in Rome. Great. So we move back to Atlanta. They weren't going to pursue it anyway. I could have stayed in Rome. But if I'd stayed in Rome, I'm afraid I'd still be married to Lenore.

FOUR

Atlanta/San Francisco

1988–1992

I had scaled the heights of my talent . . . and knew . . . what it felt
like to be famous. It didn't feel like much at all.

PAT CONROY, *The Prince of Tides*

He was distraught. He felt there was no way out. And when
somebody feels that way, that's when they become suicidal. But he
didn't really want to kill himself. He wanted to live.

MARION O'NEILL, Ph.D., ABPP, clinical psychologist

When we moved back to Atlanta, I got involved in too much when I
should have gotten involved in nothing. That's when the Atlanta paper
hired Bill Kovach of the *New York Times* to come make the Atlanta
newspaper world class, and then forced him out. I got embroiled with
all that—more chaos to my life. I've been in a million fights with the
Atlanta paper. I wrote a bunch of outraged letters to the editor. One is
so long it embarrasses me. Then there was a march for Kovach; there was
all that bullshit. I've often thought I should have just stayed in Rome.

In Atlanta, Lenore got rid of every friend I ever had. She got rid of
Bernie. She got rid of Cliff. She attacked friend after friend. I had to go
grovel and get them back after I left her. I had to go on a penitential tour
and crawl back apologizing to my friends Lenore had insulted to the
degree they would spit over their shoulder when they heard my name.
All this I have to say is my fault. I allowed it to happen. Cliff she humiliated socially when he came over to get some books. She had some
socialites at the house, and she told him not to come through the front
door. Cliff was horrified. He had enough of that Jewish contempt for
himself, and of course, so does Lenore, and she was playing into that.

When we came back from Rome, Annie gave a Southern luncheon to welcome Lenore home. She invited Cliff's wife and some of the other wives, different people like that. Lenore announced at the lunch that she had no one in Atlanta she liked at all; she was completely friendless. So, all the guests are thinking: What are we, horsemeat? Annie told me later that Lenore made it very, very uncomfortable for everybody.

Now, I've loved Annie Rivers Siddons since the moment I met her. We were always great friends. Women have been a great source of joy to me, and friendship. They open up as friends much more easily than men do; women enjoy talking more. Annie has been fun to talk to my whole life, but there was never anything sexual between us. Yet this flirtation would go on. Annie's got a Southern-woman way of flirtation. We used to tell each other things like, "I want to put a hickey on your throat." We'll laugh our asses off. And, "I want to kiss your belly button while you're getting dressed," and shit like that. Okay, Lenore sees this and does not like any of it at all. Also, Annie was a great beauty— a humdinger—and Lenore did not like that at all. She could not cut me off completely from Annie, but she made it very difficult.

Then, one of my best friends in Atlanta was a lawyer I'd hired about five or six years earlier to explain the particulars of every contract I signed. One day Lenore bushwhacks me and says, "I have proof that he's been stealing from you for many years. I'm going to take out a warrant for his arrest and alert the newspapers." I said, no, you're not. She said, "I've been with the accountants, and we can prove this." I called him right then, said, "I'm firing you as my lawyer. Thanks for all the help you've been." Click. This was a great, great loss in my life. I didn't get to tell him that story until five years after I left her.

He said, "Can you tell me why you did it?"

I said, "I had to think quick because Lenore was acting, and I was afraid it would have been front page news in Atlanta and your career would have been over."

Bernie made the mistake of teaching Emily. That was his job, but he did not know and I did not know she was going to get rid of Bernie from our life. This was after the story of Emily's abuse had come out, so Bernie's working with her. In middle school, Bernie got students to write like you've never seen. Bernie would pull it out and pull it out, something that was bothering them, how they reacted to their grand-father's death; one of them realized he was gay. He finally was getting stuff out of Emily. She was writing about her sexual abuse, and when she finished, she read it aloud to the class. The class gave her a standing ovation. Emily broke down; the class broke down.

Bernie was also counseling Lenore all through this and saying "You're going to have to change the way you treat this poor kid. Try taking a walk around the park with Emily after school, talk to her, get to know her, do things with her." So he would call up, and "Did you walk around the park?" Lenore would say, "I sprained my ankle today, Bernie." So they clashed bitterly and horribly. I just said, "I cannot deal." And we were moving anyway, so when I moved out to San Francisco, I didn't have a friend in my life.

When her son Gregory was going to college in California, Lenore brings me the news that we need to go out and help Tim Belk, who had moved from Beaufort to San Francisco and was dying of AIDS. Tim Belk was a strong argument with me, because I knew he was dying. He went down to eighty pounds before they found that drug cocktail, and he was just dying in front of me. He didn't have any family, and I'd been worrying about Tim dying of AIDS alone. "I want to be near Gregory; you want to be near Tim; let's go to San Francisco." So that's why we moved to San Francisco, where it all fell apart. Anyway, I left for San Francisco when Lenore said she had the room for me to write in ready in the new house on 115 Presidio Avenue. Of course, she didn't because my wives never have rooms for me to write in. This is always an ongoing theme.

I insisted before I went to San Francisco I was going to have some place in the South I could come to, to write. Moving west, I felt un-sheathed from my home; I felt unearthed from the place I felt most comfortable in. So I bought a house on Fripp Island. It's not a great house, but it's a pretty house on the lagoon, and I think it saved my life later. I had just closed on this house on Fripp, and we're getting on a plane in Atlanta to move to San Francisco. In the airport, Lenore does not understand why I'm so concerned about this hurricane I'm seeing on the televisions. It looked like a new planet is forming on earth, and I said Jesus God Almighty. So we head out there, we land,

and I race for CNN. It's a classic scene; the news guy's hair is blowing. I think they only do one of those and show it for the next hundred years. The first thing I heard when I got off, the man says, "According to the latest calculations, meteorologists are saying that Hurricane Hugo will make landfall at a place called Fripp Island, South Carolina." And I scream out in the San Francisco airport, "I'm fucked!" Lenore says, "It's just a storm." I said, "Look at that storm." It veered north right before it got to Fripp and hit Charleston and north of Charleston, so it got my attention.

~

By this time I had become very famous with *The Prince of Tides*. One reason my fame blew up was I spoke at the American Booksellers Association convention in New Orleans. The ABA was a big deal at that time. Walter Cronkite was giving the first talk, Carol Burnett was giving the third talk, with me squeezed in the middle. But it worked out for me very well.

Those things were so unbelievably boring, they were happy to have Walter Cronkite, and happy to have Carol Burnett. Nobody knew who the fuck I was; the Southeastern Booksellers Association—in particular a South Carolina bookseller, Rhett Jackson—had fought to have me included. Of course Nan was worried that nobody would understand why. They'd be mad that I was in—she didn't say that to me, but, you know, they'd be mad that I was picked over some better-known author. Also, she got really disturbed when people came up to take pictures. Back then, they didn't have these cameras like they do now. They were all flashbulbs, and when they came up to take pictures, they would ignore me and do the people on either side of me. This really upset Nan. I said, "Nan, let me give you the old Citadel answer, okay?" And I said, "My blood is up, and I'm excited about this. Let's see who they're taking pictures of after the program is over." It was one of my braggadocio moments when I realized Santini had risen.

I saw Carol Burnett shaking and actually trembling.

I said, "Miss Burnett, you seem nervous. You shouldn't be."

She turns to me and says, "These are intellectuals."

I said, "Ah, they're not intellectuals. Don't worry about that."

She said, "Oh, they're intellectuals. I've never spoken to intellectuals."

I said, "These are dopes. They're all idiots. Don't worry about it. They'll enjoy you. They love your show. That's why you're here, so relax. You've been on stage before. You've been on Broadway. That would be scary; this is nothing."

But she couldn't relax; she just couldn't. I saw her fall apart that day. I'm thinking, you know, my God, if she's nervous, I should be a wreck. But I was, for some reason, as calm as I can be. I was okay. I knew true tragedy in my life by then. I was married to Lenore, so I had already fucked my life up. There was nothing much more I could do to make it worse.

In my speech, I talked about Mom, who had just died, and I was still emotional about her death. I talked about the printing end of *The Boo* and told the story of getting *The Water Is Wide* published, which they found, of course, hilarious, along with my befuddled first trip to New York. The speech went so well that Carol Burnett, when she got up, said, "I've got to follow that?" Afterward, I was mobbed. It took a while to get out of there. When I finally got down on the floor, as they call it, they're waiting in line. The first person in line was Walter Cronkite, and my life had changed.

But it was Lenore who saw how famous I'd gotten with *The Prince of Tides* long before I did. I just did not get it, because I'd sit in a room all day writing. When we got to San Francisco, she had lined up society people that she wanted to be with and told me I had to give her a year because I had ruined her social life in Atlanta. I never wanted to have a social life in Atlanta, and had no idea she wanted to have a social life in Atlanta, but how I ruined it for her: There was a huge article in the Atlanta paper before the Olympics came to town about the history of the Piedmont Driving Club. Everybody knew the Piedmont Driving Club had to do something, because the world population was coming to Atlanta, and its most important business organization did not allow black membership, women membership, or Jewish membership. At that time, the club was male and white and WASP, and that was it. The article gave the whole history of the club, and at the end it quoted a guy named Sims Bray, one of the past presidents of the Piedmont Driving Club. When he was asked why Jews were not allowed entrance, he said, "A club is like a home, and I would never invite my Jew friends to my home."

For a Southern gentleman, that was crudely put. Then I found out that a Jewish friend's thirteen-year-old son read it in the paper and was weeping at the kitchen table. I told her, "I will make sure Sims Bray has my name on his lips when he dies."

So I wrote a letter to the editor which I think could have gotten me elected chief rabbi of Atlanta. I said, I would like to invite all my Jew friends to my home anytime they want to come, and all my black friends, please feel free to come. And all my women friends, come on in my home, you'll be welcomed anytime you come. I like anybody to be able to walk into my home, because home means something different to me than it does to Sims Bray. I said because of Sims Bray's statement, I am sending a donation to the National Organization for Women, and the NAACP, and I'm having a hundred trees planted in the State of Israel. They are calling it the Sims Bray Memorial Forest.

The letter was one of my overdone, bring-me-their-heads moments, there's no question about it. Well, *kaboom*, that hit. Next day this guy appears at the door enraged—Sims Bray Jr.—and I said, "Sims Bray Jr., I'd like to welcome you to my home."

He said, "My father's not an anti-Semite."

I said, "I'm sure this is embarrassing to you."

It was an explosive thing, with letters to the editor for weeks. But one thing I don't care about: I don't mind what people say about me. They can say what they want. They're Americans; I'm fine with it. I don't give a shit about people giving me shit. It is not a requirement to like old Conroy.

But Lenore is utterly dying. She said, "Now you've truly destroyed my social life in Atlanta."

I said, "We have no social life in Atlanta that I know about. How can I ruin it?"

"You ruined it for good."

"Lenore, I'm trying to be a writer. I don't want a social life."

I did not know Lenore wanted a social life, but boy did I find out. In San Francisco, she told me I owed her a year for the pain I caused her socially in Atlanta.

I said, "Lenore, you know me well enough by now. I don't give much of a shit about that."

She said, "Well I do, and you owe me a year."

Next thing you know, I'm invited to every party by the upper crust in San Francisco that I had no desire to meet or socialize with. The year I got out there, we went to a society dinner every night of our lives. Finally she had a place where she could make a great social life for herself. So we went to the mayor's house; we went to the governor's house; we went to this house; we went to that. Head of Pacific Electric Power, ambassador so-and-so. I went around every Goddamn dinner party on earth, meeting with the richest people in San Francisco. She loved it, enjoyed it, reveled in it. I have to admit the people I met were nice. They were great. What I could not stand is why Lenore wished to be around them. That I never got over. If she had said it's the party of the year one more time, I was going to throw myself off the Golden Gate Bridge.

I also admit I am absolutely fascinated by the tribe because I have never been good enough to breathe any air that was available on earth. I came from such a dog-shit social situation that I realized everything was cut off for me, and everything always would be cut off for me. But what I can do is simply observe and enjoy. I've always liked the articulation and the rituals of the upper class a great deal. These beautiful houses, the sense of history, the sense of being part of history, the sense of being part of a legacy, of passing a torch—I liked all that. I liked the way they lived. I liked the things they had. I liked walking into a room where things were properly placed and things had certain value. I was always attracted to that. Where the upper class disappoint is they almost never embrace what is new, or different, or radical, or somebody who would rock their world or change them in any way. They are not people to do that. Anytime I was in one of my fights in my life, I look around, and those people are never there. I looked around, and they were never there. And I don't think they like the iconoclasts they produce.

There was one time at one party I went to, I saw a guy sitting alone so I went over to him, started talking. We had a great conversation. He was being ignored by everyone. The next day I come down to breakfast, and Lenore says, "Pat, you're a genius. I don't know how you do it, but you're a genius." I said, "What are you talking about?" Lenore, I did not know this, read the society page first. We were all over it that first year, to my horror and embarrassment.

But the guy I was talking to was married to the society editor, and she praised me to the sky, because of her husband she dragged along to these things. No one would ever talk to him. He was not important to anybody. And my genius was I spotted the social editor's woebegone husband sitting in a corner and wooed him because I knew it would do Lenore great service in the society pages of San Francisco.

Anyway—parties—I was not meant for them. I could have been a quiet, contemplative Trappist monk eating canned peaches. I would have liked that. I think I would have enjoyed praying and having no one bother me. Except of course I would piss off the director general somehow and be thrown out of the order.

~

The first time I had seen Tim Belk in San Francisco was after he moved there with his wife Diane when I was still living in Beaufort. At that time, I didn't know what gay was; we were so naïve then. I certainly didn't know what guys did to each other. Tim says even now, Pat, you don't know they're gay unless they're wearing a dress. He knew when he was three, he told us later, but still he got married to Diane. A year after they were married, she said "Pat, can I ask you a personal question?"

"Sure, Diane, go ahead."

She said, "I just want to ask you how long in theory does it take for a man and a woman to make love after they get married?"

I said, "Well, it depends, Diane. It depends on a lot of different factors. I mean, you have the ceremony and you ride away in the car to where the honeymoon is. This could be, you know, hours away. Then you get to the room and sign in. You go in there, you get undressed, and after you get in the room, I'd say at the longest, ten, fifteen minutes."

Her face just dropped, and she says, "Pat, Tim's never made love to me yet."

I said, "Well, you know, he's shy."

And she said, "He says he's just not ready yet."

I said, "Yeah, different guys take different amounts of time." But I felt terrible for her.

Later Tim would say the reason he got his divorce with his wife, Diane, is, "Pat, we had irreconcilable similarities."

It was after I had been fired from Daufuskie Island that I got a Ford Foundation grant to study nontraditional schools in San Francisco for three months to see if that was something that would be good for the South. They called it a leadership development fellowship, and the idea was to develop leaders in the South by giving us a different experience outside the South and then sending us back to the South where we would lead our asses off for the rest of our lives and then die. I want to say the Ford Foundation Fellowship came through in the spring or summer of 1971, after I'd lost the trial to get my job back. It paid $7,500, which saved us. This grant pulled me out of the first desperate situation we were in, but I had to move three kids and Barbara and two fucking dogs . . .

My job was to look at these hippie schools in the communes around Oakland and Berkeley and San Francisco. They weren't worth a shit. I remember sitting around in a circle with the students, and their teacher's passing a joint. This is a biology class; the teacher's saying, "Now, yesterday, when we had the microscope here, did any of you have any feelings when you saw that paramecium dude eat that amoeba?" So these kids, "You know, yeah, I felt some compassion for the amoeba." I'm listening to all this horseshit, and I thought it was just ridiculous. And of course, I'm from South Carolina with a Citadel degree: everything these people hated and were against in American society. But anyway, I went to about five schools there and made a devastating report about them when I got back.

I thought, What a bunch of idiots, wasting these children's time and my time. But I got to see Tim Belk.

At night, Tim would tell the girls, Barbara and Diane, y'all need a night out, you girls, on the town. Pat and I will babysit. He meant Pat will babysit and I will go to gay bars. Then Tim started taking me out. We'd go to a restaurant, and then we'd go barhopping. Tim played in a piano bar called the Curtain Call, and one night Marlene Dietrich walks in and sings "Lili Marlene," one of the magic moments of all of our lives. It was just a great thing.

Tim had a lot of fans at the Curtain Call. I did not notice that all the people in the bar were men. And I didn't know they were gay because they didn't wear dresses. So Tim and I are sitting at the bar, and we're talking. We'd always talk about literature and music, which, in the world according to Santini, was pretty gay talk. Anyway, I feel a tap on my shoulder, and one of Tim's fans from the Curtain Call says, "Pat, can I have this dance?" I take a look around, and through this gauzy curtain I see all these guys dancing with each other. And I said, "Yeah, I can do this." So we go through the gauze. When we get there, I say, "Do you mind if I lead?" He said, "A pleasure." So, I twirl around. He kisses me on the cheek; I kiss him back. I sit back beside Tim, and I said, "Tim, you got something you need to tell me?" And Tim goes outside, he cries, and he said he's been this way since he's three.

That was the beginning of just diving into gay life out in San Francisco. He took me everywhere to show me the gay netherworld. He took me to leather bars, and he took me to Southern gay bars. We went to all kinds of places, with the guys wearing chains, and my favorite was a leather bar, tough guys wearing spike armbands on their biceps. They all looked like Green Bay Packers. Tim said, "Don't mess with these guys." I said, "Do not worry." One of them walked up with his lover, and I had never seen this in my life. He's got this big dog collar on this guy and a huge belt. He walks the guy up and says, "Heel." And the poor guy heels. He ties the guy up outside and says "Stay." So I go outside and say, "You want to talk about how this happened to you?" Tim nearly died. He's fighting and wrestling me to get me away.

He says, "That's exactly what I didn't want you to do. You said you'd be open-minded."

I said, "I am open-minded. I just want to know what happened to the guy."

But it was a new world for me, and I enjoyed it. The guys were wonderful. They couldn't have been nicer to me.

Tim got mad at me a couple years ago when I thanked him in one of the dedications, "For my gay friend in San Francisco."

He calls me and said, "You outed me."

I said, "Oh, yeah, Tim. You've kept it a big secret. No one would ever suspect you're gay."

He said, "Well, they don't know it in South Carolina."

I said, "Tim, puh-leeze. If there's anybody in America who doesn't know you're gay, let me know; I'll give them a phone call. We can get rid of the last one."

With *South of Broad* he said, "You made me too much of a queen."

I said, "I couldn't make you enough of a queen if I'd put a crown on your head."

When the AIDS epidemic broke out, I called Tim from Atlanta. I said, "Tim, I want you to stop whatever you're doing. Just quit right now."

"Pat, Pat, it's a new Tim. You're talking to Sister Mary Immaculata. I run past cucumbers at the market now. I don't even think the dirty, dirty thoughts that kept me going as a young man."

But he'd already got it.

Because of Tim Belk, I got involved in the AIDS epidemic when I moved out to San Francisco. We had our part to play in that, which was like nothing I'd ever seen. Nothing has quite made me that sad. Every knock I'd make on the door, a guy would open; he'd be dying. We would hear about Southern boys abandoned by their Southern families, dying alone in San Francisco. We looked for about ten of them. We almost always found them in the most squalid conditions, dying. I found one kid dead. And these are the best-looking guys—or they were before AIDS got them—the best-looking men you've ever seen in your life. They were all impoverished, and we would try to make their lives better. I would call all their parents, and the parents—you can just imagine. Some of these people were pathetic: farm people and religious people who just did not understand. Then I met with the director of Open Hand and delivered meals for a while. It turned out to be a large job, much bigger than I thought it was going to be. That took up a lot of time. Tim—I was worried about him all the time. He was dying. There was no question. He was dying. A few years later he was one of the first to get that new drug cocktail which saved his life, but at that time he was dying in front of my eyes.

Tim and I saw each other every Sunday at brunch down at the Washington Square Bar & Grill, where we got to know the people. It was a wonderful place in North Beach—eccentric—so we ate and drank down there. It was my dream of San Francisco. Tim had his table and would hold court every weekend. The waitress was a love and a half.

One time we were sitting there when another gay guy comes up to us, and he said there was a kid from Turbeville, South Carolina, who had been lost, and they were looking for him. He'd been kicked out of the family, and he was totally abandoned, without money. So I said, "Turbeville, South Carolina. I'm the only one in the fucking world who has been there, except for this kid." And this kid's name—if I remember right—was Eddie Truluck. So we went looking for Eddie through all the hospitals.

We finally found him living about a mile from my house. I walked up to him, and somebody said, "He's out in the garden smoking," and "Be careful, he's totally blind." Eddie was twenty years old. I walked up to him and said, "Eddie Truluck. Hi, I'm Pat Conroy." I said, "This may be bad, but it could be worse. You could be home in Turbeville." The guy laughs his ass off. He said, "How in the hell do you know Turbeville?" I told him. So we brought him stuff until he died an agonizing death.

When he died, his poor mother and her daughter came out and picked him up in a limo to take his body back to the plane. They were going to fly him to South Carolina. I took them over to the funeral home, and they insisted the guy not lock the casket before they went.

I said, "You may be sorry you did that."

And this poor woman says, "My boy, wasn't he a handsome boy? He was always so handsome."

I said, "Ma'am, I'm sure he was, but you're not going to believe what this disease did to him."

She said, "Cancer's a terrible thing."

I said, "Now, ma'am. This wasn't cancer. This was AIDS."

"I just can't tell my husband."

I said, "You can tell him whatever you want, but it's important for you to know. This is AIDS."

It's killing me to see the sight of this mother, unprepared for this, walking up to the casket, thinking she's going to see her handsome kid. The mother's knees buckled when she saw how that disease had ravaged her son.

Later, I met the sister at a party in Charleston. She came up to me. This is ten, fifteen years later, and she says, "You won't remember me, I'm so-and-so." Then she said, "I'm originally from Turbeville, South Carolina."

I said, "Darling, I know exactly who you are."

She said, "Please forgive my family. We didn't know anything."

I said, "I wish you all had learned faster."

But she said that it changed their lives. Her mother had gone back, and she changed her life. She said it made them better people, and I said, "I certainly hope so."

But I got too caught up in the AIDS epidemic in San Francisco while I was writing *Beach Music,* and I was starting to lose it. Everybody was dying. Every one of Tim's friends died, and we ended up taking care of them. The aura of death was everywhere. I remember wondering why I was called to do this, working with these guys with AIDS, trying to find them, trying to call their parents. It was disturbing and horrifying, and everybody died. Finally I got it, why I'm into every battle there is: I'm a warrior's son. When I was growing up, it was drilled into us that in the Marine Corps you were giving yourself up for something higher, keeping our nation safe. Well, I couldn't do that, so I became a champion of the underdog. I sail in, the warrior. I was born to fight, and that's all I do. I realized this is what went into Marion O'Neill's thinking about the hero-rescuer thing which has helped fuck up my life in many, many ways. I made a trail of tears out of my own life because I kept charging into situations I not only found impossible but unlivable.

This was also the time when I got home, I had to put on a tux or suit to go to a dinner party of people richer and more famous than I'd ever hung around before. I saw Jerry Brown at about twenty dinner parties I went to that year, also Joe Alioto, the old mayor of San Francisco. People I liked, certainly, but not people I'd get close to on a lifelong basis. They seemed interesting, smart California people. But it was "Hi, how are you doing, great to see you, you too." I was grinning and smiling and fat and drunk. Never heard from them again; never called them again. It was agony for me, but Lenore was in hog heaven. I think my depression in San Francisco was all based on my happiness with Lenore. There was terrible anxiety and great sadness, which led to much overdrinking and overeating. But I was trying not to get divorced again; I didn't want to be a serial divorcé.

~

I did the first screenplay for *The Prince of Tides* with Barbra Streisand, who was producer, director, actress, everything. She was the whole thing. People ask me why I sold my books to the movies, and I say, one time I said I wasn't going to do it, and then they raised the price. I said I still wasn't going to do it, and they raised it again. Eventually they hit Conroy's breaking point. That's how Hollywood generally does everything they want. But I've been pleased with all the movies of my books because I've seen what Hollywood is capable of doing to books. I've been very lucky. I didn't think *The Lords of Discipline* worked as a movie because it's just the plebe system all the way through; there's no woman. So that movie worked the least well of all. The other three I've liked a lot.

It was fun working with Barbra. I enjoyed it. She's as professional as anybody I've ever met, a perfectionist in all ways. She's burned bridges in Hollywood, both regrets it and doesn't give a shit. She's a better artist than they are, and that was where her problems all came in. Thank God that is not my life; that would drive me crazy. And what I learned instantly is that she's lonely. She has thousands of people walking by to see her house in Malibu, tourists coming and going. If we left her place, by the time she finished hiding herself, it was like she was wearing a burqa, all wrapped up, with sunglasses. But with her profile, that's it. You can still see it's her. Tourists follow her, their mouths wide open, whispering "Is that her?" That kind of fame: I do not know how one endures that in life.

I was nervous when I went to meet her, and Dad said, "Hey son, I hear she eats writers alive."

I said, "Hey, thanks, Dad. I appreciate you once again helping me with my career." When I get to her place, I tell her, "Let me tell you what my dad said."

She hears that and says, "How long has your father known me?"

I said, "Good answer. I like that." We got along great from there. I told her, "When the psychiatrist is talking, you do it. When the Southern coach is talking, let me do it, because I don't know of any Southern coaches who go *oy vey.*"

"What is *oy vey?*"

I said, "Fuck."

But she's a pro. She was always a pro. She auditioned a world-famous violinist for the scene where the guys play "Dixie." So he started, da-da-da-nah-nah, and she finally says no, no, no, you're not playing it right. And he says, "Barbra, how do you play Dixie wrong?"

She says, "We want it satirical and mocking. You're not mocking it," so he tries again, and she says no, that's terrible, that's awful. I'm not going to hire you.

"You're not going to hire me because I cannot play Dixie?"

She hired somebody else, somebody who wasn't famous but got it.

Anyway, I think it's good for a writer to do a screenplay, because you learn a lot. And oh, my God, you're paid like you've never been paid. Here's what you learn. You learn economy, you learn restraint, you learn how to do a scene without saying a thing, you learn how to get people in and out of rooms, you learn how to say a thing most efficiently. It's a good vehicle to learn how to control novels. Screenwriting is an art form I have come to admire as much as any other art form in the world. But these screenwriters are driven crazy about not being "real" writers. They have to scream and fight and roar to get what they want. It doesn't seem like much of a way to live.

Barbra and I wrote one screenplay, two screenplays, three screenplays; we're doing the rewrites. Then the other producer called me in and fired me. When I asked why, he said, "We don't think you understand the story." I said, "Yeah, you may be right." But I'd completed my contract, they paid me a lot of money, I went home, wishing I understood the story better, but I just didn't. It didn't bother me because by then I'd labored for two years on the screenplay about Bill Kovach, and it never got made because Bill wasn't fired by the Atlanta newspaper. He quit. In Hollywood, heroes don't quit. I had learned from that experience that screenplay writing is a stupid way to spend a life. It pays well, but unless the movie's made, it's worthless. But I always like it when I can learn something about America from these experiences.

I don't think I should have been nominated for an Academy Award, because I don't think there was much of my work in the final screenplay. They hired about seven or eight screenwriters after Barbra and me and hired lawyers to figure out the credits. The girl who was nominated with me told me, "I think I am responsible for 39.2 percent of the screenplay." I looked at her, said "Excuse me?" Barbra had tried for the screen credit, too. I had tried not to get one. But I certainly rode the comet tail of Barbra Streisand's fame with this. It took me to a level I had not been to before. *The Great Santini* didn't sell anything, and eventually, *The Prince of Tides,* with the movie, sold over five million copies, so that was my big success.

~

But once again, the unexpected was waiting around the corner in ambush. When *The Prince of Tides* was coming out as a movie, this is when Emily began her incredible string of suicide attempts. Of course, Lenore takes it personally and thinks that Emily is only trying to commit suicide to ruin her great week in San Francisco when the movie's coming out. This was going to be the height of Lenore's social life. Some big shots invited us to a dinner party at their house the night before the premiere. It was the Gettys, so they had more money than God, and Lenore was in a beauty parlor for weeks. The movie came out at the end of December 1991. At this time exactly, when the party of parties was being given for me by the Gettys in their mansion on Pacific Avenue, that is the day Emily makes her first suicide attempt. Emily was up on the roof of her high school wanting to hurl herself down. I visited her that afternoon in the hospital.

I called Lenore and said, "You've got to come down here. Somebody's got to be with her."

"I'm not coming. We have the party."

I said, "Lenore, one of us has to be here."

And she said, "I'm not coming. I'm going to the party."

I said, "Okay, I'll stay."

She said, "Well, you can't. You can't not go to the party because it's for you."

"We got a kid who tried to commit suicide. What kind of family chooses a party over that?"

Finally, begrudgingly, Lenore went to the mental hospital. She was absolutely pissed off. So I go to this party at the Gettys' house, and I was perfectly fucking miserable because Emily is in the hospital having just tried to kill herself. This woman comes up to me and says with her husband right beside her, "Pat, I hope you don't take this the wrong way, but I just told my husband I plan to leave him at this party and marry you." Here's what I remember from this moment. I sat there considering it so seriously, thinking "This woman looks nice." She actually did end up divorcing her husband and later married the president of *USA Today.* They have a place on Hilton Head. But my God, I remember the temptation of that night, because all of a sudden it was clear to me: I was married to a vain and shallow woman, a woman whose daughter was threatening suicide, trying to commit suicide, and all she was worried about was missing the party.

And this *was* the party of the year, so of course, Lenore sees this the next day in the paper and goes crazy. We have the premiere that night. They had one premiere in San Francisco, one in L.A., one in New York, and they had one in Beaufort. I get this phone call from the *Beaufort Gazette,* and the reporter is all huffy and puffy.

"Mr. Conroy, could you explain to me why you are going to an opening of *The Prince of Tides* in San Francisco and ignoring your hometown of Beaufort, South Carolina, the town that gave you *The Prince of Tides?*"

I said, "Yes, I'll be happy to."

And she said, "Well, I'd love to hear it."

I said, "By the way, I want to congratulate you, young lady. You are the first person from the *Beaufort Gazette* who has ever interviewed me in my life."

She said, "I find that hard to believe."

I said, "A smart reporter like you? You can find out pretty fast. I was controversial there, and they do not interview controversial people."

She said, "But can you tell me why you're not coming to Beaufort's opening?"

I said, "I can give you the inside scoop on that, and I guarantee you'll have a scoop: I was not invited."

She says, "I hardly believe that can be true."

I said, "A smart reporter like you can find out with one phone call."

So I get another call, "Mr. Conroy, we are horrified. We are absolutely horrified. We don't know how this happened."

I said, "Don't worry about it. Y'all have a ball. I have to be here in San Francisco."

So that night we went to the opening in San Francisco. I was so uncomfortable: they made me wear a cape, and the audience serenaded me. I was the Prince of San Francisco for that night, some horseshit. If I could have, I would've fed myself to a white shark off the coast, but I had to put up with it. I had to do it, and I did it, but it was one of the worst nights of my life. I can't remember seeing the movie. I sat there with Barbra Streisand sitting right behind me. When the audience laughed, I laughed. When the audience grew silent, I grew silent. I don't remember a thing about the movie today.

When we got back home that night, the babysitter's at the door. She had called the ambulance because Emily tried to kill herself by taking a whole bottle of pills. I go to the hospital; they've pumped her stomach.

I say, "Emily, you don't seem to be enjoying life very much."

She said, "Very fucking funny, Pat. You think you're a fucking comedian, don't you?" Then she laughs her ass off.

At that time I guess there should have been great celebration over the movie, but Emily was looking like a real tragedy in the making. Going from parties and premieres to isolation wards in the hospital where Emily had a suicide watch on colored those times a great deal. Then there was a mirroring going on between my life and Emily's. When Emily started her suicide attempts, this translated to me, and I started feeling suicidal. The marriage was coming apart. Lenore was quite happy among her society friends in San Francisco; I was miserable among them. I wanted to get back to Fripp and continue my work on

Beach Music, and there were clashes about that. But I knew that if I left her she'd never let me see Susannah. A lot of great emotional components were flashing in the night around me. And I couldn't go to that many parties. I mean, I just could not do it.

~

Then I got hit by a car and hurt my back. I was in bed for two months. I was in real pain, hurting terribly each day, and they did not know what was wrong. Lenore would wake up, "How do you feel today?"

I'd say, "Not too good," and I'm fairly stoical, not a whiner.

And she'd go, "Oh fuck."

One of the kids would bring breakfast up, the Filipino maid would bring lunch up, and sometimes the kids would bring supper. I could not get out of bed except to go to the bathroom, and that was agonizing. I noticed that Lenore didn't come to check on me once during the day during the two months I was on my back. I'd see her when she got up in the morning, she'd say is it better, I'd say no, she'd go "Oh, fuck," and then she would go downstairs, and I wouldn't see her for the rest of the day. It was like a billboard saying I do not love you except for what I can get from you; I will not take care of you; I will not comfort you. She was angry at me that I was sick, angry that I was in bed, angry that I was helpless. It was a great time of reading for me, because I read *Remembrance of Things Past* during that time, and while I always try to use my sicknesses well, I was in a terrible decline. In the middle of that I say to myself—it was like a command that comes roaring out of myself every once in a while—"You will not die with this woman."

By then I'd met Sylvia, and it was at this time that Sylvia and I on the phone began what became our affair. She called me every day, because she knew I was sick, that I was in bed and I was hurting. And she was a great talker. I loved talking to her because I wasn't talking to anybody else and nobody was coming to see me. I just needed companionship then.

Sylvia had entered my life in a bang. I didn't know her, never heard of her, but I got to be friends with Peter Coyote, an actor, whose kids went to the same school our kids did. He would hang around movie people, and Lenore really, really liked hanging around the actors and all these directors. She thought that was wonderful. I didn't know who these people were. Once this guy came up to me, so I said, "Hi, I'm Pat Conroy, who are you?"

He says, "Oh, c'mon man."

I said, "What do you mean?"

He says, "You don't know who I am?"

I said, "Well, I'm afraid not. I'm sorry."

"You don't know who I am, man?"

I said no.

He says, "I'm Huey Newton."

I had no idea who that was. That happened twice. The other guy was supposedly an intellectual. I thought he was an idiot. He filmed these monologues of himself. So he comes up to me at another one of these things. Hi, how are you doing? I have no idea who he is, but he knows who I am. He's shocked, offended. I say, "It must be a great surprise for you; you get to introduce yourself brand new. If you're going to start a new personality, go to me."

"Man, I can't believe this. You're putting me on, man."

"Well, I wish I was, but I do not know anybody here."

He said, "My name's Spalding Gray."

I didn't know who that was. It's always interesting with those people. They knew who I was, but I didn't know who they were; that's what made them so mad. I never pretended to get it much.

Sylvia was part of this world because she was married to a guy named Dale Chihuly, the famous glass blower. She was a gorgeous girl. Tall, brown hair; absolutely a scintillating person, charismatic. She was one that came up to me at Alice Waters's restaurant. I didn't know her, had never met her. I had become famous but I had no particular grip on the fact that I *was* that. It shocked me every time somebody came up to me knowing who I was.

Sylvia was with Peter Coyote, his wife, a Brazilian director, and a French actor. Lenore was down at the other end of the table, and I was with Peter Coyote's wife. In the middle of dinner, this pretty girl comes and sits herself down from me. Marilyn Coyote is talking to somebody else, and this girl looks over at me and says, "You know, everybody at this table is perfectly aware that your wife hates your guts."

I said, "I didn't know that."

She said, "It's perfectly clear, Pat, and if you don't know that, you need to open your eyes and look around."

What an opening. I mean, it got my attention. It started with Sylvia with that sentence, which I found a very arresting sentence, a very notable sentence, and perfectly timed in the life I was in the middle of living. It was like somebody's telling me the truth out of nowhere, and letting me know what I felt deepest inside me. I was completely stunned by that. Then, she was one of the great talkers. She knew everything about *The Prince of Tides* and could ask good questions. I thought she was brilliant.

During those two months I was in bed miserable, Lenore could not have treated me worse, and Sylvia was calling me every day, "How are you doing?" She hated her husband, and almost as soon as she met me, she started the process of divorce. I was crazy over her, but probably nothing would have happened, except I got hurt and was in bed for two months.

When the doctors finally found what was hurting me, I had a back operation. I started crying when Lenore was bringing me home. She told people I was crying because I was so happy to be coming home. I was not; I was crying because I was so unhappy. I felt like I was dying of aloneness and solitude.

Then I had something very interesting happen to me. I had a room where I wrote; I saw the Golden Gate Bridge in the distance. The longer I was there, I kept hearing that bridge—I wouldn't say calling my name—but I was starting to be attracted to that bridge, and that scared the shit out of me. I thought, so that's the pull. That's how it works. That had never happened to me before, for that bridge to begin its love song, and what it offers is a complete, absolute, and extraordinarily efficient way of killing yourself. I saw how it works for the first time. I'd never understood jumping from the Golden Gate Bridge, and then suddenly, I understood it perfectly. I remember thinking: All you have to do is walk to the bridge, which is not hard. We were close to it, and it wasn't hard to do. It becomes obsessional as a marvelous death.

I am so ashamed of the life I've lived. It started off, I'm getting beaten up when I'm in diapers, and then I'm looking at the Golden Gate Bridge thinking it'll help me out of something. I realized, okay, I have got to get out of here. Before my back had healed, I was on a plane flying to Fripp Island. I just wanted to put myself on a sea island where no one could get to me. Fripp is so isolated Salman Rushdie could hide out there. Also, it's hard to kill yourself from a height in the lowcountry. And the West Coast has never been a comfort zone to me at all. The sun sets on the wrong side there, the ocean is to your left instead of to your right, and I'm watching football games at ten in the morning, which has never made sense to me.

FIVE

Fripp Island/Beaufort, South Carolina

1992–2016

Where can a man run or where can he hide when he looks behind him and sees that he is pursued only by himself?

PAT CONROY, *The Prince of Tides*

First of all, I insisted that he see me every day, which was a long drive for him, and that he not drink. Then I had him sign a pledge that he wouldn't kill himself. I told him the reason he couldn't kill himself is that he would ruin my reputation.

MARION O'NEILL, Ph.D., ABPP, clinical psychologist

I really screwed up my life with my second marriage—I blew my own life out of the water—and I will always be recovering from that. I felt a little bit like the suburbs of Nagasaki after the bomb went off. Of course, it all occurs in our tragic middle age. It seemed like life had caught up with me and caught me in the open fields, and I was paying back for a life poorly lived and certainly poorly planned. I'd completely made a total mess out of my life, as only I could do. God, what a squirrely way I've had of destroying my own life in every way possible. Marrying Lenore was the stupidest thing I did in my life, and I knew it going in. Some things I had no choice about; the Citadel I had no choice about. I was face-to-face with my fate. But there was choice in Lenore, and I knew at the time it was not the right choice. Even when I first married Lenore, I knew I had destroyed something in myself. First of all, I had taken away a freedom that I had worked so hard to get. I knew I was an idiot, but I did it. And once I do something, say I'll do it, all right, you know, I asked for this, I walked into it, I made my vows, and I'll try to do my best with it. And I did my best for as long as

257

I could. And then I said, fuck this, this is no way to live. By then she had driven me absolutely nuts.

My answer was always to return to South Carolina, return to the beach, so I ran to Fripp Island. I ran. What I wanted to do was get into salt water every day and let that salt water heal my back. That scar became symbolic to me of my marriage.

Sylvia came out and stayed for a couple of weeks. I was in love with her and knew it but thought it was the wrong time to be in love. Sylvia wanted to get married, and I knew that divorcing Lenore would be the greatest hell I'd ever known. Also, my constant fear was if I divorced Lenore, I would never see Susannah again.

I'm in the middle of writing *Beach Music,* and Lenore was on me every night, calling every night, hammering me. Emily was still suicidal and in heavy therapy. Lenore had the big artillery guns out there, because she had started going to a shrink, and that shrink was saying, "You don't have a marriage; you don't have a husband. You let him go to Fripp. What's he doing in Fripp? Why isn't he writing in your house?"

I said, "Lenore, you know that I have to go off to write. This has happened since we've been married; it's happened my whole career." I would try to defend myself. "Lenore, did you tell her how much your house costs to live in? Did you tell her that you're playing the stock market? There is a husband, and he is at work, because all your kids are going to the most expensive schools in the world, and how are they doing that?"

All I remember is a nightmarish time trying to write this book and trying to afford Lenore, who lived in a very expensive house and dressed like a queen. So I'm making this pathetic defense, and I'm still hurting because of my back. But each night she just kept drilling and drilling and drilling. Lenore calling and blasting me every day did not push me up the ladder of mental health. It was a dreadful time at a time of only dreadful times.

It all started weighing down on me. I had to finish this book; I was running out of money. And I'm writing about not happy subjects. I'm writing about the Holocaust, about Mom's death. I'm writing about all these things that are going to normally depress one in the normal course of events.

Also, I was seeing nobody. I didn't even tell Gene Norris that I was back, I was so depressed. I thought I'd upset Gene. I had not told my brothers and sisters I'd gone back to Fripp. I had not told my father. At that time, I think my mind and body had had it, and I had truly retreated from the world into my books and my reading as I never had before. I now look back and can't imagine being that much of a loner, but I was. My body was telling me to rest the old machine for a while. Every afternoon about six o'clock I watched *The Waltons,* to try to heal myself just to get back what human kindness looked like. It was tonic for my soul. That seems so hokey, but that's what I needed right then—hokeyness—some blessed way of living. I was still writing the book somehow, I was drinking too much, and I would await these phone calls from Lenore with dread, just absolute dread.

Then this breakdown started, where I had days just crying and nothing else. It all added up until I couldn't write and didn't seem able to think, and eventually that led me to something like despair. I started storing up pills. I had everything set up, the pills and the alcohol. Then, finally one night, took them. It was after a phone call from Lenore when she just nailed me. "What a lousy husband, what a lousy father," and when Lenore got really mad, I also became a lousy writer.

Again, suicide seemed great to me. There was no fear involved with it. It just seemed like the best thing I could do for everybody. It would solve everybody's problems. My not being around would solve everything. And it would especially solve it for me. I remember when I took all these drugs, I felt happy doing it, like I wouldn't have to feel this thing in my stomach, I wouldn't have to be bent over with anxiety and sleeplessness. So I took the pills and woke up two days later. I think that's the time I threw up. I believe that's what saved me that time. When I look back, I think I kind of semiplanned it, keeping drugs around, hoping I had enough to do the job, feeling very rational when I was doing that. Of course I now feel lucky that I didn't do it, that I never took enough. I threw up twice, not knowing my body would have a response, saying fuck you, I want to stay around. My favorite days are the ones when I realize I've just survived my latest suicide attempt.

I knew I was in serious, serious trouble. My doctor then was Dr. Keyserling, who had been my doctor when I was a kid in Beaufort and delivered two of my children. But anytime I would go to him and say, "Doc, I'm feeling bad," he'd say, "I know why you're feeling bad. You're too fucking fat, and you're gaining too much fucking weight."

"Doc, I tried to kill myself."

"Well, you ought to go ahead and do it, get it over with."

That was his style, and I didn't quite need that at that moment, I didn't think.

I was thinking about going to Atlanta to see Marion O'Neill, and then it occurred to me: several years ago she'd moved to Hilton Head. So I called her immediately. I said, "Marion, I am in deep fucking trouble. It's bad. I am suicidal." My voice was doing that fucked-up thing she recognized. It's so pathetic and weak and beaten down, not that strong Churchillian voice rallying people against the Germans. Marion knew that voice and said, "Get over here right now. And be prepared to stay for a while."

It was a two-hour trip to Marion O'Neill's office on Hilton Head. When I first got over there that day, I walked in still really, really shaky, and I hear screaming. I recognize the screaming. Marion is on the phone with Lenore. I still don't know how Lenore got word that I was going to see Marion, and Marion didn't have any idea. That has always been a mystery. But when I walked into Marion's office and found Lenore on the fucking phone, that was the low point of my life. She was abusive to Marion; I could hear her cussing in her pissed-offed-ness.

Her demand was, "You put him on a plane right now. I demand as his wife you put him on a plane. He's not your patient. I've hired a doctor out here who is his doctor now."

Lenore wanted me back in San Francisco so she could put me in a mental hospital. I thought I was a dead man at that moment. I thought, That's it. I'll never come back from that.

When Marion saw me she waved me into her office, pointed and said, "Get in my room." When I went, I heard Marion get that cold voice of steel. "I'm very sorry, Lenore. But Pat is now officially my patient under my care. I will decide what is best for my patient, not you or the doctor you've hired in San Francisco. He will not be flying back tonight; that I can assure you. Thank you very much for calling."

She comes in, and I'm having my typical manly breakdown, crying and bawling uncontrollably. She shuts the door, sits down, sees me bawling. She lets me bawl for a long time. Then she said, "Could you explain to me why you married that fucking asshole?"

I cried most of the session. There was no manliness connected with this particular breakdown at all. I had simply come apart, come loose. Whenever I have a breakdown, my manhood goes into the toilet; my head goes into the oven.

Marion said, "Now Pat, you've got to promise me, if I become your doctor, you are not going to kill yourself under my care." She said, "You'll ruin my practice. No one will ever come to the doctor where the author of *The Prince of Tides* committed suicide under her care. So you've got to promise me, and you've got to sign it."

She puts this paper out, and I sign it with the blood of my dick.

I think I was with Marion the rest of the time it took me to finish *Beach Music*—I want to say two years. I went every day, five days a week, for five months. I'd still go swimming twice a day in the ocean, and I would often think I could just swim, keep swimming, keep swimming, and then cut my artery somewhere when I got out deep enough. I had all these fantasies of how I could make it look like an accident. But Marion saved me. I think that pledge I signed was a powerful thing. She made me take it seriously, and I saw her point. She knew how to get to me. She was asking me not to kill myself because of her. I may not have been able to do it for myself. So she got me, hooked me on that first day. Marion was a smart girl. And there's no question if not for her I'd be dead by now.

We'd been there before, and we went back in. She goes into this thing about me and women, which she always thought was ridiculous. Said, "Pat, can you ever fall in love with a woman you're not rescuing? Why do you have to fall in love with a woman without hope?" She went as deeply as she could into this. Mary Alice was certainly one she'd bring up a lot. "Pat, what do you think that was? That was pure rescue. She was abandoned, pregnant, living with an abusive mother. You find out about it, and bingo. What happier moment in any girl's life than your sorry ass coming along?" And she was right. Mary Alice's life was a total, complete mess. And I saw that. Why didn't I say, "Oh, what a total mess?" Marion felt as sorry for the women I fell in love with, the victims of my rescue, as she did for me. I think she thought I was exalting myself by putting myself in the position of rescuing a woman who needed help. So I'm there for the wrong reasons, not to love a woman, but to help a woman. One day Marion said, "Let's do a hypothetical, Pat. Another underdog comes along. Do you have to help the underdog every time?" And she said, "Yes, you do." There is still that thing in me: the woman in trouble has a great appeal to me.

Marion was so afraid I was going to kill myself, she made me stop off in places on my way back to Fripp. It was a long road trip, two hours there, two hours back. She'd make me stop at these different people's houses so they could report—I didn't know this—that I was still alive. I had not driven off into a creek and drowned myself or run into an abutment.

One was a woman I ended up doing the cookbook with, Suzanne Pollak. That was my first stop. I didn't know it, but she'd call Marion O'Neill: "He got here." The second place was Gene Norris at the junior high school in Beaufort. Gene would step out: "He got here." Third place, I had to make friends on Fripp Island. I had no friends, didn't see anybody. Marion said, "Make some friends." I went to Gregg and Mary Smith. I said, "Hi, how are you doing?" And sat down and became best friends with them, and they would end up calling her: "He made it home."

I had to get up early to get to Marion, and she thought as long as I was seeing people afterward, I would be okay, because, she said, "You always act like you're normal. You like to put on an act, Pat. You act happy." She said I never liked to disappoint people socially. When I go out into the world, I present myself cheerfully whether I'm suicidal or not. I always have the outward appearance of not being depressed. That's just Southern courtesy, and my courtesies are strong because of Mom. And generally, I'm always happy to see people. If I go out in public that thing switches on: I have a need to be nice. I've been in ambulances a couple of times in my life, and I have a need to be nice to the guy lifting me in the ambulance.

"Thank you very much, sir. I appreciate it. Where are you from?"

"Sir, we just want to get you stabilized here."

"You can still tell me where you're from."

But when I am in my morose, suicidal mood, what I usually do is retreat heavily. At that time I was avoiding people, didn't want to see anyone, and with me, I go into the great read. I can use my sadness to read, just read; I can read forever, and it can be a danger sign for me when I do that. Marion said, "Pat, you've turned yourself into a hermit. You don't see anybody; you don't talk to anybody. This is dangerous for you." That's another reason why Marion O'Neill made me start going out to see people after I left her office, because I think she knew if she could get me back to dealing with people, something would jumpstart in me that could get me interested in life again. She was right.

After the first day Marion said, "Okay, Pat, you like cooking. I know that. I have a friend who likes cooking. Her name's Suzanne Pollak. I want you to stop by and cook a meal, take it home and eat it at night. I want to make sure you're eating." So I started going to Suzanne's house, and we cooked something for lunch every day. She was a good cook and taught me great stuff, like how to make fresh pasta. I'd go over there after meeting with Marion, and there'd be eggs and flour, and I'd just start making the dough for the pasta, rolling it out. It was delicious. We made wonderful meals, and that's how we got the idea of doing a cookbook, which still sells for the oddest reason. Old ladies love buying it. There's no suicide in the book; there's no horror; nobody goes screaming naked down the street with their peckers dragging in the dust. Nobody slits their wrist, slits their throat; nobody throws hydrochloric acid at each other's faces. Just people calmly gathering materials and fixing good food and me telling winsome stories. So that book has done something for my reputation among those who cannot open another one of my books because they are so appalled by what they find inside, my suicided-filled literature, my death-infused prose. A common question I'm still getting now: "When are you going to write another cookbook?"

Marion thought my love of food was silly, and she didn't understand this love of cooking. She is not a sensualist in that way. But it was getting me out among people. Next was Gene Norris, and with Gene, I'd go into his office at the school. Sometimes, when I first started going there,

I'd just cry in his office all day. Gene would come in and pretend he was doing something else, and then he'd finally say something like, "You know, sometimes it's better just to cry and get it out. Don't try to keep it in. This is a good place to do it. I come back here to think and pray."

And that's when Mary and Gregg Smith came into my life. Marion said, "Pick some people at Fripp." Mary owned the T. T. Bones little general store, which was always friendly when I went in there. I liked her. Her husband was working the cash register one day, and I see a Citadel ring. I said, "Are you a Citadel guy?" He was there as a freshman when I was a senior. So I started going over there. And Marion said, "Okay, you're going over to their house every night." I said, "I don't know these people well enough." But I would show up, they would seem glad to have me. So they became two of my best friends. Then when I got home, Gene was calling every night. He felt it was very important that I check in with him every night. Then I had to get up and see Marion the next day. That was my life. And if that was what survival looked like, then give me something else.

After about I think six months with Marion, I started feeling something lifting. She slowly built me back up, and it helped that the book was coming. That always is a help for me, when a book starts rolling along. And so I'm in that interior life, and then she takes me to another interior life when I go in to see her. I had the feeling that block by block, Marion was building me back up again. Also, I have this other part of me which is the survivor. I think it's extraordinarily strong in me, and that comes roaring up. There's the soldier in me, the warrior in me who comes out fighting.

One thing Marion did convince me of is, "Your sadness and depression are well earned. But you've become aware of it, learned how to handle it; you'll be fine. Just understand that the sadness is always going to be there. But what you can do that other people can't do is you can write it out. You can get it out. You can get those poisons out of you by writing it on paper." And she said, "What you don't know you do, Pat, when you write it, you talk for a zillion people who are feeling the same thing but are helpless to get it out. They don't know these things, and you help them see these things. Unfortunately, you have to suffer to be aware of these things."

I said ah, yes, yes, that's the great part. But it's true I have become the patron saint of people in agony. Everybody has suffered. Nobody gets away from it. When people tell me they haven't suffered, it takes just a couple of questions to get to the truth. "Ma'am, how far do we have to go to get to the first crazy on your family tree?" The tragedy is that because all of us know how to write, everybody thinks they can write a book. If you have a bad experience and you know how to write an English sentence, you think you can write a book about it. This is usually not true. And that's what makes me saddest of all, for someone to have this suffering and have nowhere to go with it.

Also about this time, a friend of mine, Dickie Jones was his name, mayor of Mount Pleasant, South Carolina, a former point guard on the Citadel basketball team who was there when I was recruited to the Citadel, committed suicide. Dickie was a sunshiny guy, always up, always the-leader-of-a-pep-rally kind of guy, and he committed suicide on a park bench in Mount Pleasant; horrified everybody that knew him. Nobody had any idea he had gotten himself into deep financial holes. And when I called up about that, I heard his children screaming in the background and could hear the adults trying to console them. I burst into tears. The guy on the phone said, "Pat, a lot of people loved Dickie."

I said, "I didn't know Dickie well enough to love him; it's something else."

He said, "He affected people that way."

And what I was thinking of is I did not want to affect my children that way, and it was a great, great example for me of what I did not want to happen in my kids' lives. So I think Dickie Jones helped save me too.

⌣

When I first saw Marion, I was on an antidepressant. It was called a dry martini. Or five. She took me off that. One thing Marion told me when I walked in her office in Hilton Head: "I'm not going to see you if you're drinking. Quit drinking." She said, "I don't deal with alcoholics." I was not a full-fledged alcoholic when I saw her the first time in Atlanta. I was the second time. I was drowning in dry martinis with olives floating at the top.

I didn't drink when I was at the Citadel, and did not drink when I got out. Guys at the Citadel tell me they can't remember me at one party ever. If you drank at the Citadel, you were kicked out of school; if you had liquor in the barracks, you're gone. I think I had two or three beers the whole time I was at the Citadel, and that's it.

Here's where Bernie Schein comes into my life. Bernie now says, "Yes, it was me who turned Pat into an alcoholic." Not only that, he introduced me to Lenore Fleischer. But that first month we were all teaching, Mike and George and Bernie came over to my apartment and said, "Why didn't you come to the party?" I was going to a prayer group with Gene Norris and not drinking at that time. I started drinking when I became friends with them and began going to their parties, where I was standing there like a eunuch with no brain power watching the harem. I learned that if I had a drink with Bernie and the guys, they would start talking, and I would start talking. When I drank alcohol for the first time, I noticed a loosening up, being able to have fun, to dance.

It also loosened me up to think in ways I had not allowed myself to think. It opened for me a world I was forbidden to enter on my own, and I've always been grateful to alcohol for that. I'm not sure I could have gotten there without it. It was only by drinking I could cut through that very uptight, puritanical Southern boy that I was. Alcohol is the only thing that helped me escape that Roman Catholic military brat and altar boy, the Citadel-trained do-gooder. Rarely has there been a do-gooder kid like me. When I drank, my free thinking came loose, and I realized, "I don't have to think like this; I don't have to be like this. What is all this bullshit about?" Alcohol became part of that freeing up of what was hidden in me by my upbringing.

I really started on a steady diet of drinking when I married Barbara. She and Wes, her first husband, had a ritual of having a drink at five o'clock when he got home from work. I thought it seemed very grown up, but of course then I took this modest habit and used it to drink a Bering Sea's worth of liquor over my next forty years. I poured liquor down my throat in Nile-like proportions.

I was the type to drink and not show it much. Cliff Graubart claims he's only seen me drunk once in my life, and Cliff has seen me a lot in my life. The great drunkards I've known are horrifying and monstrous, and they change when they drink; they become these outrageous figures of brutality, crushing things in front of them and beating their wives and children. I never became like that; I never became violent. I was not a stumbling drunk or a guy who got picked up for drunk driving. I did not stagger; I did not drive crazy. I didn't slur or stumble. I wasn't destructive. I didn't beat people up; I didn't get into fights. I didn't stick my hand down the front of women's dresses. I was never that guy. I was a functioning alcoholic. I made it to planes; I made it to speeches. I could always still get work done, and at that time that was the most important thing. Aftereffects were never bad for me, unlike with Bernie; if he had too much to drink, he'd be moaning and groaning the next day like someone who'd just survived a plane crash barely.

The main thing alcohol did for me that I've always appreciated a great deal: I could think things I was denied the right to think when I was a child, when I was going to the Citadel. I could enter a world I was not supposed to ever go to, and it loosed something in my writing I could not have found without it, just like therapy. Drinking gave me a way into the writing life, and a way into the secret life I had repressed. It was the only way I had to go back into my childhood, because we were taught by my mother to protect Dad and not let our story out. That story would destroy our family, destroy his career and everything else. It was deeply ingrained in me that our number-one job was to keep the family's secret. I could never talk about it with anybody, with the exception of Carol. When Dad hurled the glass at me across the table and it shattered above my eye, Mom tells me on the way over to the emergency room that if Dad is ever arrested, his career is over and none of us will go to college. That was the huge threat she held over me.

So drinking helped me enter those realms. Later, so did Marion O'Neill, but for a tightly wound Catholic boy with Southern trappings, the first entry came through drinking. There were a lot of trap doors I had to get through before I could get to what was bothering me greatly. Drinking freed me to go there, to that region where I was forbidden access my whole childhood. This may seem like the alcoholic's excuse or lament, but alcohol took me into my imagination.

And alcohol could calm my brain down after a day of writing. The stomach always seemed to be in some kind of pain after I wrote, like a lining of pain. When I took that first drink, I could feel the alcohol going down the throat, entering the stomach, and removing that lining of pain as it went around the stomach. Drinking was the only thing I knew of that could ever cut into that. Whatever pain I was feeling, eventually I would not feel it, and it seemed like the greatest medicine God ever invented.

And after I got fired up with writing, my problem was always slowing my brain down afterward. When you go into that state you go into to write, you disappear from yourself, and when you come back out, the writing keeps going, especially if you've written well and written long. Whatever was stirred up in the brain would keep going and going and going until I had that first drink. Alcohol was something that could turn off my brain when it was still racing absolutely out of control. I think so many writers have been drunks because they have to stop that process, and there are very few ways to do it. You have to sometime come out and deal with your family. Eventually you have to walk out into the naked light of day. Oh, my God, I have children. I forgot that. And oh, I married somebody; what's her name? The drink in the evening can settle that down and even make you glad you've gotten away from the writing table. It provides a perfect bridge. What is nicer after a day's work than a glass of wine? Tell me that's not divine and pleasurable. My problem was my inability to get away from the bottle. After I finished writing for the day, I used it like an I.V. pouring gallons of bourbon or gin into me for the rest of the night until I was forklifted to the bedroom. This made Lenore possible for me. And I still had these children to raise; I still had these books to write. Thank God for alcohol.

When I went back to Marion for the first time and she was on the phone, Lenore was telling her I was a complete and hopeless alcoholic. Lenore never threw that in my face much, but after I left San Francisco, it became the reason she lost me. That became her great crutch. Of course, Hammersmith O'Neill made me go off liquor immediately because she did not want it to interfere with my talk therapy. She told me, "If you're an alcoholic, Pat, I can't treat you until you do something about that." So I said okay.

She made me go from her office to an Alcoholics Anonymous meeting, and when I came back the next day, I said if I have to go to that,

I'm going to drink myself to death with great pleasure and joy. I have never heard such boring stories, and you could see every drink they'd ever taken written in graffiti on their faces and their trembling hands. Those guys will depress me for the rest of my life. I ain't doing that. I wanted no part of that strange world of abstinence that has such piety connected to it.

But I had to quit drinking, so I did. She had told me she wasn't going to see me if I didn't quit, but what she did not tell me is she thought it would take a month or two. She did not mean for me to quit in one night. I didn't tell her I was going to do it, and I went through hideous nightmares which she thinks may have been delirium tremens. I had several bad nights. She was pissed that I didn't go off slowly.

I said, "You told me to get off or you wouldn't see me."

She said, "I didn't mean that night. You didn't tell me you were going to do that."

I said, "I didn't know I was going to do it."

But I could always put myself back in a situation where I didn't drink and try to pretend that's where I am now. I always pretend like I'm a freshman at the Citadel; I can't drink. I pretend I'm a basketball player, and I didn't drink when I was an athlete.

For three or four years, I didn't drink anything, and I should have stayed with it. But then I realized I wasn't going to see Susannah the rest of my life, and that became an agony I could not take. Susannah is the great unhealed wound in me. She was about eleven when the separation started; she was just coming into her own powers of beauty and smartness and wit. It was wonderful to see.

After the divorce, I saw her for just a few weeks over the next ten years. She was a little girl the last time I saw her, then she was a teenager when I got a phone call from her unexpectedly one summer, saying she wanted to come to Fripp for two weeks. I pick her up from the airport. She appears to me brittle, unforthcoming, but pretty and nice and certainly well behaved and respectful. I try to talk to her. I don't get as far as I'd like. She does not want me to talk about her mother, which I don't do and I wouldn't do. I wouldn't say bad things about Lenore in front of her. We were hunting for things to say, and I was trying desperately not to say anything that would piss her off. I took her to Charleston and Savannah. We went to the movies a couple of times. I took her to dinner a couple of times. Not much came out of any of that. I've always gotten along well with most people, but I could not make a single breakthrough with her.

When she was getting ready to leave, I said, "Why don't you come back for Christmas? I'd love to have you."

And she said to me in sort of a snappish way, "Oh come on, Dad, you know it's a family tradition that we go to Hawaii every Christmas."

I said, "Let me let you know how long this family tradition has been going on. I've never been to Hawaii, Susannah."

But she started going when she was still young with Lenore. She thought it was the family tradition.

Then she came to Megan's wedding in 1999, and that was the last time I saw her. I think Susannah was about seventeen at the time. She came with her brother Gregory, who was pulling guard duty. She didn't speak to me, didn't speak to her sisters, didn't speak to anybody, left without speaking, and I have not seen or heard from her since then. It's been a long time. I wouldn't recognize her if she walked through the front door.

I lost my daughter, and I think that may be the worst thing that ever happened to me. I'd go back to Dad in a minute: beat me up. I'd go back to the Citadel: do whatever you want to me. The greatest blow of my life has been Susannah. I didn't get to raise her; I didn't get to mold her; I didn't get to love her enough. When I see fathers with their daughters in a store, I get weak at the knees. I can never get over the fact that she's half me, and that somewhere in there, somewhere there is me trying to get out of her, trying to speak to her, trying to guide her, and it is useless to her.

I knew Lenore was not going to let me see Susannah after the divorce, but it never occurred to me Susannah would not make contact when she turned eighteen. I thought there was hope that when she was eighteen, she would knock at my door. And of course there wasn't. It remains one of the great shocks of my life. I can come up with no scenario why Susannah's doing this to me and everyone else, except that she's been baptized in the church of Lenore. She's cut herself off completely from my family, my brothers, sisters, her sisters, her nieces. She doesn't even know them. It's a complete cutoff of everybody who knew me, and I don't know how to break through that.

Knowing Lenore, I knew this was the weapon she was going to use to get back at me. She was going to prove that I was a worse father than the Great Santini—you know: "He can talk a good game, but his own daughter will not even speak with him." This was the hellcat missile she fired toward my plane that was going to hit me directly. This one would really hurt. And it has. This is the one that has broken me; this is the one that has killed me.

I mean, my God, I have no idea if she's ever dated, if she graduated from college. I don't know what she's doing with her life. I don't know if she's ever read a word I've written. I keep hoping she'll read my books or something will change. When I put Susannah into *Beach Music* to let her know what our relationship was at the exact year we split, I had done the best I could to tell her there was something worthy of preservation, but if she could not get that bottle tossed into the waves and retrieve that message somehow, there was not much else I could do.

Right after the divorce, there was a time when I wrote her letters or postcards every day, but I'm not sure she got one of them. I sent her gifts all the time but never got thank you for this, thank you for that. When they moved back to Atlanta, I went by to see her a couple of times, but when she saw I was out there, she wouldn't open the door. Once I saw her get out of the car when I was across the street. I said, "Susannah, can I talk to you?" and she ran into the house like I was going to beat her up. Whenever I'm in Atlanta I'll knock on the door; I'll feel people looking at me, won't get an answer, leave a letter on her windshield. I'll write her periodically and send flowers on her birthday, but I get nothing, absolutely nothing. I have no phone number for her, no e-mail address. I don't know what to do about it; I'm paralyzed. I could take a pup tent and camp out on Lenore's front lawn, but that is not what I want. I don't want that for Susannah; I don't want that for myself. I don't want the cops; I don't want to be on national news the next morning. And something in me says that Susannah has a perfect right not to see me if she doesn't want to. I could argue with her about the reason, except I wouldn't know her if she crossed the street in front of me.

So it has been simply agonizing, and I think my drinking took off again because I could not take the anxiety of that. That's my excuse—we all have these little stories we tell to make ourselves look better. So it's an excuse, because I love alcohol and took great pleasure out of it. There was nothing that turned into liquor or wine that I did not adore. Also, there's never been a pill or drug on the market or sold legally anywhere that I did not absolutely love. I have adored everything that makes me not feel that I'm alive, but I've always been perfectly happy with liquor.

So I went back to drinking, and that ended when I almost died two years ago in 2012. My body reacted, and I was dying of what they thought was congestive heart disease. My stomach was filled up, my legs were filled up, and my lungs were starting to fill up. That's when I went to the hospital, and they pumped the fluid out of my body. I lost eleven pounds in ten minutes. I'm going to write a diet book, *Lose Eleven Pounds in Ten Minutes,* by Pat Conroy.

I knew I was dying, and I knew I had to quit drinking forever. I had known this for a long time. But I think who saved my life was a doctor up at the University of South Carolina hospital in Charleston. I hated his guts. He looked at me, he says, "I know your type. You'll be back up here, crawling on your hands and knees, begging me to take you into my program. I may take you; I may not; I may get you to write a book that will finally mean something to somebody."

I'm watching this guy, not feeling like taking this shit too much. And he said, "We'll send you home, you'll start drinking again, you'll be back up, you'll crawl on your hands and knees into our program, we'll try to cure you; we may do it for a while, you'll go back, you'll be in the gutter again." He said, "I've seen drunks like you a million times. You'll be crawling back into my clinic, kissing my shoes. Maybe after I get you off alcohol, you'll finally be able to write a book that really matters."

I said, "Pal, I want you to take a good look at my fat face. You will never lay eyes on it again."

I made up my mind as I was dying that night that this guy would never see me again, and so I quit drinking that night. I'd rather have slid an anvil into my ass and leapt off a dock than go back to that guy. He also told me my liver was squeaking. I think that's a nice way to say that the liver is damaged. I had diabetes, obesity; I had done damage to my liver and kidneys, and you only get a couple of those in a lifetime, and they don't need that. They'll figure out how to die some other way, but I do not want to help them along. If I keep drinking, what I know is I'll die. What more do I need to know? When I feel that I'm going to die because of something I'm doing, I can see clearly what I have to do. There's a couple of books I'd like to write, a couple of things I'd like to do. I want to see my granddaughters get married to whatever monsters they choose. So now what I've done is exchanged alcohol for spirited games of volleyball on the beach, putt-putt golf, and ping-pong played at a brisk pace.

Now that I've quit drinking, Bernie will tell the waiter, "I'd like a martini, my wife will have this lovely red wine, his wife will have that wonderful white wine. But my friend Pat here is a hopeless alcoholic, and he cannot have anything to drink or we will have to put him into a home. Pat is simply a common drunk, and there's no other way to put it. He's also morbidly handicapped and can barely walk. God, I hate having a friend who's an invalid." Bernie goes hee-hawing away laughing his ass off.

Everybody reels back in shock. Nobody understands why I laugh, but it tickles me, because no one else would say that. Bernie is the only person on earth who would say something like that, and I can't tell you how good that was for me when I was a boy who was taught not to say anything, and it's good for me now. The freedom Bernie has presented to me of just saying anything, thinking anything, has been very, very good.

I buy this expensive bourbon for him to drink when he comes over, and Bernie will always open the bourbon, bring it over, and put it under my nose for me to smell. I will deeply inhale, and then he'll say, "Pat, I wish you could have some of this because it is so good, it is so soothing. But because you are a hopeless alcoholic you can't have any, and this is all for Bernie Schein."

Of course, my wife will get irritated and say, "Bernie, quit doing that."

But he'll say, "No, no, no, you must test Pat each day."

I go over to Bernie's, and he'll pour drinks for himself and slide it by my nose so I can smell it. Then he'll drink it and say, "Oh my God, it's so good, I wish you could taste it with me. It just tastes so good. You used to be able to partake of wonderful liquor like this, but then you became a hopeless alcoholic, and now, to save your life, you have to be for the rest of your life a teetotaler, the saddest word in the English language—teetotaler."

It's what I get. I can miss it all I want, but I was dying. This was very apparent to me: I wouldn't be around if I kept up my drinking. I did it too much, and I understand that, so I will simply suffer the rest of my life. Everybody else will be pouring liquor down their throats while I go suck on peppermint candy. Some days I prefer it when I was a hopeless drunk and had only a couple weeks to live.

~

When Lenore came to Fripp we had our great transfiguration of a marriage ender. She calls, says she's coming for a month in the summer, that her shrink says we have no marriage and we need to work on that. She said she'd let me write; she'd go to the beach. I was in the middle of a breakdown, and I don't think my judgment was good at that moment, so I said come on. Marion told me, "Don't leave anything around the house she can find to use against you." Now I know that's what she was coming for; she was on a search-and-destroy mission. She was hunting for something, some ammunition for the divorce, and I played right into it. It was my fault, and I couldn't blame anybody but myself.

I had not told anybody about Sylvia, but she made a mistake and told one of her friends, and eventually it got back to Lenore. I had also told Sylvia not to write me letters, but she would send these little love notes and sign them by some silly nickname. I had hidden them fairly well, I thought, somewhere in the attic. It was the second morning Lenore was there, when I was seeing Marion and driving back, that Lenore went through all my stuff and found the letters from Sylvia. She also found I had a local checking account.

"You have a bank account you didn't tell me about."

I said, "You'll find $500 in it. If I need to pay a bill—twenty-five bucks for the phone—it seems much easier to me."

Then I had looked at real estate; she had a real estate brochure. I said I always look at real estate. I look at real estate wherever I go. I like that.

Finally she pulls out these letters. Now, Susannah, who is eleven, is in front of us, and Lenore begins screaming out of control.

Then she turns to Susannah and starts screaming, "Your father is fucking other women! He is fucking other women! Do you know what fucking means? He is fucking other women, not your mother! Do you know what that means?"

This is like a fork to my eyeball. I go up to Susannah, kneel down and say, "Susannah, you should not have to go through this, and I promise you this is as wrong as it can be, it should not be happening, and I am sorry that it's happening to you."

And Lenore, "But he's fucking other women! He's fucking other women!"

Susannah was so sweet even in that moment. She kept saying, "Daddy, don't worry about this. This will be all right, I promise. We'll get by this, this will be okay."

I said, "Eleven is too young to be able to say that to me, but I appreciate it, kid."

And she said, "This'll be all right, this'll be all right," and of course it never was.

Lenore kept screaming, "He's fucking other women! He's fucking other women! He's fucking other women!"

I couldn't take it anymore. To put a stop to it I simply walk out of the house, get in the car, drive to Gene Norris's house, and collapse at the door. I told him what had happened and spent the night with Gene. When I got back there the next day, Lenore was gone with Susannah, and basically I've never really seen Susannah again. That was the last real human moment I had with her. My relationship with Susannah was gone forever.

And of course, tough Marion O'Neill: "Nice going, Pat. You provided Lenore with all the ammunition she came out to get." She was very happy with me when she found out about this.

Thank God Sylvia's name was not on the letters. Sylvia is a heroine in my life. She reminded me that I could love somebody and be loved in return. I feel great love and gratitude for that woman I can never repay. But she is the girl who always gets shit on. She entered my life at the wrong part of my life, and you know how that goes. The one who is there in the middle of the divorce usually gets dumped on, and I still feel terrible about that. But I told her, "Sylvia, I don't know if I'll ever divorce Lenore because I can't just throw this kid out of my life."

I would have stayed married to Lenore until Susannah was eighteen, because I knew exactly what would happen if I did not, and I was right. I didn't know how that was going to work, whether I would mostly live and write on Fripp and just go visit, but I never got to the point where I said I wanted a divorce.

The horror of that scene with Lenore still reverberates with me, and that became part of my nightmare and my inability to sleep for years. I lie there in agony in the bed at night, looking over my dreadful life, horrified by what I've done, by what I've not done, and I writhe. I lie as if I've been crucified to the bed, and I wake in caverns, study stalactites before I roll out of bed, then crawl through roach droppings. I do not bound out of bed when I awaken saying, "My God, I'm glad to be alive." There is nothing I love more than sleep, because for years I couldn't do it. Now I just adore it and can't have enough of it.

~

I have no idea how *Beach Music* got written when I returned to South Carolina from San Francisco. I had written a lot in San Francisco, but I finished up in Fripp. *Beach Music* was the book that took the longest to write, because I was married to my second wife. But here's my problem with my marriage to Lenore: I wrote *The Prince of Tides* married to her, I wrote *Beach Music* married to her, and I like both of those books a lot. Would I have written the same books if I hadn't been married to her? I'm not that sure I would have. I'm not sure. It may mean I was in the middle of the maelstrom I've always needed. I was in the middle of Santini's family. I was in the middle of whatever I needed in order to create, and that has always worried me. There's a part of me that not only thrives on chaos but needs it, looks for it, hunts it down, nets it, grabs it, brings it to me, lets it eat my entrails out as I'm trying to write. It drives me nuts that this is a possibility.

But that book, for many reasons, seems to be the most emotionally howling out of anything I've ever written. It was done under great duress.

There had been the great breakdown. There was the feeling divorce was coming down the road and nothing could be done about it. There was a feeling I'd never see Susannah again. I put Susannah as Leah in *Beach Music* because I thought I'd never see her again. I wanted to write about her as she was at the moment I thought I was losing her. I wanted to have a portrait of what our relationship was like and how I saw her before she was taken away. It was painful because I felt like I was saying good-bye to Susannah. So I was not in the best shape during that.

Also, just the sheer subject of the Holocaust, and it's difficult to be a Christian writer in the United States and deal with a subject that's so sacred to Jewish people. Many of them were: "How dare you write about our sacred subject, and can you explain why you're doing it?" I told the story of my mother, who, when I was six years old living in New Bern, North Carolina, read the *Diary of Anne Frank* to my sister and me. When you're a little boy you fall in love with Anne, and you want yourself to be in the attic instead of the others she was with. Mom reads this in her magical voice. When the book ends, Carol and I go, what happened? What happened to Anne? Where is she? And my mother starts telling us about cattle cars, gas chambers, six million Jews killed. Mom tells us that Anne Frank died in Bergen-Belsen. My sister Carol is hysterical, I'm hysterical, and my sister said, "Why did they kill Anne Frank?"

I said, "Didn't they read her book?"

And my mother says, "I want to raise a family that will hide Jews."

The next day Carol—and I don't know how she knew our neighbor was Jewish—goes next door, knocks on the door, Mrs. Orringer asks us what we want, and Carol said, "We will hide you."

This woman goes "Vhat?"

Carol says, "We will hide you. Do not worry."

My mother was absolutely obsessed with the Holocaust, and she passed that directly on to me. Because of that, I have got to write this story. I don't care who likes it or not; I have got to write it for me, for the artist I want to be. But I had to get it right. I hired Miriam Karp to interview Jews in Atlanta because a lot of the people who had been in the camps were not comfortable with a Christian asking them questions, and Miriam was well known in the Jewish community. She was just delightful, and she went around interviewing Jews who'd been in the camps and children of Holocaust survivors. I got some wonderful material from that.

When I went to the gym at the Jewish Community Center in Atlanta, I used to shower with old guys with tattoos on their forearms. After I got to know them a bit, I started to ask about them. "What happened to your families during the war? What went on?" Cliff Graubart had an aunt who died in the camps, because she didn't want to leave Warsaw until her son finished high school. And I'm thinking what a normal thing for a parent to do: after he finishes, then we'll get out. Of course by then it was too late.

I had also picked up stories over the years. I was at the Peachtree Road Race, standing in the crowd there at Ansley Park where we're living, and I started talking to the young woman next to me. We're talking, we're talking. I believe she recognized me, and that's why we were talking, but I asked her, "Where are you from?"

She said, "I'm from South Carolina, not far from you. I'm from Charleston."

I said, "Martha, a Charleston girl. Tell me about yourself, where you went to school, and I'll tell you your life story."

She said, "No, Pat, you think I'm South of Broad; I am not. I'm a Jewish girl. But a lot of those girls were my friends, and I know what you're talking about, and I know why you asked the question, but my story was different." She stunned me by saying, "Both of my parents are Holocaust survivors."

I walk her home to her apartment that day. Martha Popowski and I became friends, and I got close to her family. Her mother went out with us one night and in broken English told her story, which was the story I used in the book of the girl with the gold coins sewn into the dress. As the war went on and she traveled through Poland, she gave out gold coins to the people who helped her, the righteous Gentiles, nuns who wanted to take her into their convent, a man who had given her protection for no reason. The only thing he had to lose was his life, and his family's life, but he did it because he was a good man. Her dress started getting lighter and lighter and lighter.

We were sitting in a seafood restaurant on a little street in Atlanta, and when she finished this harrowing story, I said, "How many coins did you have when the war was over?"

I was sitting, eating with Martha, her sister, and Mrs. Popowski, and I saw the girls look at each other, and she said, "I had three." She reaches down in her dress and pulls out a gold coin on a chain, and then Martha and her sister, Sarah, pull out the other two coins.

So I looked at them all and said, "Consider that story stolen." You know, if you tell a story, it becomes like smoke in the air. It is up for grabs, and I am good at grabbing stories. Anyone who bottles it first, I'll listen.

Still, I knew what was going to happen simply because I was a Christian writing about a Jewish subject, but I've never given a rat's ass about that kind of criticism, which is just another form of censorship to me. Julian Bach thought I was getting into the land of anti-Semitism, because here I am, the goyim, who can't recognize my own anti-Semitism or the sensitivity of Jews over how they're written about.

He says, "My God, you're writing about Jews. You don't know any Jews in the South."

I said, "Julian, I got to call about a thousand people; they're hideously mistaken about their past and their upbringing."

He said, "There are no Jews until you get to Miami Beach."

I said, "Julian, there's a lot you don't know about the South. I could introduce you to Jews with a Southern accent you wouldn't believe." That's Bernie.

Julian says, "Oh, that's preposterous; we would never speak like that."

I said, "I guess I've been going around with some people who've been misrepresenting themselves as Jews since I was born."

He said, "Well, that's perfectly ridiculous, and you need to tell them that."

So I said, "Julian, what is your big problem?"

He said, "You write about Jews, you write about the Holocaust; you can't do this."

I said, "Well, I've got to do it."

And he said, "Well then, you must make all your Jews likable."

I said, "Why is that? That sounds ridiculous. I've known a lot of jerk Jews."

He says, "My God, listen to you. I noted during the football game in your book it is not the Jew who scores the winning touchdown."

I said, "You mean I've got to let the Jew score the winning touchdown? It's enough of a stretch that I have a Jew playing in the football game."

There are all these things that people will find not to like in a novel, and you don't catch it as much with a nonfiction book because you're supposedly telling the truth. The whole book I found very, very difficult to write. Then, of course, I'm going to top it off with Mom's death and Tom's suicide. Tom was going to kill himself in that book. I think I did kill him. Anyway, I had planned to kill John Hardin, who I put in as Tom, until my brother Tom actually did commit suicide. So I had to change those plans very rapidly. So Hardin survives—nice going, lad—because I didn't think the book could bear that kind of burden, and I couldn't bear putting that kind of burden into the book right after it happened. So I bailed. I hope I can be forgiven as an artist, but I bailed out of that one. It was not a wise choice; it was a choice made for me.

By this time, Nan Talese had moved to Doubleday because it was more money and prestige, I think. She got her own imprint. Again she flew me to New York and put me up in a hotel for five months. This broke up my therapy with Marion O'Neill, but I enjoyed that New York experience, and Nan wanted me right beside her while she edited. She was still a hands-on editor at that time, and we worked every day for eight hours a day in her beautiful house on East Sixty-First Street. Here's what I love about Nan: she's smarter than shit, and when she has an idea, it's not just an idea; she's got a reason for having it and can defend that idea. That's exciting to me as a writer. She would give me homework, so I'd walk home from her house to my little Surrey Hotel and do my homework that night. The new restaurateur Daniel Boulud had a little restaurant in the hotel, and that was room service, so I ate like a fucking king.

Sometimes Nan and Gay would take me over to shit-bird Elaine's with her lousy food. The best thing there was the raw oyster. But everybody was world famous and sitting around looking at other world-famous people. I got to hate Woody Allen. He and his girlfriend at the time—before he married her daughter—Mia Farrow—I'd watch them come in, and they had a special seat, as Nan and Gay had a special seat. I watched them come in there every night with their faces looking straight down at the floor. They'd walk straight as arrows to their seats and they would sit down, and only then they'd look up into each other's eyes. You know, God forbid that they may see another human being they had to say hello to. Of course I'm sitting there saying what is that fucking shit all about? Oh, there's paparazzi. There was no paparazzi in there. Everybody that went there either was somebody or wanted to be somebody or wanted to be around somebody who was somebody.

Now, I could not make Nan laugh if I put a whoopee cushion in her chair, but I've always tickled Gay. He wanted to watch the Knicks one time when we were working on the book at the house. I said sure, so we're watching the Knicks, and I'm commenting. Gay looks at me, says, "You know about basketball?" A little bit. So we keep going; he says, "No, you know a lot about basketball." Yeah, I know some things. And then finally he's going, "You know everything about basketball. Did you play basketball?" I said yeah, I played it in college. He said "Why didn't I know that?" Then he said, "John Irving has let everybody know he was a high school wrestler." But I always thought if anybody learned I was a jock in New York they wouldn't talk to me ever again.

Anyway, the editing was going well, and we had fun working together. Nan pulled that whole book together. I had given her a two-thousand-page mess, and she made that book a publishable item. She deserves that credit because I was out of my mind.

I look back now on that New York experience as a happy time. I still felt a bit queasy, but stable, as if I'd survived something, but barely, and I needed to watch myself, be careful. When Nan brought me to New York to work on that book, she was doing me a great favor because she got me out of harm's way, got me to that hotel, and then whipped me into shape for the next five months, whipped that book into shape and got it together the way she wanted and could be happy with.

She always goes crazy when I do my nature thing. I had the white porpoise in *Prince of Tides,* and in *Beach Music* I have a manta ray come flying out of the water. She wanted to cut that, and she finally says, "I'm so tired of you and your scenes about"—she's frustrated, and then she finally says—"your scenes about *seafood*." Well, I got to keep the manta ray, but I was such a weak spirit at the time I didn't fight Nan much. I basically did what she wanted me to do. But I look back on that time in New York as a great time in my writing life.

I even thought of staying in New York, but then I looked at a couple of apartments, and it was one of the most disheartening things I've ever done in my life. I hated the real estate agent; I hated the people running the buildings; I didn't like anything about New York real estate. The guys that guarded the door seemed like jerks to me. When I thought of actually living there, it didn't get me. And what am I going to do now? Start going to literary parties? No, I didn't feel like that.

~

One afternoon I was working in the Surrey Hotel, rewriting a chapter in *Beach Music*. Late in the afternoon a knock on the door came. I opened the door, and somebody threw something on the floor. That was the delivery of the divorce papers. Not everybody realizes this: Lenore asked for the divorce. I don't think I would ever have asked for one, because of Susannah. But there it was, and I had to deal with it.

A couple of days later, I get another visit from a very unprepossessing guy. He sort of looked like a bream. I said, "Hey, how you doing? How can I help you?"

He said, "Mr. Conroy, I'm from the IRS."

I said, "Come on in."

He said, "You didn't hear me. I'm from the IRS."

I said, "The Internal Revenue Service? That's how you make a living. I write books. That's how I make a living. What's the difference? You must have business with me. Come on in and sit down." And I said, "It's late in the afternoon, and I've got a full bar." I still was not drinking, so I had plenty in it. I said, "Let me fix you a drink."

He said, "Well, I'm on duty."

I said, "It's 5:30. When do you go off duty?"

"Well, officially, 5:00."

I said, "Yeah, let me fix you something."

I fixed him a drink, he sat back, and he said, "I've got bad news for you."

I said, "Generally, that is the business of the IRS. You must hate making visits like this but, you know, it's not personal. Somebody sent you to do this, so I do not resent you for it."

He says, "Mr. Conroy, you have not paid taxes for the last two years."

I said, "You know, I don't do my taxes; my wife handles all that. But I remember they always make me sign this line that says I am paying my taxes."

He said, "You signed every one of them. What has not happened is you've not sent the check along with the signature."

I said, "Well, how much do I owe?"

He said something like, "You owe us $250,000."

And I said, "So my wife—"

He said, "No checks have been sent with the forms. There's also more bad news. The IRS is fining you $200 a day until you pay this off."

I said, "I'll be glad to pay it off, but I'm going to have to finish this book, and the book's going to have to come out. But I promise, I'll pay you everything."

And so we sat. We talked about his family, we talked about my family, and when he left we shook hands. Here's what was interesting about this man. Here's what happened from that visit. He cancelled the $200 a day fine.

Unfortunately, I have never been able to involve myself with money, because that is where anxiety overwhelms me. I had so little money as a kid, and I suffered from not having some of it as a kid. You know, I did not grow up in a Sudanese refugee camp, and I know the difference of that kind of poverty. It was not poverty I grew up in. I grew up with cheapness. The Depression did something to my mother and father that made money a strange, alienating thing for them. It twisted them both in odd ways. It twisted their children in ways that were even odder.

What Mom did to us all with money is sick. I got a dime a week when I was a senior in high school. Guys on the basketball team would invite me down to Dairy Queen for a hamburger and a Coke before practice; I'd never do it, and I'd kid around, "I got to work on my

game." And it was just because, you know, a dime a week, I can't do it.
I came across a girl the other day who asked me, "Why didn't your
parents let you date in high school?" It wasn't they didn't let me date; I
didn't have enough money to date. "Hi, would you like me to buy you
a bean sprout?" My mother could utterly humiliate me with money. No
one was better than her on that. I just did not have money even to get
girls into a movie theater. "Oh, you want popcorn? My God, what a
pig. Oh, you want Coke with that? Isn't popcorn enough? Do you want
anything? Nah, my God, just concentrate on the movie."

But she really got me on the hops, our big dances. I would dread
those things. Senior year at the Citadel was the big one. We have homecoming; then we have the Ring Hop, when we receive our ring. That's
the biggest moment in a senior's life and the life of a Citadel cadet. You
walk through a huge gold replica of the ring, stop, get your picture
taken, kiss your date, and then after that go out to dinner. That's when
you get to wear your ring for the first time. It's a huge deal on campus.
I'm desperate because I don't know who to ask for a date.

Well, this girl Ann Burnett had lived a couple houses down from me
on the base in Beaufort. I was friendly to her, and she wrote me all during college. They moved to California, and she still wrote, and one day
she wrote, "Who are you taking to the Ring Hop?" I said, "Right now
nobody. You want to come?" But she's in California; it seemed like asking somebody to come from China at that time. But she worked, had a
job, so she said, "I'd love to come."

Well, I was pleased as could be, but oh God, here it comes. The letters I got from her said, "Pat, I know you don't have any money, you
can't work as a cadet, but any help you can give me on the plane ticket
or the room, the food, would be appreciated."

So I said, "Mom, I know this is going to be hard, but I think I need
some real money for this thing."

She said, "Well, Ann's got a perfectly nice job. I've written her mother,
and she makes a lot of money."

"Ma, I don't care, okay. I would like you to send me fifty bucks."

Oh, Mr. Rockefeller.

The check didn't get there. I'm going to the mailbox every day; it's
not there. It arrives the day Ann arrives. I open it up; I usually get ten

dollars a month. Mom made it a big fifteen, because of the Ring Hop. So I said oh, my God, this is going to be so humiliating. Well, we walk through the ring, Ann met the generals, and she likes that. She was a Marine's daughter so she had a good time.

Then we go out to dinner, and I'm with these other guys, my classmates, we're all going out to dinner together, and they're ordering real food, doing it big. Ann orders a Singapore sling; she ordered a salad and appetizer, escargots bathing in garlic butter. All these guys order their steaks; she orders a steak. Everybody orders a big steak except me. So she looks up, says "Pat, what are you ordering?"

I said, "Well, I got a glass of water. I'm dehydrated after basketball practice."

She says, "You got water and a green salad?"

I said, "Yeah, I just can't eat. Practice, you know, it makes me nauseated."

Then dessert comes, and whatever she ordered was on fire. When our bill arrives, I have to go borrow the money; I had to beg the money from a friend in the men's room.

I said, "I'm so sorry."

He said, "Pat, you've got quite the name as a mooch."

My worst nightmare.

Okay, that got me through dinner. Then we go to breakfast the next day. I just have a cup of coffee, and I can't even see her head, there are so many waffles between us, and now I'm borrowing from my teammates; I'm borrowing from my roommate. Then it comes time to pay the hotel room. I can offer not a cent. I take Ann back to the airport, and guess how much I can pay for her flight? I was as embarrassed as I'd ever been in my life.

Ann and I used to write regularly until that. I never wrote her again for thirty years. I disappeared from her life. She disappeared from my life. Then I was searching for her for years, because I like to have a chance to explain myself to someone. Finally somebody saw her in California. I got her address; I wrote her a letter and told her the whole story of what happened at the Ring Hop. "Ann, I did not have enough money to take you out to dinner, to buy you breakfast on Sunday. I did not have any money to help pay your plane ticket from fucking

California. Could I send you a check for $2,000? Will you let me do that for not having paid for anything for you?"

She writes back and says, "Pat, how many times do you think I've dined out on the fact I went to the Citadel Ring Hop with Pat Conroy?"

When I got her on the phone, I said, "Please let me send you $2,000. My mortification was complete."

Ann was terrific. She just said, "Pat, I don't even want to let you off. Going to the Ring Hop with you is the best thing I've ever done. You're not going to send me a cent."

But I was still horrified, after all those years.

When I was writing *The Lords of Discipline,* I had rented a place on Sullivan's Island so I could do research in Charleston. One night I went to a debutante party in Confederate Hall when I was hanging around the South of Broad crowd, them not knowing that I was cruelly amassing material that I would use to hamstring them later in their lives as they traveled their innocent ways toward death. But I was enjoying this party, and what I picked up on was that the girl who was coming out had just barely made the cut, just barely snuck in there. Her father and mother were struggling; he had had business reversals and was in trouble.

It was a nice party, the girl was enjoying herself—it was her night—and then I hear the bartender tell her father, "We're cutting off the bar. You're at your limit." I then see the girl rushing up, because guys were coming to her saying the bar was cut off. This poor father put his hands up, said, "I'm sorry, honey. We had a limit." When I saw the look on that girl's face, it almost killed me. It was hopelessness and despair, embarrassment for herself, her father letting her down on this most golden of all nights. I couldn't take it. I went over and gave the bartender my credit card and said, "Put it on that." It was the first big-wheel thing I'd ever done, and of course I was terrified they were going to find out I'd overdrawn my account by nine million dollars and they'd spit the card back at me. But the drinks started again. I couldn't stand seeing the look on that girl's face because I knew exactly what she was going through.

Now my brothers and sisters think I am hideously profligate and ridiculous in the way I use and do not use money. They consider it a serious flaw of character. They are all ants working and storing up for winter, and I am the Jurassic grasshopper. Their definition of me is Pat goes in to buy himself a Buick. Why would he buy himself a Buick? Pat has always been an old man, and old men buy Buicks, and Pat was an old man when he was eighteen.

And then they say Pat goes into a showroom, and the guy says, "Would you like me to show you a few cars?"

Pat says, "No, show me just one car."

Pat sees the car, he likes it, and the guy says, "Would you like to test drive it?"

Pat says, "No I wouldn't; I just want to buy it."

The guy says, "Well, that is $20,000," and Pat says in his fierce bargaining technique, "I'll give you $25,000."

But I didn't want to be like my mother. I really did not want to be like that. And I didn't want to be a bathroom guy, the guy who runs from the check. He sees the check walking toward us, and he suddenly finds himself in desperate need of the men's room. I call this the money shadow. People can seem perfectly normal, even fabulous human beings, until we come to the point when the check arrives.

But I have been an expert at finding people who could go through my money like it was nothing. What an idiot I was. God, what an idiot. It is a long, involved, stupid story where all the worst parts of my personality come out and gather up in a force that was irresistible and unturnable, and of course ruined my life.

~

Jim Roe was my financial counselor, my investment guy; he handled all my money, and he was one of those crashing towers in my life. He was the most successful cadet at the Citadel when I was there. He was regimental executive officer, second in command of the corps. He was vice president of the class. He was best military. Every military honor you could win, he won. The most coveted thing in our class is the Willson Ring. He won the Willson Ring. He was the perfect Christian boy from Rome, Georgia. Went to Harvard Law School from the Citadel, which ain't easy, and was head of the Southern Club at Harvard Law School.

He and I were not friends at all. He was very military: militantly military, not my type of guy at the Citadel, but I didn't have many types of guys at the Citadel. I was a lonely lad there. John Warley told me this later, that he and Jim went their freshman year to General Mark Clark, our famous president, and both of them wanted to know how to go about stopping communism.

I said, "No wonder you boys got such high rank. That's pretty good for freshmen, knowing how to brownnose a world famous general who'd written a book on anticommunism."

That's how ambitious Jim was. Jim was as ambitious as anybody in our class. He looked like he was going to eat the world alive. Freshman year, his mother came to Scott Graber and said, "You should attach your destiny to my son. He is going to be a great man."

I got to know him a little more, in sophomore year, when four sophomores were selected for the Roundtable, which was the intellectual discussion society of the Citadel. Only four sophomores were allowed to blacken its ranks. I had distinguished myself in no way at the Citadel at this time, but for some odd reason I was elected by the Roundtable. Why, I do not know, but there I was, intellectually discussing with dimwits whatever they brought up. Usually it was right-wing Nazi politics. Later, I learned it was the valedictorian of that graduating class who'd spotted me. He'd been in the public speaking course with me and heard me do a paper on Thomas Wolfe. So I was in the Roundtable with these three military guys from the sophomore class: Steve Grubb, Bill Meck, and Jim Roe.

The intellectual discussion club at the Citadel seemed to me like the most right-wing organization I could ever join. Many of the students on it were prosegregation. I don't remember anyone saying a good word about integration the three years I was on the Roundtable. In my junior year, I went on one of my little rants. This one was about the integration of the Citadel. I said, "That's coming, kids. You can talk all you want; you can make philosophical arguments. The Supreme Court has ruled. It's the law of the land. And I don't see why we're not getting ready for it." I was passionate about it.

It was not particularly well received. Jim totally disagreed with me, but when we go out, back to the barracks, he told a friend of mine,

"You know, Conroy's a jock, but he actually seemed smart tonight. Never occurred to me he might be smart. I always thought he was just a jock. Do you think he read something?"

That was my relationship with Jim.

Later, our senior year, Steve Grubb, Jim Roe, and I were elected to the Honor Court, if you can believe there's an honor system in a place where they torture young boys. I did not particularly want to be on the Honor Court, but there I was, elected. I thought, "Oh, great. I get to throw kids out of school; can't wait." But I told myself, look, I agreed to this when I came to this school. These are the rules I agreed to. And I tried to abide by them; I did.

First of all, Jim was nominated chairman, but he said there was so much he had to do: he had become regimental executive officer; he had become something with the Summerall Guards; he had become something on the Sword Drill. He was everything. I mean, Jim was everything, so he had to decline. They elected Steve Grubb, who was a good friend of mine, very high ranked, as chairman, and then they stunned me by electing me vice chairman, which meant that I was going to have to sit on every trial. I had not had a leadership role at the Citadel at all, but I had to take one, and it was agonizing for me.

So anyway, Jim is the second-highest ranked cadet in our class. First Citadel cadet ever to get into Harvard Law School. That was a great victory for our campus, and we all exulted in that and celebrated that. So Jim Roe goes off to do that. Meanwhile, most of my class goes off to Vietnam. This is 1967. They walk off stage, and they are headed for Vietnam. And I become, of course, the only draft dodger in my class.

A few years later, when *The Boo* comes out, I'd said two of the people who were most responsible for getting the Boo fired were the regimental commander and the regimental executive officer of my class, 1967. I did not name them in the book. But it was Jim Probsdorfer, the regimental commander, and Jim Roe.

When I get this Ford Foundation Fellowship, Barbara and I had rented a place in San Rafael, way outside of San Francisco, because I couldn't afford anything in the city. And one day I see two guys coming up to our house on Vendola Drive in San Rafael. It is Barry Murray, who was my classmate in Romeo Company, with Jim Roe. Jim was stationed in the Army in California, and Barry was in the Air Force.

My wife Barbara, who hated all Citadel graduates, liked Jim and Barry. I had both Bo-Pig and Mike-Swine as roommates, and both were jocks, so these two were the first gentlemanly Citadel guys that Barbara had met. And Jim is the most charming man you have ever met. He paid attention to women, which is a rare thing for a Citadel guy. I mean, he paid real attention to them. Barbara was by his side just cooing, because Jim was a pleasure to be with.

But as we're talking, I'm thinking, "What are they doing?" Jim never paid me any attention at the Citadel because he saw no need to. There was nothing to be gained. Suddenly there was something to be gained. Because of *The Boo,* I had suddenly become a figure of importance in the class. Even if it was a negative renown, it was still renown.

When I walked them back to the car Jim says, "Pat, I really have a bone to pick with you about the way you said that Probsdorfer and I had something to do with the Boo being fired."

Even though I had not named him, he knew that all his classmates knew. I had besmirched his reputation by writing that the Boo was fired by the complaints of the regimental commander and the regimental executive officer. Jim had said the Boo was bad for discipline, because the senior officers like Jim would mete out punishment to the privates, and the Boo would let them off. It's always about power.

I said, "Well, that's what the Boo told me, Jim. If you have a different story and it holds up, I'll be glad to change it. I'll call the Boo tonight to see if he's made a mistake," which I did.

And the Boo says, "He's running, Bubba. They all run for the hills now, Bubba." He said, "Since your book came out, they're calling me all the time. They were all on my side. They all fought for me."

It was a great lesson to learn in life. But I liked the way Jim approached me when he said it, and we talked about it. He just wanted to say he didn't like the way he was portrayed in the book.

Anyway, a year after we moved to Atlanta, Jim Roe moved to Atlanta with his adorable, lovely wife. God, she is a lovely, lovely Smith girl, majored in Latin and the classics. She's beautiful, and we were all dazzled by her. Anyway, because of Barbara's loving them, we became instant friends. Cliff and Bernie loved Jim Roe too: the charm. They'd say, "Pat, who can make you feel like a million bucks more than Jim Roe can?"

But Jim knew where they were going much more than Barbara and I did. Jim told me he was only going to live in a certain zip code with a certain area code. Buckhead. He lives in the smallest house on earth, but has the prefix, and that's the way he begins. He enters one of the big law firms in Atlanta: Kilpatrick and Cody.

And Jim Roe's life was, I thought, set. He was a serious Baptist, and he's the kind of guy that when he joins a Baptist church, within three years he's a deacon. He joined the Rotary Club younger than anybody is ever asked to join the Rotary Club in Atlanta. He joined the Capital City Club. He joined every club there was with the prize being the Piedmont Driving Club, but you couldn't get into that until you spent a certain time on the waiting list.

But to everybody's shock, I was the first of the group to make any money. Especially to me, the shock was tremendous. Here's what happened. When I graduated from the Citadel and I was teaching, I made $4,700 the first year, and I felt like a millionaire, because my mother and father had never given me anything. I felt like I had a million bucks. With *The Water Is Wide,* they gave me an advance of $7,500. I remember Barbara dancing all over the house when that came through. *Life* magazine did an excerpt; I got some money from that. Then the movie's bought, and what their option was, it may have been about five or $7,000 too. We felt like millionaires at that time. When they made the movie, that was $50,000. Huge back then. *The Great Santini* comes out, didn't sell much, but sold to the movies, another $7,500 option.

This is all happening when Jim Roe makes a career shift. He calls me in and says, "Pat, law is not a very satisfying way to make a living." So he tells me he's going to start one of the first financial investment firms in Atlanta, which he does, Roe, Martin, and Neiman. So Jim starts his firm. I'm not only one of the first clients; I am one of the first investors in the firm. And Jim says, "Pat, this'll be your retirement. The money you invest in my firm is going to be like the first investor in Coca-Cola," you know, that kind of horseshit. But I trusted Jim, and they became one of the leading investment finance firms in Atlanta.

Meanwhile, who joins the firm? Steve Grubb. Steve and Jim were very close. That lasts for about two years, when Steve pulls out of the firm, which should have been a red flag to me, but still, there was great prosperity. Also, Jane Lefco was hired by this firm, and she became my friend for life.

Now, there were certain little fault lines. Jim would call me up and say, "Pat, I can't meet the payroll this month. Can I go into your account and pay you back 10 percent?" So I said sure. As far as I know, he always went back and paid the 10 percent. But there were little cracks in the wall like that.

The paperback rights for *The Lords of Discipline* sold for about $700,000. Jim may have put me in a tax shelter. Avocado farms ring a bell to me. He may have put me in something like that, but of course I don't check this much. You know, I'm not the type, "My God, I want to look over the balance sheet, Jim."

Well, in 1986 Reagan passed a tax code that mostly eliminated the write-offs that Jim Roe's firm was specializing in. The avocado farms, the alfalfa farms. Whatever they were doing, he cut it out. It sent Jim's firm into a tailspin.

Jim, meanwhile, had been moving up in houses. They get to the nicer Buckhead houses, much nicer dresses, much nicer parties. He finally ends up in a house on Tuxedo Road. That is serious Buckhead and serious homes, and this one, God, I think was on four acres of land. The most beautiful swimming pool you've ever seen, a huge mansion, absolutely huge. This was the ultimate, and Jim was driving a Jaguar. By this time he had gotten into the Piedmont Driving Club.

He says, "Pat, all this is for the business. It's all for the business."

I said, "Jim, is business still doing as well?"

Now, they could have gone into stocks and done a zillion dollars' worth of other things after the tax code changed. They had a lot of clients. But what Jim did then is the weirdest thing. He announces that he had hooked up with a gold expert who realized there was more gold in Nevada sand than anywhere else. It was the largest gold deposit on earth. So he and these partners ended up buying acres of this land to be dug up, and Jim gets all these investors, the most important men in Atlanta. I went to the meeting.

I said, "Jim, I cannot invest in the Midas Project. I know more about literature than you do. This lust for gold is not unknown, and it usually comes to grief."

He said, "Pat, I'm *giving* you shares because of your support of the firm."

I didn't believe it was going to work. But Jane Lefco believed utterly in Jim. And she never quite lost it. I mean, his charm was so great she would always fall for it. She said, "Pat, do you know what he calls me? He calls me 'rich lady,' because I'm going to be so wealthy when this gold in Nevada comes through, that 'rich lady' is going to be one of the wealthiest women in the United States."

Jim would tell me in front of all these other people, "You know, I think I'm hurting a great American literary career, because Pat is going to be so wealthy he's going to have no need to sit down in front of a piece of paper to create; that's how much money he's going to have. He's going to be the richest writer in the history of the world."

I would laugh and say, "Jim, why don't you tell me that after? That would be my advice."

He said, "Pat, you don't know how to sell. You've got to build up enthusiasm."

He took Jane and me to lunch one time and said, "Rich lady, you sit there." And Jane, she's so happy she's going to be rich lady. And, "Writer, you sit over there."

We're sitting there, and he takes something out of his pocket. It looks like a hockey puck, and he spins it across the table at us. It's pure gold.

Jane looks at it and says, "Jim, where did you get it?"

He says, "We created it at the plant last week. The project works."

So Jane, she goes over, and she's kissing Jim, she's just so happy. "So the process works! It works!"

He said, "That's what it looks like, doesn't it?"

Then there's a huge meeting in a big hotel like the Ritz-Carlton, and food is served, heavy hors d'oeuvres, drinks. It's done very, very well. What Jim was good at is talking investors into investing money. I look around, and every big shot in town is there, the biggest. Because of Jim Roe's reputation for integrity and coming through and his utter charm and his salesmanship, they've all bought in to the Midas Project.

So Jim comes out and says, "We've been working on this process night and day. There's a factory out in Nevada that we have built, and we have now perfected the technology to get gold from the Nevada sand. Look at this."

He takes this puck out of his pocket and hurls this fucking piece of gold across the table. Everybody goes, "God, it works! This is wonderful!" They're all picking it up, holding it, tossing it back and forth.

He says, "Does anybody have any questions?"

I raise my hand. And so, "Pat, this is our writer, my earliest investor and the greatest believer in me. You've probably read his novels." He gives me this big introduction.

I said, "Jim, let me ask you one question. Are you telling me that this factory in Nevada has perfected the technology where a bunch of sand goes in this thing, and when you shake it up, a lot of shit pours out one way, and pure gold pours out another way?"

He said, "Pat, that's exactly what we've got."

He showed me a picture of the factory, and I said, "Jim, it looks like an abandoned doghouse." This little bitty thing, and I said, "It doesn't make any sense, Jim. It should be huge if all this sand's going to come in and you're going to shake that shit up and spurt that gold out."

Of course, the factory couldn't do what I asked, and Jim eventually moved to Nevada. He gave up his house on Tuxedo Road, the Jaguar, everything. Even that gold puck he threw across the table disappeared. And Jim disappears out into the desert with his beautiful wife. Human beings are strange, are they not? It's why writers will always have jobs.

Jane Lefco was saying, "Well, I guess rich lady's got to go back to working her fucking Jewish ass off."

And I said, "Yeah, this writer thought he was going to be farting through silk, but it looks like I'll be having to bust my ass writing books." We would laugh about it at the time, but it was not hearty laughter.

When Jim's firm imploded and folded up, all Conroy's money disappeared along with it. I lost all the money that he had invested for me, all the money I had invested in the firm. A great fortune was lost because I trusted him. I said, "Jim, I thought I was going to retire on that." I did, you know. That actually was my thought, that my investment would be fruitful, and that was a smart thing a dumb writer had done. I really don't know how much I lost. There's no telling how much I lost. I never knew how much I had. And that's my fault, not his. You know, I have signed stuff when I could have been giving my penis to science so it could be transplanted onto a chimpanzee. I have no idea what I've signed, ever.

You know, his reputation with the investment counseling firm was superb, but something went very wrong. Here's what is interesting. It's hard to fool the Citadel. You know, the Citadel was not wrong about me. I wanted nothing to do with the military. I let everybody know I wasn't going to take it seriously. But Jim Roe got the Willson Ring. So this is fooling an entire class, and this class turned out more generals than any in Citadel history. My class was impressive. And how high he rose impressed me, even though I got irritated by "I thought he was just a jock; I didn't know he could think." But that may have been why I fell for him: my need for someone in that ranking in our class to accept me.

When Jim is packing up leaving, disgraced, Lenore comes to me in tears in Atlanta and says, "Pat, I want to ask you something very personal and very important for both of us. I've been the one who followed the work of Jim Roe, and I've been the one to do the checking account and pay the bills, doing all the stuff that he did not do, and I think I've earned the right, and I hope you agree with this, to be the one who handles all our money. I've studied it with the accountant, and we've gone over the books. I'd like the opportunity to try to do this for our family."

I said, "Sure, if you want to do it, that would be great. Because I know I'm not going to do it."

I had hired Jim Roe's firm originally because I knew I needed somebody like that, and boy oh boy, I think I have never made a more expensive decision in my lifetime than to let Lenore pick up where Jim Roe left off. That was the crucial and critical moment. Of course an adult man would have said, "I must go down and speak to a banker in San Francisco and set up an account," but I was not an adult man at that point. About this time I was earning *Prince of Tides* money, and I have no idea what happened to it all. She must have felt me pulling away in San Francisco, and she was readying herself for the big break.

But Lenore divorced me; I did not divorce her. I think she thought I was at the end of my run, that she had squeezed all the money I had, and was expecting nothing to come from *Beach Music*. I don't think she expected me to finish that book because she knew I'd been suicidal. I think she thought I was crazy. Both my ex-wives thought I was crazy, and I think they were right. They were not guessing wrongly.

When the IRS came and I learned I'd paid no taxes for two years, I was completely shocked by that, because I had signed all the tax forms. Lenore would tell me, "Sign here, sign here, turn the page. Sign here, sign here, turn the page." Apparently the forms were sent in, but never the checks.

God bless these two women who kept the IRS away from me after that. Jane Lefco and Ann Torrago, who worked for Julian Bach, fought off the IRS for two years. And they had to fight off the California tax people, who they said were the meanest. They were going to put my Fripp house up for auction on the courthouse steps. That would have been nice; I would have enjoyed that. These two women kept arguing, "Why don't you put Lenore's house in San Francisco up for auction? That house is a million-something, and the house on Fripp he bought for $100,000."

The woman says, "We never go for the parasite. We always go for the host."

So one of the pressures of *Beach Music* was trying to stay out of prison for being a tax evader. I borrowed money from the bank, and Double-day paid out more of my advance to keep me afloat. *Beach Music* made money, thank God, and when the two women got me on a conference call to tell me all the back taxes had been paid, they were cheering themselves as much as they were me.

The divorce was rancorous, and on October 26, 1995, my fiftieth birthday, I was in divorce court in San Francisco. Fifty is an age that gets your attention; you're half a century old. I remember being in the bathroom of the courthouse, looking down, and thinking I'm stand-ing on a fifty-year-old foot, peeing through a fifty-year-old dick. It was kind of a shock.

I wasn't allowed to see Susannah alone during that time under court order, had to have Gregory and the shrink as a chaperone because Lenore said I was a crazy man who could not be trusted. And she was divorcing me because I was crazy, although in California, they don't much care if you're crazy.

Conrad Donner, my lawyer in San Francisco, told me I was going to lose custody of Susannah. She had reached some age—like thirteen—where she could then tell the court she did not want to see me at all. And I think that's what happened. I imagine Lenore put her up to that, but I don't know.

Lenore had suggested she needed $25,000 a month to survive at her current level. She was awarded $10,000 a month, which I thought was a lot. There were many years Lenore made more money than I did, and sometimes a lot more money than I did. The first year was a time I didn't have any money coming in, and I still had to pay her the $10,000 a month. I lived on borrowed money for at least three years. But something in me was very happy that day of the divorce. Okay, I can start my life over again at fifty. I get to start this thing over again.

~

When *Beach Music* comes out, it's 1995; I'm in divorce court; I'm having a breakdown; it's not my best year. I owe the IRS; I owe the bank. It just did not look good for the kid. The hero was limping. This took away anything I could have felt about the success of the book. But I'm on tour anyway. It was a long, exhausting tour; I went everywhere. One day I signed at a bookstore in Chapel Hill, and I got to stay with my friend Doug Marlette and his wife, Melinda.

I had met Doug in about 1976 in Charlotte, where he was the cartoonist for the *Charlotte Observer.* After *The Great Santini* came out, Jim Townsend, the founder of *Atlanta* magazine, had in his drunken stupor been hired to run *Charlotte* magazine, and Jim had run across Doug and, "I got to get you two good cats together," and that kind of bullshit that Townsend did. Doug and I were instant friends. He stayed in Charlotte till he got a job with the Atlanta paper. Doug Marlette was one of Bill Kovach's first hires, and when he moved to Atlanta we became best friends.

Here was the thing I loved about Doug: We used to talk every day. And what I'd go through with Doug, and what he'd go through with me is, when we entered these periods of depression, we were very good for each other in getting ourselves out of it. He was funny and could always make me laugh. Every day of my life, I could call up Doug, and by the end of that conversation, I would have laughed twenty-five times. I would know what was happening in every corner of the world. He had a stiletto-like mind and made conversation a kind of wonderland where we would follow each other around, what pissed us off, what was on our minds. When he was killed in a car crash, I wrote in my notebook, "Doug Marlette died today. What am I going to do the rest of my life?"

He published two novels before he died, both very good, both very well received. By then he had gone back to live in Hillsborough, North Carolina, where his family had worked in a mill. He and Melinda used the money he got for a screenplay we wrote together to buy what we have to call a mansion: a beautiful, twelve-acre Southern mansion built in about 1820. The oak trees in their yard were where the British had hung the regulators in North Carolina, and I think the first chief justice had his office in this little cabin in the yard. It was a wonderful, wonderful piece of property, and this is where I had dinner with them when I was on tour for *Beach Music*.

They were going to have a very intimate small dinner for me with their best friends. So they asked me, and I said, yeah, anybody you've got that's not a writer, it would be great to invite them. Now, the two people Doug and Melinda had become closest two were Allan Gurganus and Lee Smith. In the game, you always are told to watch out for North Carolina writers; it's a snotty group. The whole bunch of them are lurking around, and they all are stationed sort of near the Chapel Hill/Duke area, because they teach in the colleges there. I warned Doug from the very beginning that Nan Talese of all people had told me that Allan Gurganus was the most political writer she had ever met. I said, "When the Red Queen says that, pal, I would perk up." But of course, Allan fell in love with Melinda, who was beautiful, and they went around doing things that gay men and beautiful women like to do, and I think they became really good friends. And Lee Smith is known for her saintliness. Among the writers, she is saintly. Anyway, I give my advice. I would not invite either one of them.

So, it's a lovely night, we're barbecuing, I'm exhausted from this trip, and then Lee and Allan come over. Allan had on red Converse All-Stars, and Converse All-Stars were the shoes I wore as a basketball player in college, but I'd never seen red ones. After that evening, I said, "The red Converse All-Stars are mine, Marlette; they belong to me." Okay, that's the only thing we said. The dinner was incredibly sort of unenjoyable, but we all made the best of it. I got through it; I took off.

I get off the tour, I go back to Fripp Island, and Marion is seeing me every day. I am limping to what was known as a life, and Doug and I were talking every day. Meanwhile, Doug is still writing his novel. Every once in a while he'd send me a couple of chapters. After that dinner party, the Gurganus figure in the book, who was unmistakable by the way—I want to be perfectly honest in all this—he was absolutely unmistakable, and he was wearing red Converse All-Star tennis shoes. It was a laugh-out-loud parody if you knew Allan.

One reason I love Doug is he sees the horribleness of political correctness and what it could possibly lead to. He used to go through a hilarious routine where he would say, "I know how the world works now, Pat."

I'd say, "How, Doug?"

He said, "It's like this: woman—good; man—bad; black—good; white—bad; poor—good; rich—bad; gay—good; straight—bad."

He would go through a string of these, and I would be howling. He could do it all day.

In about 2000 or 2001, Doug has a finished manuscript, and he's actually sold it to Harper Collins. They send me a copy for a blurb, they send Allan a copy for a blurb, Lee a copy for a blurb, and then the shit hit the fan. Allan evidently lives down the hill from Lee, and he races up the hill, weeping uncontrollably at this dastardly portrait of himself. She takes him into her arms, and she comforts him. Then she calls Doug and tells Doug that he must know that you don't do that to friends in books. And of course Doug, loyal Doug goes, "Pat Conroy does it all the time."

Lee said, but you know, there's an unwritten code among writers that we will never do this. With Doug's sense of humor, he says, "Oh, really? Didn't I see your ex-husband in the last one? Didn't he have one eye, too, just like your ex-husband?" So Doug is not moved and like me has a temper, and her piety set it off. He called me and asked me what I did when something like this came up, and I said, "Doug, I will tell you my philosophy. It does not have to be yours. But I wouldn't change a word. That's not why I write. I certainly don't write to be edited by other writers or to be censored by other writers. Get ready for the ram. It's not going to be fun, it's not going to be pretty," and it wasn't.

When the book came out, Allan and Lee came for him, calling other writers, talking in the newspapers, complaining about the book. Word went around that the book was hideously homophobic, and some bookstores decided to cancel his book signings. It seemed to me now that liberalism had entered into the territory of censorship and book burning. And when we enter into the realm of censorship, I go off on it. I ended up blasting people with my usual delicacy for which I am well known. I am swinging the long sword with both hands, and it got to be a bloody fight.

A friend of Allan's ran the bookstore at Chapel Hill where Doug was going to have an appearance, and I was going to introduce him. She cancelled his whole appearance at the bookshop because she said the book was homophobic and they did not sell homophobic trash like that. The Center for the Study of Southern Culture got so intimidated by this gay backlash they called off a speech Doug was scheduled to give there. The bookstore in Asheville cancelled. Only afterward did the two owners, who were gay, read the book and say it wasn't homophobic.

When the word censorship was put out there, Allan and Lee realized they'd gone too far. But here's what was interesting to me. I talked to some of the people at PEN, and I told them about what had happened; they were not at all interested in pursuing it. I said, "Let me ask you a question. Why are you interested in smashing any poor Christian mother or father's natural upset over reading cusswords in a book? But you won't go after so-called liberals when they try to shut down a book? Your organization exists to help books fight that. But it's the right you jump on; the Christians you jump on. When the attack comes from the left, why do we hear nothing from you? Why don't we hear a word? It's such intellectual dishonesty I can barely stand it. Allan and Lee are not on your side. They're on the right-wingers' side; they're on the book burners' side; they are on the side of censorship.

At Doug Marlette's funeral I'm giving the usual stuff about Doug's life, his achievements, and all this crap. Then I said, "There is one thing I want to tell you about Doug Marlette that he and I disagreed on completely. He loved whenever he spotted the Santini in me. He loved when the Great Santini to my horror would roar to the surface. He loved that fighting spirit of my father that my father unfortunately passed on to me. He always encouraged more than anybody that hideous part of me. So let me bring to this eulogy some of that fighting spirit today in memory of Doug Marlette," and a cry went up from that crowd. And I said, "Here's what I really want: bring me the head of Allan Gurganus!"

Something was taken out of me in the writing of *Beach Music,* something I didn't think I'd ever get back. I didn't think I could ever write again after going through that book. It was the sheer exhaustion of seeing that one through, the pressure on me of no money, enormous debts, and the IRS all over me. I had to make that book sell if I could, because my house was going up for auction. So it was a long, long book tour where I ran my mouth trying to charm audiences.

I went to Dayton, Ohio, where I've never been in my life. So I'm sitting in Dayton, and there's a nice crowd. Anyway, I look up, and in the stacks I see my old shooting guard from the Citadel, John DeBrosse.

I look up and said, "Hey, DeBrosse, you ever been in a bookstore before?"

He looks at me and goes, "Yeah, Conroy, once. I was lost." He comes up to me afterward and says, "Conroy, would you come home with me after this is over? My family doesn't believe I know you. They don't believe I've ever met you."

I said, "I've never seen you in my life. This is the first time."

He said, "You were always a pain in the ass. Just come by, meet my wife and kids."

So, after the thing was over, we're driving to DeBrosse's house, and we start talking. It's easy, and I had not seen him in thirty years. On that book tour, my teammates started coming out of the woodwork. Jimmy Halpin in Philadelphia, and Dave Bornhorst. For some reason they just started materializing; Dan Mohr in Greensboro.

We were driving to Johnny's house, and we're talking about that last horrible basketball season. It was that night that I realized these people had been thinking as hard about that season as I had, and it was as painful to them as it was for me. I didn't think a book about something like that had ever been written, and that was the night I decided to write it. Then Nan Talese: "You want to write about a losing season? Basketball? Who cares?" But the head of our company from Germany, who was a jock, loved reading about basketball games in *Santini* and *The Lords of Discipline,* and he wanted me to do a sports book. So Nan caught the drift.

I got to visit all the guys in their homes and sit and talk. Some of the other players had great recall, had details I had forgotten. They could remember things about me that I could not remember, or I had not noticed at that time. I didn't know these guys would like me. I had no insight into that at all, but usually mine were the only books they had in their house.

I did not realize that each of these guys had been hurt and damaged by the stupid season as much as I had. Our coach really was an Ahab-like figure. He was unrelenting, a fierce man to encounter at a very fierce school. The Citadel is enough of a test without going through one more great one, and Mel Thompson was a great test for all of us. What he could do is break your spirit in ways it was hard to recover from. And what was incredible to me is all these guys had basically recovered their spirits, even though they said they'd lost it after Mel. But they found it back; they found ways back. It turned out to be a great healing for all of us who were damaged terribly in that year. We all felt this damage, and it had nearly driven us crazy.

When I got them together for our first reunion, I heard one of them say toward the end of the night, "Why in the world are we agreeing to do this? What is he going to do to us?"

Another one of the guys said, "I know what he's going to do to us. Look what he did to our fucking college."

And I've always loved this: One guy said, "Our college? Look what he did to his own father. And he's going to do the same fucking thing to us."

When I went around interviewing my teammates, I always asked, "Do you remember my father?" And they'd only met him once or twice.

He didn't come to many games, and this was over a four-year period. In fact, I think he came to only one game. But I think they saw him for a practice when I was a sophomore, something like that. Anyway, they all had the same answer. Every one of them had the same answer: "What a fucking asshole." It was a great corroboration of how Dad acted. Dad did not try to make friends with anybody. He did not consider that his job.

Al Kroboth was a teammate who had been a prisoner of war after he was shot down in Vietnam. I went up to interview him in his home, and here I am, a draft dodger interviewing a prisoner of war. So Al starts telling me his story, and I thought there was going to be a lot of tension because of what he did during the war versus what I did during the war. But Al was such a great guy, it did not come up like that ever. You know, "You did what you did, Conroy; I did what I did. Let's leave it at that."

My shock was learning that his first CO in the Marine Corps when he was in pilot training in Pensacola was Don Conroy.

"Al, you are kidding me?"

"No, I'm not, Pat."

I said, "Why didn't Dad ever tell me that? Did he know about you?"

He said, "Yes, he did. I can tell you how. When you first go into Pensacola—all the Marine and Navy pilots—you go in, and your father speaks to you. And he was a big, mean-looking, heavyset Marine."

I said, "You got him, pal."

"Mean as hell."

"Yeah, that's him."

And he said, "I thought it was him. Well anyway, Colonel Conroy makes us all stand up, say our name and where we went to college."

So Al stands up and said, "Al Kroboth. I graduated from the Citadel."

After the thing was over, Dad leans to the microphone and says, "Lieutenant Kroboth, could you report to me?"

So, Kroboth goes up to Dad and salutes. Dad salutes him back. And he said, "Kroboth, when you went to the Citadel, did you know a guy named Pat Conroy?"

Al said, "Colonel, Pat and I were on the same basketball team together. He was the captain of my team."

Dad looks at him and says, "That'll be all, Kroboth."

We call Dad from Al's house, and I repeat the story that Al told me. I said, "Dad, why didn't you and Mom invite Al to dinner, take him out to the Officers' Club? Why didn't you do anything?"

My father says, "Kroboth, are you there?"

Al gets on the phone, "Yes, Colonel, I'm here."

Dad said, "Hey, Kroboth, you're a Marine. What did you want me to do—marry you?"

Al said, "I understand completely, sir."

So that's what I grew up with. They invented the military for guys like my dad.

This book was a good project for me to do after the stress of writing *Beach Music.* There was something very healing about going around and visiting all my teammates I had not seen in years. Sharing our stories, our memories—that was good for all of us. And we learned that we all had the same nightmare experience with that basketball season, but we recovered from the damage it did to us and even took something good from it into the rest of our lives. It was great for me getting back with all these guys. I've gotten to where I love my connections with the past, because military brats don't have as many as most people do. The past has become very important to me, because I didn't think I had one.

~

After I was divorced from Lenore, a young girl came up to me in Beaufort to ask me out to dinner. She was beautiful. I said, "How old are you?"

She says, "I'm thirty."

I said, "I'm ninety-five. I can't go out with you."

She says, "Why not?"

I said, "I'm trying to think of how I walk into a room holding your hand, 'I'd like you to meet Tiffany,' and my three daughters do not fall to their knees laughing their asses off at their old fart father."

I've always wanted to be with women my own age. Once Barbara and I got divorced, I wouldn't date a woman who did not have any children because I didn't think it was fair to bring her into a family where there were already three children. And I thought, you know, let them get married to somebody who doesn't have complications like that.

I met Sandra in 1995 when I was up at the Surrey Hotel doing the rewrites for Nan of *Beach Music*. Nan announces to me that I will be going to accept an award at the Hoover Library in Birmingham, Alabama, and I said I'm not going; I don't want to go; you can't make me go. She said, "We've already accepted; you're going; it's a lifetime achievement award."

On the second night in Birmingham, there is a party with writers who seemed happier than most writers, so I'm enjoying myself. I start talking with Bill Cobb, a writer and teacher at Montevallo, and he said, "I'd like you to meet my student Sandra." Sandra turns around, he says, "Sandra, this is Pat Conroy."

Her mouth is full of food, she's eating, and she says something like "Great God Almighty," in the Southern vernacular that comes from growing up on a farm in lower Alabama.

Sandra's cute as hell, and we had a great talk. Bill says, "She's got a book coming out. Why don't you blurb it?"

I said, "You're asking the right guy. I'm a blurb slut."

The next day, when I ask someone about Sandra, I get, "Oh, she's a Methodist minister's wife, very happily married for twenty-five years." Once again, Conroy hones in on the one who is most impossible. But when I called her with the blurb, she told me she was separated from her husband and in the process of divorce. The Methodist minister did not want her to write, and this had been an ambition her whole life. He would tell her, "You need to take care of your family and forget about your personal hobbies." Being a '50s woman, and that being her husband's decree, she went along with it. But by the time we met, she was separated and had this teaching job at Gadsden State, on tenure track and with health care.

We started dating and got fairly serious right away; I liked her a ton, and she seemed to like me. But Gadsden—that place was bleak, and of course it was only twenty miles away from Piedmont, where my mother's family grew up. Then my father was dying, so I could not travel to Gadsden that often to see her. I think it took about two years before we decided to get together. I told her, "I have to take care of my dad while he's dying, but I'd like to see you, so I want you to do something bold and brave. You will not be sorry. One thing I promise you is a room with a view for you to write your books." She said she'd think about it, so she called about a week later and said, "I'll be getting in on Sunday."

She helped me all the way through Dad's dying and was a good person with good character even in the middle of my own family drama. When I told her, "I just don't think I'm capable of making a woman feel loved," she said that was all right; she didn't think she was capable of making a man feel liked. We both laughed our ass off. When we were talking about getting married, she was worried about things like being too old for me.

I said, "What are you talking about? You're my age."

"But I thought you'd want to marry someone much younger."

I said, "Can we do each other this one favor? Can we let ourselves grow old without hating each other and ourselves for it? Can we not obsess about the lost blossom of youth?"

She says, "I never had a blossom of youth to lose."

I said, "Good. You're not obsessed about muscles or what used to be lean and strong that now packs only whale blubber to carry me along on my final voyage. I've got to marry somebody who won't mind growing old; who will let us grow old together. That's what it seems to me we both need, Sandra. Gosh, you're not going to look like you did when you were a teenager? I won't even show you pictures of me as a teenager. You won't even recognize me. I don't recognize myself." I find that rare, people letting each other grow old.

And she has betrayed me only once. There's a book on Southern writers that my fat ass is in, and in this book, there is a lascivious picture of another writer and his wife in bed. So when Sandra and I first started dating, she saw this, and I said, "If you ever ask me to get in a bed to take a picture with you, I want you to listen to the divorce bells swinging in the wind." Okay, when her book *The Same Sweet Girls* was out, some magazine was doing an interview. So I come into the room, innocent as I could be, and oh, God. Sandra says, "Pat, they want to take a picture in the bedroom," and I said, "Are those bells I hear? Are those divorce bells I hear?" So she said, "I knew you'd react like this, but they told me they have to have it." I said, "It's going to be like being in bed with a corpse, only the corpse is going to be me." But I did it for love.

~

After I got married, when Doug Marlette came to visit me on Fripp, he fell to his knees laughing. I'm a guy, you know, and my house wasn't decorated, it looked like shit, and after Sandra worked her magic, Doug thought it was hysterical when he saw what she had done. With Sandra, order and civilization had come into my life.

Then an inspector told me my chimney was so fucked up he couldn't see how my house didn't burn down every time I lit a fire. He said, "I think the only reason it didn't burn down was the roof was not properly put on, and it was so wet it couldn't catch fire. But every guest who ever came through your door was in imminent danger of death." And I have a thing about hospitality. When I'm not on the road, I like to be hospitable. So he was talking about my kids, my brothers, my father. I mean, he was talking about a lot of different people who had come through.

A kid I had taught in high school, Mike Sargent, was a master builder who redid our house. He was such a pain in the ass in psychology, I used to have to quiet him and Joe Simkins down before I could start the class. "Uh, excuse me, would my two dimwits shut up so I can get on with this class? You don't have to listen to me. Look out the window, do whatever you want, but I've got to start the class." But he was really a sweetheart and had a father like mine. Then his father was killed in Vietnam. He told me later, he says, "Mr. Conroy, my father beat me badly. When I read your book, I thought holy God." And he said, "I hated my father."

Mike did a masterful job on our house. He told me, "Mr. Conroy, I'm doing it with the best woods. Galvanized nails. The best of everything. And everything will be inspected. Everything will be perfect." And it was. Mike was just a master. Then he committed suicide.

I talked to him the night he did it, and it's two or three in the morning. First it's his son, "Dad's going to commit suicide." Mike's wife had just left him. So I get Mike on the phone, and I said, "Mike, listen to me, you little cocksucker. Why didn't you pay more attention in my Goddamn psychology class? You didn't listen to a word I said, and now it could help you." He always called me Mr. Conroy. I said, "Would you quit calling me Mr. Conroy?"

"Well, Mr. Conroy, I—"

I said, "I'm going to come over and stay with you tonight because your son says you're suicidal."

He said, "I was. Look, I took some pills. I shouldn't have done it. But I'm over it. I'm okay."

We talked for an hour. I said, "Look, I'll come in. I'll sleep with you tonight."

He's one of these, you know, "Oh, you want to sleep with me?"

I said, "Look, I know it's your first time. I'll be gentle and you'll barely notice it. You may even like it as much as I do."

So I'm getting Mike to laugh. I said, "Mike, I'll come over right now. I'll be with you, I'll hold your hand, I'll stay up with you drinking coffee. Anything that will get you to daylight, so we can get you some help."

"Mr. Conroy, Mr. Conroy, let me give you back to my son."

Mike's son was staying at the house with his father, so I felt better about that. I asked him, "Can you handle this?"

He says, "Pat, I think I can. I really do. I think you've calmed Dad down."

But when he hangs up from me, he goes in the bathroom and Mike is pouring something down his throat. So he calls 911; they take him by ambulance. And of course, this I don't hear until the next day. They take him by ambulance to the hospital and put him on suicide watch. But they let him go to the bathroom, and since he was a builder, he knew how to find a beam in the ceiling. So he strung up a towel and hung himself.

Apparently he was devastated when his wife left him. He told me, he said, "I've never had another girlfriend in my life. I wouldn't even know how to ask a girl out. I don't know what to do." But his suicide had deep, deep roots, going back to his father. I understand this, because through all the other self-inflicted trauma of my life, my own suicide would have had deep, deep roots going back to my father. I am lucky that somehow I managed to make it to daylight.

〜

A few years ago, Sandra and I moved back to Beaufort because the drive to and from Fripp was getting long. The distance is not bad if you go infrequently, but if you go every day it's a long way. With traffic it got to be about a half hour each way. Also, Sandra wanted a house that did not have Lenore's taint on it, and the Fripp house was haunted for me by that nightmare scene with Lenore.

When we were out on a friend's boat one day, we went past a house on the river that was for sale. I couldn't see that much of it through the oak trees, but I loved the location on Battery Creek, which is an off-shoot of the Beaufort River. Sandra jumped on it the next day and ended up putting money down almost immediately because she just went crazy over this house. We both love it. Then Sandra wanted to sell the house on Fripp, but I said, "Sandra, I owe this house something. I think it saved my life." My children have loved it; my grandchildren have loved it. So we have people stay there. I love having people come and stay there. It's a nice thing to be able to offer.

Sandra has been a very stabilizing force in my life and is the only woman I have ever been attracted to in my whole life who came without complete psychodrama. She did not need to be rescued. Two years ago, there was a time she had started to feel bad. This is what led to the discovery of her cancer, but she thought she was having heart attacks. Sandra is so independent she's not going to let me know something like this. It might worry me somewhat that my wife is dying. I knew she didn't feel well, but nothing big, and "Do you need me to get you anything?" "No, no, no, no." Sandra is that type of sufferer, but so am I, so there's not much I can say about that.

So loud-mouth Bernie comes over one night. He brings his cigars, and we are up on the top balcony. Sandra's on the bottom one. She often goes there to read and write until she comes up to bed at about eleven o'clock. So Bernie and I were arguing about something. I am arguing brilliantly and wittily, and Bernie is sounding like the dumbass he always is, and I am defeating him soundly in whatever literary argument we are having, and Bernie is gesticulating wildly and waving. He is drinking my liquor, and then he brings it over and says, "Pat, it's a shame you can't have it." He puts it under my nose, and "Doesn't that smell great? My God, I wish you could have some. It goes down your throat, and you feel it instantly. It goes into your stomach, and you get that slight burning feeling. It's the joy of drinking. It relaxes you, and you'll never be relaxed again, and I will. And by the way, you're running out of liquor; you need to get me another bottle."

So it's that typical Bernie scene. Bernie is screaming; Bernie drinks; he gets louder and more obnoxious. We're having a ball. Bernie and I love talking and arguing with each other. We've been doing it since we were kids. The other day, Mina, the Okinawan drill sergeant who tries to get me in shape, said, "Mr. Pat, did no one ever tell you to shut up? You talk more than anybody I know. In your whole life did you ever shut up?" I said, you know, "I've been around Bernie a lot." Then she said, "That means you never learned how to shut up. That explains everything to me that Mr. Bernie became your friend when you were only fifteen years old. Both of you just talk, and neither stop talking since you two met."

Eventually Bernie: "Oh my God, Martha. I forgot about Martha. Holy shit, I was supposed to meet her for dinner at six. It's nine. Tell her I passed out, Pat. Call her and tell her I passed out. Tell her it wasn't liquor; that I wasn't drinking." So we go downstairs. I have to drive him home because Martha dropped him off.

But as we go down, I went in to say, "Sandra, I'll be right back. I'm going to go drive Bernie home." Okay, I go in, and Sandra, who is a quiet girl anyway—let me emphasize her quietude and placidity and noiselessness. That's how she lives; her life is a noiseless life. So I go in to tell her that I was taking Bernie home, I look in, and she is not there. I knew she'd been sick. I'm thinking, Where is she? So I go check the bathrooms. She's not there. I then go check the TV room and the computer room, the library. I go check my writing room.

I said, "Bernie, Sandra's not here."

He says, "She's got to be here. Where the fuck else would she be?"

So we started looking around, and Bernie gets nervous because we know she's so strict in her habits. Finally we start going through the neighborhood yelling for her. We go next door and ask the neighbors if they'd seen her. "No." We're yelling, and then I'm thinking, "Oh my God. She committed suicide. Finally a woman got so sick of living with me she dragged herself to the end of the dock and simply slipped off into Battery Creek and is being swept out to sea." Bernie—with his stupid and outmoded literary theories—and finally, I—have done it to a woman. This was my destiny, and it has caught up to me, and my wife has killed herself because I was such a monster to live with.

I'm completely horrified, panic-stricken. We're going all through the house, the neighborhood; we're calling people.

Then Bernie says, "Pat, I think we should call 911."

This absolutely terrified me. I said, "Bernie, you're not giving up are you?"

He says, "She ain't fucking here. What are we supposed to do? Let's call 911."

I said, "You call. I can't call 911."

So he calls 911, and then Bernie hands me the phone. Of course, what I expect, because I have an imagination: "Mr. Conroy, your wife's lifeless body floated by the station, and it has been eaten by crabs and attacked by sharks several times. There was nothing left of her face." But what he said was, "Mr. Conroy, we have very good news for you. Your wife is in Beaufort Memorial Hospital."

What?

I said, "How do you know that?"

He said, "Well, the ambulance came by your house."

"The ambulance came by my house? Why didn't they turn on their signal?"

"The siren was on. It was going in your driveway, red lights and everything. And they looked for you. She said you were upstairs, and a guy went and looked in. They didn't see you."

Of course, Bernie and I were out on the balcony, the door was closed. So I said, "We didn't hear a thing," but Bernie and I are both deaf. We found out later: Sandra was throwing up, feeling terrible, and thinking she was having a heart attack. She yelled up for me and Bernie, but her voice was so weak, and we were so deaf and arguing, we couldn't hear her, but she could hear us arguing. So she had finally given up and called 911 instead. And they were shocked that there were two adult males who could not have assisted her at the time.

Anyway, I said, "Thank God, this is great news." I said, "Bernie, I've got to go down to the hospital."

He says, "You've got to take me home first."

What added ridiculousness to an already silly situation is I had just bought a new car that day. Well, I had never driven it. It had all this new shit. And it's dark. So I turn the car on, and I was glad to see lights come on. I didn't have any idea why the lights came on, but they did. So I said, "That works." I put it in reverse, and Bernie's sitting there, "God-damn, hurry up." Then it starts raining. I mean, really raining hard.

Bernie says, "Turn on the windshield wipers."

I said, "I don't know how to."

He says, "What do you mean you don't know how to? It's your car!"

"I just got it today, Bernie, so shut up."

"You didn't even learn how to turn your windshield wipers on?"

So I'm trying this, I'm doing that to find the wipers. Lights are flicking on all over the car. The radio's coming on. Finally I have to roll down the window. I don't know how to roll down the window. I'm locking the door; the mirror's moving all over. Finally I flipped this switch, and the window rolls down. So I stick my head out the window in this rain you would not believe. It was raining like a bastard, and I stick my head out, I can barely see, my head is wet, and I finally drive the whole way with my head out the window, and I'm soaked.

Bernie says, "I'm going to run in and tell Martha that I'm going to go back to the hospital with you."

I said, "I'll come in with you."

He said, "No, don't come in, your head's too wet. You'll get the house wet."

So I waited out there, and Bernie comes back. "Okay, I cleared it with Martha. We're going to go over together because I have a better bedside manner than you, and Sandra is much more sexually attracted to me than to you, and I will bring her peace of mind."

I said, "Bernie, just get in the car and shut up."

We drive to the hospital with my head out of the window; it's raining like a son of a bitch. We drive into the parking lot; it's mobbed, of course. Bernie said, "Just let me out at the front, and you go find a parking place because I don't want to get wet, and it doesn't matter if you get wet or not."

So I let Bernie out. He goes in. I go find a parking place. I walk back into the rain. Now I'm soaked all over. I walk in and go up to the deputy and say, "My wife, Sandra, has come to the ICU, and I'd like to visit her."

He said, "I'm sorry, sir, her husband has already gone in to see her."

I said, "Do you mean that fat idiot with a beard?"

And he says, "Yes, sir, he just came in. He said his friend was parking the car and to tell you to sit down in the visitor's center while he comforts his wife."

So I said, "Sir, can you go in and throw him out? There's been a mistake here."

He says, "Well, I've got it written down, and you can look in there."

There's my name, Pat Conroy, signed in. So I waited. Bernie stayed with Sandra for an hour before he came out and says, "There's no reason to go in, Pat. She's exhausted. The doctor says she's talked too much tonight so you can come back tomorrow."

I said, "Fuck you, Bernie."

I ended up going back there, and Bernie had totally exhausted her. But what she thought was a heart attack eventually led to them finding out that she had some kind of cancer, which turned out to be completely treatable, thank God.

When I first met Sandra, I knew she was the right one, and she was. I told myself I needed to marry a really nice girl, and I found her in Sandra. She has brought a measure of calmness that has enabled me to continue writing even as I've become this bent, arthritic, crab-like figure who wanders the second story of my house railing at the tides.

Epilogue

Beaufort, South Carolina

Pat was a very good patient. He put himself down more than he should have, but he was able to look into himself. He was as honest with me as he could be. He never responded angrily, although there's no way to be in therapy and be comfortable. Like most of us, he is his own worst enemy, but he's got a lot of strength. At some point he realized he had to do something about his life, and he did it.

MARION O'NEILL, Ph.D., ABPP, clinical psychologist

I needed to reconnect to something I had lost. Somewhere I had lost touch with the kind of man I had the potential of being. I needed to effect a reconciliation with that unborn man and try to coax him gently toward his maturity.

PAT CONROY, *The Prince of Tides*

So I am in Beaufort, South Carolina, living the slow life, and although I look like a sea cucumber that sometimes washes up on the beach—motionless, shapeless—I am perfectly happy. I know where I want to be; I know where I don't want to be; I know whose company I want to be in. If I'm reading a book that I'm loving, I do not even need to go out of the house except to exercise my fat, cholesterol-laden body. I do not want it said that I cast a shadow over Southern literature not because of my talent but because of my hulk.

For several weeks in the summer the invasion of the children and the grandchildren comes flying in like a plague of locusts. They take turns staying at the house on Fripp. And I like it, being a grandfather, although I've come to believe that summers are highly overrated events.

The summer becomes a time when Dad does not have a job, and we have to make up for all the lost time we have missed out on during the year, and there's nothing I can do about it. There's a conspiracy at work night and day to keep me from writing. My children make sure I have quality time with each of their children, in which the quality time consists of me being with a grandchild as my children stare at me to make sure I am giving enough quality from myself to their precious children, so I am under the gun. I finally have to say, "Girls, I can't say, 'Oh, isn't that cute?' one more time. And by the way, I don't need a complete day-by-day, hour-by-hour, minute-by-minute description of my grandchildren, okay?"

But I now am sorry that I did not quit writing while the kids were growing up so I could just stare at them in amazement twenty-four hours a day and appreciate them in ways I did not do because I was young and stupid and didn't know what I was doing. If we did not have our work to drive us crazy, we could live through our children, be proud of our kids, proud of the way we raised them. Unfortunately, we have these other hungers which drive us nuts. But I will always think there is something missing from anyone who does not raise children. I think it puts you into the great flow of man and mankind to be part of that. It ratifies your part in the planetary motion. And there is something about the raising of a child: it does change you. It is a different way of looking at the world, not through me but trying to look at the world to make it safe for them. If we all did that, it would humanize the whole world.

Meanwhile, Father's Day comes and goes, and unlike Mother's Day, which is a fucking feast day, with calls, adoration, gifts, and worship, the girls will say Father's Day is a manufactured Hallmark greeting card event. I do not hear the *beep-beep-beep* as a forklift backs up moving in with my gifts. I have a wife who only gives me gifts that she later gives to other people, so they simply come through my life for a few days, and then Sandra rewraps them and gives them to someone else she loves more. I have not been allowed to keep one gift that Sandra has ever given me, and this includes dogs.

But I am grateful that Sandra pretends to love me and my children do not throw up when they see me. I have not been flushed down the toilet like a used Kleenex or thrown out the window like a diaper on the highway. I'm sort of a house fixture, like an outdoor lamp. My grand-children look at me like Ahab looked at Moby Dick, waiting to carve up my blubber and sell the ambergris on the black market. As for me, I seethe with happiness.

Summer is the typical sort of Conroy-esque madness, the carnival season when there's no reason to have a carnival. It's like we have a pep rally for everything the kids do. I'll go along with it as much as I can. I see karaoke shows featuring my grandchildren, which is a nightmare, but I do it. I never knew my life would dip quite this low, but there I am, watching this unbelievable American ritual. Two of my grand-children got into a fight because one of them listed a song she was going to sing and the other one got on stage and sang it first. Everybody was saying, "Oh, Katie, you know Stella wanted to do that," and seven year-old Katie says, "I really don't care to discuss it." Stella says, "I'm going to hate her for the rest of my life," which I find a very Conroy-like in-stinct. But then it's over. I've gone to karaoke. I've done my duty as a grandparent. I'm not letting my girls down.

When they all leave at the end of the summer, what Sandra and I do is very inappropriate and has caused hatred all throughout the fam-ily. As soon as the last ones leave, she and I perform a ritual victory dance of joy and relief. We're dancing together in the hall, throwing up our arms, thanking God that we survived this. Sandra looks like a Rockette, and for a moment in my old, crippled life, I am twirling in the air and leaping like a Russian. That being done, I can return to my life, when I used to be a writer. I will be left to my own devices, to soli-tude, to loneliness, to an oyster-like existence for the rest of my days, buried in mudflats, praying for the tide to come in and give me a little sustenance.

～

As I relive the hideous, unspeakable days of my life, they roll out in front of me, one suppuration after another wound, after another open sore. I keep waiting for the smiley face somewhere at the end of the line, knowing it will never come. It will end as a skull and bones sitting at a crossroads with my name beneath it. So I lie in bed, fat, incontinent, flatulent, impotent. I get out of bed arthritic, diabetic, with liver failure minutes away. Immediately I am beaten down and defeated, wallowing in my own excrement, retiring back into my fatness and addictions.

But in my view from the bottom of the toilet, I could not be more content with the way my career has gone. I was happy I was making a living as a writer, and surprised, very surprised, especially because I came of age when I found myself the most hated human being, the most loathed and despised and castaway being in human society: a white Southern male. A lost albino bison on the American plain. I feel lucky enough just to have been published. I am still that kid from the bases whose mother is taking out library books by the ton. I'm still the kid from a military college looking for a role model I can develop my writing career with. I'm always going to be that guy.

And I'm always going to wish I were better. That I was more talented and smarter. But there's nothing I can do about it. I was born to a dope, and I was raised in a dope-like way so I turned into a dope, and that's it. There's nothing I can do about it except do the best I can once I realized that dope-dom was my fate.

I wish I'd been more prolific. I wish I'd been less emotional. I wish I'd been more intellectual in the way I attacked work. But I was who I was, and what you write is the person you are. That is your thumbprint, your fingerprint, your soul-print.

Writers like me have chosen a life of agony. Whatever it is we get out of ourselves, whatever poisons spill out of us, you'll see the results when they're published. You've always dreamed of it, desired it, worked for it; when you get it you will loathe it and scream in agony. You'll think of George Eliot and Flaubert and Shakespeare, and you'll realize, "My God, I have contaminated the literary tradition with my little fart into the language. I've done damage to the language, to the concept of the novelist, to the human spirit." Because I have no talent; I had nothing to say; it was simply a matter of ego. I had some obsession to get my name somewhere besides on my gravestone, and there it is: *The Great Santini, The Lords of Discipline.* I have humiliated myself before the world. They are not even booing or hissing. They are simply laughing in helpless mirth at what I have presented and what I have created.

Fiction is the most agonizing because fiction is us. Nonfiction is the other. Fiction is an absolute reflection of what we have going on inside of us, or what we do not have. So I've never understood why the critics will give a break to the nonfiction writers and seem to love to humiliate the fiction writers.

My fans are the best in the world, but I've been uncomfortable with fame, really uncomfortable. It's a killing thing, fame; it corrupts everything. It doesn't seem like the way to live. I want to be in a natural environment where I'm not the center of attention. I don't want to be the entertainment for the evening. I like going to a dinner or a party where I'm not the focus. It doesn't seem like a way to think about yourself. I'm a celebrity, and you're a fucking nothing?

I can do the talking when it's necessary. Sometimes people come to hear me fucking talk. But I like to sit back, relax, and listen to someone else. I like not to be noticed. Somebody once asked Cliff Graubert why I do not seem to treasure fame, and Cliff said, "He did not want it to change anything about himself." Cliff is one of only two dumb Jews America has ever produced—the other is Bernie Schein—but Cliff got that right.

Nobody knows why what they've written starts selling, nobody. And nobody can tell you. You can sit down and say you're going to write a best seller; that doesn't mean you will. It's something uncontrollable, something invisible, and it's sort of the whims of time. Then fame goes by faster than you think. Suddenly it's here, and just as suddenly, it's past. You're wondering, "What was that all about? What just happened? What comet against the sky was that? What meteorite burned out in my system I was barely aware of?"

Writers suddenly well up and blossom, and yet they and you don't know the blossoming is going to be brief. We don't know when it's going to end, but it will always end. We do not know when we will become yesterday's porridge, but we should know that it will eventually happen. We don't know who's coming behind us, but we can be sure we've got better writers coming behind us who were just sperm cells when we were first starting out.

I tell people it's not that hard to write a novel. It's hard to have a literary career, to be long-winded enough to complete a career, to have the arc of a career. That's very difficult, and it doesn't happen I don't think that often. My theory is that lightning strikes several times and then the weather clears.

But at least I have finally reached the point in my life when I am unradioactive enough to be the grand marshal of the Beaufort waterfront parade. I will have to look kingly, and I will not feel kingly. But I will do it. I will do my thing and be the nicest person on earth. I'll be honored; I'll be sunburned; I'll get melanoma; I will die. Conroy asks for nothing, and he gets nothing in return. He simply places his head on the guillotine block and listens as it inches its way up to its highest position, waiting for it to drop.

Over the many years of dragging that oyster dredger across the sand flats of my soul, digging and grinding, hoping for some of the fruits of the sea to float to the surface, I have netted these insights. It would have all been different if I'd had a bigger dick. Not to mention, it would have been much better if I had done things differently, but I did not. So you screw up, you make mistakes, you live out a life, and then your life is flying by. It's just flying by you. The great surprise of every human life is it goes so quickly. You don't get much time.

If you're reading this, then that means Conroy sent ya. You don't look at the world from an eagle's point of view. You look at it from a scorpion's point of view, down there low in the earth, your back hunched, your spine ready. But that's good. That's good because it's really hard to make it through a life.

Postscript

Why do they not teach you that time is a fingersnap and an
eyeblink, and that you should not allow a moment to pass you by
without taking joyous, ecstatic note of it, not wasting a single
moment of its swift, breakneck circuit?

PAT CONROY, *My Losing Season*

*In the spring of 2015, nine months after our official interviews ended, Pat
Conroy's estranged daughter Susannah sent him an unexpected e-mail, beginning a process of reconciliation. Given this major development in Pat's
life, I recorded a few more interviews that focus on this situation.*

We heard that Susannah had changed jobs and moved out of Lenore's
house, but nobody knew where. When I was in Atlanta, my daughter
Megan called to say she'd found an address for Susannah on the Inter-
net, so before I left on Sunday, I went by this little apartment. It was
amazing, where it was, on Briarcliff Road, in the dead center of where
my family has been in Atlanta since the 1930s. It's within throwing distance of Stanny's house, where I was brought back when I was born—
two blocks from where I used to catch the bus to go to kindergarten.
Bernie and Martha lived on the same street. Lenore and her lovely first
husband, Alan, lived just blocks away. It was like she had entered the
territory of her birth and all our lives in Atlanta.

I left a letter at her apartment, not even knowing if it really *was* her
apartment. The note was my usual pathetic, whining self: "I just want
to see you, check on you, love to get back in touch." I gave her all my
information, although my e-mail address has been the same since I last
saw her. I never changed it in all those years. In case she wanted to reach
me, I wanted her to be able to find me.

When I left her this letter, I was expecting nothing, I have to tell you.
I've tried so many things—calling up where she works, leaving a voice

mail, going by Lenore's house, knocking on the door, ringing the door-bell, looking in the window, leaving letters on the windshield of her car. It has never worked. It's been such a black hole in my life. Then I get this e-mail from her: "Wanna have lunch?" I was completely stunned by it. I'm trying to put on my Citadel game face and retain my manly composure, but I burst into tears.

I had been needing to hear from her even more than I knew, and I didn't realize until I burst into tears how I had repressed that with my military brat reflex. When you leave someone in the military, you never see them again. Whatever friend you had is no longer a part of your life. Whatever friends you made—you'll never be able to recapture that rela-tionship. All you can do is get used to it, and that's what I tried to do with Susannah.

I found I was too emotional to write her back the first day. I just sat at the computer, wishing I knew how to type. I wrote her the next day and tried to be upbeat and charming and amusing. Sandra and Bernie and everybody tell me: Don't push any of her buttons. Of course with me, by nature I was born to push buttons. I've pushed buttons I didn't even know I was pushing with thousands of people in my past. So I've tried to include Lenore and Gregory and Emily in my e-mails, and pre-tend like Lenore is the greatest person ever in my life.

Then this book will come out, and Susannah will never speak to me as long as I live. But, our first allegiance always is to the art. Whatever art we bring to the table is sacrosanct. And I mean that. If Susannah doesn't like the book—too bad—because I don't think I've lied in it much.

Still I hope it's the beginning of something positive. There is at least communication, which we have not had in fifteen years, and I'm re-lieved at how well she writes, how well she thinks. I'm as pleased as Conroy gets. The part of me that is the darkest part—I keep beating that back into me as it tries to surface, and I'm going to let this flow freely and hope for the best.

In October 2015 Susannah was there with her sisters Jessica, Melissa, and Megan in Beaufort, South Carolina, for the "Conroy at 70" celebration. Masterminded by Jonathan Haupt of the University of South Carolina Press, this festival spanned four days and featured an extraordinary group

*of individuals from all walks of Pat Conroy's life. Editors Jonathan Galassi
and Nan Talese came from New York, along with Marly Rusoff, who took
over as the author's agent after the retirement of Julian Bach. Michael
O'Keefe, an actor in* The Great Santini, *was one of the panelists, as was
David Keith, who appeared in both* The Great Santini *and* The Lords of
Discipline. *Other attendees included Sallie Ann Robinson and her cousin
Jackie and two of the black "kids" Pat taught on Daufuskie Island; also a
former student of Pat's from Beaufort High School, Valerie Sayers, now a
writer and professor at Notre Dame. Brothers Mike, Tim, and Jim Conroy
were in attendance, as well as their sister Kathy Harvey, along with a half
dozen of Pat's grandchildren, and an assortment of nieces, nephews, and
in-laws. The irrepressible Bernie Schein was irrepressible as usual. Cliff and
Cynthia Graubert were there from Atlanta, as was Terry Leite, to whom the
adolescent Pat wrote a series of letters full of yearning and "sperm-filled
emotions." Also present were a dozen of the authors recently published by
Pat Conroy's new fiction imprint Story River Books of the University of
South Carolina Press.*

*Billy Keyserling, the mayor of Beaufort and the son of the doctor who
delivered two of Pat's daughters, gave an introduction that was so long Pat
interrupted him to report that he had turned seventy-one. Undeterred, Billy
went on to read a letter sent by Barbra Streisand, reminiscing about her
collaboration with Pat on* The Prince of Tides *movie. She wrote to him:
"First I fell in love with your books, and then I fell in love with you."*

*In a voice she must have inherited from her father, James Dickey, Bron-
wen Dickey read two of her dad's poems, one of which, "For the Last Wolverine," is among Pat's favorites. After Bronwen's reading, Pat told her: "When
I was in your daddy's class and he read 'The Last Wolverine,' what changed
my life was the line: 'Dear God of the wildness of poetry.' That is when I
thought: That's what writing should be directed at. That is the god you
should speak to always. And then the last line of that poem that you read
beautifully: 'Lord let me die, but not die out.' I think that's the love song of
every writer who has ever lived. In front of my daughters, it was an honor
to have the daughter of the greatest writer I have ever known read that
poem on this special night." And later in the evening he said, "To hear 'The
Last Wolverine' read with my wife, Cassandra, my brothers and sisters, my
daughters, my beloved daughters, my grandchildren—it moved me very*

much." Indeed, as I observed Pat while Bronwen was reading, it appeared as if he were listening to his own eulogy.

For many in attendance, one of the highlights of the festival occurred when Pat reminisced about going to Daufuskie Island and telling the poorly educated black students he found there, "They sent the right guy." He said, "I don't have any idea why I thought that at that age. I was twenty-three years old. But now that I'm seventy, I look back on that as the magic year when I discovered the man I was meant to be."

Although he said this with his tongue in his cheek, Pat explained something about himself in his closing remarks when he said, "My mother sits on my shoulder, and my mother: 'Be nice to everyone, son. Make sure you talk to everyone. Ask them a personal question, son. At least pretend like you're sincere.' And her final thing: 'Whoever you meet, make sure they leave your presence happy to have met you.'" I know I was not alone in thinking that Pat Conroy followed his mother's orders throughout his life, did so without his tongue in his cheek, with unfeigned sincerity, and everyone who met him was more than happy to have done so.

At the very end of the festival, Pat addressed his audience with this speech: "Here is where my life as a writer has been unlike anybody I have ever met. My readers are extraordinary. . . . It's been the singular, most wonderful, fabulous part of my writing life. What I wanted to be as a writer, I wanted to be a complete brave man that I am not in my real life. . . . When I sat down to write, I wanted to talk to that god of the wildness of poetry, and I wanted that voice in me if I had it to speak to people like you. And I thought if your lives were anything like mine, you were suffering. You were going through things I have gone through. Do you doubt yourself constantly? Which I do. I have doubted myself every day of my life. You go through life struggling for happiness, for joy, for anything you can to help you get through life at that day. I have been lucky with my friends; I have been lucky with my family. My family I think knows I adore them. My daughters—oh, my daughters—my fabulous daughters. My grandchildren, who thought I was nothing. Right, kids? But I've written the books because I thought if I explained my own life, somehow I could explain some of your life to you. And I thought if I could write about my pain, my struggles, I could help readers like you. What I want for myself on this night, and the nights that go on, I want to write as well as I can as long as I can, as long as I can maintain the *passion that put me at the writing desk at first. I want to honor the teachers who taught me. I want to honor this family I was luckier than anybody in the world in coming into. I want to honor my children and grandchildren. I want them to be proud of me."*

Then in January 2016, I received a phone call from Pat, who identified himself as the "soon-to-be-dead subject" of my oral biography. Pat regularly joked about his impending doom or death, most hilariously in one of our interviews, when he said: "Soon Conroy will sit like a cantaloupe in a nursing home, unavailable for comment. He will try to roll himself off the dock into Battery Creek, but the nurses will roll him back and put him on his dish. In his will he will ask that his feeding tube supply dry martinis on a twenty-four-hour basis so he will feel nothing, know nothing, and sort of like the last few years of his life." But this time it was no joke, even if he was still making a joke out of it. However, he was on his way back from the hospital, where he'd undergone a biopsy for "cancery" lesions. Two days later he was diagnosed with stage 4 pancreatic cancer.

On March 4 Pat Conroy passed away as the sun went down on Battery Creek in Beaufort, South Carolina.

The family, friends, classmates, teammates, and colleagues who knew Pat Conroy enjoyed the privilege of knowing a great man. When a person as special as Pat Conroy enters your life, the experience of knowing him expands your entire being as well as your existence beyond their ordinary boundaries. We are larger in spirit, broader in mind, and better at heart for having been welcomed into the "full Conroy embrace." But his absence will leave a gaping void in all those lives he entered. For the many who knew him and will forever mourn his loss, and for those who never knew the joy of Pat's presence in their lives, I hope this book will help preserve that great man and keep him in some small way still with us.

Author's Note and Acknowledgments

This book is the product of several special collaborations in addition to the one between Pat Conroy and me. Not long after Pat observed that I'd have a book if I'd been recording all our conversations, he suffered the almost-fatal health emergency he recounts in this narrative. Afterward he told me the experience had forced him to take stock of what he wanted to do before his death, and this list included the desire to cooperate with a biographer. I wasn't the one to do a scholarly biography, I told him, but said I'd love for us to do the kind of book I did with Eugene Walter. "Let's do it," he said.

Soon after, I spoke with the then head of the University of South Carolina Press, Jonathan Haupt, with whom I'd already been in contact regarding the publication of my Mountain Brook novel series through Pat Conroy's Story River Books imprint. Not only did Jonathan express immediate interest in publishing the proposed oral biography, but he enlisted the help of Dean Thomas McNally of the University of South Carolina Libraries to provide transcription services for my recordings. This offer was a monumental boon to my project. When I collaborated with the black Alabama midwife, I watched precious years of her elderly life slip away as I tried in vain to secure a publishing contract so I'd have advance money to spend on transcription. Eugene Walter was dead before I got a contract for our book. After Pat's health scare, I did not want to flounder around in vain again as precious time elapsed and recordings remained untranscribed. I salute the press and the Libraries of the University of South Carolina for stepping up immediately with an offer of publication and a proposal for making that happen as expeditiously as possible.

Dean McNally assigned two stellar individuals of his library staff to coordinate with me: the head of IT, Glenn Bunton, and the resident oral historian, Andrea L'Hommedieu. Together they have been responsible for transferring my recordings and organizing them along with the transcripts as part of the Conroy archive. The transcriptionist that Andrea handpicked, Nicci Leamon of Casco, Maine, is someone she had used in the past on her own oral history projects. Nicci proved to be the most professional and exceptional transcriptionist I've ever worked with. Not only was she incredibly thorough and accurate, but she brought a researcher's due diligence to the task. Her preliminary spell-checking and fact-checking saved me countless hours. When the need arose for a second transcriptionist, Stephanie Sword came through with an equally admirable job. Meanwhile, Andrea L'Hommedieu has given me the full benefit of her expertise as an official oral historian without once imposing herself on the situation.

A good 90 percent of the material in this book comes from the recorded interviews. But I started keeping a notebook soon after I started having phone conversations with Pat, years before we discussed this oral biography. As we chatted I jotted down the insights and turns of phrase that struck me as quirks of Pat's special conversational style and the personality from which it flowed. In between calls I enjoyed reading over the words I'd collected. Much of that material has found a home in this book.

In the course of our interviews, Pat was anxious for me to make contact with his former psychologist, Dr. Marion O'Neill. Pat believed that Dr. O'Neill had gotten to the root of him and his troubles in the course of their therapy, and he believed she could help me get to the root of him in my interviews. He was correct. After Pat sent in a notarized waiver of patient confidentiality, Dr. O'Neill spoke on the phone with me for six interviews, which I recorded. The quotations from Dr. O'Neill that accompany each section of the book are drawn from these interviews. Pat wanted Dr. O'Neill's voice to be a part of this narrative, and this is how we have fulfilled his request. I am grateful to her for the time Dr. O'Neill took with me, the effort she made, and the extraordinary insights that once helped Pat achieve a better understanding of himself, and then helped me become a better interviewer.

When my manuscript was complete, I had the benefit of two peerless peer reviewers. The first was "the other K/Catherine," a.k.a. Catherine Seltzer, also the other Conroy biographer. At the time she read my manuscript, she had recently published *Understanding Pat Conroy* and had just embarked on her scholarly biography. In the Conroy family, we are known as "the two K/Catherines," and Pat enjoys calling one or the other of us "the lesser K/Catherine," as the mood strikes him. In return I enjoy pointing out that some men have two women who share the same name; Pat Conroy has two biographers who share the same name. At any rate Catherine Seltzer was a great peer reviewer. Although I was nervous about submitting my work to her scholarly scrutiny, I benefited from it in every way and appreciate that she shared the knowledge gleaned from her years of research. I also gained a lot of confidence after my manuscript passed muster with her. During the revision process, I went back to her again and again with questions and concerns, and she could not have been more generous with her time, advice, and insights.

My other peer reviewer was John Sledge, former books page editor for the *Mobile Press-Register,* for which I wrote reviews until the page was discontinued. It was actually through John that I first met Pat Conroy, when I received the plum assignment of interviewing the author for a profile. That initial conversation I had with Pat essentially never ended and ultimately culminated in the conversations that constitute this book. Besides being my editor for the fifteen years I wrote book reviews, John was also the peer reviewer for my four Mountain Brook novels, published through the Story River Books imprint at the University of South Carolina Press. Over the years I have come to rely on John for both his unguarded enthusiasm and careful criticism, which have always helped steer me in the direction of what works and away from what doesn't work in my writing. Once again I am beholden to John for being there for me and coming through when I needed him.

Margaret Evans, editor of the *Lowcountry Weekly,* and long-term researcher and assistant to Pat Conroy, distinguished herself as a remarkable resource in fact-checking Pat's recollections. Although an oral biography features memories and storytelling rather than scholarship, proper names should still be spelled correctly, dates verified, and episodes corroborated to the degree possible. I also wanted to investigate items I had reason to believe Pat would have clarified or verified before including in a published book. However, I usually implemented only minimal changes pertaining to basic facts, names, and dates in the record Pat gave me. A good example of this approach is the handling of Pat's story about visiting Jonathan Galassi at Random House. While Galassi corroborates the incident, his memory diverges from Pat's on significant points. But the only thing I changed after receiving his feedback was to make the correction to Bob Bernstein's status. Pat thought he was vice president at the time, but Galassi reports he was president, so I corrected this error of fact. But when it comes to different memories and perspectives, my responsibility is to share Pat's version. If, in our interviews, Pat gave himself a heroic response to Bob Bernstein's insult that Jonathan Galassi reports did not occur, then that could demonstrate something Pat and others have pointed out about his need to be a hero. If he sharpened the conflicts and drama of the episode throughout his retelling, that shows how the writer's imagination seizes on events and reworks them for aesthetic effect. In this way an oral biography stays true to its central character and voice, and conveys these to the reader in an unfiltered and unmediated form. In any case I am fortunate that this painstaking job of verification was undertaken by Margaret Evans, who had many years of experience working for Pat and knew just where to find the sources and information we needed. Thanks for special assistance during the fact-checking process go to: Lara Alexander, Jay Bender, Barbara Conroy, Shannon Faulkner, Jonathan Galassi, Sandy Goldberg, Scott Graber, Cliff Graubert, Steve Gross, Steve Grubb, Stan Lefco, Bernie Schein, and John Warley.

I also want to thank Pat's wife, the incomparable Cassandra King Conroy, for the unflagging support and assistance that helped this project come to fruition. A helpmate to the oral biography from the beginning, she also rendered hands-on daily tactical assistance. As Pat admits, he was one of those people who had trouble getting to sleep, and then had trouble waking up. Sandra made sure Pat was ready each morning for our phone call and brought him coffee in bed as we talked. I had planned on reviewing this manuscript with Pat himself and letting him direct the revisions. Although Pat claims he never reads anything about himself and had already told me he was not going to read this oral biography, I was determined that he would read it and help me perfect it if I had to go to Beaufort and force it on him. In fact this was precisely my intention. But by the time the manuscript was fit to be seen, Pat had just been diagnosed with cancer. In one of our last conversations, I said, "Now, I know you told me you didn't want to read it, but—" Pat interrupted me: "I said that when I thought I was going to live." Somehow he made this as funny as any other exchange we ever had, and it gave me hope that he would become stable and comfortable enough for me to visit and go over the manuscript with him. Alas, this was not to be. After his death Sandra had a thousand matters to tend to in the midst of her grief. I assumed there was no way she could take on Pat's role of vetting the manuscript and was flabbergasted when she did so a month after he passed away. I was also thrilled when she declared that the book sounded "just like him." Over the next several months, Sandra gave me the benefit of her wisdom, her intimate understanding of Pat Conroy, and her painstaking examination of the oral biography. While she did not agree with every editorial decision I made in the book, Sandra remained unfailingly respectful of me both personally and professionally. One of the best by-products of my collaboration with Pat Conroy is that it has brought me in close contact with a kindred Alabama spirit and fellow novelist, Cassandra King, whose friendship I value and cherish deeply.

Jonathan Haupt was the vital spark that enabled an abstract idea to become a published book. I will be eternally grateful for the alacrity with which he seized on the idea for this book and how he wasted no time in making it happen, especially as it turned out there was no time to waste.

Also Jonathan's brilliant idea to celebrate "Conroy at 70" became even more brilliant in retrospect, after Pat's diagnosis a mere three months later. This unique festival was the product of Jonathan's genius for sweeping creative vision as well as meticulous attention to even the smallest details. It required two years of extensive planning and preparation.

People from every stage of Pat's life, from his oldest friends to his most recent protégés, were in attendance. The town of Beaufort—"that golden place under the sun" Pat adopted as his chosen hometown—turned out to embrace the man who had once been shunned at the beginning of his "radical" writing career. As much as we all reveled in participating in this glorious culminating moment, we have become even more grateful afterward to have had that opportunity to affirm the life and career of a great American individual when he was hale and hearty and very much alive. Once again, Jonathan, I salute you.

I have two first readers, Tom Uskali of New Orleans and Sean Smith of Atlanta, who have helped me with all the manuscripts of my novels and provided invaluable assistance on this project as well. These are the two people who help me overcome the struggles, fears, doubts, obstacles, and setbacks involved in the production of any manuscript. Tom is an English teacher and department chairman, a writer, reviewer, and editor with exquisite taste, judgment, and sensitivity. I don't put anything out there to anyone that Tom hasn't seen first. Sean Smith is a history and lit major turned First Amendment attorney who is also serving as my agent for this work, and I thank him for casting an expert lawyerly as well as a writerly eye over the book.

And then there is Brandon, who puts up with it all and makes it all possible.